SEDUCTION, DRIVE AND REPETITION

FREUD'S METAPHYSICS OF TRAUMA

FIGURES OF THE UNCONSCIOUS 23

SEDUCTION, DRIVE AND REPETITION

Freud's Metaphysics of Trauma

Herman Westerink and Philippe Van Haute

LEUVEN UNIVERSITY PRESS

Original title: *Verleiding, drift en herhaling: Freuds metafysica van het trauma.*
Authorized translation from the Dutch language edition published by Uitgeverij Boom, Amsterdam.

ISBN 978 94 6270 486 2 (paperback)
eISBN 978 94 6166 688 8 (ePDF)
eISBN 978 94 6166 689 5 (ePUB)
https://doi.org/10.11116/9789461666888
D/2025/1869/29
NUR: 770
Typesetting: Friedemann Vervoort
Cover design: Anton Lecock

GPRC Guaranteed Peer Reviewed Content www.gprc.be

Contents

Acknowledgements

The Dutch original of this book was published by Boom in Amsterdam in 2022 as a monograph entitled *Verleiding, drift en herhaling: Freuds metafysica van het trauma*. This monograph was the last joint publication after many years of close collaboration in our investigations of the philosophical potential of Freud's clinical and meta-psychological studies. After all, in November 2022, Philippe van Haute passed away, and unfortunately our teamwork came to an early and abrupt end. In the period after that (between 2022 and 2024) texts were published – partly posthumously – that built on this monograph. These mainly concern texts that emerged from chapters on *Beyond the Pleasure Principle* and *Moses and Monotheism*. The initiative for a volume that has been published in 2024 in collaboration with Jenny Willner entitled *Towards the Limits of Freudian Thinking: Critical Edition and Readings of 'Beyond the Pleasure Principle'* had already been taken in 2021. We had planned this volume as a preliminary study for the next joint project: a commentary on the different versions of *Beyond the Pleasure Principle* in the style of our study on the different editions of *Three Essays on the Theory of Sexuality*, published by Routledge in 2021…

We would like to thank all those who in one way or another contributed to the content of this book through conversations and discussions in research meetings, during symposia and in conferences where we brought forward our initial intuitions and ideas. We would like to thank in particular the members of the *Center for Contemporary European Philosophy* of the Radboud University Nijmegen, the members of the *Freud Research Group* of the *International Society for Psychoanalysis and Philosophy*, and participants at the *International Symposium for Phenomenology* in Perugia for their critical and stimulating suggestions and comments. We are indebted to Joey Kok for her translation of the text and to the editorial team of Leuven University Press. Finally, we would like to thank the Faculty of Philosophy, Theology and Religious Studies of Radboud University and the Philosophy Department of the University of Pretoria for their financial support.

Introduction

The seduction theory

"I no longer believe in my neurotica", Freud wrote to his friend Wilhelm Fliess on 21 September 1897.[1] This statement is perhaps one of the most commented-upon fragments in his work. With it, Freud does not imply that he no longer believes in his seduction theory on the aetiology of the neuroses. This theory posited that all psychopathology, and hysteria in particular, is the result of sexual trauma in childhood – more specifically, abuse by the father.[2] The abandonment of the seduction theory of neurosis has been the subject of much debate over the years, and the content and tenor of this debate have significantly shaped Freud's reception in wider society and culture. Several authors have alleged Freud abandoned his theory for opportunistic reasons. After all, the seduction theory implies that there must be more incestuous, perverse fathers than neurotics; not everyone who is abused will later develop hysteria or neurosis. The epidemic incidence of hysteria at the end of the nineteenth century[3] therefore suggests the worst: there must be an enormous number of perverse fathers. Freud would have found this difficult to accept. For this reason, he would have come to regard the traumatic tales of his patients as phantasies with an oedipal content. The traumatic tales about abuse would therefore be nothing other than the distorted expression of a desire for the father. Since this desire was unacceptable for the patients, it could only become conscious in distorted form – as a story about abuse. In this way, the Oedipus complex would have acquired a central role in Freud's aetiology of neurosis.

In a very general sense, this reference to the Oedipus complex implies that the drive-laden representations that structure and determine our relationships with our parents are, on the one hand, decisive for the formation of one's own identity and more particularly for its inscription in culture and, on the other hand, at the root of various psychopathologies. Working through this complex makes it possible to play one's role as 'man' towards a 'woman' (and vice versa) in a relationship that is defined as heterosexual. Freud's opportunism would thus result in an oedipal theory in which the bourgeois family is not only the context and model for the formation of an identity but is in fact also the desired outcome of normal, healthy development. Freud could thus be labeled an ideologist of patriarchy and bourgeoisie who based his theories on misconceptions and ideological positions.[4]

We will not rehash this discussion in this book. We will merely point out that most historians, psychoanalysis and philosophers who rely on Freud's work or who have studied it share the basic assumption of this historical analysis. They assume that Freud replaces his trauma theory in 1897 with a reference to the Oedipus complex and phantasy life.[5] The well-known English psychoanalyst Adam Phillips summarizes this interpretation well:

> The great discoveries of these years were a growing sense of the power and provenance of fantasy, a method for interpreting dreams, and an understanding of the Oedipus complex which linked together became a story about sexuality and an unconscious mind, a part of the mind that thought differently.[6]

Whether one is for or against Freud, according to most authors, the oedipalization of psychoanalytical theory already took place at the end of the 19th century and is the reverse of the abandonment of the seduction theory.[7]

This reading has led to the question about the place and meaning of trauma in Freud's later work being neglected in many studies of his work. Why would one examine the role of seduction and trauma after 1897, when Freud himself indicates that it is minimal or non-existent? It has of course been acknowledged that there are texts in which he seems to take up trauma theory again – notably 'From the History of an Infantile Neurosis ['The Wolf Man']' and *Moses and Monotheism* – but there has been little or no attempt to situate these texts from the perspective of the problematic of trauma within the development of Freud's thought.[8] On the contrary, these texts are usually read as part of a theory formation of the Oedipus complex. Much attention is simultaneously paid to the study of ways in which Freud presented his original seduction theory in later texts to obscure the true, opportunistic origin of his psychoanalytical theories.[9]

In this book, we want to show, by means of a careful reading of a number of case studies and meta-psychological texts, that the various references to seduction theory in Freud's texts testify to the progressive influence of trauma theory in his oeuvre. The thesis of this book is therefore that Freud never abandoned his trauma theory but over time supplemented it with new theoretical components and in the process reformulated it time and again. In this way, trauma theory not only forms a common thread through Freud's work but also plays a key role in his clinical reflections and meta-psychological theory formation. What is more, in his later writings, his trauma theory becomes the core of a tragic view of humans and life that in many respects ties in with the cultural criticism of, for example, Friedrich Nietzsche. The trauma theory in relation to his tragic view of humankind is the theme of this book.

The assumption that Freud abandons his seduction theory and replaces it with an oedipal theory of phantasm is problematic when we consider that Freud first mentions the Oedipus complex as such in 1910 in one of his lesser-known texts.[10] It is then in *Totem and Taboo* that Freud begins to assign the Oedipus complex a central place in his theorization, when he argues that this complex is "the nuclear complex of the neuroses".[11] If indeed this complex only now begins to play a central and decisive role in the Freudian aetiology of the neuroses, what was Freud's *neurotica* in the period between the infamous 1897 letter to Fliess and the publication of *Totem and Taboo*? What are the most important and relevant theoretical steps in this period? The main step is clearly formulated by Freud himself: if a psychological theory of trauma (theory of seduction) has to be abandoned, the hereditary and constitutional factors in the aetiology of the neuroses come to the fore again.[12] As we shall discuss, this evolution is connected to the discovery of infantile sexuality. In the same period, Freud starts working on his *Three Essays on the Theory of Sexuality* in which he describes a general human sexual constitution that underlies psychopathology.[13] The rediscovery of constitutional and hereditary elements consequently makes the aetiology of neuroses a general anthropological problem. The study of psychopathology now becomes a study of human existence as such. The re-evaluation of hereditary elements does not, however, mean that all reference to traumatic events disappears from Freud's theory. Both in theoretical texts such as 'My Views on the Part Played by Sexuality in the Aetiology of the Neuroses' and in the case studies Freud released after the publication of *Three Essays* in 1905, such events play a crucial role.[14] What is new here is above all that the effects and effectiveness of these traumas can only be understood from an essential interaction with hereditary (constitutional) and dispositional aspects. In this way, it becomes somewhat clear why Freud, for example writes in the case about Dora that he never gave up the theory of seduction but only adapted it because he found it incomplete.[15] Freud explicitly situates this case study in the extension of the original trauma theory, which he approvingly recalls. The same happens in the study of the Rat Man.[16] There is therefore every reason to assume that Freud did not so much abandon his original *neurotica* as adapt it in relation to constitutional factors. On the one hand, this means that the place of the Oedipus complex and of references to the Oedipus legend in Freud's work must be rethought, while on the other hand it must be made clear in what way the problematic of trauma and seduction continues to determine Freud's aetiological thinking after 1897.

In the context of this problematic, we must not only consider the interaction between constitutional elements and accidental events but also the role of phantasy life. The abandonment of the seduction theory is often, for understandable reasons, associated with the progressive development of a theory of phantasm that began in correspondence with Fliess from 1896 onwards. It is important to emphasize, however, that Freud is not specifically talking about oedipal phantasies here. In fact, in this period and actually until the publication of 'A Child is Being Beaten' in 1919, he attributes a purely defensive function to phantasm. The latter implies that the phantasm, whether or not it was oedipal, was not initially the driving force behind the pathology. On the contrary, Freud writes that numerous seduction phantasies should be interpreted as attempts to ward off the memory of one's own sexual activity (infantile masturbation).[17]

The importance of phylogeny

In the second half of the 1980s, the discovery of an unpublished manuscript in the estate of his pupil Sandor Ferenczi led to renewed attention for the place of trauma in Freud's texts. This manuscript – 'Overview of the Transference Neuroses' – describes human history as a succession of catastrophes (traumas), which the various neurotic dispositions repeat as it were.[18] Freud relies her on the evolutionary-biological theories that we will later return to in detail in this book. In the various neuroses and the instinctive constellations that underpin them, the history of the human race resonates. The publisher of 'Overview of the Transference Neuroses', Ilse Grubrich-Simitis, concludes in an article accompanying this publication that the drive model and the trauma model, which at first seemed to contradict each other, appear here as two sides of the same coin. There is no absolute opposition between real traumas and (oedipally or otherwise determined) instinctual representations. The structure of our drives is grounded in the traumatic history of the human species.[19] Moreover, individual traumas can be seen as repetitions of traumas from the earliest history of humanity.

Although evolutionary ideas had occupied Freud since his student days and are a point of reference in the letters to Fliess at the end of the 19th century, it was mainly after the publication of *Totem and Taboo* in 1913 that they start to play a prominent role in Freud's published texts. In *Totem and Taboo* Freud formulates the hypothesis of a murder of the primal father by his sons. The consequences of this murder, such as castration anxiety and an irreversible sense of guilt, continue through the generations and continue to determine our experience.[20] They only wait for the appropriate (traumatic) accidental events to be activated, that is, to order and reorganize the individual experiences in such a way that they fit into the phylogenetic scheme. In 'From the History of an Infantile Neurosis', which dates largely from 1914, Freud uses these insights for the first time to understand a concrete case study. He then integrates these insights into the new drive theory on the death and life drives that he develops in *Beyond the Pleasure Principle* from 1920. Especially in the clinical texts from the last period of Freud's life and work, phylogenetic considerations play a crucial role. The latter is modelled in *Moses and Monotheism*, which can be read as a case study of the Jewish people.

In previous publications, we have argued extensively that Freud did not introduce or discover the Oedipus complex in the letters to Fliess.[21] Freud's reflections on the Oedipus complex are, on the contrary, intrinsically interwoven with his renewed focus on obsessional neurosis following the publication in 1905 of *Three Essays on the Theory of Sexuality*. Obsessional neurosis explicitly confronted Freud for the first time with the problems of identification, aggression, prohibition and guilt that had remained much more in the background in hysteria, which he had used as an example until then. The problematics of prohibition, guilt and aggression are also central elements of the Oedipus complex. Freud's reflections on obsessional neurosis are first expressed in 'Notes Upon a Case of Obsessional Neurosis [The 'Rat Man']', which appeared in 1909. The problems of prohibition and guilt are also central to Freud's theory of culture and religion, which he develops in parallel with the study of obsessional neurosis. The study of this neurosis and the origins of culture and religion meet in *Totem and Taboo*, in which Freud's phylogenetic approach reaches its first climax. It is in the context of this phylogenetic argumentation that the Oedipus complex is introduced. The study of the Wolf Man, which dates back to the same time period, is, as we shall see, the most striking clinical illustration of this.

In the years following these publications, the evolutionary elaboration of the constitutional and hereditary aspects in the aetiology of the psychoneuroses is further developed and radicalized. Freud's metapsychology now acquires more and more metaphysical allures that transcend anthropology. Freud bases the unabridged sexually instinctual constitution from *Totem and Taboo* onwards in the history of the human species. In *Beyond the Pleasure Principle*, he adds to this that the drive (and thus life itself) came into being from the inorganic by a first external "force of whose nature we can form no conception".[22] The structure of our instinctual constitution is itself the result of a series of traumatic events that determined the history of the hominids and of all living beings. These events had led to psychical and physical changes that shaped the various species into what they are today. The drive thus becomes a fundamental principle that not only allows us to understand the phenomena we are confronted with in clinical practice in a coherent way but also to thematize the most basic characteristics of all living beings.

According to Freud, drive is not directed towards change and development from an inner lawfulness. It wants to restore the former state from which it emerged and which it had to leave or was distracted from by external forces (traumas). The drives are essentially conservative and regressive. They are governed by a repetition compulsion that aims at restoring the former state at all costs. In the end, they aim at a return to the inorganic. Seduction (trauma and diversion), drive and repetition thus become key concepts of Freud's metaphysics. This progressive broadening and deepening of Freud's psychological and anthropological theory leads to an unambiguous affirmation of a tragic human vision that cannot be reduced to the ambivalences of the oedipal object relations. Human existence for Freud is nothing but a 'detour' to death in which the traumatic fates of our species are repeated. In this way, we can place Freud's thinking in a long tradition of philosophical reflection on the drive as a causative force. This tradition begins with Aristotle and runs via, among others, Spinoza, Leibniz, Schopenhauer and Nietzsche to Foucault, Deleuze and Guattari.[23] Freud's tragic human vision – in which the problems of trauma, drive and repetition are central – can be understood in dialogue with this tradition.

Reading Freud

Most commentators seek in Freud's text a meaning that is in principle unambiguous and that progressively develops and externalizes itself. From this perspective, these texts could be read as a coherent whole, as the steady unfolding of what ultimately forms a systematic theory – Freudian psychoanalysis. In our view, this is not the most interesting approach to study Freud. After all, Freud had no difficulty in republishing texts with additions that contain new insights that are not necessarily in agreement with earlier editions of the same text. Coherence was not always his main concern. Of all Freud's most important texts – think for example of *The Interpretation of Dreams*, *Three Essays on the Theory of Sexuality* and *Beyond the Pleasure Principle* – there are different versions and editions that cannot easily be reconciled with each other.[24] In a recent study of *Three Essays on the Theory of Sexuality*, we have shown that it is important to confront the different editions and versions of the same text with each other in order to identify the issues with which Freud struggled, rather than determine unambiguous answers that he would have formulated in his question.[25] A reading that considers the different editions, shows the tensions between them and the inconsistencies sometimes arising from this allows Freud's work to be revived and sometimes leads to unexpected insights and perspectives.

In our study of *Three Essays on the Theory of Sexuality*, it leads to the insight that the original draft of this text is, as it were, overgrown by later editions and that the view of the radical critique of heteronormativity that it contains is thus obscured. What applies to *Three Essays* applies equally to, for example, the case of the Wolf Man ('From the History of an Infantile Neurosis') as to *Beyond the Pleasure Principle* and *Moses and Monotheism*, to which we will devote a great deal of attention in this book. These texts are also compositions of first versions and later additions. Here too, we are dealing with texts where this composite character, when thoroughly studied, acquires an inconsistency or, at least, a kind of tension. By naming and thematizing the different editions of the different texts, the additions and omissions, we gain a better view of Freudian psychoanalysis as a field of interrelated problematics that still gives food for thought today. Only from such a perspective – and thus averse to any attempt to capture Freudian thought once and for all in a set of dogmatic positions – can the Freudian corpus be fruitfully confronted with philosophical[26] and psychoanalytic[27] reflections on trauma.

In our first chapter, we discuss the origins of seduction theory in the correspondence with Wilhelm Fliess and in some programmatic texts from 1896. We situate Freud's thinking in the context of the progressive psychologization of the notion of trauma in the second half of the nineteenth century and show the specificity of Freud's approach. In particular, we also discuss the neuroticization (internalization and sexualization) the classical traumatic neurosis undergoes in his work. This problematic 'neuroticization' is a crucial part of Freud's seduction theory and confronts this theory with its own limits from the outset.

In the first chapter we also discuss in more detail the alleged 'abandonment' of the seduction theory. We show that this is an adaptation of this theory to new insights, which at least party arise from the theoretical problems that this theory raises, and not its replacement by an oedipal theory of neurosis. In the following chapters about some of Freud's most important case studies – 'Dora', the 'Rat Man' and the 'Wolf Man – we show how this adapted seduction theory continues to determine Freud's clinical and aetiological understanding of neurosis even after 1897.

The study of the Wolf Man, which is the subject of our fourth chapter, is in many ways a pivotal text in the development of Freud's thinking about drive and trauma. Not only is it the first clinical study in which Freud invokes the Oedipus and castration complex as (part of an) explanation for neurosis, but it is also the first clinical text in which Freud systematically refers to phylogenetic elements as the basis of neurosis. This reference is a further specification of the sexual constitution Freud had already systematically described in 1905 in his *Three Essays*. In this chapter, we subject the connection between trauma, oedipal and phylogenetic elements to a careful examination.

The references to phylogenetics and the importance of an evolutionary-biological theory formation becomes increasingly significant in Freud's work after the publication of *Totem and Taboo*. They are given an elaborated and central place in *Beyond the Pleasure Principle*, which is the subject of our sixth chapter. In order to understand this text properly, it is necessary to first map out the sources of inspiration and the basic intuitions of Freud's references to biology. This is the subject of our fifth chapter, which precedes the chapter on *Beyond the Pleasure Principle*.

In *Beyond the Pleasure Principle*, Freud introduces a new drive theory that departs from the fundamental ideas that had determined his thinking about drives up to that point. Like he did 25 years earlier in the context of the original seduction theory, Freud here again takes traumatic neurosis as point of departure for his reflections on trauma and drive. He refers more specifically to the nightmares suffered by patients who are victims of a traumatic neurosis. In these nightmares, they repeatedly experience the traumatic event – explosion, the violent death of a friend – that is at the origin of their pathology. Freud's 'far-fetched speculation' about these phenomena leads him to conclude that drive is not so much aimed at change but has an essentially regressive and therefore repetitive character.[28] He also establishes that its fundamental structure is determined by the traumatic events to which the human species (but also other animal species) fell victim during the course of its history. Trauma, drive and hereditary constitution are thus described as two sides of the same reality. They form the core elements of Freud's tragic human vision he defends in *Beyond the Pleasure Principle*. At the same time, it is striking that the study of traumatic neurosis confronts Freud once more with the limits of his model and, more specifically, of the primacy of sexuality.

In a general sense, the model in which trauma and repetition take central stage prevails in the clinical texts Freud published after *Beyond the Pleasure Principle*.[29] This is particularly the case in *Inhibitions, Symptoms and Anxiety*, which we will discuss in the last paragraph of our sixth chapter.[30] This text is an excellent transition to our last chapter about *Moses and Monotheism*. We read this text as a case study of the Jewish people.[31] This case study is the ultimate illustration of the fact that to the end of his life, Freud remained true to a modified version of the theory of seduction. From its origins to its end, Freudian psychoanalysis is a clinical and metaphysical theory of trauma.

Chapter 1

The psychologization of trauma and the origination of seduction theory

1. From railway-spine to traumatic hysteria

In our time and age, we take the existence of something like psychical trauma for granted. However, up until the middle of the 19th century, the word 'trauma' was used exclusively for physical injuries caused by accidents or violence. 'Traumatology', then, was a subdiscipline of surgery. It treated and studied physical injuries. The expansion of trauma into the psychological domain has been the result of a fascinating history that has been studied extensively over the past few decades.[1] The importance of this expansion can hardly be underestimated. Up until the mid-19th century it was impossible to understand humans as traumatizable – let alone as essentially 'traumatized' – psychological beings. The expansion of the concept of trauma, in other words, opened a new possibility for individuals (and groups) to understand themselves. At the same time, this opportunity went hand in hand with a thorough reconsideration and reformulation of psychiatric theory, psychiatric diagnosis and their corresponding treatments. In this evolution, the work of Freud generally, and particularly the introduction of his seduction theory, played an important and in many respects a decisive role.[2] The possibility of a new self-understanding and the reconsideration of psychiatric diagnosis and theory go together in Freud's work. It is important to discuss some key positions in this debate before we turn to the work of Freud and his place in this development.

In 1866, the English surgeon John Erichsen (1818-1896) published his first edition of *On Railway and other Injuries of the Nervous System*.[3] In the middle of the 19th century, railroads were coming into full swing. They were symbolic of industrialization and modern progress.[4] Observers soon noticed that survivors of the many rail accidents developed all sorts of 'nervous' symptoms for which no discernible organic basis could be found. People for instance suffered from insomnia and inexplicable aches of the back, arms and hands. Before long, the term *railway spine* had gained traction.[5] Erichsen, however, rejects the exclusive link between railroad accidents and a specific psychopathology associated with this type of accident implied in the notion of *railway spine*.[6] He points out that even before the development of the train in the 19th century, we fell victim to mechanical shocks: falling from horses or being run over by carriages.[7] Erichsen further describes how the development of the train as well as the industry led to a significant increase in collective accidents. With this comes more of a focus on a large group of patients who develop specific pathology after these accidents. He prefers describing this pathology with the term *concussion of the spine* rather than *railway spine*. He associates it mainly with hemorrhage or inflammation of the spinal cord flowing from the external violence caused by the shock. Erichsen's book was enormously successful and had a great influence on the psychiatry of his time. In the considerably expanded later edition from 1875 entitled *On Concussion of the Spine, Nervous Shock, and Other Obscure Injuries of the Nervous System in Their Clinical and Medico-legal Aspects*, the focus shifts from the spinal cord to the brain (*railway-brain*) and from organic injuries to damage to the molecular structure of the nervous system.[8]

However, we would be wrong to reduce Erichsen's theory to its somatic aspects. Erichsen, like most theorists after him, did have a keen eye for the psychological aspects of the problematic, especially in the 1875 text. In particular, he mentions the influence of fright (*terror*) that could also have a direct impact on the nervous system. In patients who only experienced a lighter, general shock that does not directly affect the head or spinal cord, the fright – that is: a purely psychological factor – can, according to Erichsen, have a decisive influence on the course of the illness. These patients show mainly emotional and possibly 'hysterical' symptoms that, in contrast to the organic symptoms of *railway-spine*, occur immediately after the accident. Once they have recovered from the shock, these patients are very agitated and difficult to calm down, Erichsen writes: "It is this condition that is so apt to lead to an emotional state, which, for want of a better term, may be called hysteria".[9]

We cannot discuss Erichsen's reflections on hysteria here – "that word that serves as a cloak to ignorance" – as distinct from *concussion of the spine*.[10] It suffices to conclude that Erichsen treated *concussion of the spine* as a separate diagnosis distinct from hysteria. In addition, and on the other hand, Erichsen does have a keen eye for psychological factors – psychical causality – in the development of psychopathology and with regards to the meaning of trauma.

With this, two basic interrelated problems are identified that have played a decisive role in the further history of the concept of railway spine or railway brain: the delineation of hysteria and its origin, psychical or otherwise.

During the 1880s, the German neurologist Hermann Oppenheim (1858-1919) introduced the concept of 'traumatic neurosis' that would soon absorb and replace Erichsen's notion of concussion of the spine. In 1889 Oppenheim's seminal book *Die traumatischen Neurosen* was published. It is clear for Oppenheim that traumatic neurosis is a separate diagnostic category that must be clearly distinguished from hysteria. Traumatic neurosis, according to him, is caused in particular by the mechanical shock (*Erschütterung*) trauma consists of. This shock causes a functional disturbance[11] at the level of the cerebral cortex.[12] This does not, however, mean that Oppenheim would have been unaware of psychical elements in the origins of traumatic neurosis. Like Erichsen, he in this context points mainly to the role of anxiety or, better still, fright.[13] Fright, as Freud would argue more fully at a later stage, refers in contrast to anxiety to the element of 'surprise' – that is, the total lack of preparation – with which trauma is associated.[14] In a 1915 text, Oppenheim summarizes his views on the role and place of psychical factors in the development of traumatic neurosis as follows:

> I too had underlined its great significance from the outset. But I also thought I should always maintain that the mechanical lesion should not be underestimated. It seemed indisputable to me that the delicate organization of the nervous tissue could be damaged directly or indirectly – in a way quite other than materially through hemorrhage, inflammation, degeneration or death. I was thinking of more delicate processes as we know them from physics and referred to the example of the iron core, the structure of which does not change perceptibly when that core becomes magnetically charged or loses this charge.[15]

In this citation, one sees that Oppenheim by no means denies the existence and importance of psychical traumas but also that it remains unclear how their connection with organic factors should be imagined. How could psychical traumas have any meaningful influence on the organic structure at all?[16]

However, Erichsen as well as Oppenheim distinguish concussion of the spine and traumatic neurosis from hysteria respectively. They assume that it concerns a separate illness with its own aetiology. Specifically, they point to mechanical shock and its effects on the nervous system. They therefore rather explain this pathology from an actual trauma than from a hereditary predisposition.[17]

Another view is found in Jean-Martin Charcot (1825-1893), with whom Freud went on a study trip to Paris in 1885-1886 at the hospital of Salpétrière. Charcot no longer regards traumatic neurosis as a separate illness like Erichsen and Oppenheim but as a subcategory of hysteria. Up until the 1870s, Charcot had done mainly clinical-anatomical research; from that time, however, and to the end of his life, he had turned to the study of hysteria and would soon become one of its greatest specialists and advocates, both in France and far beyond its borders. Charcot considers hysteria as a disturbance of the neuro-sensitive function.[18] In his famous *Leçons du mardi*, Charcot provides very detailed descriptions of his hysterical patients. These descriptions are regularly interspersed with theoretical reflections on the development of hysterical symptoms – conversions and convulsions ('hysterical attacks' the course of which Charcot meticulously described in four 'stages'), anesthesia, movement disorders (abasia and astasia)[19] – and the aetiology of this pathology. We cannot discuss Charcot's insights into hysteria and his detailed descriptions at length here. We will limit ourselves to Charcot's concept of 'traumatic hysteria' that in principle coincides with what Erichsen called concussion of the spine and Oppenheim called 'traumatic neurosis'.[20] In the last part of his life, Charcot developed this concept to indicate hysterical symptoms and states that occurred after serious traumatic events and specifically after accidents involving 'mechanical shock'. Here he refers explicitly to Erichsen (railway-spine) and to Oppenheim's standard work.[21] Unlike Erichsen and Oppenheim, Charcot does not think actual trauma is the cause of the hysterical pathology that follows on from it. Trauma is only an *agent provocateur* – an instigator – which, in those with the inherited predisposition, gives way to the development of hysterical pathology. The cause of traumatic hysteria is in other words neither the trauma itself – nor the other possible catalysts we mentioned – but the underlying neuropathic disposition: "It is therefore doubtless not a question of receptivity (and we have already said that we do not consider hysteria a disease coming from without) but a special morbid predisposing condition inherent in the individual".[22] He further connects this disposition with the degeneration theory of Morel and Magan (Morel, *Traité des maladies mentales*, 1860), which was very popular in the second half of the 19th century. This theory held that intoxication and addiction, but also for instance syphilis,[23] could give way from one generation to the next to pathologies such as hysteria and epilepsy, perversions or learning disabilities.[24]

This degeneration theory was largely based on Lamarck's evolutionary-biological theory on the inheritance of acquired characteristics.[25]

The role of hereditary disposition is also aptly illustrated by the way in which Charcot connects hysteria and hypnosis. Hypnosis plays an important role in Charcot's theory, from a theoretical as well as from a clinical standpoint. In Charcot's time, hypnosis was a serious and important scientific theme that fascinated more than just physicians and psychiatrists. Charcot demonstrates how through hypnosis one can both evoke symptoms (paralysis, anesthesias) and make them disappear again. He assumes hypnosis is an artificially induced change in the nervous system that could only be induced in hysterical patients. Charcot considers this 'hypnotizability' as a fundamental characteristic of hysteria.[26] It is part of the underlying neuropathic disposition. Accordingly, the hypnotizability illustrates that accidental rather than dispositional factors are decisive in the development of hysteria.

A clinical illustration can further illuminate the role and significance of hypnosis for pathogenesis of *traumato-hystérie*. In the second volume of his *Leçons du mardi*, Charcot discusses a patient he calls 'Le Log'. This patient had been hit by a carriage and thrown onto the sidewalk. In the process he lost consciousness and had no memory of the accident. Eyewitnesses confirmed that the carriage did not run him over. He also showed no visible physical injuries. However, 'Le Log' held firm to his belief in another story that also frequently appeared in his dreams.[27] In this story, the carriage came past making a lot of noise, the horse fell on him, and his chest collided with the horse's head. 'Le Log' would then have fallen, and the carriage would have ridden over the upper part of his thighs. In his dreams – rather, nightmares – he wakes up screaming at this point in the story.[28] 'Le Log' suffers, among other things, from paralysis of the lower limbs, where he feels no sensation.[29] Charcot shows that the distribution of this numbness or anesthesia over the body clearly differs from the anesthesias occurring in organic lesions.[30] In other words, the numbness does not follow the distribution one would expect based on the course of the nerve pathways. At the same time, Charcot determines that the distribution of anesthesia across 'Le Log's' body is identical to that which occurs in 'hypnotizable hemi-anesthetic[31] hysterical subjects' (sic) where paralysis was induced in the lower limbs through hypnosis. There is thus no clinical difference between 'Le Log's' paralyses and that of the 'hysterical subjects' just mentioned. From this Charcot concludes that the paralysis in both cases must have come about in an analogous manner.[32]

According to Charcot, the fall and accompanying loss of consciousness brought 'Le Log' into a state that made him particularly susceptible to (auto-) suggestion, according to the model of hypnotic somnambulism (sleepwalking) in a stricter sense.[33] The shock of collision gave way to a feeling of numbness in the affected limbs, which, after an incubation period of a few days, could induce in 'Le Log' through auto-suggestion the idea that he was paralyzed. The shock and the loss of consciousness indeed lead to an elimination of the ego, as occurs in hypnosis. The idea of paralysis can, according to Charcot, in these circumstances occupy all brain activity and lead to a real paralysis.[34] He adds that this process runs unconsciously. Thus, even if patients are in a certain sense deluding themselves, they do so without realizing it and without having a grip on the process. Charcot further points out that a 'local shock' is not the only starting point for suggestion; fright could have the same effect. He refers in this context to what German writers have called *Schrecklahmungen*. The 'cerebral nervous shock' brought about by fright may, in those who are predisposed, lead to a transient emotional weakening ('paresis') transforming into a permanent paralysis of the lower limbs ('paraplegia').[35]

Two views are thus contrasted. On the one hand are Erichsen and Oppenheim, who consider traumatic neurosis as a separate diagnostic category or illness caused by an actual external trauma. This trauma, a mechanical shock such as for example an accident, leads to damage of the finer nerve tissue that cannot (or at least not yet), however, be empirically determined. Charcot, on the other hand, does not view traumatic neurosis as a separate category, rather as a sub-category of hysteria. He talks about traumatic hysteria. Charcot also understands trauma as an external mechanical shock (accident), but this shock is according to him not the cause of the pathology. It is just the catalyst or the trigger (*agent provocateur*) that activates an existing neuropathic disposition. 'Hypnotizability', according to Charcot, constitutes an integral part of this disposition. Moreover, the efficacy of these traumas is, according to Charcot, to a large extent unconscious and can be characterized by an incubation that can take from a few days to several weeks.[36] All of this, however, does not prevent both Erichsen and Oppenheim, and Charcot from paying attention to the psychological aspects contributing to the development of what they call traumatic neurosis or traumatic hysteria. In particular, the role and significance of fright that occurs during trauma is noted by all these authors as an important psychological element. Charcot is moreover aware that the physical location of hysterical paralyses and anesthesia differs from the actual course of the nerve pathways. However, he does not infer from this that hysteria could unreservedly be treated as a psychological problem. This is a step that Freud will take. On the one hand, like Charcot, he views traumatic neurosis as a form of hysteria, but he will at the same time, in contrast to Charcot, refer to the psychological factors to explain its manifestation.

2. From neurology to psychology: hysterical versus organic paralyses

Although Charcot, even more than Erichsen and Oppenheim, emphasizes the importance of psychical factors in the development of the pathologies we are discussing here, he remains a neurologist. Hysteria is a functional disorder that, in the conceptualization of the end of the 19th century, means that it has an organic, and in Charcot's case, hereditary cause that cannot, however, be anatomically localized. Following this logic, Charcot relates hysterical paralyses to what he calls a 'dynamic' or functional lesion. It is an injury for which no trace can be found in the cadaver '*post mortem*'.[37] Charcot's psychological speculations thus nevertheless always remain framed in a neurological context. Regardless, hysteria is a nervous disorder. Freud on the other hand will take the step initiated, but not taken, by Charcot: hysteria is not a neurological but a *psychological* problem.[38]

We already know that Charcot thought hysterical paralysis and anesthesia do not consider the anatomy of the nervous system. For example, Charcot writes about 'Guertz', a patient from the Parisian hospital of La Salpêtrière, and that the area of her shoulder where she had lost feeling took the shape of a shoulder piece of a sixteenth century harness.[39] The hysterical body thus appears to be imaginary or depicted rather than neurological. Freud takes this line even further in an early article discussing the differences between organic and hysterical motor paralyses. It has often been pointed out that hysterical paralyses *simulate* organic ones.[40] Yet hysterical paralyses are not carbon copies of organic, cerebral ones. For example, in the latter, the peripheral element (hand or foot) is always more severely affected than the central element (shoulder). With hysterical paralyses we often see, according to Freud, the opposite. The thigh can be more severely paralyzed than the foot. 'Le Log' for instance had no feeling in his lower limbs, except in his toes. But also in other respects, hysterical differs from organic paralysis. For example, hysterical paralysis only reproduces paralysis in a leg or arm instead of one half of the body, as in organic hemiplegia. Certainly, more intense organic paralyses of a single arm or leg (monoplegias) are never clearly delineated. When an arm is paralyzed, there are also lesser traces of paralysis in the face and leg. A purely cortical monoplegia always has a moderate intensity. As soon as this intensity increases, disorders in the leg and face also appear: "*It [the paralysis] cannot at the same time become absolute and retain its delimitation*".[41] The sensibility or sensitivity disturbances accompanying the paralysis also differ in the two cases. In hysteria, these disorders are deeper and more frequent than in organic paralyses.

The problem Freud now faces is the following: either functional lesions are real organic ones and respect the anatomy of the nervous system, or they refer to a causality that escapes neurology. Freud concludes:

> I, on the contrary, assert that the lesion in hysterical paralyses must be completely independent of the anatomy of the nervous system, since *in its paralyses and other manifestations hysteria behaves as though anatomy did not exist or as though it had no knowledge of it* (…). It takes the organs in the ordinary, popular sense of the names they bear: the leg is the leg as far up as its insertion into the hip, the arm is the upper limb as it is visible under the clothing.[42]

Hysteria demands more than a neurological explanation: "I only ask permission to move on to psychological ground – which can scarcely be avoided in dealing with hysteria".[43] Unlike Erichsen, Oppenheim and Charcot, Freud leaves the domain of neurology and goes in search of an exclusively psychological explanation.

3. Hysterics suffer from reminiscences

In the last part of his text on the distinction between hysterical and organic paralyses, Freud for the first time provides an exclusively psychological explanation of hysterical symptoms. In many respects, this explanation is in line with Charcot's vision and, as Freud himself notes, with the views of the French psychologist Pierre Janet (1859-1947) on dissociation.[44] We recall how in Charcot's patient 'Le Log', the feeling of numbness in the lower limbs gave way to the idea of paralysis that, because of the simultaneous elimination of the ego, could occupy all brain activity. Thus, the idea of paralysis could not be incorporated as a consistent center of synthesis. It led, as it were, to an autonomous (disassociated or split off) existence over which the conscious had no control.

Freud firstly takes this perspective further. He wants to inquire how a functional change – paralysis, for example – can occur without an accompanying organic lesion. When hysterical paralyses do not consider the anatomy of the nervous system, the lesion at the origin of such paralysis must be a change in the mental representation of, for example, an arm. This change exists in the dissociation of this representation from the other ideas the ego forms: "The lesion would therefore be *the abolition of the associative accessibility of the conception of the arm*".[45] This representation must have become inaccessible, without being damaged or destroyed in the material substrate.

The idea of associative inaccessibility is still close to Charcot's thinking.[46] But in the text we are discussing here, Freud takes a new and decisive step in the progressive psychologization of trauma we are attempting to reconstruct. Every psychological impression or experience, he writes, is equipped with a certain affect value from which the ego needs to rid itself via a motor reaction (weeping or hitting, for example) or associative psychical act (speaking about it, for example). When this does not happen, the memory of the impression or experience gains the weight of trauma and becomes the cause of lasting symptoms.[47] Freud illustrates this process by referring to the amusing story of a man who never wanted to wash his hand as it had touched the king. The relationship between his hand and the king was so important for this man that he refused it contact with anything else. Similarly, the representation of an arm or leg could become connected to an impression of or an association with great affect value – an accident, for example – separating it from other associations. This separation occurs according to Freud "because the whole of its [of the representation – HW/PvH] associative affinity, so to say, is saturated in a subconscious association with the memory of the event, the trauma, which produced the paralysis".[48] The affected body part regains its freedom when this affect can be discharged *in extremis* by an adequate motor response or through conscious psychical effort. The latter is, according to Freud, at once the ultimate proof of his theory.[49]

The psychologization of trauma is thus essentially complete. For Freud, trauma is no longer an external physical shock that brings about symptoms by virtue of the supposed organic lesions it causes. On the contrary, it is a memory that attacks us, as it were, from within and whose traumatic character is determined by its accompanying affect. It is exactly this affect that explains why this memory is separated from other associations and representations. "*Hysterics*", Freud concludes, "*suffer mainly from reminiscences*".

4. *Hysteria and trauma*

In the same year, 1895, in which 'Some Points for a Comparative Study of Organic and Hysterical Motor Paralyses' appeared, Breuer and Freud's 'On the Psychical Mechanism of Hysterical Phenomena: Preliminary Communication' was published. A reprint of this text was later added as an introduction to *Studies on Hysteria*. The 'Preliminary Communication', together with the text on 'organic and hysterical paralyses' marks the period in which Freud makes the move into psychology. This development would be completed in *Studies on Hysteria* and more so in three programmatic texts from 1896 that comprise the canonical version of his seduction theory.[50] In 'Preliminary Communication', Freud first completes several important changes that were of particular importance for the further development of his theory.

In the first place, Freud here reaffirms the rejection of the strict distinction between traumatic neurosis and traumatic hysteria that we have already discussed. Traumatic neurosis is not caused by physical shock or lesion, as Oppenheim for example thought, but by the 'fright affect', that is, by a psychical trauma. In the same way, Freud continues, research shows that in most if not all cases, hysterical symptoms are also caused by psychical traumas. This undermines the distinction between traumatic neurosis and traumatic hysteria. Every incident that evokes affects such as fright, shame or psychical suffering can generate a traumatic effect. In 'common hysteria' it often concerns "a number of partial traumas forming a group of provoking causes. These have only been able to exercise a traumatic effect by summation and they belong together in so far as they are in part components of a single story of suffering".[51]

Following Charcot, Freud then further distinguishes in the text between 'disposed hysteria' and 'acquired hysteria'. The former is preceded by hypnoid, abnormal states of consciousness underlying the separation of a representation. Patients prone to this are, as it were, predestined to become hysterical. But according to Freud, this dissociation can also come about after severe traumas such as in traumatic neurosis or after a difficult suppression such as a sexual affect. Here Freud speaks about a '*psychically acquired* hysteria'. He writes: "Between the extremes of these two forms we must assume the existence of a series of cases within which the liability to dissociation in the subject and the affective magnitude of the trauma vary inversely".[52] This clarification is not trivial. After all, it suggests that the distinction between 'disposed hysteria' and 'traumatic hysteria' is but relative. In other words, it not only brings traumatic neurosis within the ambit of hysteria but, at the same time, it fundamentally connects with trauma[53] and in principle determines it independently of predisposed hypnoid conditions.

The evolution described up till now can be summarized as follows. Concussion of the spine and traumatic neuroses discussed by Erichsen and Oppenheim was clearly distinct from hysteria and caused by a mechanical shock that resulted in a change in the nervous system. Charcot interpreted traumatic neurosis as traumatic hysteria. According to Charcot, traumatic hysteria was not the result of an actual trauma but of a neuropathic disposition. Freud now relativizes the distinction between 'traumatic' and 'disposed' hysteria. All forms of hysteria are, in principle, traumatic. Trauma itself is no longer an actual external event but the memory of an affect-laden one. For now, trauma here remains nonspecific: it may concern an accident, sexual seduction or something experienced as particularly shameful. In other words, it concerns any event with special affect value that cannot be disposed of and is therefore split off. The nonspecific nature of trauma in the texts of this period is related to Freud's insistence, for the time being, on Charcot's – and Pierre Janet's – theory of dissociation as mechanism of hysterical symptoms. At the end of 'Preliminary Communication', he writes, however: "we cannot conceal (…) that this has brought us nearer to an understanding only of the *mechanism* of hysterical symptoms and not of the internal causes of hysteria".[54]

Freud will soon find these 'inner causes' in a conflict that is essentially sexual. This is what his seduction theory of psychopathology is all about. It concerns a further radicalization of the psychologization of the trauma being discussed here. At the same time, Freud will leave dissociation theory behind and replace it with a theory on the repression of psychic conflict.

5. Seduction theory and the sexualization of trauma

In the years between the first publication of 'Preliminary Communication' in 1893 and the publication, in the run of 1896, of the three programmatic texts on seduction theory we mentioned earlier, there are two parallel developments with respect to the status of trauma. On the one hand, trauma is progressively sexualized, and on the other, this trauma at the same time obtains a more complicated, *temporal* structure. A discussion of both these evolutions will also allow us to show how and why Freud's confirmation of the primacy of sexual trauma is consistent with the *internal* development of his *own theory*.

In 'Preliminary Communication' Freud still primarily thinks of the aetiology of hysteria in terms of a simple model of cause and effect. A single traumatic event causes one or more hysterical symptoms. Unlike Charcot, Freud does not consider this trauma as a trigger (*agent provocateur*) that activates a neuropathical disposition but as a "foreign body" (*Fremdkörper*) that continues to determine the symptom even after its actual occurrence as a memory.[55] According to Freud, this is evidenced by the fact that hysterical symptoms disappear immediately when this cause can be recalled in the analysis.[56]

Freud soon abandons this overly simplified model, however. Multiple symptoms cannot be derived from a single event. On the contrary, these symptoms refer to a complex network of interconnected events and scenes. We find a good example of this problematic in the third observation from *Studies on Hysteria* in which Freud discusses the case of 'Miss Lucy R'.[57] Lucy suffers from recurring olfactory hallucinations. What it amounts to, Freud writes, is to find an experience in which these olfactory sensations that have now become subjective also existed objectively. In fact, these olfactory sensations should be regarded as a memory symbol of trauma.[58] The smell that most haunts Lucy is the smell of burned pudding. Freud takes this smell as point of departure for his analysis, and thus finds a first traumatic scene. As Lucy was busy cooking with the children of her employer, a wealthy industrialist whose wife had died some time before, the post came, including a letter from her mother. The children wrestled the letter from her hands and said they would keep it for her so she could read it on her birthday. While the children were dancing around her, she noticed the smell of burned pudding abandoned by the children. From this time, she was haunted by this smell. Freud points out that two conflicting affects are expressed in this scene. On the one hand, her love for the children, but also on the other, her desire to return to her own mother. Her love for the children is strengthened further in that she promised their mother on her deathbed she would care for them. And she told Freud that her desire to return to her mother related to conflicts between herself and some colleagues and with the fact that the father of the children would not have sufficiently supported her in the process. In reconstructing the causes of Lucy's pathology, in other words, Freud does not encounter dissociation and fragmentation but inner affective conflicts.[59] Freud concludes: "The conflict between her affects had elevated the moment (…) into a trauma, and the sensation of smell that was associated with trauma persisted".[60]

But this explanation still leaves much to be desired. It is neither yet clear why smell was chosen as mnemic symbol, nor why "these agitations and this conflict of affects should have led to hysteria".[61] Regarding the former, Freud refers to the process of repression, which from now on would unequivocally replace dissociation as the explanatory mechanism. In 'Some Points for a Comparative Study of Organic and Hysterical Motor Paralyses', Freud, in line with Charcot and Janet, still assumed hysterical paralysis arises from *the abolition of the associative accessibility* of the conception of the affected limb (for example, the arm).

This inability is related to the hypnoid condition in which the patient finds themselves at the moment of trauma or that is induced by it. Also in the 'Preliminary Communication', this is the model ('*splitting of consciousness*'). Dissociation is, especially for Charcot and Janet, a deficit. The traumatic experience leads to disintegration of the ego. Repression, on the other hand, is an *active* defense mechanism. The ego comes into conflict with the affect-laden representation that actively pushes it away to the unconscious. In the first instance, Freud still regarded repression as a deliberate activity, and he talks about an act of volition or also a 'hysterical counter-will'.[62] The ground for repression can, according to Freud, only be a sensation of unpleasure. What is repressed is a representation that is incompatible with the ego. But what then is the unacceptable representation that Miss Lucy wants to repress? Freud suspects that Miss Lucy did not tell him the whole story. Behind her story hides unrequited love for the father of the children and the desire to take their mother's place with the father. The conflicts with her colleagues are an expression of the anxiety that they might notice her attachment to and infatuation with her employer. It is this representation she does not want to be reminded of because it is unpleasurable, and that she wants to banish from her consciousness or repress. At the same time, the amount of excitation with which this representation is connected and that is, as it were, the index for the importance Lucy attaches to it is invested in the body (conversion).

The fact that it is specifically the sensation of smell that is chosen as mnemonic symbol has everything to do, according to Freud, with the chronic nasal condition she suffers from and that at times prevent her from smelling anything. However, the smell of burned pudding could have broken this incapacity. In his study of Dora, Freud speaks of a '*somatic compliance*' (*somatisches Entgegenkommen*) in this context:[63] the sum of excitation is converted into a pre-existing 'somatic innervation' and the consequent gain is the "incompatibility between the single idea that is to be repressed and the dominant mass of ideas constituting the ego".[64]

However, the elucidation of this olfactory hallucination does not lead to its disappearance. Freud also suspects that this "symbol (...) in addition to the main scene (...) had taken over the representation of the many minor traumas".[65] One day, Lucy tells Freud that the smell of burned pudding had disappeared but had been replaced by the smell of cigar smoke. This smell was also there before the burned pudding. The analysis of this new smell sensation leads to another scene where the main accountant of the children's father's business wanted to kiss the children goodbye. The father jumped up and yelled: 'Don't kiss the children'. Lucy then felt 'a stab in her heart', and because the men were smoking, this smell had been burned into her memory.[66]

But the meaning of this scene also raises questions. Specifically, it is not clear why Lucy feels a 'stab in her heart' at the father's vehement reaction to something she has no real part in anyway. An even older scene brings more clarity here. When she was still hoping that the rich industrialist would react positively to her infatuation, he reacted vehemently towards her after a lady friend kissed the children goodbye on the mouth. He threatened to fire her should it happen again. All her hopes for a future with this man went up in smoke in this scene. 'If he can lash out at me like that for something insignificant for which I also cannot be held responsible, then surely he has never loved me'. This memory occurred to her when the accountant wanted to kiss the children and explains her reaction – 'a stab in her heart' – during this later scene. At this point in the analysis, the olfactory hallucinations and also the depression from which she simultaneously suffered disappeared.

Freud relates Lucy's successive hysterical symptoms with various traumatic scenes. The actual traumatic moment is the event that comes last, the scene in which the father is angered by the kisses of the lady friend and the accompanying libidinal disillusionment. Although this scene is repressed, it initially remains without effect, even if Freud notes that Lucy's dejection may have begun at that point. The symptoms do not occur until later, when other events that "may be described as 'auxiliary'", such as the scene with the accountant, calls the former back into consciousness.[67] This may give the auxiliary event a traumatic meaning. In the incident with the accountant, Lucy accordingly behaves "as though she had got rid of everything connected with her devotion to her employer".[68] She feels 'a stab at the heart' that concerned the (assumed) spurned love for her employer. The traumatic meaning of this and other scenes is grounded in the sensations of unpleasure they evoke. Hysterical patients thus suffer not only from memories but equally from an inner and thus psychical conflict between an affect associated with this memory and the ego.

Of particular importance here, however, is the following: not only has trauma acquired an exclusively psychical meaning, but it is also no longer a single event that as exclusive cause explains the manifestation of the pathology. On the contrary, it concerns in this instance *a succession of interconnected* events that can explain the pathogenesis in their temporal coherence. Moreover, the unacceptable representation that is being repressed is libidinal in nature. This also applies in principle to the other cases discussed in *Studies on Hysteria*. We are thus only a step away from the classic formulation of the theory of seduction.

Freud formulates the seduction theory of hysteria in the three canonical texts from 1896 we mentioned earlier. In 'The Aetiology of Hysteria', he argues that when a hysterical symptom – vomiting, for instance – can be traced in the first instance to the fright at a railway accident, this accident inevitably triggered another event that is better able to explain this symptom, for example, the sight of a cadaver. Freud in this regard distinguishes between the *suitability as a determinant* of a trauma and the *traumatic force* that emanates from it.[69] The fright experienced during a railway accident is perhaps intense enough to be traumatizing, but it has no substantive connection to hysterical vomiting. The sight of a rotting cadaver, on the other hand, does. But Freud immediately goes a step further. As of now it is known that if we go back far enough along the chain of interconnected memories, we sooner or later inevitably end up in the realm of sexuality.[70] Hysterics in other words suffer from memories of sexual experiences, and these memories, Freud adds, usually relate to adolescence. However, according to Freud, the pubescent events discussed in analysis often lack any traumatic force: an innocent touch of a leg or an obscene remark. Sometimes the 'suitability to determination' is also absent. In other words, these events stemming from puberty often do not adequately explain hysterical symptoms. The latter presupposes that we go back even further to "earliest childhood (…) before the development of sexual life".[71]

How should we imagine this now? In his 'Project for a Scientific Psychology' from 1895, Freud describes the case of Emma Eckstein who was abused by a drugstore assistant at the age of eight – that is, before the onset of puberty. The assistant touched her genitals through her clothes. This event initially had seemingly no pathogenic effect.[72] An effect does not occur until Emma enters a clothing store at age twelve – and thus at the onset of puberty. She sees two men, one of whom she sees as sexually attractive, laughing. The man's smile reminds her of the grin on the drugstore assistant's face when he groped her. This memory now surfaces at the edge of her consciousness. But Emma is an adolescent, and she now understands the sexual meaning of what happened a few years before. She also connects this meaning with her own interest in one of the two shop assistants.[73] She finds this representation unacceptable and unpleasurable. It is repressed, and Emma then develops a phobia of stores. She no longer dares enter them alone.[74]

The history of Emma Eckstein reminds us of the one of Lucy R. According to Freud, in both cases, the hysterical pathology is caused by interconnected traumatic events, and it implies a conflict between the ego and affect-laden representations associated with this event.[75] Repression is the result of the conflict. In both cases, the original trauma also initially remains without effect. According to Freud, this is the case because sexuality does not make its appearance until adolescence. Therefore, trauma only has an effect if it is *remembered* in conjunction with a new event at the onset of puberty and can take on a sexual meaning. The case of Emma Eckstein provides a striking illustration. The first event takes place in a pre-sexual period in which Emma cannot yet understand what is happening to her. This changes at the onset of adolescence. Only now – in retrospect (*nachträglich)*, says Freud – does the original event obtain sexual significance.[76] The defense reaction occurs only in this second moment because the sexual meaning and content of this event can only be understood then. Freud writes that infantile sexual experiences "create the hysterical symptoms, but that they do not do so immediately, but remain without effect to begin with and only exercise a pathogenic action later, when they have been aroused after puberty in the form of unconscious memories".[77]

The seduction theory states that all 'neuroses of defense' are caused by sexual traumas. Freud's examples of seduction often relate to abuse in a strict sense. He identifies seduction with being overpowered by another (often or usually the father). This overpowering is according to Freud unpleasurable, as it is passively endured. The original seduction in hysteria is a scene in which the child is passive and for this reason experiences unpleasure. Freudian seduction can, however, not be limited to abuse. As we will explore further in detail in our discussion of the studies of Dora and especially the Wolf Man, *Verführung/verführen* in Freud's work often refers to *ablenken*, that is, 'to deviate from the normal course'. Sexual abuse disrupts sexual development and diverts it from its 'normal' path. But according to Freud other events can have the same effect: observing sexual scenes (of animals or people), sexual games of children or even the (early) acquisition of knowledge of sexuality have equal potential to disrupt 'normal' development. Seduction and abuse are thus by no means synonyms in Freud's work.

Freud also thinks that obsessional neurosis and paranoia could be explained from the paradigm of seduction.[78] In this light, whether someone becomes hysterical, develops obsessional neurosis or paranoia relates to the timing of the trauma and whether it was experienced actively or passively. Obsessional neurosis and paranoia would not be caused by a passive experience, but by an active and pleasurable sexual experience during later childhood. The existence of active, pleasurable experiences in childhood compels Freud to explain how and why these experiences can at a later stage obtain an unpleasurable character and give rise to an obsessional neurotic or paranoid problematic. In line with the general tenets of seduction theory, Freud postulates to explain this transformation as a passive, unpleasurable experience that would have preceded the active, pleasurable experience.[79]

6. Some reflections on the primacy of sexuality

Psychologization and sexualization of trauma go hand in hand in Freud. They are two sides of the same coin. How can this be understood? What are the motives that convinced Freud of the *exclusively* sexual aetiology of neurosis, as expressed in seduction theory? A conclusive answer to this question is difficult, but perhaps we could formulate some hypotheses that can shed some light on this problematic.

We described in the preceding part the increasing psychologization of the concept of trauma from Erichsen to Freud. This psychologization is also an internalization. Even though, as we discussed earlier, Charcot and Janet contributed significantly to the psychologization of the concept of trauma, trauma for them remained an external event. Moreover, this trauma has no intersubjective character. It does not involve someone who does something in relation to someone else. In the seduction theory, the latter is indeed the case.[80] According to Freud, moreover, it is not the external event that is traumatizing but rather the memory thereof insofar it implies a conflict between an affect-laden representation and the ego. The pathogenic effect of the memory presupposes an initial event that remains without significant effect, and this, he believes, is only possible in the sphere of sexuality. Indeed, at the time, Freud still believes there is no such thing as infantile sexuality.[81] In children, the sexual drives have not yet been activated, and the sexual organs are not yet developed to maturity. This explains why events of a sexual nature, according to Freud, can have no immediate effect in children. After all, there is no infantile (pre-pubescent) sexuality. At the onset of puberty, these events then evoke a traumatic effect *nachträglich*:

> An inverted relation of this sort between real experience and memory seems to contain the psychological precondition for the occurrence of a repression. Sexual life affords—through the retardation of pubertal maturity as compared with the psychical functions—the only possibility that occurs for this inversion of relative effectiveness. *The traumas of childhood operate in a deferred fashion as though they were fresh experiences; but they do so unconsciously.*[82]

Elsewhere Freud writes in the same perspective that only in the domain of sexuality a memory has "a greater releasing power subsequently than had been produced by the experience corresponding to it".[83]

This view also fits nicely with another a priori of Freudian thought and science of Freud's time. Freud and many of his contemporaries, such as Krafft-Ebing and Moll, thought and operated from a Darwinist frame of reference. According to Darwin, evolution is determined by two fundamental principles: natural selection (struggle for existence) and sexual selection (struggle for reproduction).[84] In his later texts, and especially from *Three Essays on the Theory of Sexuality* from 1905, Freud translates this distinction to psychology.[85] There are two, and only two, fundamental drives: self-preservation drives and sexual drives. From the publication of *Three Essays*, Freud will argue that psychic life is determined by a fundamental conflict between both these drives. The conflict between the ego and a memory of a sexual nature that is at the center of seduction theory is, as it were, an antecedent to this contradiction, and it dovetails seamlessly with Freud's Darwinian thought.[86]

7. The problem with the seduction theory and the discovery of infantile sexuality

Freud did not defend the theory of seduction in its canonical form for very long. In actual fact, it is a theory that he adhered to in this form for only a year. In the letter to his friend Wilhelm Fliess dated 21 September 1897, he already writes that he no longer believes in his *neurotica*.[87] With *neurotica*, Freud means his 'theory of the neurosis' and thus seduction theory. He gives several reasons why he no longer believes in this theory. In the first place, he refers to his inability to bring an analysis to a proper and complete conclusion and thus achieve a complete cure. Next Freud had found that in most cases the father was blamed for perverse abuse. If this abuse lies at the origin of hysteria, then we must assume that it occurs even more frequently than hysteria itself. After all, pathology does not occur with occasional abuse and, moreover, assumes that defense mechanisms have failed, which is not always the case. However, according to Freud, it is hard to believe that there could be so many perverse fathers. Seduction theory thus loses credibility. Third, we can never rule out that seduction fantasies are shaped during puberty with the help of the knowledge of sexuality then present, and subsequently projected back onto childhood from there. After all, the unconscious does not distinguish between reality and an affect-laden fiction. And finally, it is notable that even in the deepest psychosis where the unconscious is fully exposed as it were, the theme of sexual abuse is not broached. If this were the case, how could one then hope to retrieve these memories through analysis?[88]

It is especially the second and third reasons that Freud mentions in his letter to Fliess for abandoning the theory of seduction, and that played a significant part in Freud's perception and interpretation. We already noted in our introduction that both Freud-adepts and Freud-exegetes invariably assume that Freud in 1897 would have replaced the theory of seduction with an oedipal theory of phantasm. The stories of abuse by the father would be nothing but the distorted expression of sexual desire for the father. In other words, there are not an inordinate number of perverse fathers, but the desire for the father is, particularly in young girls, a structural fact. Psychoanalysis, so it is thought, is born the moment Freud discovers the essentially oedipal structure of the unconscious desire. In this way, trauma and desire are understood as each other's opposites.[89]

In the following chapters, we shall see that these interpretations are at the very least unsubtle and perhaps simply incorrect. For now, we just want to underline that Freud himself did not emphasize the oedipal problematic as much as reintroduce a reference to dispositional aspects and heredity as basic conditions for the development of neurosis. Freud writes: "And with this the factor of a hereditary disposition regains a sphere of influence from which I had made it my task to expel it".[90] *Expressis verbis* against Charcot, seduction theory wanted to be a *pure* psychological theory. The rediscovery of the importance of heredity is the logical outcome of several paradoxes and problems that undermined the theory of seduction from the beginning.

Seduction theory is a general theory of neurosis.[91] It exposes not only the cause of hysteria but also the cause of obsessional neurosis and paranoia. So,

Freud must also explain *within the framework of the theory of seduction* why someone becomes hysterical rather than compulsively neurotic or paranoid. Freud now argues, as we indicated earlier, that the original seduction in hysteria is a scene in which the child remained passive and that was experienced as unpleasurable. In obsessional neurosis, on the other hand, the child is according to him actively involved in the original seduction, and it is also a source of pleasure.[92] In obsessional neurosis, this seduction is later repressed because of the self-reproaches the memory of it evokes.

In this way, however, the pathogenesis of obsessional neurosis seems to imply the existence of infantile sexuality.[93] After all, how could the small child actively pursue sexual desire if infantile sexuality did not exist? At the same time, the asexuality of the infantile period was a cornerstone of the seduction theory, according to Freud. To solve this problem, he introduces a phasing in of childhood. Seduction must be situated earlier in the case of hysteria (up to age four) than in the case of obsessional neurosis (between four and eight years).[94] The strictly asexual period is thus pushed back to the period up to four years of age, but a new problem arises immediately. How can the memory of a pleasure experience induce unpleasure? Freud, as we already know, initially solves this problem by arguing that in the case of obsessional neurosis the pleasurable experience is preceded by an earlier unpleasurable and painful experience: "We may suppose that it is the later convergence of this passive experience with the experience of pleasure that adds the unpleasure to the pleasurable memory and makes repression possible".[95]

Decisive in this discussion on infantile sexuality is also and perhaps especially the problematic of the aetiology of the perversions. Sexual perversions inevitably take Freud beyond the theory of seduction. One would normally expect pleasurable sexual experience from childhood to evoke even greater pleasure when remembered at the onset of puberty. It is precisely what happens in perversion: the perverse subject feels compelled to repeat endlessly the infantile experience of pleasure and the perverse acts that caused it. For Freud, the perversion is related to an experience of pleasure that begins before the age of four years and continues in the period between four and eight years. The memory of these experiences is intensified at the onset of puberty, resulting in perversion and sexual compulsion. But this theory of perversion implies the existence of infantile sexuality. After all, one can only be affected if one is also 'affectable'.[96] A perverse seduction can only affect someone who can experience pleasure at the erogenous zones.[97] Thus, in a letter to Fliess written in the period straight after the supposed abandonment of the theory of seduction, Freud argues that infantile sexuality is not provoked by seduction but should be seen as a spontaneous organic process.[98] Freud's explanation of perversion destroys one of the foundations of the original seduction theory: the asexuality and passivity of the child.

8. Towards a theory of sexuality

We are now in a better position to understand what Freud means in his letter of 21 September 1897 when he writes that abandoning his *neurotica* brought hereditary and dispositional factors back to the fore. The discovery of infantile sexuality made it necessary to clearly chart its constitutional elements. At the same time these hereditary and dispositional factors had to provide insight into the way in which pleasurable infantile sexual activities could *nachträglich* be experienced as unpleasure during adolescence. After all, Freud could hardly explain this transformation from pleasure into unpleasure from pure psychological theory. He expected a final explanation from an organic theory of sexuality. In manuscript K, which he sent to Wilhelm Fliess in January 1896, he wrote: "So long as there is no correct theory of the sexual process, the question of the origin of the unpleasure operating in repression remains unanswered".[99]

Even before explicitly abandoning seduction theory in the letter of 21 September 1897 to Fliess,[100] Freud seeks an answer to this problem in an organic theory of sexuality. At first Freud hoped that Fliess would provide him with such a theory,[101] but he gradually realized that he would have to do this himself. Freud's efforts eventually culminated in the first edition of his *Three Essays on the Theory of Sexuality*, which was published in 1905. *Three Essays* articulates an 'organic-sexual' theory that forms the biological base for Freud's psychological theory of neurosis.[102] In a letter to Fliess of 22 September 1898, Freud writes in this regard: "I am not at all in disagreement with you, not at all inclined to leave the psychology hanging in the air without an organic basis".[103] The contours of this organic foundation already become clear in the exchange of letters with Wilhelm Fliess at the turn of the 20th century.

A first important element from the organic-sexual theory is the idea that humans are essentially bisexual.[104] Freud derived this insight in part from Wilhelm Fliess, and he held to it until the end of his life. In *Three Essays on the Theory of Sexuality* he will use this, for example, to explain that there are both homo- and heterosexual inclinations in every human being. A second important element is the theory of organic repression. Freud writes about this in an important letter of 14 November 1897: "I have often suspected that something organic played a part in repression; I was able once before to tell you that it was a question of the abandonment of former sexual zones".[105] In the young child, the oral and anal zones of the body, as with animals, are sources of unproblematic pleasure experiences. The body is a constant source of pleasurable stimulation in which certain specific *erogenous* zones play a special role. In humans, unlike animals, these erogenous zones are given up during psycho-sexual development. When these zones are at a later stage – for example during puberty – libidinally reoccupied, it does not lead to "a release of libido but of an unpleasure, an internal situation which is analogous to disgust in the case of an object".[106] Just as we turn away in disgust from a foul-smelling object, the preconscious now turns away from the memory of the erogenous experience of pleasure: "To put it crudely, the current memory stinks just as an actual object stinks; and as we turn away our sense organ in disgust, so do our preconscious and our conscious sense turn away from the memory. This is *repression*".[107]

This theory answers the question of the spontaneous conversion of pleasure into unpleasure that had become a crucial problem for Freud's theory of neurosis. According to Freud, this conversion and thus repression is not the result of neurosis – it is therefore no pathological process – but the result of a *general-human spontaneous process* that is founded in our biological constitution. That is why Freud speaks of an *organic* repression. According to Freud, this repression is at the same time "the affective basis for a multitude of intellectual processes of development, such as morality, shame, etc. Thus the whole of this arises at the expense of extinct (potential) sexuality".[108] Only a being capable of shame and disgust can also develop moral sensitivity. In *Three Essays on the Theory of Sexuality*, Freud notes shame, disgust and moral 'reaction-formations' that are formed spontaneously at the expense of infantile sexuality.[109]

In chapter five, we will see in further detail that Freud, in his explorations of a biological constitution and of organic processes, draws on insights from evolutionary biology – insights with which he had been very familiar since his student days.[110] According to Freud, the conversion of pleasure into unpleasure can best be understood from an evolutionary perspective. Evolution from animal to human is accompanied by physical changes such as a clear distinction between excretory- and reproductive organs. Also, humans are characterized by walking upright, with a consequent changing role of smell and the emergence of disgust for the trails of excretion that humans (and animals) leave on the ground. Because Freud, following Ernst Haeckel and many other contemporaries, assumes that this evolution repeats itself in short form in every individual, the body in each individual is, in principle, a source of pleasurable stimulation and experience at various erogenous zones, but this pleasurable experience becomes the object of disgust and shame as early as infancy. Sexuality, consequently, is essentially conflictual. This conflict is not rooted in the opposition between sexuality and culture but finds its origin in sexual physicality itself.

Freud further argues that sexuality in childhood is essentially autoerotic. In a letter of 9 December 1899, he confirms: "The lowest sexual stratum is auto-erotism, which does without any psychosexual aim and demands only local feelings of satisfaction It is succeeded by allo-erotism (homo- and hetero-erotism)".[111] In *Three Essays*, Freud confirms this statement: infantile sexuality is essentially *autoerotic*, that is to say, 'without object' and thus also without fantasy.[112] Indeed, according to Freud, fantasy always implies a scene in which the object plays a role. This also means that, according to Freud, infantile sexuality can be described in exclusively physiological terms. It is not mediated by phantasmatic representations. Infantile sexuality is nothing but non-functional corporeal experiences of pleasure. It is profoundly no more than pleasurable tickling without psychical (phantasmatic) processing or support. At the onset of puberty, infantile sexuality is replaced by object-oriented adult sexuality. Sexuality will now explicitly focus on the search for an object, but this search is now more specifically motivated by a new type of sexual desire that was impossible until then: orgasm ('end pleasure'). Either way, it is not the nature of the object (man or woman) that primarily determines its meaning, but the pleasure it promises.[113]

9. Sexuality and fantasy

The autoerotic character of infantile sexuality is at once one of the most important arguments against the idea that Freud would have replaced seduction theory with a theory of oedipal phantasm as early as 1897. Since phantasm is inevitably object-oriented, oedipal phantasm and desire are only possible once sexuality becomes 'allo-erotic', that is, actively oriented towards the object. This is not yet the case in the infantile period. Sexuality becomes explicitly object-oriented only at the onset of puberty. Up until this time, the object plays a purely instrumental role and is not sought for its own sake.[114]

This does not, however, prevent Freud, during the time following his supposed abandonment of seduction theory, from also seeking a theory of fantasy life in line with the new biological theory of sexuality. If seduction could be seen unequivocally as a reality through which an asexual child is prematurely introduced to sexuality by a perverse adult, infantile fantasy life was not a special problem. Its perverse content could be explained by real seduction. However, Freud now no longer understands the stories about perverse seductions and other sexual experiences exclusively as 'memories',[115] but also as 'fantasies'. These fantasies are, as we read in a letter of 3 January 1899 "products of later periods and are projected back from the then present on the earliest childhood".[116] A few days later Freud adds: "Puberty is becoming ever more central; fantasy as the key holds fast".[117] Freud specifies the thought that fantasies are products of later periods and specifically of puberty as the period in which fantasy is "projected back into the past so that the new persons become aligned with the old ones, who become their prototypes".[118]

That 'fantasizing' is essentially 'fantasizing back' is intrinsically related to the autoerotic character of infantile sexuality. When the latter can be described in purely physiological terms, it also immediately means that a psychological meaning can be given to it only later. One thinks here again of Emma Eckstein and the problematic of *nachträglichkeit* that we raised there. In the case of Emma Eckstein, the memory was first sexualized at the onset of puberty. It is true that Freud recognized the existence of infantile sexuality after 1897, but its autoerotic character implies that the original pleasurable sexual experience is only associated with concrete sexual representations and objects for the first time when puberty begins. At that moment, the original erogenous zones are reinvested through object-oriented adolescent sexuality. Explicitly perverse fantasies and representations result from this. In the case of Dora, which we discuss in more detail in the next chapter, Freud for instance writes that Dora frantically sucked her thumb as a small child. From this he concludes that the oral zone was very strongly developed in her. During infancy, however, experiences of oral pleasure are not yet associated with objects or fantasies about objects. It is only in puberty that sexuality – including oral sexuality – becomes object-oriented. Thus, when Dora is almost nineteen years old, she will develop a fellatio fantasy. Again, this involves the oral drive, but this time, this drive is focused on an object. According to Freud, this is a reinvestment of the oral zone from adult sexuality. So, it would be a misconception to speak of an infantile fantasy here. After all, the infantile period itself was characterized only by a preference for oral pleasure experiences.[119]

10. Sexuality and the pleasure principle

We have encountered the problem of pleasure in various ways in this chapter's account. Very early on, Freud was confronted by the problem of how an experience that at first has hardly any effect (the first time of trauma) or is experienced as pleasurable (for instance in obsessional neurosis) can become unpleasurable at a later stage and especially during puberty. To explain this phenomenon, Freud introduces organic repression. It is this transformation of a pleasurable or affective neutral experience into an unpleasurable memory that explains why the latter is repressed. Even in the early years of psychoanalysis, the motive for repressing a representation is always the unpleasure it would cause in the ego if it were to become conscious. One thinks here, for example, of the Emma Eckstein case: it is only at the onset of puberty that the memory of the assault by the grocer acquires a sexual meaning and becomes unpleasurable. The repression thus illustrates the general tendency of the psychic apparatus to avoid unpleasure. Thus, in his early works, Freud speaks of an unpleasure principle in this regard; later he renames it the pleasure principle.[120] This unpleasure- or pleasure principle automatically regulates the psychic apparatus, that is, it determines the function of the (pre-)conscious as well as the unconscious system. Freud furthermore identifies 'pleasure' with a decrease in tension, and unpleasure with an increase thereof.[121] The qualitative properties that determine the psychic system (pleasure-unpleasure) are thus made dependent on purely quantitative factors: increase or decrease in tension.

The Freudian (un-)pleasure principle is undoubtedly worthy of a separate study. We cannot discuss it in depth here. We want to highlight only a few aspects that are relevant to the theme we discuss in this book. First, we need to distinguish the pleasure principle from the constancy principle. In 'Project for a Scientific Psychology' from 1895, Freud posits a primary trend of the psychic apparatus to fully release tension. This pleasure principle is "the principle of neuronal inertia" of which the constancy principle is an adaptation.[122] According to Freud, this constancy principle expresses the tendency to keep the tension at as low and constant a level as possible. It is a modification of the 'principle of neuronal inertia' that comes about under pressure from the necessities of life.[123] Indeed, if the organism were directed only to a total reduction of tension, it could not survive for long. Consequently, to avoid its own destruction, it must be transformed into a constancy principle.

Freud formulates a strong connection between the (un-)pleasure and the primacy of sexuality that we discussed. In manuscript K, for example, which he wrote to Wilhelm Fliess on 1 January 1896, he writes that the tendency to keep the tension as low as possible (constancy) related only to memories and thoughts, but not on observations of external reality. This tendency is harmless when focused on representations that at the time were associated with unpleasure but are incapable of acquiring current unpleasure (except remembered unpleasure). However, the constancy mechanism becomes harmful – that is, it gives rise to repression and thus to pathology – when it targets sexual representations or memories. The latter is the result of the fact that only sexual memories can induce greater unpleasure at the time they are remembered (puberty) than at the time they were actually experienced.

Later, when Freud would increasingly emphasize, in addition to the role of traumatic sexual events, perverse and other forbidden drive impulses that are repressed to the unconscious, this issue becomes a little more complex. After all, the realization of these drive impulses is essentially pleasurable. It is only unpleasurable for the ego and the higher (moral) agencies. In *Beyond the Pleasure Principle*, Freud will summarize this situation as follows: what is pleasurable for one system (the realization of perverse impulses) is unpleasurable for the other (for example the conscience) and vice versa.[124] Drive renunciation (unpleasure) can indeed be pleasurable for the conscience.

We will return to this issue in more detail in the chapter on *Beyond the Pleasure Principle*. For now, it suffices to say that the pleasure principle is closely linked to the primacy of sexuality. After all, the pleasure principle finds its privileged field of action in the realm of sexuality.

11. Trauma and constitution

The abandonment of seduction theory involves a reconfirmation of the importance of hereditary and dispositional elements in the aetiology of neurosis. These elements are thematized in their interrelatedness in Freud's sexual theory, which he develops from 1897 and which is systematically set out in *Three Essays on the Theory of Sexuality*. However, the rediscovery of hereditary and dispositional factors for the development of neurosis does not mean the complete disappearance of aetiological references to accidental infantile and sexual trauma or traumas. Neither does it mean that these traumas are from here on out always reduced to phantasmatic constructions. What it does mean is that these traumas are no longer seen as the exclusive cause of neurosis? From this point, their function is considered and understood from an intrinsic interaction with innate dispositional and hereditary elements. The three case studies we discuss in the following chapters testify to this.

Before analyzing these studies in greater detail, we would like to determine the general aetiological framework from which Freud would understand the pathology of his patients going forward. He formulates this framework in *Three Essays* and in a short text from 1906 that he wrote shortly thereafter, 'My Views on the Part Played by Sexuality in the Aetiology of the Neuroses'. In *Three Essays*, Freud writes the following, with regards to seduction theory:

> I cannot admit that in my paper on 'The Aetiology of Hysteria' I exaggerated the frequency or importance of that influence, though I did not then know that persons who remain normal may have had the same experiences in their childhood, and though I consequently overrated the importance of seduction in comparison with the factors of sexual constitution and development. Obviously seduction is not required in order to arouse a child's sexual life; that can also come about spontaneously from internal causes.[125]

The reference to an innate sexual constitution means that seduction is no longer needed to explain infantile sexuality. A highly developed constitution in which for instance anal or oral drives and their repression ('internal causes') are strongly represented may in principle be enough to provide insight into a specific pathology.[126] At the same time, the fact that abuse does not always lead to pathology raises the suspicion that the effect of sexual traumas cannot be understood separately from a predetermined constitution. In a general sense, Freud determines the relationship between inherited constitution and disposition on the one hand and accidental events on the other as a complemental series "in which the diminishing intensity of one factor is balanced by the increasing intensity of the other".[127] At both extremes of the series, cases are possible that are exclusively determined by one or both (accidental or hereditary) elements.[128]

We should also not lose sight here of the fact that Freud initially approached repression as a conscious and thus also as a purely psychological process.[129] The reference to an organic repression changed this. Repression and thus conflict comprise an intrinsic part of our sexual constitution. Whether an accidental event will be experienced as traumatic or not then depends completely on our reaction to it, that is, if we react by repression or not. During further development, the repressed pleasurable sexual excitations from infancy connect – especially at the onset of puberty – with perverse fantasies and fantasies about (parental or other) abuse that moves between the symptoms and infantile impressions. In this way, fantasy life does not oppose the external reality in an absolute sense.[130] It is after all constructed from what the child has heard and seen. According to Freud, the unconscious does not distinguish between affectively invested phantasmic construction and reality.

12. Conclusion

In this chapter, we unpacked the origins of Freud's seduction theory in relation to the discussions on the status of traumatic neurosis in psychiatry of particularly the last quarter of the 19th century. Like Charcot, Freud situates traumatic neurosis within hysteria. Moreover, he tries to "bridge the gap between Charcot's traumatic hysteria and common non-traumatic hysteria".[131] Thus, Freud completes the psychologization of trauma that already commenced in the work of Erichsen on *concussion of the spine* and in Oppenheim on traumatic neurosis. This psychologization is in Freud also an internalization, and it is accompanied by a real sexualization: neurosis is caused by the unpleasurable memory of sexual trauma and the accompanying psychical conflict. Internalization and sexualization go hand in hand for Freud: after all, it is only in the sexual sphere – remember the importance and role of adolescence – that the memory of an event can be more intense and threatening than the event itself.

In this psychologization of trauma, Oppenheim's traumatic neurosis becomes completely 'neurotized'. After all, from 1897, Freud thinks that an external event can only be traumatizing when it connects to an existing conflict in which sexuality plays a significant role. This is indeed not evident.[132] Why could, for example, being in or witnessing a terrible accident – Freud calls them 'ordinary traumas' – not be traumatizing *in itself*? Put differently, why should we assume that every trauma goes back to a sexual problematic?

Freud does not consider this question and this problem, however. We see that after the *Studies on Hysteria* and up until World War I in 1914, the reference to traumatic neurosis almost completely disappears from his work. Perhaps it was also clear to Freud that traumatic neurosis was a special problem for seduction theory in that it set or appeared to set a limit for generalizing the sexual conflict model. This conflict model is, however, the *shibboleth* of Freudian psychoanalysis. We could then also ask ourselves if the problematic of traumatic neurosis does not inevitably confront us with the limits of Freudian thought. Later in this book, we will again take up the problematic of traumatic neurosis and its relation to psychoanalysis. In *Beyond the Pleasure Principle*, this pathology indeed once more becomes a central point of attention of Freud's reflections. The many soldiers who became victims of traumatic neurosis during the war years between 1914 and 1918 rekindled the discussion on the status of this problematic within psychiatry.[133] Freud was hereby obliged to take up this problematic once again. He would do so by substantially reconsidering the relationship between drive and trauma within the framework of a tragic human vision that places trauma at the center of organic life. Also, in *Moses and Monotheism* Freud would return to traumatic neurosis, this time to analyze the impact of an aggressive act, the murder of Moses.

Until then, Freud concentrated on elaborating his theory of neurosis. We mentioned that in traditional historiography, it is usually claimed that after 1897, Freud replaced his theory of seduction – *ergo*, his trauma theory – with a theory of (oedipal) fantasy life. However, we can only note that Freud never repeated the 1897 claim that he no 'longer believes in his *neurotica*'. On the contrary, Freud did not reject the reference to trauma but rather integrated its efficacy into a complex network of aetiological factors. Freud, therefore, does not mention abandoning this theory in his published texts but rather speaks about its 'insufficiencies', which he could now complete and correct.[134] Precisely what this completion and correction entails can best be traced in a detailed reading of some of Freud's major case studies – Dora, the Rat Man and the Wolf Man. These case studies are therefore the subject of the next three chapters of this book.

CHAPTER 2

Seduction and hysterical disposition: Dora[1]

1. Introduction

Towards the end of 1900, Freud started the analytic treatment of Ida Bauer – the sister of Otto Bauer, who would later become an influential social-democratic politician.[2] In the psychoanalytical history, Ida Bauer would become known by the name Freud gave her in his case study: 'Dora'. According to Freud, Dora suffered from *petite hystérie*.[3] The spectacular attacks Charcot had described in detail and defined were absent from Dora's syndrome, but she had suffered, from her childhood, from a whole range of more innocent hysterical symptoms: bedwetting, headaches, difficulties with breathing, a nervous cough that just did not want to go away. Freud calls these symptoms 'hysterical' because they cannot be associated with any specific organic lesion. Dora's father brought her to Freud in September 1900 after at the age of seventeen she left a letter lying around announcing her suicide. She had also recently fainted after an argument with her father about his affair with Frau K. Dora herself was not particularly enthusiastic about the idea of going for therapy with Freud, and she soon put an end to it. On 31 December 1900, she informed Freud that she would not return.[4] This is the very reason why Freud speaks in the title about a 'fragment' of the analysis of a case of hysteria. The text of the case study was already ready for publication in 1901. Yet Freud – presumably to be discrete – would wait until 1905 to publish the text for the first time, in the *Monatschrift für Psychiatrie und Neurologie*.

2. Dora and seduction

For those familiar with the classic historiography of Freudian psychoanalysis, the opening lines might come as a surprise:

> In 1895 and 1896 I put forward certain views upon the pathogenesis of hysterical symptoms and upon the mental processes occurring in hysteria. Since that time several years have passed. In now proposing, therefore, to substantiate those views by giving a detailed report of the history of a case and its treatment, I cannot avoid making a few introductory remarks.[5]

So, Freud himself immediately – as much as eight years after supposedly abandoning the theory of seduction – makes a direct connection between this new study and his earlier insights into the pathogenesis of hysteria. Later we will see that the same goes for the other major case studies – the Rat Man and the Wolf Man – which we will also discuss in our book. Therefore, over the years Freud continued to defend the continuity between his early theories on seduction (and the importance of trauma) and his later work. In the study of 'Dora', Freud specifies this continuity as follows:

> Since then [since the publication of *Studies on Hysteria* – HW/PvH] I have seen an abundance of cases of hysteria, and I have been occupied with each case for a number of days, weeks, or years. In not a single one of them have I failed to discover the psychological determinants which were postulated in the *Studies*, namely, a psychical trauma, a conflict of affects, and—an additional factor which I brought forward in later publications—a disturbance in the sphere of sexuality.[6]

'Fragment of an Analysis of a Case of Hysteria' shows how, together, accidental, traumatic events, psychological structure and an organic sexual constitution ('a disturbance in the sphere of sexuality') determine the appearance and course of a concrete case of hysteria. This text therefore does not signal the farewell of the old theory of seduction and the trauma model. In a footnote in the text, Freud, on the contrary, declares that he has gone beyond the limits of this model without abandoning it, however: "All that I have abandoned is the emphasis laid upon the so-called 'hypnoid state', which was supposed to be occasioned in the patient by the trauma, and to be the foundation for all the psychologically abnormal events which followed."[7]

Freud refers in the passages that we just cited to 'later publications' in which he unpacked the 'organic sexual constitution'. In the first instance, this concerns *Three Essays on the Theory of Sexuality*, which is published in the same year as the study of Dora and, as we know, contains a systematic exposition of the polymorphic perverted constitution underlying neurosis in general and hysteria in particular. A year later, Freud added 'My Views on the Part Played by Sexuality in the Aetiology of the Neuroses'. In this text Freud posits, as we already know, that his initial unilateral attention to accidental factors in the aetiology of the neuroses was the result of the fact that his "scanty" material at "that time (…) happened by chance to include a disproportionately large number of cases in which sexual seduction by an adult or by older children played the chief part in the history of the patient's childhood".[8] He immediately adds that the seduction in these cases was 'not open to doubt'. He further argues that the overvaluation of accidental factors had to do with the fact that in the early years he was not able "to distinguish with certainty between falsifications made by hysterics in their memories of childhood and traces of real events".[9] Phantasies of seduction could indeed also be demystified "as attempts at fending off memories of the subject's *own* sexual activity (infantile masturbation)".[10] This discovery of the defensive function of phantasma also leads to a redetermination of the mechanism of hysterical symptoms:

> They were now no longer to be regarded as direct derivatives of the repressed memories of childhood experiences; but between the symptoms and the childish impressions there were inserted the patient's *phantasies* (or imaginary memories), mostly produced during the years of puberty, which on the one side were built up out of and over the childhood memories and on the other side were transformed directly into the symptoms.[11]

According to Freud, the growing insight into the importance of phantasy life in pathogenesis leads not only to the relativization of the aetiological meaning of real traumas but also mainly to "factors of constitution and heredity (gaining) the upper hand once more".[12] These passages clearly show that Freud denies neither reality nor the importance of real traumas but that he now understands their aetiological role and meaning from a complex interplay with phantasy life and constitutional factors. These constitutional factors have a relative predominance.

'Fragment of an Analysis of a Case of Hysteria' should be read as a clinical complement to or illustration of *Three Essays on the Theory of Sexuality* and 'My Views on the Part Played by Sexuality in the Aetiology of the Neuroses'. It shows, by way of a concrete case, the complex interplay of aetiological factors the theoretical texts speak about and that imply a reformulation of the original theory of seduction. According to Freud, this clinical study is "the subtlest thing I have written so far".[13] In what follows, we first discuss the meta-psychological input of 'Fragment of an Analysis of a Case of Hysteria'. Thereafter we discuss the basic symptom of Dora's pathology, dispositional disgust with the sexual. We then delve deeper into the origin of this disgust. Hereby it will become clear in which way the text about Dora illustrates the reformulation of the original theory of seduction, also illuminating it in a striking way.[14]

3. Clinical and meta-psychological aims

In the history of psychoanalysis, the Dora case is especially well-known because of the problem of (counter)transference.[15] In the postscript to the text, Freud describes, for the first time, how transference, which until then he considered a mere obstacle to psychoanalysis, can also become her 'most powerful ally'.[16] Transference, according to Freud, is the inevitable 'latest creation' of the illness in which impulses and fantasies relating to someone from the patient's earlier life are relived in the current relationship with the psychoanalyst.[17] At first glance, the transference thus stands in the way of the memory of the repressed, which is the goal of therapy. At the same time, however, the transference allows the analyst to identify and discuss elements of the repressed that the patient cannot allow to penetrate consciousness. In this way, the psychoanalyst makes a virtue from necessity, and the transference can be conducive to the treatment. Freud further acknowledges that he only noticed Dora's transference too late. Beside her father, Freud also took the place of Herr K., with whom she was in love and who disappointed her in various ways. Dora took revenge on Freud and broke off the relationship. She broke contact with Freud *as if* Freud were Herr K.: "Thus, she *acted out* an essential part of her recollections and phantasies instead of reproducing it in the treatment".[18] In a footnote the same postscript, Freud later writes that he had not noticed the homosexual bond that connected Dora with the spouse of Herr K. Freud admits that he paid little or no attention to the fact that Dora often shared the room with Frau K., that they were confidants, and that Dora spoke of Frau K.'s 'adorable white body' as if they were in love with each other. Freud's positive opinion about Herr K. and his heteronormative prejudices led him to want to link Dora to Herr K., thereby healing her. In other words, these biases (countertransference) prevented Freud from recognizing and analyzing the homosexual aspects of Dora's hysterical problematic.[19]

We will not discuss the transference problematic any further. In the postscript to the text, we are discussing here, Freud also writes that his study was intended not so much to deal with the technique of analysis, and thus transference, to expose the internal structure of a case of hysteria.[20] Furthermore, Freud wants to show how this structure and the formation of symptoms that express it can be traced through the patient's dreams. He was interested in the study of dreams because he was convinced that "the dream is one of the roads along which consciousness can be reached by the psychical material which, on account of the opposition aroused by its content, has been cut off from consciousness and repressed, and has thus become pathogenic".[21] In this way, dreams also make it possible to gain insight into the psychical mechanisms that determine the formation of neurotic symptoms. Consequently, the study on Dora wants to show as "supplement (to) my book on the interpretation of dreams (…) how an art, which would otherwise be useless, can be turned to account for the discovery of the hidden and repressed parts of mental life".[22] Freud even initially wanted to call his study "*Traum und Hysterie*".[23]

According to Freud, the fact that this study of Dora is mainly psychological does not prevent it from illustrating the importance of an organic sexual basis for a solid understanding of the neurosis. "It is the therapeutic technique alone", he wrote, "that is purely psychological; the theory does not by any means fail to point out that neuroses have an organic basis—though it is true that it does not look for that basis in any pathological anatomical changes."[24] As we know, Freud identifies this organic basis with the polymorphous perverse disposition described in *Three Essays on the Theory of Sexuality*. "Fragment of an analysis of a case of hysteria" draws "attention (…) to the points at which the analysis comes into contact with these organic bases of the symptoms".[25] In other words, The study of Dora shows the intertwining of the psychological and organic aspects of hysteria. It thus confirms the growing importance of the hereditary and dispositional elements he already announced in the 21 September 1897 letter to Fliess on abandoning the theory of seduction.

4. *Une petite hystérie: methodological considerations*

We have pointed out that Dora bears no resemblance to Charcot's famous patients with their spectacular symptomatology[26]: hysterical attacks, hallucinations, and dramatic conversion symptoms. Compared to Charcot's patients, there was hardly anything sensational about Dora's symptomatology. Dora has no seizures and only showed minimal conversion symptoms: a cough that does not want to let up, periodic aphonia (inability to speak), migraine attacks, nervous asthma ('dyspnea'), enuresis (bedwetting) and feelings of depression. Some of these symptoms started appearing very early, from the time she was eight, Freud writes. He speaks about a *petite hystérie* distinct from the *grande hystérie* Charcot made famous. It is clear to Freud that for a better understanding of hysteria, we need to turn to *petite hystérie*.

This insight somewhat anticipates the approach Eugen Bleuler would propose for *dementia praecox* some years later. According to Bleuler, to study *dementia praecox* – or schizophrenia, as he first called this pathology[27] – it is better to look not at the positive (*akzessorische*) symptoms but at the negative or basic (*Grund)* ones (apathy, anhedonia and so on). 'Positive' symptoms refer to the patient's new creations, such as delusion. These symptoms can also occur in other pathologies, even if they express themselves in a specific way in schizophrenia. 'Negative' symptoms refer to something that is absent or has fallen away (for example, the possibility to still experience the body as a source of pleasure[28]). These basic symptoms are characteristic of schizophrenia. Freud makes a similar move with hysteria. To understand the latter, we should not look at spectacular symptoms such as convulsions but focus our attention on day-to-day, less obvious symptoms. Freud adds that hysteria is characterized especially by a symptom that in many ways seems to correspond with what Bleuler would later call basic symptoms. According to Freud, hysterical patients no longer experience sexual enjoyment.[29] Hysteria is fundamentally characterized by a spontaneous rejection of sexuality that evokes only disgust:

> I should without question consider a person hysterical in whom an occasion for sexual excitement elicited feelings that were preponderantly or exclusively unpleasurable; and I should do so whether or no the person were capable of producing somatic symptoms.[30]

From this perspective, acquiring insight in hysteria firstly means understanding what concretely caused this 'affect reversal' from a pleasurable experience to disgust in sexuality.

Sexuality disgusts Dora as she associates it with the excremental. In *Three Essays on the Theory of Sexuality* Freud posits that every human being is inevitably confronted with the task of separating the sexual from the excremental. Freud repeats this view in his study of Dora. According to him, disgust is our original and spontaneous reaction to the smell and later also to the sight of excrements. Genitals can elicit the same reaction. It is especially true of the male genitals that after all also serve to release urine. Freud continues:

> Thus it happens that disgust becomes one of the means of affective expression in the sphere of sexual life. The Early Christian Father's *'inter urinas et faeces nascimur'* clings to sexual life and cannot be detached from it in spite of every effort at idealization.[31]

Put differently, the possible contamination of the sexual by the excremental is an intrinsic part of human sexuality. Freud writes in this regard: "It is scarcely possible to exaggerate the pathogenic significance of the comprehensive tie uniting the sexual and the excremental, a tie which is at the basis of a very large number of hysterical phobias".[32] But a possibility is no necessity. Most people successfully make the psychical effort (idealizing) necessary to separate sexual the excremental. Hysterics do not succeed with this. Freud writes:

> The fact that this association [of the sexual with the excremental – HW/PvH] *can* be called up does not show that it actually *will* be called up. And indeed in normal circumstances it will not be. A knowledge of the paths does not render less necessary a knowledge of the forces which travel along them.[33]

To understand the disgust for the sexual, which is the *shibboleth* of hysteria, therefore implies an understanding of the that gave rise to this association. Disgust for the sexual also plays a crucial role with Dora. How can we understand it, and how did it emerge in this concrete case? In Freud's response to this question, real traumatic events continue to play an important role.

5. The bi-temporality of trauma

Freud's analyst's report on Dora is built on two dreams and the insights they offer to understand Dora's hysterical problem. This is consistent with Freud's intention to illuminate in 'Fragment of an Analysis of a Case of Hysteria' the role of dreams in the psychoanalytical process. Most of the secondary literature is also aimed at a discussion of these dreams. What is sometimes forgotten is the central role of two traumas in Dora's medical history. Even though these traumas, as we shall see, no longer play an exclusive role in the aetiology of the neurosis, we should by no means underestimate their importance. Freud moreover does not doubt their reality for a second.

Which traumas are these? Dora's father told Freud about an incident that occurred when Dora was sixteen. Herr K. dared to declare his love to Dora during a boat trip on the lake. This upset Dora. In return, she slapped Herr K. in the face and ran away from him. However, Freud immediately noted that this trauma is not able to reveal the specificity of Dora's symptoms. It is impossible, he writes, to uncover a coherence between these two events and Dora's oral symptoms (nervous cough, aphonia, and so on), many of which already presented long before this event. Some even first occurred, as we know, when Dora was only eight years old. Consequently, the declaration of love at the lake had no explanatory value for Dora's pathological condition. According to Freud, the latter rings even more true because Dora was in love with Herr K. She should, Freud declares quite expeditiously, have experienced pleasure and excitement instead of aversion. Dora's reaction is therefore inconsistent: she rejects that which, according to Freud, she should desire. We should, Freud concludes, go back further in time to find another incident that is better able to explain Dora's symptoms.[34]

Once the first difficulties of the treatment had been overcome, Dora related another incident involving the same Herr K. This second incident is better suited to fulfil the role of the sexual trauma for which we are searching. When Dora was fourteen, Herr K. managed to be alone with her in his store. On this occasion, he pressed the girl against him and kissed her on the lips. Freud assumes that Dora must have felt an analogous change in her clitoris at this moment. However, she did not feel pleasure in this moment, only disgust. Freud writes that Dora felt deep disgust at that moment, and he already calls her reaction on this occasion 'completely hysterical'.[35] This 'reversal of affect' is further accompanied by a shift in sensation. Instead of a pleasurable genital sensation, Dora "was overcome by the unpleasurable feeling which is proper to the tract of mucous membrane at the entrance to the alimentary canal—that is by disgust".[36] Freud explains this shift by emphasizing the fact that as a child Dora fanatically sucked her thumb. Dora had a pronounced preference for oral experiences of pleasure. The power of the oral drive component is an important characteristic of Dora's sexual constitution. It is at the root of the numerous oral symptoms that determine Dora's clinical picture.[37]

Freud writes that this first trauma hardly had lasting consequences. Disgust did not become a permanent symptom, and trauma had no permanent repercussions on her relationship with Herr K. Neither of them ever mentioned the incident, and Dora paid it little attention afterwards. According to Freud, this trauma had little effect because at that moment – even though she was on the threshold of puberty – Dora did not yet possess the sexual knowledge and concrete conceptions that would have allowed her to adequately understand what happened to her. Thus, the first trauma only takes its full meaning from the perspective of the other trauma (*nachträglich*) that recalls the first and occurs at a time when Dora can fully understand this first trauma. Freud argues that at the time of the scene in the store, Dora was not familiar with the physical signs of arousal in a man.[38] Her reaction in the moment is not grounded in any specific sexual image or fantasy. It is the expression of the *general, unspecific and pre-representational* identification of sexuality with filth that we noted before as a basic symptom of hysteria. 'Filth' here paradigmatically refers to the excremental but, as we shall see, could indicate every kind of bodily excretion.

Herr K.'s declaration of love at the lake brought the first trauma back to consciousness. This scene reminded Dora of the scene in Herr K.'s store and disgust immediately raised its head again. But Dora had now entered puberty. In the meantime, she acquired more detailed knowledge of 'facts in the region of sexual knowledge' and, more specifically, she also now realized that other parts of the body than the genitals can be used for sexual behavior.[39] This newly acquired knowledge came with increasing attention on the extra-marital relation between her father with Frau K. According to Freud, Dora also actively participated in this herself as an accomplice in very different ways. For example, she regularly offered to mind Herr and Frau K.'s children, which gave her father and Frau K. the opportunity to spend time together (Freud 1905e: 47). It also does not come as any surprise then, Freud writes, that Dora

> with her spasmodic cough, which, as is usual, was referred for its exciting stimulus to a tickling in her throat, (…) pictured to herself a scene of sexual gratification *per os* between the two people whose love-affair occupied her mind so incessantly.[40]

Thus, it becomes clear how the retroactive interaction between the two traumas enables the association of Dora's symptoms with explicitly sexual representations. When the first trauma occurred, Dora was not yet a teenager. We know from our previous chapter that in this period, sexuality does not yet have an autoerotic character. Infantile sexuality is not actively focused on or searching for an external object. It is only looking for pleasure. Infantile sexuality can be described in exclusively physiological terms. The rejection thereof in the pre-pubescent period is consequently also not aimed at one specific object or (phantasmatic) representation. In fact, it concerns *the sphere* or *the element* of sexuality as such without any reference to concrete fantasies or objects. When the first scene is recalled in a second moment (*nachträglich*), however, Dora has entered puberty. Now she can link sexuality – and thus also her disgust – with concrete representations or fantasies. At the onset of puberty, the erogenous zones are after all re-invested through the libido that is now actively aimed at objects. It is only from puberty that sexuality and thus also its eventual rejection is explicitly and intentionally related to objects. From now on, Dora's disgust and the oral symptoms associated with it, such as the nervous cough, are motivated by the fellatio phantasy that did not emerge until later – at almost nineteen years of age, Freud writes.[41] Consequently, the traumas we discussed no longer have aetiological meaning in themselves, as was the case in the original theory of seduction, but they actualize and transform a previous hysterical disposition that is the very basis of hysteria.

In the case of Dora, trauma retains the same temporal structure as in the original theory of seduction. However, the role of these traumas is being thoroughly reconsidered. In 'The Aetiology of Hysteria' (1896) the first trauma is still compared to a 'disposition' that only resorts to an effect in a second moment, *nachträglich*. In Dora, on the contrary, the first trauma already has an immediate effect, even if it is not lasting. It awakens an already pre-existing disposition: Dora immediately reacts with disgust to the sexual advances of Herr K. The trauma no longer fulfils an exclusively aetiological role here. It only activates a disposition that takes over this aetiological role. Yet one should not interpret it as a return to the old Charcotian model. According to Charcot, hysteria is caused by a neuropathic disposition for which trauma purely functions as catalyst. In 'My Views on the Part Played by Sexuality in the Aetiology of the Neuroses', Freud writes about this:

> the factors of constitution and heredity necessarily gained the upper hand once more; but there was this difference between my views and those prevailing in other quarters, that on my theory the 'sexual constitution' took the place of a 'general neuropathic disposition'.[42]

In Freud, trauma moreover remains a *Fremdkörper* that indeed activates a pre-existing disposition but simultaneously also has a lasting impact on the course and shape of the hysterical pathology. It thus concerns more than a pure *agent provocateur* or catalyst the impact of which disappears as soon as it has acted, like in Charcot. Dora's traumas determine, together with her sexual constitution (among which oral drive), the shape and course of the illness.

6. Hysterical disposition and the importance of masturbation

In Dora's case, the first trauma activates a pre-existing sexual disposition, in which the oral drive component plays a central role. The contamination of the sphere of sexuality with the excremental must already have been established prior to the traumatic events in the store of Herr K. Dora's first symptoms also already occurred when she was only eight years old. We can thus not fully understand her *petite hystérie* by only considering what happened shortly before and during Dora's puberty. The interaction we discussed in the previous section does not explain the commencement of Dora's hysteria, only its activation during puberty. We consequently need to go back in Dora's life history to provide insight into the early symptoms and the origin of the aversion to sexuality. These early symptoms and the onset of aversion should also be understood from a collaboration between traumatic (accidental) and hereditary factors: "In neurotics their sexual constitution, under which the effects of heredity are included, operates in combination with any accidental influences in their life which may disturb the development of normal sexuality".[43]

To respond to the question about the commencement of Dora's hysterical disposition, we will turn to the first of the two dreams that structure Freud's analysis of Dora's pathology. Shortly after the scene in Herr K.'s store where he embraced her against her will, Dora dreams that the family home is ablaze. In this dream, she is awoken by her father who leans over her. Her mother does not want to leave the house before first saving her jewel-case. However, her father answers: *"I refuse to let myself and my two children be burnt for the sake of your jewel-case"*.[44] Freud understands this dream as a reaction to the incident in the store of Herr K. In the dream, Dora's father protects her from the fire. According to Freud, this 'fire' does not refer only to the burning house but also to Dora's love for Herr K. She is 'on fire' for him. In the dream Dora is awoken by her father, just like he woke her up when she was a child to prevent her from wetting her bed. Freud concludes from this that Dora hopes her father would protect her as before, this time not from bed-wetting but from her desire and love for Herr K.[45]

We have already noted Dora's enuresis that, according to Freud, should be considered a hysterical symptom. As strange as it may sound nowadays, Freud like many psychiatrists of his time explicitly associates bedwetting with masturbation. Children, Freud writes, also make this connection themselves, and Dora is no exception. Freud associates this general insight with the fact that Dora overheard her parents speaking about her father's syphilis[46] and that she had heard an old aunt tell her mother 'He was ill before his marriage, you know'. The old aunt added a few comments that Dora did not immediately understand but that she later associated with 'improper subjects'.[47] Dora suspected her father's frivolous lifestyle was to blame for his illness and that she had inherited it from him. Also when Dora accompanied her mother, who suffered from abdominal pains and catarrh, to a spa in Franzenbad, she assumed her father had caused the problem and sexually transmitted his infection. Freud adds that Dora made a novice mistake by confusing both gonorrhoea with syphilis and infection with hereditary transmission. On this occasion, Dora identifies with her mother. This raises the question for Freud if she herself did not also contract a sexually transmitted infection. Dora confides in him that she suffers from a vaginal discharge, and she does not remember when it started. Leucorrhoea, Freud teaches her, is the result of masturbation.[48]

From all of this, Freud concluded that Dora's criticism of her father's debauched lifestyle is fundamentally self-reproach. Here Dora is on the way to, Freud writes, "finding an answer to her own question of why it was that precisely she had fallen ill—by confessing that she had masturbated, probably in childhood".[49] She rejects Freud's statement on a conscious level. But according to Freud, a symptomatic act during the analysis – Dora brought a small reticule to the consultation "as she lay on the sofa and talked, she kept playing with it—opening it, putting a finger into it, shutting it again, and so on" – is an unconscious confirmation of his conclusion.[50] Masturbation is the secret Dora did not want to reveal to her doctors and did not want to talk about with anyone.

The analysis of Dora's first dream puts Freud on the trail of the problematic of masturbation. But what exactly is the role he ascribes to masturbation? Freud points out that Dora's bedwetting, for which he considers masturbation responsible, continued until shortly before the appearance of the 'nervous asthma' (dyspnea: shortness of breath) when she was eight years old. Freud continues:

> Hysterical symptoms hardly ever appear so long as children are masturbating, but only afterwards, when a period of abstinence has set in; they form a substitute for masturbatory satisfaction, the desire for which continues to persist in the unconscious until another and more normal kind of satisfaction appears—where that is still attainable.[51]

This means that the symptoms Dora developed before the first trauma occurred when she was fourteen, should, according to Freud, be seen as substitutes for masturbation, that is, for an autoerotic sexual activity. In a next step this means for Freud that we, to understand Dora's pathology, should explain why she abandoned this pleasurable activity. Put differently, for Freud, the question why she stopped masturbating operationalizes the question of how sexuality became problematic and an object of disgust for her. This question can only be sufficiently answered by identifying the traumatic events at the root of the abandonment of masturbation (and thus of the disgust with pleasurable sexual physicality):

> *If, therefore, the trauma theory is not to be abandoned*, we must go back to her childhood and look about there for any influences or impressions which might have had an effect analogous *to that of a trauma*. Moreover, it deserves to be remarked that in the investigation even of cases in which the first symptoms had not already set in in childhood I have been driven to trace back the patients' life history to their earliest years.[52]

We cannot repeat it enough, Freud did not simply abandon trauma theory. He only reformulated it.[53]

We already pointed out the continuity between Freud's texts from the last decade of the 19th century and 'Fragment of an Analysis of a Case of Hysteria'. In his response to the question about the origin of Dora's rejection of sexuality?, Freud once more refers to his earlier work, specifically to an article entitled 'On the Grounds for Detaching a Particular Syndrome from Neurasthenia under the Description "Anxiety Neurosis"' from 1895, in which he linked dyspnea and heart palpitations with fragments of the sexual act and coitus. Certainly, according to Freud Dora's symptoms and numerous other signs he does not further specify allows Freud to conclude that she must have hear her parents making love. Dora had to have understood the sexual meaning of what she heard, since "the movements expressive of sexual excitement lie within them ready to hand, as innate pieces of mechanism".[54] And Freud concludes: "The sympathetic excitement which may be supposed to have occurred in Dora on such an occasion may very easily have made the child's sexuality veer round and have replaced her inclination to masturbation by an inclination to anxiety".[55]

But why would this be the case? Freud does not really elaborate in this point in 'Fragment', but perhaps *Three Essays*, which is published in the same year, can help us further here. We have already recalled that Freud in the first edition of *Three Essays* takes great pains to make it clear that infantile sexuality is autoerotic in the strictest sense of the word and can be described in exclusively physiological terms. This could explain why Dora could not bind the excitement Freud reckons she must have felt overhearing her parents making love to sexual representations. The libidinal tension and energy that was released thus remains present unbound or, as Freud also says, 'free-floating'.[56] So it becomes clear how hearing the sexual activities of her parents is the traumatic event through which (autoerotic) sexuality for Dora is bound to anxiety rather than pleasure. As always with Freud, this trauma comes from within: it is the own unbound sexual energy that works traumatizingly, not eavesdropping on the parents as such.

In the context occupying us here Freud writes that Dora repeated the sounds that came from her parents' room as an asthma-attack at a later instance. Dora missed her dearly beloved father while he was away on a business trip. According to Freud we can easily reconstruct her unconscious argumentation that led to the creation of this symptom if we take as departure point the incident during which it occurred for the first time. Dora had her first asthma attack when she was out of breath following a walk in the mountains.[57] From this point a complex reasoning can be reconstructed: her father, who also suffered from shortness of breath, was not allowed to walk in the mountains for fear of exerting himself too much; but did he not exert himself too much during the sexual activities with his spouse that Dora involuntarily witnessed? And finally, did Dora in turn not exert herself too much while she masturbated? This latter activity is also after all associated with shortness of breath. Finally, the dyspnea returns as an intensified symptom expressing Dora's identification with her father.[58]

But all this still does not suffice to understand Dora's rejection of experiencing sexual pleasure. We now understand how and why sexuality is associated with anxiety, but it does not explain the actual disgust with sexuality. Remember

Freud's argument that her vaginal discharge is a result of masturbation? According to Freud, leucorrhoea and hysterical symptoms are closely related. He writes in this regard that "in the case of hysterical patients suffering from leucorrhoea any increase in the catarrh was regularly followed by an intensification of the hysterical troubles, and especially of loss of appetite and vomiting".[59] Although Freud does not completely exclude the gynecological hypothesis that this association could have an organic foundation, he still prefers a psychological explanation. Pathologies of the genital apparatus evoke feelings of repulsion and disgust. They lower the patient's self-esteem: "An abnormal secretion of the mucous membrane of the vagina is looked upon as a source of disgust".[60] In this regard Freud also refers to Dora's governess who taught her that all men were frivolous and untrustworthy. For Dora, Freud suspects, this meant that all men, like her father, are frivolous and that fort his reason they suffer from a sexually transmitted disease. But Dora could only understand these diseases by analogy to her own experiences. Consequently, she equated sexually transmitted diseases with disgusting excretions. This reconstruction of Dora's unconscious reasoning allows one to understand the disgust she feels after Herr K. embraced her in his store and she felt his erect penis against her: "the disgust which was transferred on to the contact of the man would be a feeling which had been projected according to the primitive mechanism I have already mentioned (…) and would be related ultimately to her own leucorrhoea".[61]

In all of this it is striking that hysteria in Dora's case actually develops in two episodes. The temporal structure of the two traumas we have already discussed marks the transition from the first to the second episode.[62] A first period takes place completely during childhood, the second in puberty and adulthood. The second period further builds on the problems that were constructed in and central to the infantile period. This dichotomy was still absent from the original seduction theory, which did not consider any specific developments in the infantile period.[63] Everything revolved around an original trauma that got, at the onset of puberty, a traumatic meaning as a memory. Emma Eckstein was the model for this. In the case of Dora, on the other hand, what comes about in the second (pubertal) period can only be understood from the perspective of the specific psychosexual developments in the first (infantile) period. This dichotomy in Dora's clinical history anticipates Freud's later views, which will be covered in more detail in the chapters on the Rat Man and the Wolf Man and according to which adult neurosis can only come about and be understood based on an infantile neurosis.

7. An oedipal interpretation?

We now understand how the hysterical disposition came about in the case of Dora, as well as how it was activated in a second moment. Freud explains Dora's pathology and more specifically her disgust with the experience of sexual pleasure beyond every reference to the Oedipus complex. In this last case, the disgust for the sexual would, incidentally, concern the violation of the barrier against incest, which is hardly mentioned in the text about Dora.[64] The so-called abandonment of the theory of seduction in 1897 does thus not coincide with the discovery of the Oedipus complex but with a re-evaluation of constitutional and dispositional elements in the aetiology of neurosis. Yet numerous commentators not only defended an oedipal reading of this case study but also ascribed this oedipal reading to Freud.

It is undoubtedly correct, as many critics have argued, that Freud, during his analysis of Dora constantly attempts to fit her into the conventional framework of heterosexual seduction.[65] An important part of Freud's efforts is aimed at convincing her of her own part in the relationship between her father and Frau K. Freud accepted that a silent agreement existed between Dora's father and Herr K. According to this agreement, her father could have his way with Frau K., provided that he did not comment on Herr K.'s attempts to seduce Dora.[66] Freud writes that she accepted this situation for a long time without protest. Indeed, Dora only starts criticizing her father after the scene at the lake when she is sixteen years old. The reason is simple, Freud says: she herself had been in love with Herr K. for years. Her father's adventure with Frau K. gave her an opportunity to spend more time with Herr K. Consequently, her reproaches and criticism of her father were equally self-reproaches.[67] One of Freud's arguments fort his interpretation is Dora's periodic aphonia: Dora loses her voice during the absence of Herr K. and miraculously regains it upon his return. This symptom has a mirrored reaction in Frau K.: when Herr K. came home, he found his spouse still ill in bed, despite her being in peak health the previous day.

However, this biased emphasis on the heterosexual matrix is not the same as an oedipal interpretation or an interpretation in terms of the Oedipus complex. Freud's analysis of the dream we referred to earlier clearly shows that Freud is not yet thinking in oedipal terms in this text and that, as far as he is concerned, modified seduction theory suffices to understand Dora's pathology. In this dream Dora's mother refuses leave the burning house without her jewel-case. Her father, however, says he does not want the children to be left behind in the fire because of this case.[68] Following this dream Dora tells Freud that her parents recently argued about a piece of jewelry. Her mother wanted pearl drop earrings and her father gave her a bracelet instead. Freud then introduces an association between 'jewel-case' (and jewelry in general) and female genitals. He also posits that Dora's mother was in the past a rival in the battle for the father's affection and that Dora perhaps wants to give the father that which the mother refused him: her 'jewelry'.[69] There is thus clearly an oedipal theme in this dream. Freud writes about this:

> I have shown at length elsewhere at what an early age sexual attraction makes itself felt between parents and children, and I have explained that the legend of Oedipus is probably to be regarded as a poetical rendering of what is typical in these relations. Distinct traces are probably to be found in most people of an early partiality of this kind—on the part of a daughter for her father, or on the part of a son for his mother; but it must be assumed to be more intense from the very first in the case of those children whose constitution marks them down for a neurosis, who develop prematurely and have a craving for love.[70]

It immediately follows that this dream bears evidence of a reliving of germinal feelings from childhood that have an oedipal character. But does discovering an oedipal theme equal giving an oedipal explanation?

Various elements must be noted here. In the above citation Freud implicitly refers to his book on dreams that appeared in November 1899. In *The Interpretation of Dreams* Freud discusses the Oedipus legend in the chapter on typical dreams.[71] In this chapter, Freud calls this legend a poetic arrangement of the way in which parents and children generally relate to each other.[72] According to Freud it also explains why it still touches us today:

> His [Oedipus's] destiny moves us only because it might have been ours—because the oracle laid the same curse upon us before our birth as upon him. It is the fate of all of us, perhaps, to direct our first sexual impulse towards our mother and our first hatred and our first murderous wish against our father. Our dreams convince us that that is so.[73]

However, Freud does not use the Oedipus myth in *The Interpretation of Dreams* to explain the formation and meaning of our dreams in general. Neither does he use it to explain psychopathology. There is no mention yet in *The Interpretation of Dreams* of a psychological complex that constitutes the core of the unconscious and that regulates our access to culture. In the first edition of *Three Essays* as well as in 'Fragment', Freud refers to these passages from *The Interpretation of Dreams*. These references can thus not be used as evidence for an oedipal reading of the text.[74]

In the text on Dora, Freud also remains unclear about the sexual – in this context referring to 'genital' – character of early childhood relationships between parents and children. It is important because this sexual character is assumed in the Oedipus complex. In the terms of this complex, the young boy has a sexual (genital) desire for the mother and the same goes for the relationship of the young girl for her father. This desire does not differ substantially from adult sexual desire.[75] Yet Freud writes in 'Fragment' that this 'rudimentary feeling of love' that binds children to their parents develops into a sexual (genital) inclination only in response to certain influences – for example seduction or masturbation – in childhood or only during puberty.[76] This idea is in line with the insight from the first edition of *Three Essays*, that the sexualization of object relations and subsequently the oedipal problematic in principle only comes about at the onset of puberty:[77]

> the parents' affection for their child may awaken his sexual instinct prematurely (…) to such a degree that the mental excitation breaks through in an unmistakable fashion to the genital system. If, on the other hand, they are fortunate enough to avoid this, then their affection can perform its task of directing the child in his choice of a sexual object when he reaches maturity. No doubt the simplest course for the child would be to choose as his sexual objects the same persons whom, since his childhood, he has loved with what may be described as damped-down libido. But, by the postponing of sexual maturation, time has been gained in which the child can erect, among other restraints on sexuality, the barrier against incest, and can thus take up into himself the moral precepts which expressly exclude from his object-choice, as being blood-relations, the persons whom he has loved in his childhood.[78]

Up until the onset of puberty childhood sexuality remains autoerotic and not essentially genitally oriented. All this means Freud at this stage of his thinking also adheres to a strict distinction between infantile and adult (adolescent) sexuality, where oedipal relationships in principle strictly belong to adolescent sexuality.[79]

But in our current context, the latter is perhaps not even the most important. Dora tells Freud that a few days before the 'oedipal' dream she herself also received a very expensive jewel-case from Her K. Freud assumes for

Dora this means she has to offer Herr K. a 'return gift'. Consequently, Dora's mother replaces Frau K. in the dream, according to Freud. The meaning of the dream becomes clear in this way: "So you are ready to give Herr K. what his wife withholds from him. That is the thought which has had to be repressed with so much energy, and which has made it necessary for every one of its elements to be turned into its opposite".[80] The question then becomes how this repression came about.

Freud links, as we know, the idea that Dora's father tried to save her from the burning house with the fact that the latter often woke her in the middle of the night when she was still a child to protect her against bedwetting. Freud further also suggests that 'fire' could also have, beside its usual meaning, a sexual one. According to Freud, in the dream Dora's father replaces Herr K. for whom Dora is 'on fire'. Dora's father needs to protect her from this 'fire' in the same way he protected her from bedwetting before. Freud concludes: "that she had at that point summoned up an infantile affection for her father so as to be able to keep her repressed love for Herr K. in its state of repression".[81] That is pretty much the opposite of an oedipal declaration. An oedipal declaration implies after all implies that an actual love (for Herr K., for example) is understood as a reissue of an old love for the father ('You may think you are in love with Herr K., but in fact you desire your father'). In this case, the unconscious sexual desire for the father would also be the cause of disgust for sexuality. According to Freud, it is about something else with Dora. At the heart of Dora's problematic is her *actual* infatuation with Herr K., and the memory of her love for her father must protect her against this. The latter has only a reactive function. The dream about the burning house illustrates Freud's insight that fantasy life primarily has a defensive function against one's own sexual activity. Freud therefore never claims that 'oedipal relationships' are at the origin of Dora's *petite hystérie* and particularly her disgust for sexuality.[82]

It is, however, not the full story yet. At the beginning of this chapter, we already noted that Freud admits his failure to notice Dora's homosexual desire for Frau K. This inability gave way to the rash termination of the analysis after four months. Indeed, Freud did overlook essential aspects of Dora's behavior. We have pointed out before that Dora often shared the room with Frau K. and that she talked about her 'adorable white body'.[83] Dora and Frau K. clearly had a very intimate relationship. Even when Frau K. deeply disappointed Dora by not wanting to believe that Herr K. was trying to seduce her, Dora remained faithful to her. And when she was accused of an unhealthy interest in 'sexual matters', Dora did not reveal that she acquired this knowledge in a significant way through Frau K.[84] All this casts Dora's interest in the relationship between her father and Frau K. in a new light. This interest does not originate in oedipally motivated jealousy. In fact, it concerns Frau K. herself: the childhood infatuation with her father is awakened to enable repression of the love for Herr K., but simultaneously, and more fundamentally, this hides Dora's desire for Frau K. and 'her adorable white body'. In the background we also discover the problematic of bisexuality, which, as we know from our previous chapter, is part of the human constitution as such, according to Freud.[85]

8. *Conclusion*

The literature often suggests that the theory of seduction is absent from 'Fragment of an Analysis of a Case of Hysteria'. This is consistent with the idea that Freud would have abandoned this theory as early as 1897.[86] Our explanation shows that this reading is highly problematic. In his analysis, Freud thoroughly refers to traumatic events that occurred prior to the age of fourteen that had a disruptive effect on Dora's development (*Verführung*). Moreover, Freud clearly indicates that he wants not only to (re)confirm the theory of seduction but also actually wants to adjust it. This adjustment concerns the relationship between accidental (traumatic) events and the sexual constitution on the one hand and, on the other, rejection of every reference to hypnoid conditions that would occur in patients because of trauma and that would contribute to the forming of hysterical symptoms. About this latter aspect, we can be brief. Freud no longer notes these hypnoid conditions in the Dora case. Regarding the former point, Freud's discussion of Dora's clinical history is completely in line with what he had stated in 'The Aetiology of Hysteria'.[87] Indeed, Freud's discussion does not stop with the traumas that occur shortly before and after puberty. Instead, he searches for the childhood sexual traumas upon which Dora's pathology is based. Based on the interaction between this trauma (hearing the sexual activity of her parents) as well as accidental (for example Dora's leucorrhea) and constitutional (for example her strong oral libido) factors, the disposition established in the first period becomes psychically active in the second period following the seduction in the store of Herr K. This 'activation' itself happens over two phases, where the disgust for the sexual is only bound to specific representations in the second phase. The temporality of the trauma is here not only way more complex than in the original theory of seduction but also no longer founded in an asexual childhood, as for example was still the case in Emma. In this way Freud reconciles the original theory of seduction with the discovery of a polymorphic perverted constitution.

The case study on Dora anticipates in different ways the case studies on the Rat Man and the Wolf Man that we discuss in the following two chapters. In our discussion of Dora, we already noted the psychical development during the pre-pubescent period that in the shape of childhood neurosis takes on great significance in both these studies.[88] In addition, in the case of Dora, there is the problematic of what Freud already calls 'primal scenes' in Manuscript L on the architecture and analysis of hysteria: bearing witness to the coitus or sexual activity of the parents. Freud writes there: "The aim seems to be to reach the earliest [sexual] scenes. In a few cases this is achieved directly, but in others only by a detour via fantasies. For fantasies are psychic facades produced in order to bar access to these memories".[89] Freud does not use the word 'primal scene' in the text on Dora, but hearing the sexual activities of the parents is also the 'first' trauma in a chain of traumas that helped make Dora's *petite hystérie* possible. In the study of the Wolf Man, the reference to the primal scene will expand to a central element in Freud's clinical theory.

In the years after the publication of *Three Essays* and the 'Fragment', Freud's attention progressively shifts from hysteria to obsessional neurosis.[90] In 1909 he publishes 'Notes Upon a Case of Obsessional Neurosis [The 'Rat Man']', which discusses the analysis of a compulsive patient, Ernst Lanzer. As in the case of Dora, the historiographical tradition read this case study as confirmation of the hypothesis that the theory of seduction was replaced in 1897 with a theory of oedipal phantasm. We will show in our next chapter that the problematic of the Rat Man, like this one of Dora, should be understood from a reworked theory of seduction. At the same time, our reading of the Rat Man case study will again confront us with the boundaries of Freud's theory on sexual trauma.

Chapter 3

Trauma, aggression and father complex: The Rat Man

1. *Introduction*

Our analysis of 'Fragment of an Analysis of a Case of Hysteria' shows that Freud's abandonment of the seduction theory has a different meaning than is claimed in classic historiography of Freudian psychoanalysis. More concretely, it does not mean that the reference to the traumatic origin of the various neuroses is replaced by a reference to their oedipal genesis. In fact, even though Freud no longer considers trauma as the exclusive cause of hysteria, it retains an important role in its pathogenesis. It is no different in Freud's reflections on obsessional neurosis. Also, in the study of obsessional neurosis, trauma and thus a modified seduction theory continues to play an important role. In this chapter, we want to illustrate this based on 'Notes Upon a Case of Obsessional Neurosis [The 'Rat Man']'.[1]

This study of an obsessional patient appeared in 1909 and commences, just like the study of Dora, with reference to seduction theory.[2] Freud writes that his text contains "some disconnected statements of an aphoristic character upon the genesis and finer psychological mechanism of obsessional processes, and I shall thus hope *to develop* my first observations on the subject".[3] Later in this study, Freud admittedly criticizes the text he refers to in this citation ('Further Remarks on the Neuro-Psychoses of Defence'), but this criticism does not concern the idea of seduction as much as the description of the obsessive-compulsive syndrome of this earlier text.[4] Yet the study of the Rat Man is not really known for trauma's role therein. To the contrary, in fact, this case study is linked to the introduction of the father complex, which would be a crucial aspect of the Oedipus complex.[5] This father complex refers to the ambivalent feelings of the young boy towards his father, who denies him access to experiences of sexual pleasure in general and to the mother in particular. Because of the references to the father complex, the study of the

Rat Man is mostly interpreted and read in oedipal terms.[6] We will show that this interpretation is not obvious and that, even in the case of the Rat Man, Freud remains much closer to the theory of seduction than is often assumed. Or better yet, also in the case of the Rat Man, Freud explains the pathology based on an interplay of traumatic, phantasmatic and dispositional factors. The reference to Oedipus plays a minor role here, which we will have to clarify in the course of this chapter.[7]

The study of the Rat Man is also important as it shows that it is only with some effort that Freud can maintain the sexualization of trauma, which we discussed in the first chapter and that seemed obvious in the case of Dora. In other words, Freud already pushes the limits of his model in obsessional neurosis. The latter concerns the central role of anger and aggression in the obsessional neurosis problem. Without the reference to anger and aggression, the trauma cannot be understood in the study of the Rat Man. The question then becomes why anger and aggression would essentially be sexual. Freud's response in 'Notes Upon a Case of Obsessional Neurosis' is not really satisfying. He will only settle the question of the relationship between the two in *Beyond the Pleasure Principle* in 1920.[8] But first we discuss the case history of the Rat Man.

2. *Some remarks on the case history*

Ernst Lanzer visited Freud for the first time on 1 October 1907 following a panic attack. He suffered this attack after hearing of horrible punishment used in the East in which a pot containing a rat was turned upside down on someone's buttocks. This rat then bore its way out of the pot via the victim's anus. Upon hearing this tale, Lanzer was overcome by the thought that this torment would befall someone very dear to him – his father or a lady whom he was in love with for many years.[9] The importance of this tale in his medical history gave Lanzer his nickname: the Rat Man.

Lanzer lost his pince-nez during military maneuvers and in the interest of time ordered a new one from his optician in Vienna with the request to send them by post. On the evening of the same day on which he heard the rat tale, a cruel officer handed him his new pince-nez with the message to refund lieutenant A., who would have advanced the payment for the glasses. At that moment the thought took shape as a command: "*that he was not to pay back the money* or it would happen – (that is, the phantasy about rats would come true as regards his father and the lady)".[10] This order was already peculiar as his father had passed away some years before. Immediately after the first command, however, came the opposite: "You must pay back the 3.80 Kronen to Lieutenant A".[11] The theory that it was not Lieutenant A. but a female postal clerk who advanced the money does not change anything here. It does not deter him from fanatically clinging to the apparently senseless vow to refund Lieutenant A. In the days that follow, Lanzer develops one strange strategy after the other to honor his vow, just to subsequently make it impossible again. This leaves him in utter confusion.

The fear that something terrible could happen to his lady, and even more so to his father, whom he admired, plays a central role in Ernst Lanzer's the life.[12] He also suffered from numerous compulsive thoughts and compulsive impulses. For example, on the day his lady friend had to leave, Ernst accidentally knocked his foot on a stone in the road. When he realizes his lady friend would also soon be coming past this spot, he feels obliged to put the stone out of the way by the side of the road, as he fears it would damage her carriage. He subsequently realizes it is nonsensical and feels the irresistible compulsion to put the stone back. According to Freud, we can only understand this double action as the expression of a frantic

> battle between love and hate (…) and the object of both these feelings was one and the same person. The battle was represented in a plastic form by his compulsive and symbolic act of removing the stone from the road along which she was to drive, and then of undoing this deed of love by replacing the stone where it had lain, so that her carriage might come to grief against it and she herself be hurt.[13]

According to Freud, the vehemence of Ernst Lanzer's opposing impulses is expressed even more clearly in the following example. When, at a time that Lanzer was busy with a particularly difficult piece of work, his lady had to go to and nurse her ill grandmother, the idea suddenly occurred to him: "If you received a command to take your examination this term at the first possible opportunity, you might manage to obey it. But if you were commanded to cut your throat with a razor, what then?".[14] When he then wanted to take up the razor, it occurred to him to go to the grandmother and cut her throat. The origin of this compulsive idea forced itself upon him in reverse order. The aggressive impulse against the grandmother occurred first, but in Ernst Lanzer's consciousness, it is preceded by the punitive order to cut his own throat.

According to Freud, hostile impulses play a central role in the syndrome of the Rat Man. Following the departure of his beloved, Lanzer is for instance overwhelmed by an obsession to understand. He questions everyone to the last detail to be sure he heard them right: 'What is it you are saying exactly?' This obsession originated in a statement his lady made; he understood her to mean she wanted to deny his advances in public. It later became clear that the contrary was true. The compulsion to understand thus becomes comprehensible: 'if you want to spare yourself unnecessary heartache, you have to be sure that you completely understand what you are being told'. Yet this does not explain everything, Freud reckons. Lanzer was, after all, never satisfied with the answer he received to his repeated demands for clarification. He remained uncertain. So there had to be another element at work here. According to Freud, the compulsion to understand something correctly is again an expression of his uncertainty about his lady's love and his anger about it.[15]

Compulsive acts often occur in two stages, according to Freud. These stages express the endless battle between love and hate. In contrast to hysteria, where the symptom is a compromise between various conscious and unconscious tendencies, here both tendencies are satisfied separately, one after the other.[16]

3. *The elementary organism of neurosis*

Ernst Lanzer constantly fears that some terrible thing, such as the rat torture, will happen to someone he holds dear. More than his lady, this fear concerns his father. The anxiety that his father might die has been with him since childhood.[17] There are thus plenty of reasons to examine this childhood more closely.

As early as during the first session of his treatment, Ernst Lanzer tells Freud that as a child he had a 'burning and tormenting curiosity' to see women naked. This desire came about after he was allowed one evening to creep under the skirt of and fondle a pretty young governess, Fräulein Peter.[18] He was also later very active sexually. When he was six years old, he waited excitedly for the moment when another governess, Fräulein Lina, pressed out the abscesses on her buttocks. He allowed himself to take many liberties with her and was also heavily burdened during this time by erections, bemoaning these to his mother. In short, Ernst Lanzer's childhood is characterized by much sexual activity and pleasure experiences. Completely in line with the old seduction theory, Freud writes in this regard: "Such cases [of obsessional neurosis –

HW/PvH], unlike those of hysteria, invariably possess the characteristic of premature sexual activity".[19]

But this is not all. Whenever the desire arose to see girls and women our patient was fond of naked, the fear crept in that something bad would happen because of these thoughts. He was also afraid that he would have to take appropriate measures to combat these thoughts. Lanzer saw all of this as the onset of his illness. According to Freud, it on the contrary already concerned the actual illness itself. The child is after all in the grip of strong sexual drive impulses. Although these do not yet have a compulsive character during infancy, this is only because they are for the time being still experienced as ego-syntonic. Yet a conflict is already being formed: alongside the wish, there is an obsessional fear that is linked to this wish. Whenever the desire to see women naked arises, the Rat Man fears something bad will happen. Even if this 'bad' remains vague at first, according to Freud it does not take much effort to discover that this generalization is intended to hide the fact that it concerns the death of the father: 'If I think that, my father has to die'. Freud concludes:

> We find accordingly: an erotic instinct and a revolt against it; a wish which has not yet become compulsive and, struggling against it, a fear which is already compulsive; a distressing affect and an impulsion towards the performance of defensive acts. The inventory of the neurosis has reached its full muster.[20]

This is what Freud calls the "*elementary organism*" of Ernst Lanzer's obsessional neurosis, "the study of which could alone enable us to obtain a grasp of the complicated organization of his subsequent illness".[21]

4. *The source of the hatred*

The structure of the elementary organism of Lanzer's obsessional neurosis discussed above is recognizable through Freud's description of the case history and of the analysis. When at twelve years of age, he is in love with a girl who reacted tepidly to his advances, Ernst suddenly thought that she would show him affection if his father happened to die.[22] And in a completely similar way, a few months before his father's death, the thought crossed his mind that his death would help create the material conditions that would allow him to marry his lady. These and similar ideas surprise Ernst Lanzer very much and seem unbelievable because he never desired the death of his father. His father was after all his best, his closest friend whom he held most dear. Ernst still had an excellent relationship with his father. To this, Freud responds that it is precisely this intense love that is the precondition of the repressed hatred.[23] The idea that his father would die is a distorted expression of the wish that this would happen, and according to Freud, this wish shows Ernst Lanzer's hatred towards his father. The intensity of his love does not, however, allow this hatred to remain conscious. The hatred is repressed to the unconscious.

To this, Ernst Lanzer adds that he indeed loved his lady very much, but that the sensual wishes such as those felt during his youth were missing with her. In fact, his sensual wishes were generally much stronger during his childhood than later.[24] According to Freud, Lanzer thus indicates the source of the hostility towards his father. This source apparently concerns sensual desire. Moreover, since the preoccupation with death and thus the hostility towards his father has tormented him since he was six years old, this source must involve a conflict between the infantile sexuality on the one hand and the childish love for the father that interferes with infantile satisfaction on the other. Or, more precisely, the hostility originates in a premature conflict with the power or the instance interfering with the satisfaction of the infantile sensual desire.[25]

Freud now advances the following argument that is crucial to our own:

> If we apply *knowledge gained elsewhere* (…) we shall not be able to avoid a suspicion that in this instance as in others (that is to say, before the child had reached his sixth year) there had been conflicts and repressions, which had themselves been overtaken by amnesia, but had left behind them as a residuum the particular content of this obsessive fear.[26]

Freud does not specify precisely what the 'elsewhere' in this citation refers to, but considering both the previous references in this text as well as the content of this citation, it is difficult not to think of 'Further Remarks on the Neuro-Psychoses of Defence' from 1896 and thus of the old seduction theory. We cannot understand Ernst Lanzer's pathology without or outside of the old seduction theory.

What then is the traumatic experience that, according to Freud, underlies Ernst Lanzer's obsessional-neurotic pathology? Lanzer himself has no direct memory of this incident, but his mother often tells him about it. When he was still very young, he must have done something very bad. It remains somewhat unclear what exactly Lanzer had done. Freud suspects it concerns masturbation (autoerotic sexuality), but the mother recalls that he had bitten someone. In any case, his father had treated him very severely and beaten him. Little Ernst reacted with great rage to this punishment. Since he was not yet familiar with any bad language, Ernst lambasted his father with the few words he knew: "'You lamp! You towel! You plate!' and so on". This incident would leave a lasting impression on him as well as on his father.[27] Not only was it the last time his father beat him, but Ernst also felt this incident to be at the basis of a character change: from here, *fearing his own rage*, he became a coward.

We must briefly pause at the structure of this traumatic event. The father's interdict is not directly responsible for the unpleasure and repression of infantile sexual activity that underlie the self-blame and obsessive thoughts that are so characteristic of Lanzer's syndrome. According to Freud, what makes this incident traumatic is *the fear of the violence of his own rage* and not the prohibition of the father as such.[28] It is also this fear that explains the character change he so bitterly bemoans. Since the incident with his father, he has indeed become a coward. According to him, this cowardice expresses itself in many ways. He is afraid of beatings and cannot bear to see other children being beaten. But the cowardice also shows itself in other ways. For example, Ernst invents complex and senseless strategies to pay his debt to the counter clerk without breaking his vow to reimburse Lieutenant A. From cowardice, he says, he allows these strategies to fail that he does not have to reveal their embarrassing senselessness in public. But honoring his vow would also be an expression of cowardice. He would only be trying to get rid of his obsessive thoughts like this.[29]

The traumatic conflict with his father during his childhood lies at the origin of what Freud calls the *father complex* that characterizes obsessional neurosis (Freud 1909d: 200-220). This notion refers to the ambivalent relationship with the father who is loved on the one hand ('he was my best friend') but simultaneously hated on the other (he prevents autoerotic pleasure). According to Freud, the hatred of the father is repressed to the unconscious to avoid open conflict between these two tendencies, while conscious love is simultaneously intensified to maintain this repression.[30] This father complex structures Ernst Lanzer's syndrome. According to Freud, only this complex can clarify his most characteristic compulsive thoughts and obsessional symptoms.

5. Clinical significance of the father complex

A few illustrations could shed further light on Freud's clinical logic concerning the father complex. They can, for example, make it clear why certain events could have such a profound impact on the life of the Rat Man. For example, Ernst Lanzer's mother told him one day that her wealthy cousin is willing to give him his daughter's hand in marriage if he completes his studies. This marriage would open great professional prospects. It would, however, imply giving up his love for his lady, who was less fortunate financially. In this way, Ernst suddenly found himself in a similar situation in which his father also once found himself. His father also had to choose between a poor woman he had been in love with and a wealthy heiress who would later become Ernst Lanzer's mother. A conflict was ignited. Should Ernst be loyal to his poor beloved, or should he follow in the footsteps of his father, with whom he identifies?[31] This conflict forms the core of Lanzer's pathology. He must choose between his beloved and the continuing influence of his father, who prohibits this love (and the sensuality). It repeats the childhood trauma we discussed earlier. Lanzer tries to resolve this conflict by fleeing to illness.[32]

The father complex also makes it possible to further comment on and clarify the great impact of the tale of the torment to which Lanzer owes his nickname, the 'Rat Man'. In this context, Freud speaks of 'complexive sensitiveness'.[33] Partly through the ambiguity of the word 'rat', this word hit a nerve in the unconscious of Ernst Lanzer. For example, the word conjures a memory about one of his father's stories. When he was in the army, he would have had big trouble if a friend had not advanced money to repay a small gambling debt. His father was a *Spielratte* (a fanatic player). Lanzer took the cruel captain's words that he must settle his debt with Lieutenant A. as an allusion to his own father's unpaid debt.

We cannot elaborate the ambiguous connections of the word 'rat' with Ernst Lanzer's unconscious.[34] So, we limit ourselves to a few essential aspects of the more general relationship between the story of the torment and the childhood incident we discussed earlier. According to Freud, Lanzer quickly associated the story about the punishment with the childhood scene that involved him masturbating or biting someone. The captain, who was able to promote such punishments, also became the father's substitute and absorbed at least some of the resentment and hatred Lanzer felt towards his father when he was punished as a child. According to Freud, the idea that this punishment could also happen to someone dear to him should be translated as 'something like that should happen to you', and here this thought was instantly aimed at his father, since the captain was his substitute.[35] When the cruel captain orders him some time later to refund Lieutenant A., the Rat Man already knows that Lieutenant A. is mistaken. It would therefore have been obvious that Ernst Lanzer would have spontaneously reacted with a derisive remark: 'Hey, what are you thinking?' But under the influence of the childhood scene and the father complex, he links the derisive comment to an unfulfillable, absurd condition: 'I will pay back, if my father (who already died) and my beloved (who had a vasectomy) have children'. The derisive incantation to the two people he loves the most is, however, unacceptable for the Rat Man. Now that this crime has been committed, the punishment will inevitably follow. This punishment consists of the obligation to respect a vow that is impossible to keep and that he simultaneously knows is based on false premises.[36]

All of this clarifies that the traumatic event underlying the Rat Man's pathology meets all the conditions of a trauma according to the original seduction theory. In 'The Aetiology of Hysteria' from 1896, at the height of seduction theory, Freud indicated that a trauma must possess *a suitability to serve as a determinant* as well as the necessary *traumatic force* to serve as the explanatory cause of hysterical and obsessive neurotic symptoms.[37] We can be brief about the traumatic force of the childhood event that determined Ernst Lanzer's life and that underlies the father complex. As it leads to a change in character, its force is difficult to doubt. But this event equally possesses the suitability to serve as the determinant Freud calls for. Our discussion of the Rat Man's characteristic symptoms and of his relation to the cruel captain shows that they are also substantively determined by this trauma. There is a clear connection between (the structure of) this trauma and the *content* of the various obsessive symptoms. This is precisely what the 'suitability to serve as a determinant' refers to.

6. The seduction theory in the case study

It of course does not follow from all this that Freud would fully defend his old seduction theory in his study of the Rat Man. But it has at least also become clear that a simple reference to the Oedipus complex also does not suffice to understand Freud's position on obsessional neurosis in this text. However, we cannot further expand and understand the problematic of the Oedipus complex in the case of the Rat Man before first deepening Freud's use of the seduction theory in 'Notes'.

We know from the preceding chapters that in the post-1897 texts, childhood trauma can in principle only still work in relation to constitutional and dispositional factors. From 'The Disposition to Obsessional Neurosis' from 1913 and in the third edition of his *Three Essays on the Theory of Sexuality* from 1915, Freud links obsessional neurosis with anal erotism and sadism. In these texts, he will raise an anal-sadistic organizational libidinal form that is a necessary and inevitable developmental libidinal phase. In this phase, anal pleasure experiences and aggressive, controlling tendencies play a main role. The obsessive neurotic disposition refers to a fixation in this phase to which the libido can return when there are difficulties in development (for example the father's interdict).

The idea of an obsessional neurotic disposition is as such still missing from the case study that we discuss in this chapter. A handful of its essential elements are, however, already present. Freud writes, for example, that the rat punishment stirs up the anal erotism that played a significant part in Ernst Lanzer's childhood and that is maintained as he had suffered from worms for years. In addition, Freud states that in obsessional neurosis in general and particularly in the Rat Man, the sadistic component of the libido is strongly developed "and have consequently undergone a premature and all too thorough suppression".[38] The interference of the father reactivates and stimulates this sadistic component, which explains Ernst's anger, according to Freud. Thus, the action of the trauma as we have described it cannot be understood separately from pre-existing constitutional impulses. The anger that frightens Ernst and determines the traumatic quality of the childhood incident is an expression thereof. Indeed, the trauma no longer plays the same causal role as in the original seduction theory, but it remains decisive for the pathology in a dynamic exchange with constitutional elements.

We remember how in 'Fragment' the hysterical disposition came about because of the interaction between constitutional elements and accidental factors. We find the same interaction in the study on the Rat Man. Here too, Freud argues that the obsessive disposition is shaped by the collaboration of the constitutional (for instance, a strongly developed sadistic component of the libido) and accidental elements (for instance, the confrontation with the father at the age of six). This disposition fundamentally determines the way in which the Rat Man reacts to later (traumatic) situations. The aggressive reaction to the grandmother when his beloved visits her at a moment the Rat

Man also needs her is a good example of such a dispositionally determined reaction.

In 'The Disposition to Obsessional Neurosis' Freud assigns responsibility for the choice of neurosis (*Neurosenwahl*) to these constitutional and dispositional elements – for example regression to and fixation on the anal-sadistic phase of the libido. It is not for nothing that the subtitle of this text is 'A Contribution to the Problem of Choice of Neurosis'. In 'Notes', Freud however argues that we need to propose "that in *every* neurosis [hysteria, obsessional neurosis and paranoia – HW/PvH] we come upon *the same* suppressed instincts behind the symptoms".[39] In this perspective, the difference between the neuroses only concerns the way in which impulses are warded off: "What is characteristic of this neurosis – what differentiates it from hysteria – is not, in my opinion, to be found in instinctual life but in the psychological field".[40] Thus, the choice of neurosis only depends on the specific defensive mechanisms, not on *which* impulses are warded off. At the same time, however, Freud cannot deny a very specific impulse problematic coming to the fore in obsessional neurosis: an overwrought love that must repress an unconscious hate. About this, Freud writes "it is gratifying to find how easily we can now follow the puzzling processes of an obsessional neurosis by bringing them into relation with this one factor".[41] So, he ignores his own warning and connects obsessional neurosis with a specific dispositional impulse problematic, the battle between love and hate. This is intrinsically bound to constitutionally strengthened sadism.[42]

7. The father complex and the oedipal problematic

What is it about the father complex, which is often interpreted as a precursor to the Oedipus complex? It is obvious to interpret the libidinal desires the father denies Ernst in an oedipal context: the father is a competitor in the battle for the mother, and the hate is a consequence thereof. It would instantly imply that the father's interdict *would surface* an *already existing* (oedipally motivated) ambivalence. However, Freud exclusively talks about the auto-erotic and onanistic activities the father forbids Ernst.[43] Also, nowhere in the case history is the father presented as a competitor in a battle to possess the mother. This is also not the case in Freud's notes in this case, even if the mother plays a larger role here compared to the published version. Moreover, the mother is also presented in these notes as an obstacle to Ernst's sexual activities and hence in this regard a successor to the father after his death.[44]

Freud's description of the *nuclear complex* of the neurosis also does not answer, in the text on the Rat Man, to the classic Oedipus complex. After all, it lacks every reference to the mother, and Freud again mentions only a ban on autoeroticism: "It is entirely characteristic of the nuclear complex of infancy that the child's father should be assigned the part of a sexual opponent and of an interferer with autoerotic sexual activities; and real events are usually to a large extent responsible for bringing this about".[45]

To further this relationship between the father complex and the Oedipus complex in 'Notes', it makes sense to consider how Freud analyzes the oedipal relationships in texts from the same time. In 'On the Sexual Theories of Children', which is released a year before the study of the Rat Man, he calls the presence of the parents "a reality which needs no further enquiry".[46] It would also be Freud's point of departure in the brief text 'Family Romances', which appeared shortly before the study on the Rat Man: the parents are a given, their presence and their role are not questioned, let alone interpreted in sexual terms. It is only later, at the onset of puberty, that the relationship with the parents is transformed and 'sexualized'. This is particularly evident in the relationship with the mother, which now becomes the object of incestuous fantasies.[47] Freud's text on the family romance plays a crucial role in the progressive oedipalization of his thoughts.[48] We must therefore investigate it in more detail in this context.

'Family Romances' forms part of a series of publications on studies of infantile object relations and transformations during puberty. Freud examines this problematic by directing his attention to a drive he did not mention in the first edition of *Three Essays*: the epistemophilic instinct or 'drive for knowledge or research'.[49] In his text "On the Sexual Theories of Children" from 1908 Freud argues that this drive is awoken from egoist motives through the birth of a brother or sister.[50] The epistemophilic drive is subsequently not rooted in an aspiration to sexual desire but in the fear of losing parental care. According to Freud, the mystery 'Where do children come from?' should, however, remain unsolved because the small child has no knowledge of the existence of the vagina and the role of the sperm cells.[51] Neither does the child know the meaning and role of coitus. This is precisely why it is only able to formulate inadequate theories linking fertilization and birth to activities and experiences with which it is familiar, namely eating and defecating. Children believe that one falls pregnant by eating something and that birth happens through excrement through the gut.[52] The first childhood theories about adult sexuality are consequently misconceptions that flow from the infantile sexual constitution and the polymorphous perverse activities that are associated with it: "We can say in general of the sexual theories of children that they are reflections of their own sexual constitution".[53] 'Little Hans', whose case study Freud published in the same year as 'Notes Upon a Case of Obsessional Neurosis', taught Freud that infantile sexual theories are based on the premise that all living creatures, including women, possess a penis.[54] This premise is crucial because, according to Freud, it explains why the child does not arrive at an understanding of the existence of the vagina and thus cannot comprehend the process of fertilization and birth. This childish phallocentrism – or better, widdlercentrism – that underpins infantile sexual theories is the only reason why Freud terms these theories 'sexual'.

In 'Family Romances', Freud goes a step further. The term 'family romance' refers to phantasms in which children, because of the disappointments they inevitably encounter in the relationship with their real parents (they are for example less wealthy, large or powerful than the small child had thought), adjusts their relationship to them in an imaginary way. The small child would now for example fantasize about being given up by prestigious parents who will come and reclaim them. Compared to infantile sexual theories, this 'romance' is not 'sexual' in the sense that it would mirror the polymorphous-perverse activities of the child. It is also not 'sexual' because the child has no sense yet of sexual differences, the vagina, sperm, intercourse and procreation. Freud on the contrary refers here only to loving and ambitious goals pursued in fantasies about other, more highly placed or sophisticated parents.[55] Family romances concern, in other words, the different aspects of infantile and pre-pubescent theories on (a relationship to the) parents beyond any reference to infantile sexuality. According to Freud, these relationships are only sexualized in puberty and then also immediately oedipalized. This sexualization and oedipalization of object relations can be explained through new knowledge about genital difference[56], procreation and origin acquired at the onset of puberty, according to Freud. It is this knowledge – in which the relationship to the mother is absolutely certain and beyond any doubt, and the father is regarded as fundamentally insecure – which leads to a sexualization of the family romances. The following citation clearly illustrates this process:

> When presently the child comes to know the difference in the parts played by fathers and mothers in their sexual relations, and realizes that '*pater semper incertus est*', while the mother is '*certissima*', the family romance undergoes a curious curtailment: it contents itself with exalting the child's father, but no longer casts any doubts on his maternal origin,

> which is regarded as something unalterable. This *second (sexual) stage of the family romance* is actuated by another motive as well, which is absent in the first (asexual) stage. The child, having *learnt* about sexual processes, tends to picture to himself erotic situations and relations, the motive force behind this being his desire to bring his mother (who is the subject of the most intense sexual curiosity) into situations of secret infidelity and into secret love-affairs. *In this way the child's phantasies, which started by being, as it were, asexual, are brought up to the level of his later knowledge.*[57]

This citation illuminates the way in which Freud's thinking evolved during the years following the publication of *Three Essays on the Theory of Sexuality*. In the text on family romances, puberty is the most important turning point in the development of the individual. During the pre-pubescent period, the child only has loving feelings towards the parental objects. These objects are sexualized when puberty begins for the reasons we have set out. At first sight, 'Family Romances' is in this way on a par with *Three Essays*, in which puberty is also a turning point. But in *Three Essays*, infancy was of course not 'asexually' determined as in the text we are discussing here. There it was not a matter of contrast between an 'asexual' and a 'sexual' period but between an an-objectal, autoerotic sexual period and objectal, genitally oriented puberal sexuality. Infantile sexuality was 'without object' and, therefore, the object relations were 'asexual' and only supported by selfish motives (food consumption, care). The new interest in objects at the onset of puberty is simultaneously also motivated by a search for a new type of sexual pleasure that was impossible until then: the orgasm ('end pleasure').[58] In 'Family Romances', on the other hand, the most important developmental task confronting the child is not the subjugation of the various erogenous zones to the primacy of genitality. The most important task for the child is rather to become independent of the authority of the parents.[59] The most important motives for this development are under no circumstances sexual but belong exclusively to the sphere of self-preservation drives. At the same time, sexuality is drawn into an intrinsic connection with (knowledge of) sexual difference, which was expressly not the case in the first edition of *Three Essays*.

In the case of the Rat Man, the discussion on the relationship between parents – particularly the father – and children links the way Freud thematizes it in 'Family Romances'. Parents are also for the Rat Man a given in the first place. Their presence is in the first instance "a reality which needs no further enquiry".[60] The relationship with the parents can by no means be understood in terms of the Oedipus complex. In a footnote in the text on the Rat Man, Freud argues "that people's 'childhood memories' are only consolidated at a later period, usually at the age of puberty; and that this involves a complicated process of remodelling, analogous in every way to the process by which a nation constructs legends about its early history".[61] The allusions in Ernst Lanzer's dreams to sexual desires towards the mother, which Freud mentions in the same footnote, must also be understood from this perspective. Indeed, Freud states that in his phantasies about his infancy, the growing individual tries to obscure the memory of his own autoerotic activity "by exalting their memory-traces to the level of object-love, just as a real historian will view the past in the light of the present".[62]

Moreover, also the version of the role of the father remains sexually neutral. It is a correct man and role model for his son with whom he had a good and loving relationship. Only when the father prohibits the autoerotic activity of little Ernst everything changes. From this moment, the father becomes the object of a strong sadistic impulse (and hate) that constitutes an integral part of the libido. Only at this point does the father consequently become a fully fledged part of the libidinal economy of the Rat Man. The prohibition (and trauma) lead to a *premature* sexualization of the relationship with the father (and the parents) and not vice versa. The latter is, however, presupposed in an oedipal reading.

8. Seduction, trauma and the Oedipus complex

In the original theory of seduction, Freud explains both hysteria and obsessional neurosis as effects of a sexual trauma during childhood. This theory generally holds that hysteria is caused by a trauma that is passively experienced and was thus not pleasurable, while obsessional neurosis was the result of a trauma in which the patient was actively involved and that was experienced as pleasure. This trauma occurred at a somewhat later age, but according to Freud, behind the event in which the small child played an active role, a passive unpleasurable scene could always be found.

Both the preceding chapters made it clear that in the years after 1897, Freud also linked neurosis in its hysterical and obsessive form with traumatic events that help determine its course. As far as we know, this is Freud's explicit view. Trauma admittedly loses its exclusive aetiological role, but it remains an essential element in a modified theory of seduction. In both cases, this modification concerns the new emphasis on constitutional and dispositional elements of a sexual nature that are the real cause of pathology. Thus, the Rat Man's character change, which lies at the basis of his pathology, is an effect of the interaction between constitutional (a strongly developed sadistic impulse) and accidental elements (the intervention of the father and his own reaction to it). This does, however, not mean that trauma is purely reduced to a catalyst, such as with Charcot. It remains a foreign body (*Fremdkörper*) without which we cannot understand the course and face of neurosis.[63] Thus, the various conflicts that determine the rhythm and structure of the Rat Man's life are, for example, new editions of the original trauma.

Even if Freud does not explicitly thematize this problem in the texts we discuss here, the distinction between 'passive' and 'active' events still plays an important part, just as in the original theory of seduction. With Dora (hysteria), from the beginning – eavesdropping on the sexual activities of her parents – it is firstly about passive traumas she experienced as unpleasurable, for the reasons we set out. The Rat Man (the patient with obsessional neurosis), on the other hand, is actively involved in the scene that acquires a traumatic meaning for him. Moreover, the traumatic force here does not lie in the external event as such but rather in the internal processing or the absence thereof. Overhearing her parents' sexual activities takes on a traumatic meaning for Dora because she cannot bind the sexual energy that is released to modified representations. Thus, this 'free-floating' sexual energy threatens the integrity of the ego from within. What traumatizes the Rat Man is not so much the interdict of the father as such but the fear of his own angry reaction to it. The first fright after seeing the force of his anger pushes through in a continuous anticipation of a fit of rage coming from the fear of the explosive force of the own anger.[64]

Whichever way one looks at it, neither in the study of Dora, nor in that of the Rat Man does the Oedipus complex play a meaningful aetiological role. With Dora, oedipal motives and fantasies are evoked to repress an important aspect of her problematic – the love for Herr K. and, ultimately, also the homosexual desires for Frau K. – and in the case of the Rat Man, the sexualization of relations to the parents is the result and not the cause of the father's no. In these texts, then, oedipal phantasies primarily have a defensive meaning. One cannot emphasize enough that in Freud's work, not every reference to oedipal themes may be interpreted in terms of the Oedipus complex. Generally, one could argue that certainly in the period up to 1910, the Oedipus complex is a problem that belongs to the (beginning of the) puberal period, according to Freud. After all, the Oedipus complex presupposes sexualized object relations, and up until then Freud had denied its existence in childhood. Freudian psychoanalysis is, especially regarding the aetiology of the neuroses, not oedipal until 1910.

9. Trauma, aggression and sexuality

Freud's original theory of seduction implies that trauma is sexual in essence. This applied to both hysteria and obsessive neurosis. Since the obsessive-neurotic patient is involved in the trauma and in principle also derives pleasure from it, Freud still has to explain why this experience of pleasure is repressed. Freud refers for this to the fusion of the active experience with an earlier passive experience, as in hysteria.[65] In this perspective, Freud calls obsessional neurosis a dialect of hysteria.[66] The Rat Man too is actively involved in sexual acts with women and girls from his immediate environment. He is not just a passive victim thereof. At the same time, the sexual content of the traumatic experience that underlies the obsessional neurosis of the Rat Man remains uncertain at first glance. According to his mother, he bit someone. However, Freud thinks he was punished by his father because he masturbated. Moreover, he does not refer here to an earlier passive experience to explain the repression. What makes the conflict with the father traumatic is the fear of his own anger. So, one could ask how Freud can keep on saying that trauma is also essentially sexual in obsessional neurosis. Fundamentally, Freud seems to ground this insight in the belief that the Rat Man's anger is an expression of hate that is bound to a strongly developed sadistic component of the libido. By casting anger, hate and sadism as extensions of each other in this way, Freud succeeds in giving trauma an unequivocally sexual meaning.

Yet we need to question the legitimacy of the connection Freud makes between anger, hate and sadism. Anger and hate differ substantially. We can be angry with a friend without hating them. Anger has an explosive character. It implies a sudden eruption that can bring relief as well as destruction. Anger always has a paroxysmal character; it is an affective outburst hence stands in the way of cold-bloodedness, which is necessary for revenge. Anger is an affect. It overwhelms and brings us beside ourselves. It also disappears when the situation that evoked it is no longer present or when it was taken out. Anger does occur in relation to a specific object but can easily be transferred to other objects. In the theoretical part of *Studies on Hysteria*, Breuer had given the example of Bismarck who must suppress his anger towards the emperor, but the moment he is alone again, he smashes a valuable vase.[67] Thus, anger is explosive and does not depend on a single specific object for its satisfaction. It is entirely different with hate. Hate is a passion. Like a grudge, it can be cultivated. Hate deepens itself. Hate maintains itself in relation to a specific object that cannot be replaced by another. Hate lives in us, we feed it, it gives our existence stability and ensures that we do not lose ourselves.[68] It has the latter in common with love.

Reading 'Notes', one notices that Freud in the *description* of the history of an illness is concerned mostly with anger, while in his *theoretical* contemplations, he systematically interprets this anger as an expression of hatred. In the clinical history of the Rat Man, it repeatedly concerns a sudden rebellious anger towards someone interfering with pleasure: his father, an old professor in the sanatorium who occupies the room neighboring the room of the nurse he desires, his fiancée and her ill grandmother, and so forth.[69]

Again and again, it concerns a situationally determined momentary affect. Freud also describes these fortunes of the Rat Man with words such as 'a restrained anger drive', 'a tremendous feeling of rage, which was inaccessible to the patient's consciousness and was directed against someone who had cropped up as an interference with the course of his love'.[70] But in his theoretical considerations, Freud translates this anger in terms of hate and sadism. He thus describes the drive constellation that is characteristic of obsessional neurosis as follows:

> in the cases of unconscious hatred with which we are concerned the sadistic components of love have, from constitutional causes, been exceptionally strongly developed, and have consequently undergone a premature and all too thorough suppression, and that the neurotic phenomena we have observed arise on the one hand from conscious feelings of affection which have become exaggerated as a reaction, and on the other hand from sadism persisting in the unconscious in the form of hatred.[71]

The repressed anger is interpreted here without detours and without further argument as a sadism that continues in the unconscious. This equation between anger and hate is not inconsequential.

When anger is interpreted according to the logic of hate, the Rat Man's successive fits of rage must be oriented at the same object. The objects of these fits consequently only appear diverse. In the case of the Rat Man, this gives the father enormous weight. According to Freud, the hate is indeed originally oriented at the father. The old professor, the army officers, the grandmother of his lady are in fact nothing but father substitutes. The hate against the father is transmitted to these objects. The father complex in this way appears as an effect of a conceptual confusion between anger and hate. Again and again, the Rat Man is overwhelmed by a blind rage when someone thwarts his sexual desires. The infantile fit of rage against his father is indeed the prototype and model of similar situations, but it by no means implies that that it would inevitably also be the origin of an unconscious hate. When Freud – and the Freudian tradition – had considered the distinction between anger and hate, the introduction of the father complex – and with it the usual oedipal reading of this case study? – would perhaps have seemed less obvious.

But there is more. In the first edition of *Three Essays on the Theory of Sexuality*, Freud still had linked aggression with the 'instinct for mastery' or the mastery drive, which by itself is not sexual.[72] According to Freud, cruel impulses arise from sources that are indeed independent from sexuality but that can, via a process of anastomosis (cross-connection), become united early on close to their points of origin. According to Freud, this mastery drive arises from non-sexual motor impulses that discharge in muscle activity those that are paradigmatically expressed in infantile romps. The cross-connections between both can be established when the muscle activity coincides with erogenous pleasure.[73] In the third edition of *Three Essays*, but also already in the case of the Rat Man, Freud still exclusively thinks of aggression as an expression of a sadistic impulse of libido. Hate and aggression are sexualized in this way.[74] In the Rat Man, Freud does not really argue the link between sadism and hate. He does not proceed further than the explanation that unconscious hatred and a strongly developed sadistic component of the libido reflexively imply each other.[75] This smooth connection between hate and sadism is, however, far from evident. Thus, a child who treats a pet sadistically does not hate, and neither is it clear why this sadism should at once be seen as libidinal. For Freud's argumentation in 'Notes', this sexualization is perhaps also important because it allows him to understand the mother's memory of conflict with the father – the Rat Man would have bitten someone – as an expression of sadistic libido.

Freud ensures the sexual status of the trauma by sexualizing both the activity of the Rat Man for which he is punished as well as his reaction to it. This sexualization is, however, not obvious. Hate and anger answer to a different logic, and the relation between sadism and hate remains problematic. Finally, it is not clear – Freud was still, as we have argued, deeply under the impression of this problem in the first edition of *Three Essays* – why aggression and sadism would always have a sexual meaning. One recalls in this regard that Freud in his original seduction theory assumes that sexual trauma is introduced at two times. In both the case of Emma and Dora, which we discussed in the previous two chapters, a first event is reinterpreted *nachträglich* at the onset of puberty that, according to Freud, is a qualitative break in the development of sexual experience. This break and the reinterpretation enabled by it are crucial for the activity of the trauma as well as characteristic of sexuality. We do not find this *nachträgliche* reinterpretation in the case of the Rat Man. Here it exclusively concerns the continuous *repetition* of always *the same* inclination. Unlike sexuality, aggression develops continuously. Its essence does not change during psychical evolution. The relationship between aggression and sexuality will continue occupying Freud in the years after 'Notes Upon a Case of Obsessional Neurosis'. As we will see, this problematics also reappears in *Beyond the Pleasure Principle* and in *Moses and Monotheism*.[76]

9. Conclusion

This chapter taught us that in the years following the first appearance of *Three Essays on the Theory of Sexuality*, Freud continues to understand not only hysteria (Dora) but also obsessional neurosis (the Rat Man) from a modified seduction theory. The aetiological meaning of trauma is also contained in connection with obsessional neurosis, but trauma simultaneously continues to play a role in the aetiology of neurosis, albeit consistent with constitutional and dispositional elements having the upper hand, as in the case of Dora. Freud continues to emphasize the sexual character of trauma (and the sexual aetiology of the neurosis), even if he must fully understand the problematic of rage and aggression from the point of sexuality. We showed that both this equalization and the sexual character of trauma are perhaps less certain here than Freud indicates.

This also means the oedipal explanation of the compulsive pathology, which in most of the publications on the Rat Man replaces the reference to seduction theory, does not withstand a thorough reading of the texts. Sexualization of the relationship with the father is, in Freud's text, an effect of trauma and does not lie at the origin of the conflict. Moreover, according to *Three Essays*, the problematic of sexual difference (and of oedipal relations) only becomes relevant at the onset of puberty and thus cannot underpin infantile neurosis.

In *Three Essays*, Freud took apart sexuality, gender difference and procreation. With precision, Freud shows that these problematics do not mutually imply one another. Sexuality refers, on the contrary, to a non-functional pleasure experience that is not essentially oriented to reproduction. In the years after *Three Essays* was first published, Freud will again link sexuality to the problematic of genital difference and more specifically to infantile phallocentrism. He even distinguishes, in 'Family Romances', an asexual (infantile) period that is followed by a sexual (puberal) period revolving around sexual differentiation and the Oedipus complex. In subsequent texts, he will further strengthen this tendency by progressively describing sexual difference and the Oedipus complex that is associated with it as structural elements of infantile sexuality itself.[77] That is the line Freud will follow from now on. The study of the Wolf Man, 'From the History of an Infantile Neurosis', which we will discuss in the next chapter, is a striking illustration of Freud's attempts at rethinking childhood sexuality in terms of puberal sexuality, or what was until then considered puberal sexuality. In the last edition from 1924 of *Three Essays*, Freud summarizes this development as follows:

> we must also suppose that the choice of an object, such as we have shown to be characteristic of the pubertal phase of development, has already frequently or habitually been effected during the years of childhood: that is to say, the whole of the sexual currents have become directed towards a single person in relation to whom they seek to achieve their aims. This then is the closest approximation possible in childhood to the final form taken by sexual life after puberty.[78]

This does not mean, however, that Freud will abandon every reference to trauma and seduction theory in 'From the History of an Infantile Neurosis'. On the contrary, beside the problematic of castration and the Oedipus complex, Freud explicitly reconfirms the reality of sexual trauma in conjunction with constitutional and dispositional elements. With regards to the latter, the study on the Wolf Man shows an important shift, which will remain crucial for the further development of our book. From the moment Freud starts to gather followers, he tries to 'conquer psychiatry' via Eugen Bleuler, Karl Abraham and especially Carl Gustav Jung, and introduce psychoanalytic theory, but he simultaneously shows a growing interest in 'applied psychoanalysis' that must help reveal the origin of culture, particularly religion.[79] In this context, psycho-Lamarckism – the doctrine of the inheritance of acquired characteristics, psychic dispositions and memories – gains increasing importance in Freud's theorizing.[80] This leads particularly to a redetermination of the content and role of constitution in the human condition and psychopathology. Notably the determining (and universal) role the Oedipus complex acquires in Freud's clinical views following the publication of the Rat Man is closely related to Freud's explorations of phylogenetic factors in the human constitution. In our next chapter, we will indicate how these different themes come together in Freud's discussion of the case of the Wolf Man.

Chapter 4

Seduction, primal scene and constitution: The Wolf Man

1. Introduction

In the previous chapters, we showed that Freud modified and supplemented the theory of seduction with new insights. The case study of the Wolf Man, 'From the History of an Infantile Neurosis', can be read as the next step in which Freud supplements his trauma theory with one of constitutional, dispositional and development-psychological factors in the aetiology of neurosis. Like in the cases of Emma and Dora, the case study of the Wolf Man is structured by a trauma in two phases. The case of the Wolf Man is therewith a case in which "the old trauma theory of the neuroses (...) had suddenly come to the front once more".[1] However, this temporality of the trauma is now completely situated in early childhood, causing puberty to lose its aetiological significance. By introducing a theory of sexual development in different phases, another important element is added to the trauma theory. The trauma is decisively influenced by several disturbances (fixations, inhibitions) in the earliest sexual development. These early 'derailments' are decisive for the creation and meaning of the trauma in a second episode. At the same time, this theory is expanded with an element that Freud also introduced and explored in other texts in the same period: a theory of the significance of trauma in phylogeny and for the development of the sexual constitution. All in all, 'From the History of an Infantile Neurosis' is an extremely complex case in which numerous elements from previous case studies and meta-psychological reflections are brought together in a text that also has a place in Freud's debates with some of his students, especially Carl Gustav Jung.

2. *Treatment and context*

More than six months before Freud recorded the history of the Wolf Man's illness in October and November 1914, he had written a text on the principles and findings of psychoanalysis: 'The History of the Psychoanalytic Movement'.[2] Already on the opening page of 'From the History of an Infantile Neurosis', Freud writes that the case study connects to this text as it "supplements the polemic contained in that essay, which is in essence of a personal character, by an objective estimation of the analytic material".[3] At the time Freud wrote his text on the history of the psychoanalytic movement, the treatment of the Wolf Man was coming to an end. In February 1910, the very wealthy 23-year-old Sergei Pankejeff (coming from Odessa, Russia) commenced his analysis with Freud. The analysis would continue until July 1914. This young man had collapsed after he contracted gonorrhea at eighteen. Freud quickly concludes that his affliction should be seen as "a condition following on an obsessional neurosis which has come to an end spontaneously" in his youth.[4] According to Freud, the actual neurosis and the failure to solve real life problems could be understood almost entirely from the infantile neurosis. To understand Freud's complete focus on the infantile neurosis of the Wolf Man, we must briefly dwell on the targeted 'polemic'.

In concrete terms, this concerns the debate with Jung. In connection with Freud's ideas about a general human sexual constitution and sexual fantasies of adults about so-called traumatic events in childhood, Jung had formed his own thoughts about the aetiology of neuroses. He believes that precisely the generality of the sexual constitution implies that it cannot be pathogenic. After all, such a general constitution cannot explain anything specific. However, components of that constitution can be activated by a current and real conflict, giving the impression that the current neurosis has its origins in constitutional factors. The starting point in Jung's view of the psychoneuroses is therefore a current conflict that always revolves around an impulse of libido (drive)[5] and an obstacle raised, i.e. a difficulty that has arisen in a new life situation and that requires commitment, problem solving and adjustment to culturally defined life goals. The libido, however, avoids these current problems and tasks, activates memories and stages a clinical picture that seems to have its origins in childhood. Even though these memories seem to go back to a factual reality, they are nothing more than fantasies in which an "apparent aetiology is presented".[6] In fact, these fantasies are attempts to find excuses in the past for "work not done in the face of reality" in the present.[7] According to Jung, the memories of childhood, and more concretely of 'pre-sexual' experiences of pleasure and unpleasure in a period of (constitutional) vulnerability and sensitivity, are sexualized from a current conflict and life task. Although Jung here links up with certain of Freud's insights, it is clear that all constitutional and accidental factors in early childhood to which Freud attributed a decisive role in the aetiology are interpreted in terms of sexualizing regression and fantasy.

"What is in dispute, therefore, is the significance of the infantile factor", Freud writes in the case of the Wolf Man.[8] His response to Jung comprises an indication that this case concerns a fully fledged infantile neurosis anchored in the sexual constitution and in true traumatic impressions and experiences during early childhood. The analysis of the Wolf Man allows a descent "into the deepest and most primitive strata of mental development and in gaining from there solutions for the problems of the later formations".[9] According to Freud, the central issue of current life tasks and goals, which was central to Jung, can be ignored here. After all, the small child has no knowledge of the tasks that culture places on the individual. The infantile neurosis can therefore not be explained based on a conflict with cultural representations.

The treatment of the Wolf Man lasted more than four years and, according to Freud, was difficult. "The patient with whom I am here concerned remained for a long time unassailably entrenched behind an attitude of obliging apathy".[10] However, we know the patient disclosed at least one crucial element of the case history early in the treatment. That concerns the anxiety dream of the wolves. Freud must also have concluded in the first half of the treatment that the Wolf Man must have witnessed sexual intercourse between his parents in his earliest childhood. In 1912, in the *Zentralblatt für Psychoanalyse*, he made a brief appeal to colleagues to be alert to childhood dreams whose interpretation justifies the conclusion that "*the dreamers had been witnesses of sexual intercourse in their early years*".[11] Early in 1913, he published a short article, 'The Occurrence in Dreams of Material from Fairy Tales', including the analysis of the Wolf Man's dream.[12] The first difficult part of the Wolf Man's treatment therefore provides insight into the two central – traumatic – moments in the aetiology of his patient's infantile neurosis: the observation of sexual intercourse between the parents and the anxiety dream.

From completed 'From the History of an Infantile Neurosis' at the beginning of November 1914. The intention was to publish this text in the *Jahrbuch für Psychoanalytische und Psychopathologische Forschungen*, but the journal's lifespan was cut short by the outbreak of World War I. The text was abandoned until 1918, when it was included in Freud's *Sammlung Kleiner Schriften zur Neurosenlehre*. On that occasion, Freud added two long passages in chapters 5 and 8 to the text.[13] We will discuss those additions separately in this chapter.

3. Memories of childhood

In the article about the material from fairy tales in dreams Freud writes that his patient found a support in his early childhood memories in the fact that he moved with his parents from their 'first estate' (in Cherson at the mouth of the Dnipro) to the city (Odessa) when he was 5 years old.[14] Before that move, the Wolf Man's severe neurotic disorder begins. Just before the age of four, an animal phobia develops, and from the age of about 4½, he develops an obsessive-compulsive disorder. Although the latter disorder extends into the tenth year of life (after which it 'spontaneously' ends), the determining moments and factors for the development of the obsessive-compulsive disorder fall within the first 5 years of life. Because even though the Wolf Man has difficulty organizing chronologically the various memories of defining impressions, he places them all in this period.

The Wolf Man's parents have a happy married life that is soon overshadowed by the mother's abdominal disorders and the father's manic-depressive moods that lead to his frequent absences from home. The little boy knows about his mother's ailments. When he was about 3¼ years old, he heard his mother talking to a doctor about her pains and hemorrhages – her lamentation "I cannot go on living like this" was instilled in him, and he later used it countless times for himself.[15] He has a sister, Anna, who is two years older than him and "lively, gifted, and precociously naughty".[16] As far as he can remember, he was cared for by an uneducated old woman, his 'Nanya'. This woman treats him very tenderly and transfers her motherly love for her deceased child to him. Initially the little boy was a "a very good-natured, tractable, and even quiet child". But around the age of 3½ his character changes quite suddenly: he has become "discontented, irritable and violent, took offence on every possible occasion, and then flew into a rage and screamed like a savage".[17] This happens in a summer in which an English, often inebriated governess, Miss Oven, was employed to take care of the children. The quarrelsome nature of the governess is mainly expressed in skirmishes with the nanya. In these situations, the young boy steadfastly sides with the older woman and shows signs of hatred for the governess. However, he also recalls at other times mercilessly taunting his nanya during this period.[18]

The first question now is how the change in character can be explained. After all, this change heralds a period of essentially infantile neurosis – animal phobia and obsessional neurosis. The Wolf Man remembers that this period is inextricably linked to all kinds of events and impressions, but he initially only knows that they belong to the period before the move. For example, he talks about his fear of the image of an upright wolf in a picture book – an image with which his sister teases him again and again to take pleasure in his fear. But he is also afraid of other animals and remembers an incident where he chased a large butterfly and suddenly developed a severe fear of the animal. At the same time, he also remembers tormenting beetles and cutting caterpillars in half. His contradictory – phobic and perverse – behavior towards animals is also expressed in a fear of horses and an undoubted pleasure in hitting horses.

The Wolf Man also relates that he was very devout in his early youth, that he had to pray for a long time before going to sleep, cross himself endlessly and kiss all the images of saints in his room. He also remembers that he kept having blasphemous thoughts, such as 'God-swine' and 'God-shit'. Similar thoughts occurred when he saw three piles of horse manure during a trip and was reminded of the Trinity. At the same time, he developed the ceremonial practice of exhaling loudly when seeing beggars, old or disabled people. With this ritual, he thought he could avoid becoming like them. Furthermore, the Wolf Man recalls that, although his relationship with his father clearly deteriorated as he grew older, they were very close in his younger years. They often played together, and the small boy was proud of his father, and he wanted "to be a gentleman like him".[19]

Regarding these and other memories produced, Freud notes that sometimes the details seemed "extraordinary and incredible". That's why he requested his patient "make the strictest criticism of his recollections".[20] This comment marks the beginning of this case study in which – in the light of the debate with Jung – the question of the status and reliability of memories of infantile events occupies a crucial place. Although infantile memories may generally be 'distorted' and 'mutilated', they are key in the analysis of infantile neurosis. The memories and dreams of the adult Wolf Man point the way to early impressions and events that really happened and that turn out to be defining moments in the development of the neurosis. Just because the memory of the patient "is claiming (…) to possess the quality of reality", it is necessary to submit the concrete memories to strict criticism and distinguish them from phantasies that were produced much later. In concrete terms, Freud is thinking of the terrifying wolf dream that "relates to an occurrence that really took place and was not merely imagined" and of the sister's seduction that had 'certainly not been a phantasy'.[21]

Indeed, in the study of the Wolf Man, Freud aims to show that memories are not phantasies produced by adults and projected back into childhood, as Jung had claimed. According to Freud, Jung's theory relies on "a low estimate of the importance of early infantile impressions". Freud, on the other hand, holds on to insights from the time of seduction theory: children can register observations and process experiences psychologically at a very young age. The original observations and the activation, processing and understanding experienced a few years later in an anxiety dream can then ultimately be made conscious in a coherent manner in adulthood.[22] But what is still missing is a criterion to distinguish memories of these impressions from later phantasies. How can we be sure that a memory of a childhood experience is not a back-projected phantasy?[23]

In the study of the Wolf Man, Freud writes that the memories reproduced by his patient give reason to suppose that the English governess plays a crucial role in the young Wolf Man's personality change. He seems to confirm Freud's assumption in several dreams that contain aggressive acts against the governess and his sister. However, Freud interprets these dreams as "phantasies, which the dreamer had made on the subject of his childhood at some time or other, probably at the age of puberty".[24] When Freud comes across a memory in which his sister "seduced" the little boy "into sexual practices", and subsequently, in a second memory of his sister that emerges, she grabs his member and starts playing with it, Freud understands why these dreams must be products of later phantasies. The phantasies "were meant to efface the memory of an event which later on seemed offensive to the patient's masculine self-esteem, and they reached this end by putting an imaginary and desirable converse in the place of the historical truth".[25] Not in the difficult relationship with the quarrelsome governess but in the seductions by the sister should the decisive motive for the personality change be sought.

This is not to say that all the Wolf Man's dreams are nothing but phantasies. On the contrary, in this case study, Freud explicitly emphasizes that 'dreaming is also remembering', albeit subject to the conditions – condensation, displacements, associations with recent events – that apply to dream-formation. In dreams, childhood scenes are not directly reproduced as recollections, but these experiences can be "divined—constructed—gradually and laboriously from an aggregate of indications".[26] According to Freud, such a construction becomes possible since the patient repeatedly brings up a dream with certain factors and that the repeated interpretation of the dream in different analytical sessions leads time and again to the same 'sense of reality' of (part of) the content of the dream. As the analysis progresses, that sense of reality will strengthen the patient's "profound conviction of the reality of these primal scenes".[27] The wolf dream meets these requirements. The patient regularly returns to it during the four-year analysis, during which he was always affected by "lasting sense of reality, too, which the dream left behind it". It is precisely this fact that leads Freud to assume that this dream relates to something that actually happened in childhood. But it is about the "reality of something unknown", a "long-forgotten trace in his memory of a scene".[28]

4. Seduction and its consequences

An important moment in the analysis of the Wolf Man is the moment when he suddenly and spontaneously recalls "when he was still very small, 'on the first estate', his sister had seduced him into sexual practices".[29] It is a crucial memory in the case because, as would soon become clear, with this seduction by the sister, the Wolf Man's personality change is started. The seduction by the sister's firstly entails her suggestion that they show their bottoms to each other, and then putting these words into action. But more important than this was a second seduction scene that the Wolf Man remembered vividly and in detail. His father was away, his mother in the room adjacent to where he and his sister were playing. His sister had then "taken hold of his penis and played with it, at the same time telling him incomprehensible stories about his Nanya, as though by way of explanation. His Nanya, she said, used to do the same thing with all kinds of people—for instance, with the gardener: she used to stand him on his head, and then take hold of his genitals".[30]

The Wolf Man was 3¼ years old when the brief episode of his sister's seduction attempts began. To understand the significance of these temptations for his change in character and his infantile neurosis, Freud notes that although the little boy refuses the person tempting him, he does not refuse the thing. Apparently, his sister, who is primarily an unwelcome rival for the Wolf Man when it comes to parental appreciation and love, is not an appropriate sexual object. He now directs the sexual excitement and activity aroused in the Wolf Man towards Nanya.

> He therefore began to play with his penis in his Nanya's presence, and this, like so many other instances in which children do not conceal their masturbation, must be regarded as an attempt at seduction. His Nanya disillusioned him; she made a serious face, and explained that that wasn't good; children who did that, she added, got a 'wound' in the place.[31]

Nanya's comment could be interpreted as a threat, but for the Wolf Man it is primarily a rejection. His love for her cools as a result, and this becomes clear not long afterwards in the period after the personality change: he starts to tease and taunt her until she bursts into tears. In the meantime, he looks for another love object. The seduction by the sister "had given him the passive sexual aim of being touched on the genitals" and now that his attempts to seduce Nanya had failed, he returned to that aim, looking for another object to touch his member. This object is the father, who is often absent during that period. That father is an example the Wolf Man admires until that moment. He identifies with him and wants to be a gentleman like him. We might expect Freud to introduce the father complex or the Oedipus complex from this point on. This he does not do, however. In fact, for now, the little Wolf Man's relationship with his father is what was also true of the Rat Man. The relationship with the father is relatively uncomplicated until the moment of the anxious wolf nightmare, several months later. When he is present, they play together; the Wolf Man is proud of his father, and his father loved him very much.[32] There is no indication of a strong oedipal ambivalence towards the father here.

In the chapter focusing on the seduction by the sister, Freud notes that the first genital excitations arising from this were the impetus for all kinds of sexual explorations. He develops a strong curiosity about the genitals of others. His desire to watch is satisfied by watching his sister and her girlfriend peeing. According to Freud, we may assume that the boy here is confronted with the problem of castration. But his reaction is, according to Freud, what you usually find in other young children. What the little boy sees gives no reason to see this as confirmation of the threat of his Nanya.[33] Instead, he develops the infantile theory in which what he sees is girls' 'front bottom'.[34] The driving force behind such an infantile theory is formed by the desire to look, that is, the pleasure experienced by visual impressions, especially of the hidden parts of the body. The material from which the theories are constructed is formed by what the child already knows, in this concrete case his own and his sister's bottom.[35]

Other impressions and stories also meant that the subject of castration could occupy him without worrying him yet. For example, he heard the story from *Reynard the Fox* in which a wolf wants to fish in the winter, uses its tail as a fishing rod and then breaks it off in the ice. He also hears the names horses are called depending on whether their sexual organs are intact or not. Freud concludes: "Thus he was occupied with thoughts about castration, but as yet he had no belief in it and no dread of it".[36]

The seduction by the sister and its already-mentioned effects are crucial to understanding the change in character a few months later. After being rejected by his nanya, the little boy soon stopped masturbating. "*His sexual life, therefore, which was beginning to come under the sway of the genital zone, gave way before an external obstacle, and was thrown back by its influence into an earlier phase of pregenital organization*".[37] With the collapse of the primacy of the genital zone, the sexual life of the Wolf Man takes on an anal-sadistic character. The sadism is most clear in the taunting of his nanya and the tormenting of small animals. At the same time, a masochistic tendency emerges. The new passive goal of his pursuits is from now on colored by a sadism that turns against his own person. Fantasies emerge in which boys are beaten, "especially (…) on the penis" or on the bottom.[38] Freud concludes from this that a consciousness of guilt due to the previous masturbation played a role here. When his father returns to the estate in the autumn of that year – the Wolf Man is well over 3½ years old – after a period of absence, he becomes the object of the little boy's anger and rage. While taunting the nanya and tormenting animals were still an expression of sadism, the anger against the father, however, has a masochistic purpose. In fact, Freud notes, they were 'seduction attempts' by the little boy, attempts to entice his father to discipline him, thus satisfying him and at the same time assuaging his guilt.

The inventory of the various seduction attempts that follow on from that by his sister does not yet exhaustively address the subject. In the remainder of the case study, it appears that the seduction by the sister also continued to have an effect during the period of his infantile obsessional neurosis (from 4½ years old). During that period, he starts to see his sister as "embodiment (…) of temptation and sin". He develops a strong hostility towards her – and towards other women. He provokes quarrels with her because he suspects that she is always lurking around him "to drag him again into sin". However, those fights with her give him a new sense of sinfulness. For example, by provoking quarrels with his sister, he reproduces "the event of his seduction over and over again".[39]

More important than these repetitions of the seduction by his sister is a scene that is only remembered by the Wolf Man towards the end of the analysis (in 1914). This scene emerges after a screen memory[40] that has already been told much earlier comes to the fore again in the analysis. It concerns the memory of the swallowtail butterfly with its beautiful large yellow stripes, which he suddenly became very afraid of after it had sat on a flower and had opened and closed its wings several times. The analysis shows that behind this lies the memory of a nanny named Grusha. The Wolf Man then remembers a scene when he must have been about 2½ years old. In that scene, this nanny is on her knees scrubbing the floor. As he watches, he becomes sexually aroused and pees his pants, after which she jokingly threatened to castrate her.[41] About this, Freud writes: "His micturition on the floor was in reality an attempt at a seduction, and the girl replied to it with a threat of castration, just as though she had understood what he meant".[42] This threat has not yet made any impression on the little boy.[43] It only has an effect afterwards in the anxiety dream about the wolves.

This scene is important primarily because all subsequent love objects – often simple peasant women – will prove to be substitutes for this one person. The Grusha scene is significant because it goes a long way toward explaining the Wolf Man's later object choices. However, Freud does wonder whether this scene was not later edited and sexualized by fantasy. The situation was perhaps nothing other than banal (a girl scrubbing) and coincidental (a little boy peeing his pants). However, he sees precisely in this sexual excitement the piece of reality through which the scene expressed something important that subsequently had to be left out and blocked by a screen memory. According to Freud, this sexual arousal was made possible by the 'activation' of an even older scene – the 'primal scene'. He had then seen his mother in a similar position to the scrubbing Grusha (see below).

The fact that Freud calls the Grusha scene an attempt at seduction does not mean that this scene "disturbed and diverted" the sexual development of the young Wolf Man in the same way that the seduction by his sister did.[44] The Grusha scene marks the beginning of a formerly normal development of identification with the father and of urethral eroticism. So, the male genital already plays a role. This points to the beginning of sexual development that will be organized around the primacy of the genitals. In the seduction by his sister, this genital organization then succumbs when that temptation and the threat/rejection of his nanya give him a passive goal. The Grusha scene therefore seems hardly important for his personality change and infantile neurosis. What this seduction scene shows is a first, still unproblematic development of the primal scene.

What is the place and significance of the various seduction scenes and attempts in the aetiology of infantile neurosis as it emerges in this case? The seduction by the sister in particular is decisive for the personality change (at the age of 3½ years) that precedes the actual neurosis (from the age of 4) and without which this neurosis would not have developed. During that period, the seduction by the sister provides the Wolf Man with a passive goal (touching and chastisement of his penis), and the genital organization succumbs to the threat of castration by his nanya. Anal-sadistic tendencies are now gaining the upper hand. The father moves from being the identification object for his sexual activities (Grusha scene) to becoming the "sexual object of a passive current in his present anal-sadistic phase".[45] The seduction also stimulates the voyeurism and sexual curiosity of the small boy. Castration occupies his thoughts. Specifically, Freud writes, two 'theoretical' problems occupy the Wolf Man: the question of the origin of children where babies come from and the question about the possibility of losing the genitals.[46]

The seduction (*Verführung*) by the sister marks a crucial moment in an already 'disturbed' development that Freud describes in terms of a 'deflection', 'derailment' or 'diversion' (*ablenken*) of the assumed normal sexual development of the child.[47] By seduction Freud means here any impression and experience that is intentionally or coincidentally initiated by an object (person), which provokes a reaction of sexual excitation and exploration, and which then 'constantly' 'leads astray' (*ver-führt*) the child from and thus 'diverts' (*ablenkt*) from a normal development.[48]

This is not a new idea. In fact, Freud makes explicit here what has always been a core aspect of the notion of *Verführung* (see p. 36). An event or impression can be called traumatic when it provokes effects that lead a person away from a supposedly normal development. We already saw this in the study of Dora, especially in the reactions of disgust and fear to Herr K.'s embrace in the store when Dora was 14 years old and not yet in puberty. These reactions of disgust and fear of the sexual were partly determined by a disturbing impression in childhood – the 'primal scene' of listening to the sexual intercourse between the parents and the subsequent 'affect reversal' (see p. 71). In the Wolf Man, this line of thought is further developed. As we will shortly see, a 'primal scene' produces the first premature sexual arousal and activities. The seduction by the sister then has a lasting effect on further developments. Freud writes about this: "Under the persisting influence of this experience [the seduction by the sister, HW/PvH] he pursued a path from his sister *via* his Nanya to his father".[49] The sister's seduction marks a crucial moment in a derailment of normal development that has already started. This is first manifested in the change in character and the boy's object-choice. The traumatic anxiety dream with which the actual infantile neurosis begins further 'diverts' (*abgelenkt*) the chosen 'path'.[50]

How does such a 'diversion' or 'deflection' (*Verführung*) come about? In *Three Essays*, Freud had mentioned two constitutional factors that are decisive. The first is 'precocious sexual maturity', that is, the set of perverse sexual activities developed during a period when genital organization has not yet been developed and reaction formations have not yet been completed. With the Wolf Man we could think here of urethral eroticism and masturbation. The second factor is 'increased pertinacity or susceptibility to fixation'. Early sexual impressions and problems make such a deep impression that they 'lead' to a compulsion to repeat them. They 'lay down the path to be taken' (*Wege vorschreiben*) by the sexual drive for a whole lifetime.[51] This is how perverse fixations and neurotic disorders (inhibition, regression) arise as 'deviations' from normal sexual life.[52] The seduction by the sister leads to the experience of pleasure being so fixated on a passive goal and on the anal-sadistic phase that the developmental path is further disturbed.

Regarding the seduction by the sister and its effects, Freud thus emphasizes the 'continual influence' and 'deviations' of a presupposed 'normal' sexual development. The continuing influence of the sister's seduction must, as we will see in the continuation, make plausible how a first pleasurable experience (the primal scene) can produce intense unpleasure in a second moment (the fear dream of the wolves) and can become a traumatic experience that is decisive for the development of an infantile neurosis.

5. *Primal scene, anxiety dream and Nachträglichkeit*

Freud had already noted in *Studies on Hysteria* that seeing or hearing sexual intercourse between the two parents can make an impression with a traumatic effect. In a footnote in that text, he briefly mentioned the case of a woman whose anxiety attacks had started after she had seen her father get into bed with her mother several times and then heard something that had greatly aroused her.[53] We have seen that also in the case study on Dora, hearing about sexual intercourse between the parents plays a crucial role in the development of her hysterical syndrome. In fact, this experience already had the status of a 'primal scene' there. Already in the first half of the treatment of the Wolf Man, Freud has a strong suspicion that the anxiety dream of the wolves indicates that the Wolf Man must have witnessed sexual intercourse between his parents.

In the dream the boy is in bed – it is winter and night-time. Suddenly the window opens, and the boy is 'terrified' to see, in a large walnut tree in front of the window, six or seven white wolves sitting motionless and watching with rapt attention. They resemble foxes because of their long tails and sheepdogs because of their pointed ears. The boy is filled with fear, afraid of being eaten, and wakes up screaming. The Wolf Man first connects this dream with stories of wolves in fairy tales he had heard and images in picture books. The number seven can be associated with the fairy tale of 'Seven Little Goats'. The fact that the wolves sit in a tree and have long tails can be related to another fairy tale in which wolves build a pyramid to take revenge on a tailor who climbed a tree after tearing off one of their tails.[54] The white color of the wolves can be associated with the little white goats from the fairy tale, but also with the thousands of white sheep on the estate – sheep that had died en masse due to a botched vaccination just before the boy had the dream.

The fear of wolves immediately manifests itself in an animal phobia. Drawing on insights from his analysis of little Hans's horse phobia,[55] Freud puts forward that the wolf is a father substitute to draw the following conclusion: "His fear of his father was the strongest motive for his falling ill".[56] The most important starting points for this interpretation are the fairy tales of 'The Wolf and the Seven Little Goats' and 'Little Red Riding-Hood' because of the element of being eaten by the wolf. The Wolf Man associates this with the sweetly intended 'growling' by his father while playing and the joking threat 'I will eat you up (Freud 1918b: 106). A reconstruction of the most important fragments of the dream yields the following: "*A real occurrence—dating from a very early period—looking—immobility—sexual problems—castration—his father—something terrible*".[57] The next step in the interpretation during the treatment runs via an exploration of 'reversals': behind the attentive observation by the wolves lies an experience in which the Wolf Man watches attentively. And behind the immobility lies an impression of fervid movements. The fact that the dream was dreamed just before Christmas (Christmas tree) and therefore just before his birthday (presents on the tree) encourages Freud to explore its wishful nature. The dreamer desires gratification ('presents') – more specifically, sexual (masochistic) gratification from his father. Freud writes about this:

> The strength of this wish made it possible to revive a long-forgotten trace in his memory of a scene which was able to show him what sexual satisfaction from his father was like; and the result was terror, horror of the fulfilment of the wish, the repression of the impulse which had manifested itself by means of the wish.[58]

In the wolf dream, "unconscious memory-traces" of the "picture of copulation between his parents, copulation in circumstances which were not entirely usual and were especially favourable for observation" "sprang into activity". When the Wolf Man must have been 1½ years old, he had been sleeping in a cot in his parents' bedroom. When he wakes up, he witnesses "a coitus *a tergo* [from behind], three times repeated" where he can see his father's organ as well as the genitals of his mother.[59] Freud adds that the toddler 'understood the process as well as its significance'.[60] What and how does the Wolf Man understand what he sees? According to Freud, the Wolf Man only understands retrospectively, that is in his dream, that what he observed concerns satisfaction – something he can now conclude from "the expression of enjoyment which he saw on his mother's face", a pleasure he has come to know through the satisfaction of his own desire and sexual explorations.[61] But how then is it possible that the little toddler, even though he only learns the meaning of what is observed afterwards, becomes excited and disrupts the lovemaking by passing a stool and screaming? After all, does that excitement not also presuppose a certain 'understanding' of what has been observed? As we will see, Freud answers this question with a reference to phylogeny.

The fact that this scene can cause so much fear afterwards (*nachträglich*) at the age of 4 is because the Wolf Man discovers the consequence of his passive sexual goal of wanting to be satisfied by his father: castration. According to Freud, the fact that this primal scene is 'activated' in the dream is possible through the 'strength of the wish' to be satisfied by the father. This wish makes it possible to revive the scene "which was able to show him what sexual satisfaction from his father was like". The revival of the scene results, in the anxious dream, in the recognition of "the reality of the existence of castration".[62]

> For now he saw with his own eyes the wound of which his Nanya had spoken, and understood that its presence was a necessary condition of intercourse with his father. He could no longer confuse it with the bottom, as he had in his observation of the little girls.[63]

The question that had been occupying the Wolf Man for some time – of whether you can lose the genitals – was thus answered in a highly disturbing manner. The dream shows him that his infantile theories were incorrect, that girls do not have a 'front bottom', but 'a wound'. The observation of the 'wound' produces a 'conclusion' namely the answer to the question whether loss of the genitals is possible.[64] The discovery (observation and mental processes) that castration truly exists has far-reaching consequences.

> He discovered the vagina and the biological significance of masculine and feminine. He understood now that active was the same as masculine, while passive was the same as feminine. His passive sexual aim should now have been transformed into a feminine one, and have expressed itself as 'being copulated with by his father' instead of 'being beaten by him on the genitals or on the bottom'. This feminine aim, however, underwent repression and was obliged to let itself be replaced by fear of the wolf.[65]

The Wolf Man thus discovers as early as four years the sexual differential, the difference between male and female.[66] The dream shows the small Wolf Man that, to be satisfied by the father, he must become like his mother, that is, female and castrated. To this the boy reacts not only with fear but also resistance. The boy does not want to accept this consequence of castration.

Both parents can be connected with elements from the wolf dream. According to Freud, the mother can be recognized in the wolf without a tail on which the other wolves climb (in the tailor's fairy tale), while in the primal scene, the father assumes the position of the upright, threatening wolf he knew from the images from the book with the fairy tale of 'Little Red Riding-Hood'.

In various ways, the chapter about this anxiety dream and the primal scene activated in it re-incorporates core elements from the theory of seduction. This applies primarily to the dream as an 'event' that concludes the character change period and commences the infantile neurosis one. This event "was not an external trauma, but a dream, from which he awoke in a state of anxiety".[67] At first glance, this statement seems to imply criticism of the old trauma theory: a dream after all differs from Emma's traumatic experiences in the clothing store or Dora's confrontations with Herr K's advances. However, that is not what Freud means with this statement. According to Freud, the dream can certainly be seen as a trauma. After all, the decisive factor is that a memory of a previous traumatic experience is 'activated' in the dream.[68] As in the previous case studies, Freud emphasizes that the trauma comes from within: an activated memory of an impression generated excitation at the time.

In what follows, Freud writes that the anxiety dream is a traumatic experience that "operated like a second seduction".[69] Freud writes about this: "The activation of the picture, which, thanks to the advance in his intellectual development, he was now able to understand, operated not only like a fresh event, but like a new trauma, like an interference from outside analogous to the seduction".[70] In the dream, the primal scene becomes a traumatic experience after the fact (*nachträglich*). As with Emma and Dora, we find here a theory of the trauma in two phases. Freud even explicitly refers to the theory of seduction when he calls the dream 'a second seduction'. What then is the 'first seduction'? That is not the seduction by the sister but the primal scene. After all, in the dream, the memory traces of the observation of the parents' coitus are activated. Such an observation was already seen by Freud at the time of the seduction theory as a scene through which a child is suddenly and therefore brutally confronted with adult sexuality and with its first spontaneous reactions of pleasure and unpleasure. This is also the case in the Wolf Man study. The little toddler responds to the observation of his parents' sexual intercourse with a first sexual activity (passing a stool). This is followed by a series of premature sexual activities in which the boy initially identified with his father (Grusha scene). In the anxiety dream, the memory of this primal scene is activated, but it takes on a new meaning under the influence of the effects of the seduction by the sister (the father as object choice; the passive attitude). In the dream, the Wolf Man is confronted with the consequences of his identification with his mother and his desire to be satisfied by his father. It is this brutal confrontation with the implication of passivity and femininity (castration) that causes him intense fear, and thus has a traumatic effect. The continued influence of the seduction by the sister is thus a condition for the activation of the primal scene in an anxiety dream. After all, the young Wolf Man taking his father as a sexual object resulted from the seduction by the sister. Had this development and choice of objects not occurred, the primordial scene would probably not have become pathogenic.

Through the extensive analysis of the seduction by the sister and its immediate consequences, Freud traces the two accidental moments that structure the entire case study: the primal scene and the anxiety dream. It is the traumatic effect of these two experiences that largely determines the aetiology of the infantile neurosis. Hence Freud can write: "The old trauma theory of the neuroses, which was after all built up upon impressions gained from psycho-analytic practice, had suddenly come to the front once more".[71] He refers to the trauma theory as we know it from the cases of Emma and Dora. In both cases it concerns a theory of the temporality of trauma and its significance for the aetiology of the neurosis: a first experience in childhood and the subsequent activation (*nachträglich*) of this first experience in a second traumatic experience in adolescence.

The distance in time between the first and second trauma, compared to Emma and Dora, is radically shortened in the case of the Wolf Man. There is only 2½ years between the primal scene and the anxiety dream. The *nachträgliche* effect of the primal scene now occurs early in childhood, not in puberty. Puberty is not a factor in the aetiology of infantile neurosis. At this point, Freud can build on previously gained insights. The study of Little Hans had taught him that an animal phobia can arise and be 'resolved' in childhood.[72] The personality change of the Rat Man after his first anger attack had confirmed this. The analysis of the Wolf Man offers Freud the ideal opportunity to map out the complex aetiology of an infantile neurosis.

Because of this effect of the infantile in the later neurosis, Freud speaks of a double *Nachträglichkeit*. There is the 'deferred' activation of the primal scene in the anxiety dream. And there is, at the time of the analysis, a new activation of the primal scene that manifests itself in the understanding and 'putting into words' of what must have happened in childhood.[73]

> This is simply another instance of *deferred action* [*Nachträglichkeit*]. At the age of one and a half the child receives an impression to which he is unable to react adequately; he is only able to understand it and to be moved by it when the impression is revived in him at the age of four; and only twenty years later, during the analysis, is he able to grasp with his conscious mental processes what was then going on in him.[74]

The concepts *nachträglich* and *Nachträglichkeit* occur more often in the case study of the Wolf Man than in any of Freud's other texts.[75] That is telling. It shows that in the study of the Wolf Man, the reconstruction of the primal scene and its activation in the second trauma is 'etiologically privileged' in this study.[76] This makes it clear once again that Freud had not resolutely abandoned his trauma theory in September 1897 but reformulated it based in particular on his theory of infantile sexuality (as the whole of pleasurable sexual experiences), the urge to know (infantile sexual theories) and the sexual development of the child. When in the analysis one can 'construct' and 'extract' the traumatic primal scene from the available material, then it turns out that "all the consequences radiate out from it" as they become manifest in later moments and in the symptomatology of the infantile neurosis.[77] We also saw something similar in the case of the Rat Man: all later obsessive-compulsive symptoms can be understood from the scene of the anger attack.

6. Constitutional factors and dispositions

The 'etiological privileging' of trauma in the case of the Wolf Man could be seen as a return to the theory of seduction in which trauma was the exclusive factor in the aetiology of the neuroses.[78] The Wolf Man's choice of neuroses – his animal phobia and obsessional neurosis – would in that case be fully determined by the series of accidental factors discussed above. Without the primal scene and the seduction by the sister, the Wolf Man would never have become neurotic. But is it fair to speak, in this sense, about a 'return' to the theory of seduction?

There is ample evidence to show that with the 'abandonment' of the seduction theory, hereditary and constitutional factors became more important.[79] Freud had defined this constitution in terms of a general and impulsive sexual constitution that he had further described in *Three Essays* as a 'composition' of partial drives and components. He subsequently suggested that "the preponderating dominance of (this or that) erotogenic zone", of this or that partial drive could well be decisive for the choice of neurosis. Each drive component can "as a disposition (…) vary in its intensity" and is, as it were, waiting for accidental influences to be activated.[80] Here we find the starting point for the next step. In the case of Dora, we saw that her 'hysterical disposition' determines the experience of the trauma – in concrete terms: her disgust for sexuality, as for her it is linked to the excremental. Although Freud's terminology in this case study is still not very stable, he notes on this point that the "sexual constitution, under which the effects of heredity are included, operates in combination with any accidental influences" and in such a way that the development of normal sexuality is disturbed.[81] In the case of the Rat Man, the sadistic component of the libido turned out to be "exceptionally strongly developed" and have "consequently undergone a premature and all too thorough suppression".[82] The fate of this component of the sexual constitution therefore determined the choice of neuroses – obsessional neurosis in this case. In other words, as such, the traumatic experiences in these case studies are not decisive for the aetiology of a neurosis.[83] The determining factor is the way in which a particular drive composition (sexual constitution) expresses itself *in reaction* to a traumatic incident. Dora reacts 'hysterically' to the seduction by Herr K. because she already has a hysterical disposition.[84]

Traumatic events do not coincidentally happen to a person and throw them off course out of nowhere but are incidents that "correspond to the first activities of his innate constitutional instinctual dispositions".[85] In the study of the Wolf Man, this becomes clear in the toddler's physical reaction to observing the *coitus a tergo*. His sexual excitement manifests in passing a stool – and not in urinating, for example – and this Freud regards as "a characteristic of his congenital sexual constitution" in which an anal component is strongly developed.[86]

Constitution and phylogeny

In the case study of the Wolf Man, Freud takes the next step in this theory of sexual constitution: in this constitution, traces of the evolution of humankind and of the experiences of previous generations are preserved. For example, he notes that the sexual preference for the rear parts of the body should not necessarily be derived from the primal and Grusha scenes but is "a general characteristic of people who are inclined to an obsessional neurosis" and that this preference "is part of the fabric of the anal-erotic disposition and is one of the archaic traits which distinguish that constitution". Here Freud emphasizes the strongly developed anal component of the sexual constitution as well as an 'archaic trait' in this sexual constitution that he links with "copulation from behind—*more ferarum*" (in the fashion of wild animals) that may be phylogenetically regarded as the older form of copulation.[87] A little later in the text, he notes that these constitutional factors and the impressions of the scenes do not contradict or exclude each other but rather supplement so that there is in fact a case of 'overdetermination'. One should then consider that the Wolf Man 'inherited' these constitutional predilections from his father whom he had observed, at the age of one-and-a-half years, exercising his preference for copulation from behind.

The references, in the case study of the Wolf Man, to 'archaic traits' and phylogenetic aspects of the sexual constitution are striking. In none of the previous case studies did such references play as big a role as in this one. Freud's interest in this theme can hardly be separated from Jung's explorations of the analogies between myths, psychotic delusions and the phantasy life of neurotics. Partly thanks to this work, Freud is confronted with a factor that could well be 'a new original source of pathological productions'. The 'parallels between ontogenetic and phylogenetic developments' should therefore be further explored, he believes.[88] However, as we will see in the next chapter, Freud's interest in phylogeny cannot be reduced to a response to Jung.

We find the first major exploration of the phylogenetic factor in *Totem and Taboo*. A central question in the fourth essay of this text is how the 'traumatic' incident of the primal murder and especially the prehistoric human's first reactions to this deed (namely guilt) can have a continued influence on later generations in such a way that these reactions continue to constitute, throughout cultural history, the core of developments in religion, social organizations and morality. How is 'continuity in spiritual life' between generations possible over thousands of years? Freud writes about this: "A part of the problem seems to be met by the psychical dispositions which, however, need to be given some sort of impetus in the life of the individual before they can be roused into actual operation".[89] Continuity in spiritual life is therefore not guaranteed through oral or written transmission but by inheriting reaction formations and memory traces. Here, Freud appeals to psycho-Lamarckism. We will discuss this in detail in the next chapter.

In the case study of the Wolf Man, this train of thought is developed further. The last pages of the study dedicated to "the phylogenetically inherited schemata, which, like the categories of philosophy, are concerned with the business of 'placing' the impressions derived from actual experience".[90] These inherited schemata are seen as characteristics acquired in the course of cultural history. The Oedipus complex is "one of them – is, in fact, the best known member of the class" of schemata. In the case of the Wolf Man, this complex is referred to as a 'schemata' that orders an individual's experiences and impressions and reorganizes them in such a way that they fit into the schemata. According to Freud, we must assume that such a schemata can 'triumph' over individual experiences. In the case of the Wolf Man, this would take place when the Wolf Man's father "became the castrator and the menace of his infantile sexuality", when in fact the castration threats emanate from women – Grusha and the nanya.[91]

However, in the study of the Wolf Man, Freud wants to retain the idea that the continuation of phylogenetic material can always be traced when one assumes the accidental experiences first activated these schemata. In an added passage from 1918, Freud clarifies this point when he notes that the fear of castration initially affected the person who had made the threat (Grusha). Only then was that fear transposed "on to another person to whom it was bound to become attached in accordance with phylogenetic precedent".[92] The phylogenetic schemata is compelling here, but only in the reaction to a threat of castration.

Now we have already seen that the little Wolf Man does not believe Grusha and his nanya's threats of castration. The fear of castration only becomes manifest in full force in the wolf dream. The 'displacement' of the actor of the castration (from the women to the father) takes place here. In other words, it is only in the second trauma (the wolf dream) that this phylogenetic schema is activated, and the primal scene is interpreted in a new way, and that is as a scene in which the father is the castrator. The phylogenetic scheme does not determine of the *coitus a tergo* at the age of one and a half. The schema of the Oedipus complex in which the father is the castrator is only activated afterwards.

This is different for another aspect of the primal scene, and that is that the small toddler seems to 'instinctively' (*instinktiv*) understand the observation of the *coitus a tergo* as a sexual activity. The small toddler instinctively knows that what he sees is a 'sexual process'. We have already seen Freud claiming elsewhere in the text that the Wolf Man only 'understands' what he saw during the dream and not during the observation itself. This 'understanding' at the time of the dream is possible, Freud says, from what the Wolf Man got to know and appreciate through sexual arousal and via sexual exploration ('theory' formation). Only afterwards does what has been observed deliver 'thought results'. At the time of the first observation, there are no such 'thought results'. At that point, there is no 'theoretical' understanding. However, there is an 'instinctive knowledge' or 'primitive mental activity' – analogous to that of animals – that can help explain why the small toddler is aroused. He apparently has "some sort of hardly definable knowledge, something, as it were, preparatory to an understanding" according to which he can 'understand' the activity of the parents as a *sexual* one.[93]

According to Freud, this has consequences for the theory of trauma. He writes in this regard: "The significance of the traumas of early childhood would lie in their contributing material to this unconscious [of which the instinctual is the center – HW/PvH] which would save it from being worn away by the subsequent course of development".[94] What Freud means by this is that the repression as we find it in the neuroses implies a regression to the instinctive preliminary stage. In this case, this stage has the power to pull down higher psychical processes such as thought activities and phantasies towards itself. Trauma activates the 'instinctive' constitutional factor and grants it the power to disrupt and inhibit intellectual development – "human reason, when that faculty came to be acquired".[95] In this way, trauma prevents sublimation of drives through intellectual activities.

Dispositions and sexual development

In the previous chapters we saw that Freud's use of the concepts of constitution and disposition in their mutual relationship is still unstable and uncertain. For example, in the Dora case we already find the idea of a 'hysterical disposition' and of such an interaction between constitutional and accidental factors that this can result in a "certain stage of *inhibited development*".[96] But these concepts are not yet clearly defined in relation to each other. Freud only started doing this more systematically from 'The Disposition to Obsessional Neurosis' from 1913. In this text, he defines 'dispositions' as 'developmental disorders' through libidinal fixation.[97] The underlying hypothesis for this definition is that the psychical development normally takes place in such a way that the psychical functions, and especially the sexual functions, undergo 'a progressive change'.[98] The idea of progressive development of sexual functions is developed more systematically by Freud at this time as a theory to provide an answer to a number of problems.

The first problem can be inferred from the structure of *Three Essays* from 1905. Freud had described two clearly distinct regimes of sexuality there – infantile sexuality and sexuality as it develops from puberty.[99] What he could not explain in this text, however, is how the transformation from infantile to adult sexuality takes place, and what circumstances 'compel' a person to submit the polymorph-perverse and autoerotic drives to the primacy of genital function and to put sexual activities at the service of reproduction.[100] Freud formulated the answer to this question in 1915 in *Three Essays*: the primacy of the genital function is the end result of a 'normal' sexual development. The various components of sexual drive can be placed on a line of development, with a specific component dominating sexual organization in the different sexual phases.[101] For example, he draws a distinction between a pregenital and genital organization, and within the pregenital organization he distinguishes an oral-cannibalistic and an anal-sadistic phase.[102] In short, the theory of the two stages of sexuality is supplemented by a theory of sexual development between the two stages. In the case of the Wolf Man, we see an application of this addition to the theory of sexuality. To the old question of how an exciting and pleasurable primal scene can generate unpleasure (anxiety) in a second moment, Freud's answer is: through the intermediate 'derailments' in sexual development.

The second problem the theory of the stages of sexual development had to solve was the problem of the choice of neuroses. In the theory of seduction, Freud had put forward that the choice of neuroses depended on the age at which sexual traumas occur. Early passive experiences would then predispose to hysteria, while active experiences that occur a little later in childhood would predispose to obsessional neurosis. In *Three Essays* and in the study of Dora another vision comes to the fore when Freud writes that every step on the path of development could become 'a point of fixation' and 'inhibited development'.[103] This idea is further elaborated in 'The Disposition to Obsessional Neurosis'. A theory of sexual development makes it possible to connect the different stages of sexual development with the different moments of very early inhibitions and fixations. For obsessional neurosis – think of the Rat Man – a fixation in the anal-sadistic phase applies; it is characterized by "the striking primacy of sadism and anal erotism".[104]

We have already seen that the description of the case history of the Wolf Man is structured primarily by the bi-temporality of the trauma – the primal scene and the anxiety dream. The theory of sexual development in phases and of the possibility of a derailment of or disturbance in this development (fixation, inhibition, regression) forms a second structural element in the case study. We have already mentioned important moments framed by this theory. That his father could become his object of affection, was possible through "a link with his earlier and spontaneous phase of development" in which he had identified with his father and admired him.[105] Here we could also think of the surrender of the early, still incomplete genital organization (as an effect of seduction) and the regression to the anal-sadistic phase.

But Freud does not only refer to sexual development to understand the change in character. Discussing the wolf dream, Freud notes that the boy "had reached a new phase of his sexual organization". Until that moment, an anal-sadistic organization with masochistic features predominated. But the "activation of the primal scene in the dream now brought him back to the genital organization".[106] He discovers the vagina and therefore the biological significance of genital difference. With the change in organization, his sexual purpose also changes. Instead of being beaten by the father on the genitals or the bottom, the goal now becomes to be coitalized by the father. However, that feminine aim is immediately displaced and makes repressed and makes way for the wolf phobia. The effect of this repression is that the genital organization is rejected and collapses again. The anal-sadistic organization therefore continues to exist, first in the animal phobia and subsequently in the obsessional neurosis.

Freud's explanations about the effect of anal-sadistic organization in the disposition to animal phobia, but especially also to infantile obsessional neurosis, link to several facts we have already mentioned before: passing a stool during the anal scene and the infantile theory that the female genital is a 'front bottom'. The facts show that in particular the anal component of the anal-sadistic organization was always (that is, in and from the primal scene) a dominant factor in the sexual life of the little Wolf Man. It is clear, Freud writes, that the anal zone of the little Wolf Man becomes excited during the observation of the *coitus a tergo*. This excitement could be judged as a characteristic of his innate sexual constitution. The anal component is apparently highly developed, which is further reinforced by the intestinal symptoms that occur in early childhood – diarrhea, incontinence, constipation and intestinal pain.[107]

That the anal component comes strongly to the fore is also apparent from the way in which the infantile sexual theories take shape with the Wolf Man. Before the anxiety dream period, the small boy did not only develop the theory that girls have a 'front bottom', but he is also convinced that "the part of the female body which received the male organ was the anus". The allusions to and preoccupation with castration ensure that the anxiety dream causes him to realize that castration really exists and that women are different from men. That implies "a doubt on the '*cloacal theory*'". By rejecting the genital organization and clinging to an anal-sadistic organization, he decides "in favour of the intestine and against the vagina".[108] Besides realizing that castration really exists, he maintains his old theory in which coitus takes place anally. The fear of castration settles in "side by side with an identification with women by means of the bowel". It is this identification that, according to Freud, makes the feminine attitude equal to a homosexual attitude. "The organ by which his identification with women, his passive homosexual attitude to men, was able to express itself was the anal zone".[109]

This has far-reaching consequences. A first consequence concerns the identification with the mother. We know that she suffered from an abdominal disorder about which she once lamented to a doctor that she 'could not live like this any longer'. According to the Wolf Man, she did not suffer from an abdominal but of an intestinal disease, however. Under the influence of this primal scene, the little Wolf Man develops the theory that this disease is caused by the *coitus a tergo*. This develops into a fear of having the same ailment as the mother, and this fear is an important driving force behind his intestinal problems and the lasting fear of dying from dying of an intestinal ailment during the period of animal phobia. According to Freud, these intestinal problems could be seen as hysterical phenomena of conversion resulting from repression of homosexuality.[110] With that, these hysterical symptoms are an expression of the view that sexual intercourse takes place through the intestines.

The anal-sadistic organization is also the basis upon which the obsessional neurosis can originate. Freud notes about the transformation of animal phobia into obsessional neurosis that it does not occur spontaneously but is brought about by an outside influence – in a sense, by a new seduction. In this case, that influence comes from the mother and consists of introducing the boy to the world of religion 'in the hope of distracting him' (*abzulenken*) from what makes him irritable and anxious.[111] Obsessional neurosis thus starts from am interplay between a constitutional (anal-sadistic component of the sexual drive) and an accidental factor (seduction by the mother). The result of the mother's intervention is an obsessional neurosis with strong religious traits.

It would go too far to describe all the Wolf Man's compulsive ideas and actions here. Central is the Wolf Man's pious identification with Christ as the son of God. The relationship of the Wolf Man with this father god is extremely ambivalent, of which the simultaneous pursuit of pure love for God and having blasphemous thoughts ('God-shit', 'God-swine'), and also the preoccupations with sinful seductions are the most obvious manifestations. It suffices to point here to Freud's evaluation that the anal-sadistic organization was so strongly developed that the possibility to sublimate – and thereby also desexualize – the drive via religion ultimately failed. This allowed the various elements of the infantile obsessional neurosis to be reactivated later in life after he had contracted gonorrhea.

In the foregoing we have identified several constitutional and dispositional aspects in the aetiology of the infantile neurosis. However, in the study of the Wolf Man, Freud does not systematically address the distinction and the relationship between constitution, disposition and accident. He does so in other texts from this time, especially in some of lectures he gave at the University of Vienna during the winter semester of 1916-1917, specifically lectures 22 and 23. In these lectures, earlier intuitions are articulated more systematically. The question of whether the neuroses are the result of *exogenous* or *endogenous* conditions is answered by Freud with reference to an interplay between constitutional and accidental factors.[112] The sexual constitution (or 'inherited predisposition') and the accidental experiences together form the 'disposition by libidinal fixation'. According to Freud the relationship between disposition and constitution in the aetiology of the individual's neurosis can now simply be formulated as follows: 'disposition = constitution + accidental experience'.[113]

But that is not all. After all, the constitution itself is also the result of the interaction between 'constitutional' factors and the traumatic experiences of previous generations. In this regard, Freud speaks of 'constitutional dispositions' are the sum of acquired characteristics and as such "after-effects of experiences by ancestors in the past".[114] To the constitution of each individual, reaction patterns and memory traces of traumatic impressions of previous generations should also be added. The constitution of each individual is the result of the developments humankind has gone through and the fixations, disturbances and 'deflections' that took places in that development. That human constitution has in itself – as we will see in the following chapters – always been 'disturbed' by the traumatic experiences of earlier generations.

Complemental series

If the disposition to a neurosis is to be thought of as the sum of constitution and accidental experience, the question arises: How can the influence of constitutional and accidental influences in their mutual relationship be described? From 1895, Freud's answer to this question will in essence always be (a variant of) the same model: the 'aetiological equation' or 'complemental series' (*Ergänzungsreihe*). In 'Critique of Anxiety Neurosis', Freud had for the first time systematically dealt with the question of how the various factors in the aetiology of neuroses relate to each other. The most important factors are 'condition' ('hereditary disposition' or predisposition), the different 'specific causes' (e.g. deflection of sexual tension) and 'supporting causes' (fright, exhaustion) and the 'instigation' or 'triggering cause' (that is seduction as *agent provocateur*). The notion of aetiological equation was introduced by Freud to place the various causes not separately from each other but so that they can 'flow into each other' and the various factors can support and complement each other.[115]

In 'My Views' and later also in the third edition of *Three Essays* from 1915, Freud had simplified the model by reducing it to two factors, namely constitution (predisposition) and experience (trauma).[116] He writes about this:

> The constitutional factor must await experiences before it can make itself felt; the accidental factor must have a constitutional basis in order to come into operation. To cover the majority of cases we can picture what has been described as a 'complemental series', in which the diminishing intensity of one factor is balanced by the increasing intensity of the other; there is, how-over, no reason to deny the existence of extreme cases at the two ends of the series.[117]

As a rule, the constitutional factor can only be activated by an experience or impression (in early childhood). An experience or impression is as a rule only traumatic when it is supported by the sexual constitution or organization. At the ends of the series, however, we also find extreme cases in which only the constitutional factor (for example an inherited predisposition) or only a traumatic experience (for example, serious sexual abuse) can lead to a neurosis.

7. Primal scene and/or primal phantasy (1918)

In *The Interpretation of Dreams*, Freud had dedicated a chapter to 'typical dreams', that is, dreams one finds in several people with virtually the same content and meaning, such as the dreams about the death of loved ones.[118] In subsequent editions (1911, 1914 en 1919) the arsenal of typical dreams was expanded. Freud now includes dreams with a clearly sexual character: dreams about sexual intercourse, castration and masturbation.[119] Regarding the case of the Wolf Man, this raises a question that in principle threatens to undermine the whole construction from 1914. After all, if there are 'typical' dreams about the observation of sexual intercourse, why should it then be assumed that the primal scene was an observation of an actual *coitus a tergo*? And if that primal scene has a 'typical' character and has not really been observed, what does that mean for the reconstruction of the causes of the personality change and the aetiology of infantile neurosis?

In the continuation of the expansion of typical dreams with sexual content, Freud introduces the 'primal phantasy' concept in 1915. By this he means a group of phantasies that have a 'typical' character, that is, phantasies which can be disclosed by analysis as "unconscious phantasies of all neurotics, and probably of all human beings". In concrete terms, these are phantasies "the observation of sexual intercourse between the parents, of seduction, of castration, and others".[120] In lecture 23, Freud returns to this concept and notes that these primal phantasies are a 'phylogenetic endowment'.

> In them the individual reaches beyond his own experience into primaeval experience at points where his own experience has been too rudimentary. It seems to me quite possible that all the things that are told to us today in analysis as phantasy – the seduction of children, the inflaming of sexual excitement by observing parental intercourse, the threat of castration (or rather castration itself) – were once rreal occurrences in the primaeval times of the human family, and that children in their phantasies are simply filling in the gaps in individual truth with prehistoric truth.[121]

During this period, the typical dreams and primal phantasies are anchored by Freud in a theory of phylogeny in which prehistoric experiences are inherited as acquired psychical contents (see the next chapter).[122] In the case study of the Wolf Man, this is expressed in the passages that are added to the text in 1918. The scenes of observing parental coitus, of seduction and of the threat of castration are "unquestionably an inherited endowment, a phylogenetic heritage", but these impressions could " just as easily be acquired by personal experience".[123] With this reference to seduction as phylogenetic asset, Freud in a sense answers the question: Are the stories of patients about seductions during childhood indeed 'true'?[124] Freud's original answer was 'sometimes' when they really happened and 'often not' when they later appear to have been phantasized. The reference to phylogeny and to primal phantasies allows tor a different response: the seduction stories are always 'true', as they either really happened during in a person's childhood or really happened in the lives of previous generations. In both cases, memory traces (see the next chapter) can be activated afterwards.

On the relation between phylogenetic heritage and individual experience, Freud writes: "All that we find in the prehistory of neuroses is that a child catches hold of this phylogenetic experience where his own experience fails him" to supplement the experience.[125] From the notion of the complemental series,[126] Freud believes that the constitutional factor – the phylogenetic experience – asserts itself when there is a 'gap' in the individual experience that needs to be filled. Conversely, the individual experience needs to be supported by the phylogenetic experience to sort a – traumatic – effect. In the case of the Wolf Man, the latter can be clarified based on an event that had not yet played a significant role in the 1914 version. Freud writes in 1918 that shortly before the moment of his anxious dream, the Wolf Man probably observed large white dogs copulating – *more ferarum* – when he visited the flock of diseased sheep with his father.[127] This observation is in itself banal and commonplace, but it does link to the strongly developed desire to see the hidden parts of other people.[128] In the wolf dream this observation is 'transferred' to the parents, and the recent experience is thus supplemented with phylogenetic material. The result is a phantasized 'typical' scene of the observation of sexual intercourse between the parents *more ferarum.* In reality, however, Freud writes in 1918, the toddler was lying in his crib, woke up and then saw both his parents in white sleepwear – nothing more. This observation is the only and minimum condition for the possibility of subsequently fabricating the scene from a recent observation supplemented with phylogenetic material.

It should not be surprising that Freud questions the status of the primal scene in the passages inserted later in 1918. After all, the primal scene is a construction of a real event that cannot be remembered.[129] For that reason, every primal scene is always questionable, especially when another reconstruction of impressions and experiences also seems possible. In the alternative construction, the Wolf Man was not able to look at the genitals of his parents at the age of 1½ years and instinctively understand what was happening here. The reference to instinctive knowledge is therefore less relevant in this variant. The later comprehension of the fabricated scene during the dream can now be explained from the observation of the dogs and of girls, supplemented by infantile sexual theories and the realization that castration really does exist. That means that the seduction by the sister and its effects (the sexual explorations and activities) retain a central role in the aetiology. In the additions from 1918, Freud therefore also emphasizes that seduction is and remains 'an indisputable reality'[130]

In these additions, the Grusha scene (at the age of 2½ years) is now given a role that it did not have before. This scene now appears to be the first experience of sexual arousal (urination) and also the first confrontation with the threat of castration. The fact that according to the phylogenetic scheme, the father had to be the castrator, does not mean that Grusha, as the first person to threaten castration, leaves no trace in the period of animal phobia. On the contrary, the fear of the butterfly with the striped, yellow wings is 'analogous' to the fear of wolves. It is not derived from but is the remnant of the fear of the first castrator. It is not the primal scene that is the first trauma in this case, but the Grusha scene – a scene that was so banal and detailed that its origin could not be attributed to the child's imagination.[131] Unlike the primal scene that was a 'construction' but no memory, the Grusha scene has for Freud the great advantage of being spontaneously remembered. The new reconstruction results in Freud, despite all modifications, holding on to the temporality of trauma: the Grusha scene and the wolf dream.

8. Conclusion

We have shown in our reading of the case studies of Dora and the Rat Man that the Oedipus complex does not play a significant role in those studies in the aetiology of their respective hysteria and obsessional neurosis. That seems to change fundamentally in the case of the Wolf Man. Freud has now introduced the Oedipus complex as such in his work and in *Totem and Taboo* labeled it as "the nucleus of all neuroses".[132] However, it remains to be seen if this last statement means that the case of the Wolf Man now also allows for an oedipal reading. At first glance, one might think so. After all, the Oedipus complex assumes sexualized object relations, and this is certainly the case in the infantile neurosis of the Wolf Man. Yet the case urges us to be cautious and raises the question of what Freud actually meant by the 'nucleus of neuroses'. In *Totem and Taboo*, he further describes this nucleus as the 'acquired' quality of an emotional ambivalence – in the relationship with the father (father complex) – that was originally foreign to the emotional life of humanity but has become, through the traumatic event of the primal murder, 'a fundamental phenomenon of our emotional life'. This acquired trait therefore finds a 'powerful expression' in everyone.[133] In de Wolf Man, this idea finds a specific and also limited application, namely in the assumption that in the trauma (the anxiety dream) a phylogenetic scheme can be activated that orders the experiences of the young Wolf Man and provides them with new meaning: not the sister or the nanya but the father is the castrator. What Freud called 'core of the neuroses' therefore appears, on closer inspection, to be little more than powerful phylogenetic schemes that are awakened by private experiences that subsequently 'triumph' over these experiences. The passages about primal phantasies added in 1918 shine a bright light on the 'typical' contents of the 'core of neuroses' acquired from the human family during prehistoric times: the infantile seduction; the sexual arousal when observing sexual intercourse between the parents; the castration performed by the father.

The study of the Wolf Man thus shows that the Oedipus complex is introduced by Freud in the context of a reflection on the constitutional factors in the aetiology of the neuroses. In the Oedipus complex, various 'acquired characteristics' are brought together that comprise the core of phylogenetic property. Because this 'core' interacts with private traumatic experiences, Freud can call it the 'core of all neuroses'. Seen in this way, the Oedipus complex does not replace an 'abandoned' theory of seduction, but rather the complex is introduced into a trauma theory in which the traumatic experiences of previous generations are now also given a place. The human (sexual) constitution is itself the effect of traumatic experiences from the prehistoric times of humanity. This theme is central to the next chapter.

Chapter 5

Constitution, phylogeny and evolutionary biology

1. Introduction

The case study of the Wolf Man shows that Freud, in his thoughts on constitutional factors in the aetiology of neurosis, strongly emphasizes the influence of phylogenetic material that organizes life impressions in the form of 'innate schemas'. Here, we encounter a problematic that not only plays a prominent role in the case of the Wolf Man. After 'abandoning' his psychological seduction theory, Freud is forced to map out the constitutional and hereditary factors and their significance for the aetiology of the neuroses. He will seek connections for this with the accepted and dominant theories from evolutionary biology (embryology, paleontology, zoology) of his time – the late nineteenth century and early twentieth century. According to Freud, the constitutional and hereditary factors must be viewed as the result of a long series of physiological and psychological modifications and adaptations under the influence of external and internal forces. We will see in this chapter that his view of the constitutional and hereditary factors from this perspective will be determined by the notion of trauma. The human constitution is the result of evolutionary and cultural-historical developments in which traumatic experiences and impressions have left indelible somatic and psychological traces.

The reference to the influence of 'typical' phylogenetic schemas in the case of the Wolf Man are not surprising considering that the period in which the Wolf Man was being treated was when he began to map what phylogeny means for the human constitution and for the sexual development and ego-forming of the individual (and for the neurotic). *Totem and Taboo* is the first important result.[1] A second important text is 'Overview of the Transference Neuroses', which was written in 1915 but only published in 1985. We could say that Freud's analyses of phylogeny then culminate in *Beyond the Pleasure*

Principle and in *Moses and Monotheism* – the texts we will discuss in the next chapters. That is why we reflect in this chapter on the way in which evolutionary-biological theory formation opens the possibility for Freud to broaden his trauma theory and apply it in a theory of phylogeny. But before we discuss this in more detail, we would like to briefly consider the question of why and how Freud came to thematize the constitutional factors in the aetiology of neuroses after 1897.

2. The 'animal character' of childhood sexuality

In the first chapter we saw how and why Freud, after 'abandoning' the seduction theory, focused on constitutional and hereditary factors in the aetiology of the neuroses. The problematic of 'organic repression' and the reaction formations raised the question of the origin and the conditions in human evolution through which repression – more concretely, disgust – could become an aspect of a typically human sexual constitution and sexual development. For the answer, Freud looked to evolutionary biology. Walking upright changes the distance between the nose and the ground, resulting in a different appreciation of smell.[2] While in animals smell is the most important sense for sexual purposes, in *Homo erectus* this becomes seeing/looking.[3] In this regard Freud does not emphasize a divide between human and animal, instinct and drive or nature and culture. He emphasizes evolutionary continuity. Organic repression and reaction formations of disgust and shame are indeed typically human and can be traced back to the development in the organization of the erogenous zones and senses, but repression and reaction formations have bearing on perverse aspects of sexuality that are a 'continuation' of the 'perverse' sexuality of animals. In a number of letters to Fliess from 1897 (12 January, 8 February, 14 November), Freud suggests that childhood sexuality that is not yet limited by disgust and shame – the earliest period of infancy – has an 'animal character' due to the pleasurable interest (eating, smelling) it takes in excrement.[4]

In later texts, these intuitions are repeated and somewhat more elaborated upon. For example, in the 22nd lecture of the *Introductory Lectures on Psychoanalysis* from 1917, he remarks that the development of sexual drive and the repression of oral and anal components of drive can be understood from a phylogenetic perspective.[5] While in some animal species, the genital apparatus is closely connected with the excretion apparatus, in humans these apparatuses are clearly distinguished. However, infantile sexuality with its polymorphic-perverse character still attest to this phylogenetic entanglement of apparatuses, zones and functions. Some 'perversions' found in animals – such as the uninhibited interest in excrements – are also found in children. In other words, the perverse character of childhood sexuality shows that, from an evolutionary perspective, this sexuality is an extension of that of animals. Indeed, the oral (cannibalistic) and anal phase of childhood sexuality are organizations that are "harking back to early animal forms of life".[6] Childhood sexuality has an animal character as long as reaction formations and moral restrictions have not set limits. The first phases in sexual development form, as it were, an intermediate stage in an evolution from animal sexuality to that of an adult human. The fact that, normally, the genital apparatus will take precedence in adult sexuality from puberty (or prematurely) is, from an evolutionary perspective, 'planned out' and 'inherited' but must also be 'acquired' again by everyone through a combination of inner 'pressure' (normal sexual development with successive stages), and external demands (cultural morality). Pathological disorders, inhibitions and (perverse) fixations show that this acquisition is certainly not self-evident.

3. Haeckel's biogenetic law and its implications

It is striking, in the various passages in his work in which Freud refers to evolutionary-biological theories, that almost nowhere – with the important exception of *Beyond the Pleasure Principle* (see below) – he discusses in detail concrete theories of specific authors. It is clear that in various passages in his work) he seeks connection with the biogenetic law as formulated by zoologist Ernst Haeckel.[7] Haeckel had summarized that law in *Generelle Morphologie der Organismen* from 1866 in the thesis that "ontogeny is the short and rapid recapitulation of phylogeny".[8] By this he means that the development of each organic individual and the changes in form this individual undergoes during its development and maturation is a complete repetition of the development of the evolutionary lineage to which this individual belongs. The changes in physiological shape (as we know them from embryology) are a repetition of the complete evolutionary lineage (as we know them from paleontology) to which this individual belongs. The human embryo successively passes through the stages of single-celled organism, invertebrate, fish, reptile, mammal and primate, before finally being born as a child.[9] In *Beyond the Pleasure Principle* Freud describes this law as follows:

> We see how the germ of a living animal is obliged in the course of its development to recapitulate (even if only in a transient and abbreviated fashion) the structures of all the forms from which it is sprung, instead of proceeding quickly by the shortest path to its final shape. This behaviour is only to a very slight degree attributable to mechanical causes, and the historical explanation cannot accordingly be neglected.[10]

It is certain that Freud already acquired extensive knowledge of the various evolutionary-biological insights and the debates surrounding them during his student years and time (1875-1876) as the scientific assistant to the zoologist Carl Claus. Claus – a specialist in the evolution of crustaceans – himself played a central role in discussions with, among others, Haeckel about the genealogical categorization and evolution of organic life. Claus was particularly interested in the gradual transformations of organs and organ functions, especially in marine animals, and had his assistants conduct research in this field.[11] Freud's first scientific article is a 'Clausian' zoological study into the development of the sexual organs of eels, 'Beobachtungen über Gestaltung und feineren Bau der als Hoden beschriebenen Lappenorgane des Aals' from 1877, in which he shows that, in eels, a 'transitional form' in the evolution of the reproductive organs becomes visible.

In this context Freud also gets to know Haeckel's biogenetic law. We should note that Haeckel is certainly not the first and only one to formulate a recapitulation theory. This idea is defended in various authoritative manuals and textbooks from that time – including by Claus in his *Grundzüge der Zoologie*[12] from 1872.[13] A decisive influence on the development of this theory was Darwin, who in *On the Origin of Species* (1859) extensively discussed findings from embryology, because these would support his theory of evolution. He writes about this: "the embryo is the animal in its less modified state; and in so far it reveals the structure of its progenitor", this is, of "ancient forms of life".[14] Haeckel and others – among which, for example, Gustav Fechner and August Weismann, whom Freud discusses in *Beyond the Pleasure Principle* – elaborated on this intuition in their recapitulation theories.[15]

Haeckel's biogenetic law has several important implications and applications that we also find in Freud. First, using this law, sexual development can be anchored in an evolutionary perspective on the development of reproductive organs, the functions of the different body zones and orifices, and related somatic processes. We have already seen above that Freud argued in 1897 that every child can without much effort experience pleasure at oral and anal erogenous zones, before the first reaction formations of disgust and shame arise. We have also already seen that Freud would interpret the polymorphic-perverse aspects of infantile sexuality – more specifically, the oral and anal phases – as 'relapse into an animal form of life'. Haeckel's biogenetic law makes it possible to base the sexual character of these organizations and phases in a gradual and inescapable development from animal to human sexuality. From this perspective, infantile sexuality becomes a kind of intermediate phase[16] between a functional animal reproductive instinct and species-dependent organizations of the reproductive organs on the one hand and a later functional human sexuality that is genitally organized and serves reproduction. In every individual this phylogenetic development is repeated; the transition from animal to human sexuality takes place again and in a condensed form. However, the biogenetic law states not only that each individual organism must repeat the developmental stages of the species, but also that in each developmental step, a previous stage is necessarily and 'spontaneously' given up. [17] This implication of the law is also expressed in various texts by Freud. That's how he writes in 'The Dissolution of the Oedipus complex':

> Although the majority of human beings go through the Oedipus complex as an individual experience, it is nevertheless a phenomenon which is determined and laid down by heredity and which is bound to pass away according to programme when the next pre-ordained phase of development sets in.[18]

Second, because each individual repeats the development of an entire evolutionary lineage, all regulatory mechanisms and functions that apply to all organisms in that lineage must also apply to the individual. And conversely, any basic regulatory mechanisms and functions[19] found in the individual organism must also apply to all organisms in the same lineage. Particularly in *Beyond the Pleasure Principle,* Freud will try to base his metapsychological reflections on drives, the compulsion to repeat, binding and aversion to stimuli, with the help of Haeckel's law, in a comprehensive theory of evolution and fundamental characteristics of all organic life. Knowledge of phylogeny enables Freud to highlight fundamental aspects of being human. In *Moses and Monotheism,* the perspective is more likely to be reversed. The theory of the aetiology of the individual's neurosis is 'transferred' to mass psychology and serves as a model for a (re)construction of the history and character formation of an entire people.[20]

Thirdly, our cultural creations can be understood from the principles and functions that also apply in nature.[21] In other words, there is no radical break between nature and culture. Cultural history is an extension of the evolution of organic life, that is, it progresses from simple and 'primitive' to increasingly highly developed, more complex and more differentiated forms. For Freud, ontogeny as a recapitulation of phylogeny cannot, as is the case with Haeckel, be limited to a repetition of 'paleontology' at the level of 'embryology'. The evolution of the human species and the individual also emphatically includes cultural history. Everyone briefly and quickly repeats the entire phylogeny, including the development from primitive to highly civilized being. Freud writes the following about this in 'The Question of Lay Analysis':

> The alternative friendlier, and probably also the more pertinent view would be that in the mental life of children to-day we can still detect the same archaic factors which were once dominant generally in the primaeval days of human civilization. In his mental development the child would be repeating the history of his race in an abbreviated form, just as embryology long since recognized was the case with somatic development.[22]

This citation not only makes it clear that the evolution of nature and culture are an extension of each other and are organized by the same principles. The psychical development of the individual – more concretely, sexual development and ego-formation – are a repetition of a cultural-historical development. For example, in lecture 22 from 1917 he notes that the development of the ego and the libido is "an abbreviated form [of] the entire development of the human race, into phylogenetic prehistory too".[23] While infantile sexuality is still an extension of animal sexuality, further sexual development must be understood from the perspective of cultural history, and particularly the primal history – the 'childhood' – of humanity.

But how does one gain insight into the achievements and impressions of people in the most recent periods in the different cultures? The scarce material sources provide little insight. We find a first answer in the letters to Fliess and in *The Interpretation of Dreams*. According to Freud, traces of old familial and social relationships are preserved in myths and legends and in ancient religious cults. The child sacrifices in the cult of Moloch, the myth of Cronus who devours his sons, of Zeus who castrates his father and of Oedipus who kills his father, provide a certain insight into the 'despotic power' and 'ruthlessness' with which the primeval fathers exercised their authority and the aggression that this must have sparked in the sons.[24] This intuition is developed much more systematically in *Totem and Taboo*. Haeckel's biogenetic law makes it possible to reconstruct the primordial history – childhood – of humanity from the traces it has left behind in ontogeny. From the preface to *Totem and Taboo*, it is evident that Freud bases the possibility of analogies between primitives and children on a notion of repetition. Freud writes: "An attempt is made in this volume to deduce the original meaning of totemism from the vestiges remaining of it in childhood—from the hints of it which *emerge in the course of the growth* of our own children".[25] The argument here is as follows. Because ontogeny is a repetition of phylogeny, ontogeny can also serve as a model for the reconstruction of phylogeny – here, of the primal history of humankind.[26]

Freud can take a next step from Haeckel's biogenetic law. If the sexual development and ego-formation at an ontogenetic level is a repetition of phylogenetic developments, then the same perhaps applies for the developmental disorders we know from the analysis of psychoneuroses. According to Freud, there are not only parallels between child and primitive being but also between the child/primitive and the neurotic who is inhibited and fixed in his or her psychical development.[27] The developmental disorders of individuals can also be seen as a repetition of inherited 'disorders' and fixations that have been reflected in the general sexual constitution. The disposition to neurosis in the individual has a constitutional aspect that as such is an inherited residue of "the acquisition of our ancestors".[28] And these acquired traits comprise physical and psychical modifications resulting from reactions of the ancestors to traumatic events and impressions.

4. Cultural development and trauma

The idea of an evolution of humankind and culture through responses to traumatic influences was discussed by Freud in a speculative text written in 1915 under the title 'Overview of the Transference Neuroses'.[29] The central thesis is that the psychoneuroses bear witness to the psychical development history of the human being. Based on the psychoanalytic insight into the time and phase of sexual development in which the neurosis (through fixation) appears in the individual life, the evolutionary origin of those neuroses and their precipitation in the constitution can be reconstructed.[30] That primeval history – the period of the Ice Ages and the Stone Age – is structured and characterized by several primeval geological catastrophes, life-threatening deprivations and systemic violence in a murderous society in which prehistoric people took the destruction of others (strangers, enemies) for granted and were not hindered by an instinct not to kill and eat their own kind.[31]

Such 'accidental' factors trigger complex psychical reactions and behavioral patterns. The notion of the father as castrator, the origin of the Oedipus complex and the theory of primal murder are included by Freud in 'Overview of the Transference Neuroses' in a broader perspective on a primeval time in which the murder of the primal father does not mark the transition between an animal life and life in culture but rather corresponds to a 'state phase' in a longer 'disturbed' developmental history.[32] Primordial history is seen by Freud as a series of traumatic – partly sexual, partly non-sexual – experiences that give rise to several psychical reactions that would subsequently be inherited in the form of fixations and reaction patterns as (part of the) 'constitution'. Together, the successive state phases in primordial history form the 'hereditary dispositions' that – as a constitutional factor – are 'repeated' in the aetiology of the neuroses at the individual level (ontogeny).

So far, 'Overview of the Transference Neuroses' seems to be an elaboration of intuitions from *Totem and Taboo* about the lasting influence of prehistoric experiences and impressions on psychic life in the form of 'dispositions'. Since the traumatic experiences of prehistoric times, all humans have tended to develop in a certain direction and respond in a similar way to certain impressions, excitations and stimuli. As an example, we can refer here to the reaction formations of disgust for the excremental and of guilt in relation to feeling ambivalences. But Freud goes one step further. Not only psychical life but also physical development and somatic processes are influenced in a decisive and far-reaching way by the experiences of prehistoric times. Perhaps the most important effect of the traumatic experiences of prehistoric hominids concerns the fact that in humans – unlike in animals – sexual development is interrupted after a first flowering of infantile sexuality in which the drive pursues the autoerotic pleasure experience, but in which also various drive components fall prey to (organic and cultural-morality-reinforced) repression. The fact that the drives serve reproduction is a delayed development that only starts during puberty.[33] In a passage Freud inserts into *Three Essays* in 1915, he comments on this that the origin of this human peculiarity must be looked for "in the prehistory of the human species".[34] Here, he suggests that the interrupted sexual development due to repression, the postponed reproductive function and its significance for the aetiology of the neuroses can be seen as the deposit of prehistoric traumatic experiences in the sexual constitution and instinctual life. More concretely, this concerns a period in which castration threats and actual castrations by the leaders (primeval fathers) of the hominids living in groups lead to the postponement of sexual activities among the sons.[35] We return to this in detail in the chapter about *Moses and Monotheism*.

We can conclude from 'Overview of the Transference Neuroses' that for Freud, the human is a traumatized animal – an animal whose physical and psychological development from prehistoric times has been disturbed, interrupted (inhibited) and 'deflected', and has thus acquired the shape that will repeat itself in every individual. 'Normal' sexual development in humans is essentially 'disturbed' sexual development. From here Freud will take the next step in *Beyond the Pleasure Principle*. Not only humans have been traumatized and disturbed in their physiological and psychological development by a series of events and experiences in prehistoric times. From the origin of life from inorganic material, the evolution of all living organisms is determined by physiological modifications resulting from forces acting on organic life from without and from within.

In this context, we would like to point out a fundamental difference between the views of Haeckel (cum suis) and Freud. For Haeckel, the evolution of all living things unmistakably shows a progressive development towards completion and even perfection of individuals and species.[36] Both in the process of selection because of a struggle for existence in which the strong survive and reproduce (Darwin) and in the process of inheritance of acquired characteristics (Lamarck, see below), Haeckel believes, a 'law of nature' becomes established: species develop slowly and uninterruptedly to higher perfection.[37] In every organism we find a natural tendency to perfect its own species. This is a trend that also manifests itself in cultural history, namely in the development of increasingly 'higher' cultures. Against this, Freud will argue in *Beyond the Pleasure Principle* that this tendency cannot be found in organic life and that human and cultural development cannot be understood from a 'drive towards perfection'.[38] For Freud, progression is epiphenomenal. It is only conceivable from the reactions of organisms to life-threatening, traumatic influences from outside and from within on those organisms.[39]

5. *Acquired psychical characteristics*

Totem and Taboo and 'Overview of the Transference Neuroses' raise the question of how the primal human being's 'traumatic' experiences could have and maintain influence on later generations. How is continuity in the mental life between generations possible? About this, Freud writes: "A part of the problem seems to be met by the inheritance of psychical dispositions which, however, need to be given some sort of impetus in the life of the individual before they can be roused into actual operation".[40] For example, the fact that the incest taboo could continue to exist from generation to generation is, according to Freud, not possible based on oral tradition alone. Much more important is that this taboo has become part of an organized 'psychical endowment'.[41] So, the taboo, among the reactions to the primal murder, is a 'historical acquisition' that is established in many persons through 'organic inheritance'.[42] These contents are part of the set of inherited psychological response patterns ('emotional legacy') to the primal experiences of humanity. What is inherited is not the memory of the murder, but the set of psychological reactions to it – especially the feeling of guilt – and associated contents such as taboos. What is inherited is not the memory of the original castrator, but the 'schema' in which the fear of castration is associated with the father figure.[43]

In the secondary literature, the theory of the inheritance of psychological dispositions has usually and rightly been associated with the work of Jean-Baptiste de Lamarck. In the period when Freud began to expressly become interested in the role of phylogenetic factors in the aetiology of neuroses (from 1897 and more intensively from 1912), the theory of the inheritance of acquired traits is an important element of much evolutionary-biological theorizing. The already mentioned and influential Haeckel, for example, saw Lamarck's insights as an indispensable and fundamental part of the theory of evolution.[44] Adolf Wagner, who published his *Geschichte des Lamarckismus* in 1909 – a book that Freud owned and studied – even argued that Lamarck's theories were more current than ever, because they offered a way out of a Darwinian theory that could only conceive of the development of organic life in terms of natural selection and the coincidence in which it took place.[45]

The correspondence with Ferenczi specifically in the period from 1916-1918 shows that Freud was set on giving psychoanalysis a solid base in evolutionary biology, particularly in Lamarckism.[46] Yet he does not throw himself into this project with abandon but rather postpones a thorough reading of Lamarck's work.[47] This is perhaps not surprising when we consider that Lamarck in fact only described physiological-adaptive processes. The inheritance of acquired traits involved organs and body parts that had been developed (or diminished) through frequent and intensive use (or neglect or non-use) over the life of an x number of generations.[48] The fact that an organ was used more intensively (or less frequently) was not coincidental or random, but 'purposeful', that is, the use was for self-preservation (food intake, defense). Examples include the development of a long neck in a giraffe or – as an example of disuse – the loss of vision in a mole.[49] Out of a need to access a food source (the leaves high in a tree), the giraffe would have developed a long neck over time through frequent use. Lamarck does not link this purposeful use of body parts or organs with a notion of striving, drive or instinct, but with perception and knowledge.[50] The giraffe (here an animal without typical giraffe characteristics) perceives its environment, 'understands' what it needs to gain access to food and, based on this 'knowledge', adapts to the circumstances by developing a long neck (the hallmark of giraffes).

From the latter we can understand Freud's hesitation about Lamarck's theory of evolution. After all, Lamarck's sole focus was functionally effective physiological modifications and adaptations to the environment. Strivings and adjustments follow perception, but what is missing is a reflection on drive and/or instinct. What is therefore clearly more interesting to Freud is the psycho-Lamarckism of, among others, August Pauly who had published a book in 1905 entitled *Darwinismus und Lamarckismus*.[51] With Pauly, the attention shifts from the effective use of body parts and organs and the adaptation to circumstances to a study of the psychical mechanisms that form the conditions for somatic modifications. For example, Pauly points out the importance of inner stimuli – 'drive forces' and 'energy' that create a tension whose build-up is the condition for a physiological change. What Pauly further adds is a much more detailed analysis of the psychological factors in this process: need as a source for physical and psychical adjustments; the memory function (the totality of previous experiences); the discernment and the judgment function (the consideration of which change or adjustment best contributes to the desired satisfaction of needs). Regarding the inheritance of psychical dispositions, Pauly argues that it is not only the physiological modifications and the capacity for new modifications that are inherited, but also the whole of the 'experiences of the previous generations', that is, 'the waxing and waning of needs', the experience of the 'means of gratification' and the set of efficient and adaptive responses.[52]

In a letter to Abraham from November 1917, Freud writes that such a theory can explain how a set of needs and the search for satisfaction of those needs creates and converts organs to provide for that satisfaction.[53] According to Freud, this psycho-Lamarckism provides a biological argument for the psychoanalytical insight that unconscious thoughts have power ('omnipotence of thoughts') over the body. After all, in hysterics and other neurotic patients, we see that their physical symptoms are first and foremost fixation of experiences that occurred only in their imagination or stem from unconscious thoughts and desires.[54] What emerges in this reference to organ-creating needs and desires lies at the heart of Freud's fascination with Lamarckism: the drive is a constantly active force that creates organic forms and psychic structures from within.

At the same time, however, there is one decisive point on which Freud does not remain within the framework of psycho-Lamarckism. After all, his focus is on precisely those elements of the human constitution that are not purposefully formed from need or use but which are the result of traumatic events in cultural history and have provoked reaction patterns and developments that later generations living in other – less hostile – cultural conditions have not been able to cast off. Humanity was apparently unable to fundamentally reorganize its mental apparatus and phylogenetic schemes over the course of history out of needs and by adaptation to better conditions.[55]

6. Memory traces and the problem of inheritance

Another psycho-Lamarckist who should be mentioned is Ewald Hering for his theory of 'unconscious memory' as formulated in a lecture from 1870.[56] Distinctive for remembering, Hering believed, is not an intentional reproduction of ideas, but the remarkable fact that an awareness of past images and events can arise spontaneously, unrestrained and with the same freshness and liveliness as their original occurrence. We may assume that this reproduction of past impressions is possible because the event at the time set in motion an 'organic process' (vibrations and waves) and thus left an impression in the nervous apparatus. Under certain circumstances, that impression can be reactivated and thus recall the event again.

This model is based on the Lamarckian notion of the legacy of memories. Hering's starting point here is the idea that memories as they are organically stored in cells can be inherited by the next generation. There is a 'plasmatic memory' in which memories can be stored and passed on from generation to generation.[57] Those memories from previous generations can be activated in later generations under similar circumstances, and the response to this will be like that of the previous generation. New experiences can be added to the transgenerational memory again and again. In animals we know this as instinct; in humans we find the same instinctive patterns (particularly at the level of self- and species preservation), but higher mental abilities have also been developed that make it possible to preserve the memory of previous generations in a different way (oral and written transmission).[58]

The idea of inheriting memory-traces is only explicitly formulated in Freud's late work. In earlier texts such as *The Interpretation of Dreams*, but also in a later text such as *Beyond the Pleasure Principle*, the memory system is described as a system in which converted perceptual stimuli and associated excitations are stored as 'traces'. It is in this memory system that different representations can then be connected – associated – with each other. The more premature and powerful the impression, the more powerful the impulse or pressure from the unconscious on the psychical apparatus. It is this dynamic that makes 'hysterics suffer from their memories'. But also, what we call our character should be seen as the effect of the 'memory-traces of our impressions'.[59]

We have seen that, especially from *Totem and Taboo* and his reflection on phylogeny, Freud assumes a continuity in the psychic life of all people in the form of acquired psychical dispositions – developmental directions and reaction patterns. The study of the Wolf Man provided an important insight that made the next step possible. Sometimes reactions are not determined by what one has experienced, but a reaction is determined by a phylogenetic schema. The Wolf Man reacts with fear not only to the threat of castration, but more specifically to a threat posed by his father. This means that in addition to a disposition (anxiety in response to the threat of castration), a certain 'content' (father as castrator) is also brought in from the acquired property. For Freud, these contents cannot be anything other than acquired memory-traces of what previous generations experienced as traumatic. From the 1920s onwards,[60] he explicitly linked memory-traces to inherited psychological contents. And it will ultimately only be in *Moses and Monotheism* that he systematically elaborates and applies the notion of acquired memory-traces (psychical contents) in his analysis of the Jewish character.

How should we imagine the process of inheritance of acquired memory-traces? Where and how can psychic content be processed, stored and passed on via the germ cells at an organic level in such a way that it can be reproduced in the next generation? This is a question with which all psycho-Lamarckists struggle – and Freud too. In passages in his work where he thematizes the inheritance of psychological contents or dispositions, he says little about the mechanism of that inheritance. In *The Ego and the Id,* he briefly discusses these inherited formations – more specifically, the acquisition by the primitive human of religion and morality from the father complex – as the core of the unconscious. Freud writes about this that the experiences of the ego (the primitive human) do not seem to be heritable, but that when the same experiences are also undergone by several successive generations, "they transform themselves, so to say, into experiences of the id, the impressions of which are preserved by heredity".[61] However, Freud later has to admit that we are "not yet able to grasp" the nature and mechanism of this inheritance.[62]

There is a reason for Freud's reticence regarding this problem of the inheritance of psychic experiences, contents, formations and schemas. He seems aware of the fact that the Achilles heel of psycho-Lamarckism is the lack of an adequate theory of inheritance. Within psycho-Lamarckism there is a debate about this that has been conducted without satisfactory results ever since Hering's notion of the plasmatic inheritance of memories. Should one think of inheritance in terms of vibration or waves (Hering) or in terms of energy (force), electricity (current, charge) or chemical processes (substances, fusions) that act on the nervous apparatus?[63] And how should one relate these physiological processes to psychical contents? The eventual demise of psycho-Lamarckism with the rise of Mendelian genetics will be mainly because it had not been able to formulate a plausible, testable theory of the mechanism of the inheritance of psychic contents....

7. Inheritance, drive and the persistence of sexual trauma

Based on Freud's own theory, inheritance relates to the formation and content of the constitution. We have already seen that for Freud this constitution is primarily instinctive. It is therefore obvious that Freud connects inheritance with the drive theory. Moreover, drive is a "concept on the frontier between the mental and the somatic".[64] The drive is in essence somatic, he writes in 'Instincts and Their Vicissitudes'. But it is also the "psychical representative of the stimuli originating from within the organism and reaching the mind".[65] From within the organism, the drive acts as a constantly urging force on the 'nervous substance'. This happens in such a way that the nervous system is forced to adapt (namely to the fact that there is a constantly acting force that cannot be avoided) and develop new functions that enable it to also change the outside world with the aim of satisfying the drive. Drives therefore act from the organic on the psychological apparatus and can generate changes (adjustments) in the apparatus. But Freud also suggests the opposite. The traumatic experiences of primeval humanity have had a lasting influence through changes they bring about in the drives themselves. In 'Instincts and Their Vicissitudes', he notes that "the instincts [drives] themselves are, at least in part, precipitates of the effects of external stimulation, which in the course of phylogeny have brought about modifications in the living substance".[66]

How should we imagine this influence and change by external stimuli? In more concretely formulated words: How could the traumatic experiences in the prehistory of humanity have led to changes in the drives? And what changes are those? Freud will be able to answer these questions with a reference to the biogenetic law. In a letter to Ferenczi from July 1915, he writes that what are now the neuroses were once phases in the human condition.[67] Because the neuroses are a repetition of state phases in prehistory, the influence of prehistoric traumatic experiences and impressions on the human condition (constitution) can be reconstructed and understood from the place and meaning of the trauma in the aetiology of the various neuroses. This is elaborated by Freud in 'Overview of the Transference Neuroses'. For Freud's speculative historical reconstruction, the starting point is the reaction of anxiety to the hardships and life-threatening conditions during the Ice Age. From this anxiety, the primal human learns to "be afraid of his unsatisfied libido" (sexual drive) and is then "induced (*verleitet*) (…) to treat the unsatisfied libido as an external danger".[68] However, this is not a solution: the excess of libido constantly arouses new anxiety, and thus a first hereditary disposition (phobia, anxiety hysteria) is fixed, which as such helps determine the reaction to subsequent traumatic experiences.[69] This is the beginning of the 'phylogenetic series' of dispositions as Freud further mapped them in his text. Man is a traumatized animal. Not only do the various dispositions to the neuroses testify to this but also the disposition to drive renunciation (through inhibition, reaction formations, sublimation), inherited through cultural history, which as internal compulsion prescribes certain developmental paths.[70] Here we recognize a core element of Freud's tragic human vision.

What Freud describes here is in accordance with the meaning of the concept of seduction as we encountered it in early texts. Seduction means that the combination of an insistent and unrestrained drive and a certain impression or experience "lay down the path to be taken by the sexual instinct for a whole lifetime".[71] In 'Overview of the Transference Neuroses' he writes that the drive is deflected and led away from the pre-traumatic situation[72] and from now on leads to a repetition – again in every generation – of the enforced path. This ties in with what Freud had said in *Three Essays* on the conditions for neurotic disorders: there is a certain quantum of uninhibited libido, and there is increased adhesiveness or fixability of drives. The primal constitution that determines the reaction to the first traumatic experiences consists of nothing other than the properties of the drive itself: it is an insistent force seeking satisfaction (discharge); it can be fixated. These two traits – together with traumatic experiences – are the conditions for the emergence of various successive constitutional dispositions that together describe normal sexual development (incl. repression of oral and anal components) as well as that of neurotic disorders through fixation.[73]

Instinctual life is rethought in this way from the perspective of trauma theory.[74] Every individual repeats, in their own instinctive constitution and development, the fixations and response patterns to the traumatic experiences of primeval humanity. This creates the possibility of the next step that Freud would take in *Beyond the Pleasure Principle* and later texts such as *Inhibitions, Symptoms and Anxiety*: the instinctual character of the human constitution means that being human as such is determined by the traumatic effects of the drives.

What are the most important reasons for Freud to give the idea of the inheritance of acquired traits a central place in his thinking about phylogeny and constitution? A first reason has already been mentioned. It is the felt necessity of a foundation for psychoanalytic theory in biology. In this context, we have seen that since 1897, Freud has been appealing to findings from evolutionary biology to explain organic repression and reaction formations (disgust) in particular. Because such psychological phenomena are a general human phenomenon, Freud cannot and does not want to fall back on theories in which (psycho)pathologies are explained based on physiological abnormalities and defects, forms of degeneration or nervous weaknesses because of incidental influences such as overload (stress) or intoxication. The theory of the inheritance of acquired characteristics offers the possibility of relating dispositions to the various neuroses to a general human constitution that is in turn the disturbed result of traumatic experiences from the history of humanity and even from all organic life.

A second reason is related to this. For Freud it is of great importance to anchor ontogeny and pathogeny in a theory of the human constitution as such, that is, of sexual development, ego formation and the disorders in these developments – also at the phylogenetic and cultural-historical level. For Freud, psycho-Lamarckism, but also Haeckel's biogenetic law and Hering's notion of the inheritance of memory-traces, are part of an evolutionary-biological set of theories in which the emphasis is not on selection and chance (Darwin), but on the repetitive effect of instinctive forces, acquired psychical tendencies, reactions to experiences and adjustments to the demands of reality. According to Freud, only a theory on the inheritance of acquired physical traits makes it possible to anchor ontogeny in phylogeny, and connect the psychology of the individual with that of the masses.[75]

A third reason is that the extension of drive theory with a theory on the effect of humanity's traumatic experiences on the drives does not provide a sufficient explanation for the inheritance of dispositions, psychic contents or schemata as these are fixed and organized in the entirety of reactions to and memory-traces of experiences of previous generations. So, a theory of the inheritance of psychical contents remains necessary to bridge the fate of the drives as the determining factor in sexual development and ego formation since the Ice Age on the one hand and on the other the schemata and complexes (castration, Oedipus complex, seduction) associated with the various developmental phases and dispositions. In other words, Freud needs a theory on the inheritance of psychical dispositions and memory-traces to substantiate the influence and meaning of the castration complex and the Oedipus complex and make it plausible. We already saw this in the case of the Wolf Man: the role of the Oedipus complex in the aetiology of childhood neurosis of the Wolf Man is completely determined by the idea that this complex was acquired in prehistoric times and inherited as schema or primal phantasy and can triumph in the individual's life. If there were no inheritance of psychical contents, there would also be no 'typical' oedipal schemata to organize and give meaning to actual experiences and impressions. And these schemata are universal, not because they spontaneously arise from the human capacity to phantasize, symbolize or theorize but because they come from a multitude of contingent events all hominids experienced in prehistoric times.

Chapter 6

Traumatic neurosis, compulsion to repeat and drive theory: *Beyond the Pleasure Principle*

1. Introduction

From the first chapter, we have learned that the internalization and sexualization of trauma on which seduction theory is based simultaneously also implies that the classic traumatic neurosis can now be understood from the perspective of the seduction theory. This theory thus psychologizes and neuroticizes traumatic neurosis. In this way, it loses every specificity – it can be explained like every hysterical problematic. From here, sexual trauma replaces the 'banal' trauma that also includes train and industrial accidents.[1] From 1897, traumatic neurosis as an explicit theme also largely disappears from Freud's writing.[2] All attention will from now on be directed towards reworking the seduction theory in relation to constitutional and dispositional factors. The cases discussed in the previous chapters are testimony to this development. However, Freud's study of the Rat Man also teaches us that the sexualization of trauma is not self-evident when the domain of hysteria is exited. At least, reducing hate to sadism, which plays a central role in obsessional neurosis, is not obvious. In the discussion of the study of the Wolf Man it became clear how and why Freud, in his attempt to rescue the primate from sexual trauma, seeks connections with the dominant theories from evolutionary biology at the time. Inspired by psycho-Lamarckism, Freud now reconsiders the human constitution as resulting from traumatic events and their subsequent reactions.

With the outbreak of World War I in 1914, however, Freud is again strongly confronted with the problematic of traumatic neurosis. Not a single army was spared from an epidemic psychiatry would name shell shock, war neurosis or *Kriegshysterie*. What to make of soldiers who suddenly lost their ability to speak or hear, who claimed to be blind, who teetered through life and were unable to control their physical and emotional expressions? The same soldiers suffered from insomnia or had the most terrifying nightmares. The notion of shell shock is a direct reference to the old 'shock theory' of traumatic neurosis that we discussed in the first chapter. Some psychiatrists thought that the symptoms described here were the result of explosions to which these soldiers were exposed. The resultant physical shock would form the base of invisible scars to the nervous system or the brain. Others were more inclined to link these symptoms with degeneration, to analogy with Charcot's explanation of traumatic (male) hysteria. Although they acknowledged the importance of psychological factors, but at the same time based the ultimate etiology of shell shock on a predetermined neuropathic constitution. After all, this allowed for an explanation for the same traumatic events not always giving way to the development of a traumatic pathology. According to these psychiatrists, for your own body, fright and anxiety were naturally important psychological factors that participated here. The term *Schreckneurose* was sometimes used. From here it was but one step to developing a pure psychogenic theory. Babinski, a pupil of Charcot, had argued during the first years of the new century that Charcot made way too much of the concept of 'hysteria' and that most of his patients suffered from misunderstood neurological problems. Where it did indeed involve hysteria, this pathology was, according to Babinski, the result of (auto-)suggestion. It also subsequently had to be treated and cured through suggestion (or hypnosis). To emphasize the purely suggestive character of hysteria, Babinski no longer referred to hysteria but *pithiatism*.[3] Fully in line with Babinski's explanation of hysteria, many thought the origin of *Schreckneurose* to be wishful thinking: the soldiers want to escape from the horrors of war and for this reason developed a specific pathology. The *Schreck-* or *Kriegsneurose* was in fact a 'flight into illness' to escape the war in this way. The accusation of simulation was always lurking in the background.

The discussion of the status of this *Kriegsneurose* clearly ran parallel to the discussions, at the turn of the 19th century, of traumatic neurosis and traumatic hysteria. However, subject to psychoanalysis and the psychological mechanisms it uncovered all the while (traumatic memories, psychological conflicts being converted into physical symptoms) now making it possible for many psychiatrists to understand how wishful thinking determines the symptoms of war neurosis. Psychoanalysis in this way increasingly obtained the right to exist in psychiatric discussions, which must have been music to Freud's ears. Not only in the domain of psychosis but also in the context of war neuroses, the new theory was now being taken seriously, by the psychiatric establishment as well as the relevant government institutions.[4]

We do need to make an important note here. The nature of the traumas concerned here could give the psychiatrists the impression that they could refer to psychoanalysis and its psychological mechanisms without accepting Freud's primacy of sexuality.[5] The latter is interesting because it again suggests that it is far from clear why traumatic neurosis – appearing here in the guise of a subcategory, war neurosis – should be traced back to an essentially sexual conflict.

The symptomatology of traumatic war neurosis sets the Freudian primacy of sexuality before a special problem. Charcot already knew that, in their dreams, traumatized patients again and again repeated the casualties of which they were victims. The soldiers suffering from a war neurosis likewise relived in their dreams their traumatic experiences. This symptom – the compulsive repetition of events that could never have been pleasurable – can however not be reconciled with the pleasure principle that is, as we know from our first chapter, closely associated with the primacy of sexuality. In this way, traumatic neurosis refers to a problematic *Beyond the Pleasure Principle* and thus to a problematic of sexuality. As in the 1890s, traumatic neurosis confronts Freud with the boundaries of his own model. The reflections on these (supposed?) boundaries bring Freud to thoroughly reformulate his drive theory and introduce an original and un-retractable contradiction between death and life drives. In this chapter, we will show how this reformulation coincides with Freud's theory of trauma and more specifically also his integration thereof in the phylogenetic views we discussed in the previous chapter and in our examination of the Wolf Man case. This integration led, as we alluded to in our introduction, to the development of a tragic view of human life revolving around drive, trauma and repetition. In a last section we will finally show how Freud re-establishes the cohesion between trauma, repetition and phylogeny in *Inhibitions, Symptoms and Anxiety*. Before getting into detail, however, we first need to delve a little deeper into the origin of *Beyond the Pleasure Principle*, in which Freud raises the problematics we discuss above.

2. *Two versions of the text*

We known since the 1990s that Freud did not write the published version of *Beyond the Pleasure Principle* in one go. Ilse Grubrich-Simitis found in Freud's estate an earlier version of *Beyond the Pleasure Principle* that he had already completed in April 1919.[6] For a while, Freud did not work on the manuscript.

Only in May 1920 did he take it up again and concluded the revision in July that year. Save for a few interventions, this second draft is the text that was published later in 1920. In the reprints of 1921 and 1923, a few short but meaningful passages were added.[7]

The second version of *Beyond the Pleasure Principle* is an extension of the first. It contains *grosso modo* the first five chapters that, bar a few added passages, remained unaltered in the second version. The entire sixth chapter was added between the fifth and the original sixth and final chapter. In this way, the original sixth chapter became the seventh in the second version. This seventh chapter is a thoroughly revised version of the original chapter six. Immediately apparent from a comparison of the first two versions is the change of perspective that takes place between the fifth and the sixth chapter that was added later. Generally, this change in perspective lies in that in the fifth chapter, the classic contrast between drives for self-preservation (ego drives) and sexual drives are relativized and undermined by the idea that all drives are characterized by one and the same principle. All drives profoundly aim for a return to the inorganic and thus have a conservative and regressive character. The sixth chapter re-introduces a new drive dualism that can be seen as a response to and a correction of the conclusions of the original fifth chapter.

Most of, if not all, philosophical interpretations of this text are based on the published text from 1920 and treat it as a homogenous whole. It is assumed that Freud would have almost immediately written it in the form we know from the *Gesammelte Werke*.[8] This assumption removes the opportunity for the text's uncertainties and paradoxes to come into their own and to understand what is at stake. This approach too often forces the reader to search for more coherence than there is in the text, or to negate divergent passages. Or it leads to at least quietly assuming the entire text tries to provide an answer to *still the same question or questions* and the different chapters are equally stages in responding to and developing this one problematic.

However, when the first two versions of *Beyond the Pleasure Principle* are read side by side, it quickly becomes clear that they articulate positions that are difficult to reconcile. Moreover, all indications are that Freud put the first version aside as he found the conclusions he drew specifically in the fifth chapter unacceptable. The new sixth chapter then does not so much continue the argument commenced in the first five chapters but responds to and corrects the insights to which the discussion had led up to this point. A comparison of both manuscripts also makes clear that Freud sometimes did his very best, while rewriting in 1920, to relativize or even hide from view the contrasts between the trains of thought in the fourth and fifth chapter on the one hand and those in the sixth chapter on the other.

For *Beyond the Pleasure Principle* to truly give up its secrets, we need to ask which hypotheses and statements Freud defends in the first version and in what way these could not be anything else than problematic for him. Next, we need to check in which way the additional sixth chapter is an answer to this impasse. In this way, Freud's text appears in a new perspective that allows for a different reading than what has become customary in the literature.

3. The limits of the pleasure principle and psychoanalysis

In his theorization, Freud continued to assume that the psychic life was automatically regulated by a pleasure-, or even better, an unpleasure principle.[9] This of course does not mean that Freud had no eye for the many forms of unpleasure confronting us over the course of our life. When I fall down the stairs, or when a loved one is not there where one hopes to find her, it naturally causes unpleasure, but these events evade my grasp and are beyond my control. My reaction to these situations can be guided in the correct way through the pleasure principle. I can take pain medication after the fall or call my loved one in the hope that we can still meet up. These forms of unpleasure, then, do not contradict the pleasure principle.[10]

The problematic of psychopathology is in this regard already a more complicated problem. When psychic life automatically and spontaneously strives for pleasure, how can we explain the emergence of neurotic symptoms? These are after all not only unpleasurable, but they also often have a seriously invalidating effect on daily life. Freud believes, however, that it is not necessarily a problem for the pleasure principle. Neurotic symptoms are after all *compromise-formations*. They are a compromise between the patient's unconscious, perverse wishes and desires on the one hand and, on the other, the interests of the ego that need to consider the demands of reality and of the higher psychological functions such as conscience. This explains why Freud writes that "unpleasure for one system and (…) simultaneously satisfaction for the other".[11] The following up on moral requirements is pleasurable for the ego and the preconscious system but unavoidably require that unconscious perverse desires need to remain unsatisfied.[12] The direct satisfaction of the latter unavoidably leads to unpleasure on the level of the ego, however. Freud also writes in this regard that "all neurotic unpleasure is (…) pleasure that cannot be felt as such".[13] The satisfaction of our unconscious drive representations can after all only be experienced as unpleasurable by the Ego and the higher psychic systems.

We have, however, pointed out before that traumatic neurosis does not adhere to this scheme. The war neurotics constantly repeat in their dreams the events that lay at the base of their pathology.[14] They constantly repeat in their dreams the traumas to which they fell victim. How could this be understood? Freud had argued in his *Interpretation of Dreams* that dreams are the fulfillments of wishes. In the dream, repressed desires are represented, in a distorted way, as having been realized. There are of course dreams that seem to contradict this general law – anxiety dreams and punishment dreams, for example – but these dreams can easily be understood from the dynamic of the pleasure principle. So, Freud writes about dreams of punishment that "it has become easy to recognize in these punishment dreams the fulfilments of the wishes of the super-ego".[15] Many anxiety dreams can also be understood in this way: the anxiety is then for example linked with the fact that the repressed content threatens to surface too directly. In these explanations, the general scheme we already discussed earlier can be seen: what is pleasure for the one system is unpleasure for the other. The nightmares of traumatized patients put into question the common validity of the pleasure principle though. These dreams after all repeat events that never were pleasurable. What wishes could they be fulfilling? In the traumatic and war neuroses we come across a compulsive repetition that, according to Freud, seems to carry us 'beyond' the pleasure principle.

Freud finds this problematic of repetition not only in traumatic neurosis but also in the transference in the analytical cure.[16] At first, he views the transference as an obstacle to psychoanalysis. The psychoanalytical cure, so he argues, aims to make the past and the unconscious desires and fantasies that are an expression thereof conscious again. In transference, this past is on the contrary only repeated – and not remembered – in relation to the psychoanalyst. In the relation with the analyst the patient repeats important drive representations rooted in his/her past and lying at the basis of his/her neurotic suffering. The earlier neurosis, so Freud writes, is thus replaced by a "fresh, 'transference neurosis'".[17] At first glance, this tendency runs counter to the aim of the psychoanalytic treatment. But Freud gradually realized that the transference can also be an instrument with which to trace back the past and the unconscious. In this way, the transference became an ally of the psychoanalyst. Furthermore, Freud thought the transference relation is formed almost automatically. It is thus not really avoidable and in this sense has *a compulsive character*. It is not unimportant that Freud first introduces the notion of the *compulsion to repeat* in relation to the transference in analysis.[18]

It is clear that the transference neurosis in itself does not contradict the rule of the pleasure principle. By repeating in transference, patients want to save themselves the unpleasure associated with the becoming conscious of the unconscious, repressed drive representations. Yet Freud notes the following here:

> But we come now to a new and remarkable fact, namely that the compulsion to repeat also recalls from the past experiences which include no possibility of pleasure, and which can never, even long ago, have brought satisfaction, even to instinctual impulses [*Triebregungen*], which have since been repressed.[19]

After all, is psychic life not automatically regulated by the pleasure principle?

Even if it is especially these clinical phenomena that had convinced Freud of the existence of a repetition compulsion that carried us 'beyond' the pleasure principle, these phenomena are certainly not the only examples of repetition. Equally, the compulsion to repeat does not only appear in the context of psychopathology. In fact, in our daily lives too we are confronted by it. So, Freud discusses in the second chapter of the text a game his grandson Ernst often plays. Little Ernst tossed away a bobbin, often crying 'oooh'. The complete game became clear when the bobbin was attached to a piece of string and the little boy threw this object away while calling 'oooh' and then pulling it back to him while he saying 'aaah'. According to Freud, these cries mean *fort* (gone) and *da* (back), and he interprets this game as a portrayal of the departure (absence) and return of the mother of the small child. The problem that becomes visible here has in the meantime become known. Freud noted that the game is also played without the string attached to the bobbin to reel it back in. This means that the return of the mother cannot constitute any part of the game. The departure of the mother and her absence could, however, not have been pleasurable. How could the constant repetition of an in itself unpleasurable event be understood? Does this game not also refer to something lying 'beyond the pleasure principle'?

As with all other examples, Freud also does not let himself be immediately convinced here. He indicates that the child could have transformed this experience into a game for other motives than only the repetition of an unpleasurable event.[20] The game is perhaps the child's attempt to replace their original passive attitude with an active one. Viewed as such, the game satisfies a drive for mastery that operates apart from the question if the memory in itself is pleasurable or not. It could also concern the satisfaction of a revenge impulse towards the mother: 'All right, then, go away! I don't need you'. After all, children more often repeat experiences in their play that could hardly have been pleasurable. But in this repetition they also satisfy other desires – for instance the wish to be grown-up – that can unfasten themselves somewhat from the question whether what is repeated was pleasurable or not. In the '*Fort-da*-game', repetition of unpleasure and the pleasure principle do not exclude each other in principle: "the compulsion to repeat and instinctual satisfaction, which is immediately pleasurable seem to converge here into an intimate partnership".[21]

Regardless, at first glance Freud does not find the repetition in the children's game conclusive enough to postulate a compulsion to repeat 'beyond' the pleasure principle. Only after the clinical arguments – particularly the traumatic dreams – he discusses in the third chapter convince him of the existence of a compulsion to repeat that cannot be reduced to the pleasure principle does he decide to also retain his grandson's game as an illustration thereof. Freud writes: "Enough is left unexplained to justify the hypothesis of a compulsion to repeat–something that seems *more primitive, more elementary, more instinctual* [*triebhafter*], than the pleasure principle which it overrides".[22]

Repetition can be associated with pleasure. But this does not prevent repetition from also directly coming into conflict with the pleasure principle. If such is the case, repetition can take on a *daemonic* character. After all, in such case it no longer cares about our well-being.[23] To clarify Freud refers especially to the life of non-neurotic patients. With them, repetition makes the impression of a fate that stalks them and that Freud links to Nietzsche's notion of 'perpetual recurrence of the same thing'.[24] Here he for instance shows by way of illustration the story of a woman who was married three times, and all three times her husband died soon after the wedding, so that she repeatedly renewed her status as widow.[25]

4. Trauma and repetition

To the question of what could count as trauma, Freud answers in the first instance that it concerns a psychic shock without meaning. In this regard, he also refers to 'the old, naive theory of shock'.[26] With this he means the theory of the *concussion of the spine* and the *railway-spine* that we discussed in the first chapter. In our first chapter, we pointed out that different authors have emphasized the role of fright and threat to life in the emergence of this pathology. Freud links to this last thought. Psychic traumas are events that overwhelm us in the most literal sense. They are events that we cannot give any specific meaning because we were not prepared for them, not even with 'preparedness for anxiety'. For, according to Freud, anxiety offers an initial protection against traumatic neurosis. After all, anxiety describes a state of expecting and anticipating danger, even if it is unknown.[27] With fright, by contrast, the emphasis lies in the element of surprise. It occurs when one is exposed to danger without being prepared for it. From this Freud concludes that a traumatic shock "is caused by the lack of any preparedness for anxiety, including lack of hypercathexis of the systems that would be the first to receive the stimulus. Owing to their low cathexis those systems are not in a good position for binding the inflowing amounts of excitation".[28]

Anxiety prepares us for something that we expect to come, even if we do not know precisely what it is. In this way, it makes it possible or more comfortable to couple an event to a representation or a network of representations. In this way, the event can obtain a space in the psychological life, and we can adequately react to it, so that the traumatic effect subsides. Freud concludes: "It will be seen, then, that preparedness for anxiety (...) constitute[s] the last line of defence of the shield against stimuli".[29]

In this way the anxiety dreams of traumatic patients and war neurotics can be understood, according to Freud. These dreams endeavour retrospectively to establish the preparedness for anxiety that was missing at the time of the accident. In and through the repetition in their dream the patients attempt to produce the anxiety that must allow them to *bind* the experience to which they were so unexpectedly surrendered. When we are in anxious expectation, even of an undetermined danger, we are less easily overwhelmed and can successfully bind the 'inflowing amounts of excitation' to a (network of) time-place determined representations.[30] This binding allows an adequate – that is to say in accordance with the pleasure principle: through discharge – reaction to these amounts of excitation. When this binding is not established, like in the war neurosis, a specific memory is replaced by a continuous time- and place-less repetition of the same. The dreams of war neurotics, Freud concludes, "endeavouring to master the stimulus retrospectively, by developing the anxiety whose omission was the cause of the traumatic neurosis".[31]

5. Repetition and drive

For Freud it is clear from the start that the repetition 'beyond' the pleasure principle has an *instinctual* [*triebhaften*] character.[32] In his discussion of transference neurosis he points out that nothing in the unconscious resists becoming conscious of and the realization of the unconscious representations. The resistance against the unconscious originates in the ego and the higher psychological functions, not in the unconscious itself. According to Freud, as the unconscious also consists of instinctually invested representations, the compulsion to repeat must subsequently also have an instinctual character. The compulsion to repeat is "more primitive, elementary, instinctual [*triebhafter*]" than the pleasure principle. The transference in which this repetition originates is the work of the unconscious and thus of the drive. In compulsion to repeat, a fundamental drive characteristic appears and thus of human beings as essentially 'instinctual' beings. So, we should ask what *in the drive itself* goes beyond the pleasure principle and how it should be understood.

In classic descriptions of traumatic neurosis, a non-sexual trauma has a direct and immediate destructive effect because a person was not at all prepared. The way in which Freud describes traumatic neurosis in the first three chapters of *Beyond the Pleasure Principle* definitely seems to confirm this thesis. But we should remind ourselves that in the original as well as in the modified seduction theory, trauma comes from within. With Emma, for example, the anxiety she feels when she walks into the clothing store where she notices the two servants giggling with each other, is the result of the shopkeeper's smirk surfacing at the edge of her consciousness. Only in this second moment does Emma understand the sexual meaning of the first event and the memory becomes traumatic. Also, in the case of the Rat Man, the anxiety for his own anger determines the traumatic quality of the conflict with the father. Here, the anxiety and hence the trauma are not caused by the external event as such. It is the drive impulses that besiege Emma and the Rat Man *from within* that have a traumatizing effect and thus have to be bound.

Freud now, in the fourth chapter of *Beyond the Pleasure Principle*, returns to this thought of an internal trauma and thus takes a new course in his argumentation. He writes that we could perhaps still prepare for external stimuli but not for the drives that well up from within our bodies. He refers in this regard to the distinction between 'quiescent' ('bound') and 'mobile' energy, which Breuer had introduced in the theoretical part he wrote for

Studies on Hysteria and that he already used in his seventh metapsychological chapter of his *Interpretation of Dreams*.[33] Freud identifies 'mobile energy' as the primary process that dominates unconscious processes. In the unconscious, cathectic energy can freely pass from one representation to the next (the energy is not fixed or coupled to any one representation), thus creating links that to the waking life appear to be senseless. But at the same time, it is precisely this 'mobility' that makes it possible for the unconscious to penetrate consciousness, in this way taking the shortest possible way to satisfying or discharging the libidinal energy it carries. Dreams are a good example. An unacceptable representation can pass its cathectic energy to one or more innocent representations (displacement), or different representations can concentrate their cathectic energy in a single one (condensation) in order to circumnavigate the censorship of the Ego. These shifts in cathectic energy do not in any way consider the reality and the prevailing order like, for example, the time sequence. Therefore, the mental formations ruled by the unconscious sometimes seem so bizarre to the waking life. In a dream one can be urinating against a wall while behind oneself it gathers into an entire lake, but for waking life this is absurd.[34] This primary process aims only at achieving satisfaction at any cost, as quickly as possible and eventually in a hallucinatory way.

Freud distinguishes this primary process from the secondary process that characterizes the (pre-)conscious. In the secondary process the mobile flow of cathectic energy is contained by binding this energy in a more stable way to a network of representations. Representations are occupied in a more stable way, taking account of, for instance, the ordering relationships of time and space.[35] The representations can subsequently no longer be linked to each other freely and without limits or simply act as each other's replacement. It is perhaps particularly important that Freud also links the pleasure principle with the secondary process. Considering the explanation above this seems obvious. We previously called binding a condition for the 'dominance' of the pleasure principle.[36] This binding now appears to be characteristic of the secondary process. The pleasure principle and the secondary process therefore go hand in hand.

All this results in Freud equating the pleasure principle to the reality principle, at least implicitly, from the fourth chapter of the text. Earlier in the text, Freud had already introduced the distinction between the pleasure- and the reality principle.[37] As we know, the pleasure principle refers to the tendency of the psychic apparatus to discharge the tension as quickly as possible or keeping it as low as possible. From the perspective of the material and the cultural outside world, this principle is useless from the start and often even dangerous to the organism. Therefore, according to Freud, the original pleasure principle is succeeded by the reality principle which

> does not abandon the intention of ultimately obtaining pleasure, but it nevertheless demands and carries in to effect the postponement of satisfaction, the abandonment of a number of possibilities of gaining satisfaction and the temporary toleration of unpleasure as a step on the long indirect road to pleasure.[38]

As Freud argued years earlier in 'Formulations on the Two Principles of Mental Functioning', the reality principle is therefore a deferred pleasure principle.

Here, a tension can be traced that is important for a good understanding of Freud's argument in *Beyond the Pleasure Principle*. On the one hand, he talks about a pleasure principle that is specific to the 'primary' psychic process.[39] Herewith he refers to the spontaneous tendency to discharge the tension, at least to as low a level as possible.[40] Later in the text Freud however considers the primary process as the 'instinctual' ground for the compulsion to repeat that is up against the pleasure principle that he now says is specific to the secondary process. In this way, the pleasure principle rather seems to indicate the basic principle of the efficacy of the ego that needs to defend itself against the drive's attempts to penetrate consciousness.

In this way, the question how trauma can also, in the case of traumatic neurosis, come from within and have an 'instinctual' base remains unresolved. In the 1919 manuscript Freud still owes us the answer to this question. In some passages he added to the end of the fourth chapter in the 1920 edition, he alludes to what he wrote about the sources of sexuality in *Three Essays on the Theory of Sexuality*.[41] There he stated that mechanical shocks could cause sexual excitation. He also already associated this phenomenon with traumatic neurosis there:

> Here again we must mention, which is not yet understood, that the combination of fright and mechanical agitation produces severe, hysteriform, traumatic neurosis. It may at least be assumed that these influences, which, when they are of small intensity, become sources of sexual excitation, lead to a profound disorder in the sexual mechanism or chemistry if they operate with exaggerated force.[42]

This is at least a decidedly speculative (and not very convincing?) point of view: from the fact that the rocking of a train could lead to sexual excitation, it is hard to gather that a train accident must be the case to an extreme degree.[43] In *Beyond the Pleasure Principle*, Freud confirms this viewpoint without further commentary. This means that, according to Freud, the mechanical shock that comes with the accident generates huge quantities of sexual energy that must be bound, that is, subjugated to the power of the secondary process and thus of the pleasure principle. Freud writes:

> A failure to effect this binding would provoke a disturbance analogous to a traumatic neurosis; and only after binding has been accomplished would it be possible for the dominance of the pleasure principle (and of its modification, the reality principle) to proceed unhindered.[44]

In this way, trauma is again genuinely understood as an essentially 'internal event'. The external event on its own does not have any explanatory value for the pathology, according to Freud.

The traumatizing effect of an event cannot be understood apart from the levels of libidinal energy that is simultaneously generated. Here we retrace Freud's classical framework in which the effectivity of accidental events is intrinsically associated with constitutional and 'instinctual' factors. The efficacy of trauma is always linked to the constitutionally determined character of the drive. In this way, the traumatic neurosis in *Beyond the Pleasure Principle* can remain the model of a reflection of the status and nature of drives and the instinctual. Freud is thus also able to maintain – for now? – the primacy of sexuality.

6. Drive and phylogeny

We argued that compulsion to repeat teaches us something about the essence of the drives and the instinctual. To understand repetition, Freud introduces a new definition of drive in the fifth chapter of *Beyond the Pleasure Principle*. Here, e defines drive as "*an urge inherent in organic life to restore an earlier state of things* which the living entity has been obliged to abandon under the pressure of external disturbing forces". He compares this drive with "a kind of organic elasticity, or, to put it another way, the expression of the inertia inherent in organic life". For a proper understanding of this definition, it is best to start from the concept of drive that Freud wants to avoid or at least amend here. We have become accustomed, Freud says, to view drive as "a factor impelling towards change and development".[45] It was the vision Freud defended even shortly before in 'Instincts and Their Vicissitudes'. The following, somewhat longer citation makes it abundantly clear:

> Instinctual stimuli [*Triebreize*], which originate from within the organism, cannot be dealt with by this mechanism. Thus they make far higher demands on the nervous system and cause it to undertake involved and interconnected activities by which the external world is so changed as to afford satisfaction to the internal source of stimulation. Above all, they oblige the nervous system to renounce its ideal intention of keeping off stimuli, for they maintain an incessant and unavoidable afflux of stimulation. We may therefore well conclude that instincts [*Triebe*], and not external stimuli [*Reize*], are the true motive forces behind the advances that have led the nervous system, with its unlimited capacities, to its present high level of development.[46]

But does this depiction allow for an adequate understanding of repetition as an essential expression of the drive? After all, repetition is diametrically opposed to change and development. Those who repeat do not change and are not really included in progressive development.[47] If repetition expresses an essential aspect of drive, then the latter must have a conservative character according to Freud. He writes:

> This view of instincts [*Triebe*] strikes us as strange because we have become used to see in them a factor impelling towards change and development, whereas we are now asked to recognize in them the precise contrary—an expression of the conservative nature of living substance.[48]

In this section and the next, we shall see that the new determination of drive can only be fully understood from the growing importance of the phylogenetic theories we discussed in the previous chapter. Indeed, Freud founds this new drive theory in reflections that immediately connect with psycho-Lamarckism and Haeckel's recapitulation theory with which we are familiar. Only in this way can it become clear what exactly defines the conservative character of the drives. This foundation unfolds in several steps that we discuss one by one for the sake of good order.

First, Freud defines life itself as an effect of "the action of a force of whose nature we van form no conception" – a force that has generated life in matter.[49] He thus considers the origin of life according to the model of a trauma. And as the individual trauma generates libidinal energy that needs to be discharged, so the impact of an incomprehensible force created tension in the inorganic substance that needed to be discharged again. Freud concludes: "the tension which then arose in what had hitherto been an inanimate substance endeavoured to cancel itself out. In this way the first instinct [*Trieb*] came into being: the instinct to return to the inanimate".[50] This instinctual force that determines organic life is not directed at change or development. They are in essence conservative and regressive, that is, they want to return to their *status quo ante*. They pursue only thing: to undo as quickly as possible the imposed modifications and tensions that accompany them. This is also what Freud means when he states that the drive is governed by an inertia principle: it manifests the inertness inherent in organic life.[51] The drive does not want to move forward, it only wants to return to its (inorganic) origin.

In single-celled organisms (protists) – the first and simplest forms of life – the processes of resisting incoming forces and discharge of tension are still relatively straightforward. Due to external impulse effects, they develop an inorganic shield, a siliceous external skeleton,[52] that acts as a barrier to stimuli (*Reizschutz*).[53] The protists only had to – successfully – protect themselves against external stimuli and were at the same time able to simply eliminate internal stimuli by discharging waste products of metabolic processes.[54] In a highly developed organism such as the human being, the external skeleton has been internalized, and the senses have taken over the function of resisting and metered absorption of stimuli. However, large and intense amounts of internal excitations are also received that cannot automatically and immediately be discharged and against which there is no defense.[55] The psychic apparatus is this tasked with binding the incoming energy and insistent excitations and changing these "from a freely flowing into a quiescent state".[56]

Freud assumes that with the development of organisms to ever higher and more complex forms, the internal excitations and tensions increase, and the discharge requires greater physical and psychical effort. We need to ask how this development is possible when the drive – and thus the organism as such – strives to return to a quiescent and thus tensionless state. If there is an urge to move back to the inanimate, what explains the further development of organic life into forms that no longer 'die so smoothly and easily' and have such a 'short lifespan' as the first living organisms (protists)?[57] In the first edition of *Beyond the Pleasure Principle* from 1919 Freud argues the following in this regard. That, despite the urge for the inanimate, there is life, and that this life has further developed in more complex organisms is determined by organic life being subject to an endless series of imposed modifications and adjustments to circumstances. What we call evolution, development or progress does not originate from the drive. On the contrary, it is, Freud argues in line with Lamarck's view of evolution, a set of changes that determine the lifecycle of organisms as acquired characteristics and are repeated in subsequent generations[58] In successive developments in increasingly complex organisms, the set of imposed and acquired changes has obliged "the still surviving substance to diverge ever more widely from its original course [*Ablenkungen*] of life and to make ever more complicated *détours* [*Umwege*] before reaching its aim of death".[59] This 'aim of death' is here to be understood as the reduction of internal tension to an absolute minimum and hence the return to the inanimate. The evolution from single cell to increasingly complex organism thus makes the journey back to the inanimate longer and more laborious but does not change its fundamentally conservative and regressive character. Every organism of every kind has developed a kind of 'détour' to life's aim and wants to "die only in its own fashion", that is, to preserve itself up until it dies a 'natural death'.[60] In this regard Freud, for example, refers to specific fish (e.g., salmon) that undertake a long and complicated journey during spawning to hatch in specific waters and then die there.[61] These fish complete the development of their kind in an inverted order – here, Freud again refers to Haeckel's bio-genetic law – thus making it possible for the next generation to repeat the path (or 'détour') to be taken. Before we can elaborate on these insights, also regarding human existence, in the next section, we must first highlight another important element.

According to Freud, it was not only modifications imposed by external factors that made it possible to prolong the life of organisms – and thus the path to death. We must also assume that already quite early in evolution of life, cells were formed that could not sustain themselves independently, such as the protists that enveloped themselves in an impulse-resistant, inorganic shield and managed to rejuvenate themselves and multiply through cell division. In these cells – the so-called germ-cells – the original, vulnerable and tension-filled structure of the first living substance was preserved and, in addition to the drive to return to the inanimate, drives arose that began to seek contact with other germ-cells.[62] From this arises, Freud suggests, the ability to bind cells together to form multicellular organisms in which fragile germ-cells are surrounded by greater numbers of protective cells – the body. This possibility characterizes drives that, from the moment that sex differences and reproduction also arise, can be called sexual drives. At first sight it appears that these sexual drives counter the drives that strive to return to the inanimate as quickly as possible. And yet, even these drives are 'conservative' according to Freud, because the reproduction takes the shape of a 'restoration of an earlier state'. After all, each new multicellular organism develops from the fusion of two germ-cells into one that will then re-envelope itself with a mortal body. Reproduction is the repetition over and over again of a 'détour' to the death of a body filled with excitations and tension.

We recall how Freud defines the concept of seduction (*Verführung*) as 'deflection' or 'leading astray' (*ablenken*) of normal development. This line is continued in *Beyond the Pleasure Principle*, but this time without explicit reference to seduction. Normal development of a singular organism (ontogeny) is nothing other than repetition of one in the evolution of the kind disturbed, deflected and acquired development (phylogeny). Changes in the evolution of organic life are deflections and detours provoked by outside influences. Freud's 'cosmology' turns out to be a 'traumatology'. Life itself arises from traumatic shock; evolution is driven by enforced modifications, that is, by reactions to disturbances producing deflections that acquired as such will define the 'normal' development repeated in each generation; and the most complex organism can hardly defend itself against (and is helplessly at the mercy of) the tensions and excitations threatening it from within.

7. Lamarckism, recapitulation theory and the problem of drive monism

We are nearing the end of Freud's bold speculation or at least the first attempt at it, which he then revises in the second version of the text. Is it conceivable, Freud wonders, that *all* drives are repetitive and conservative?[63] Are there no drives then insisting on development and progress? Even if Freud does not want to completely exclude this hypothesis, he nevertheless decides to first examine all consequences of his basic hypothesis.[64] The main question Freud needs to answer here is how his new insights about the drive relate to the old dualism, which pitted drives of self-preservation (ego drives) against sexual drives. It is notable that Freud does not name death drives in the first five chapters of his text, and that the reference to Eros towards the end of the fifth chapter was also not added until 1923.[65] The only drives Freud mentions in the original version of these chapters are the drives of self-preservation and sexual drives. Although he calls the sexual drives 'life drives' in the first version of the text,[66] these 'life instincts' are then opposed to drives of self-preservation and can thus not simply have the same meaning yet as Eros later in the sixth chapter. After all, here, Eros is opposed to the death drives and not to the drives of self-preservation that are also included under Eros later in the sixth chapter.

The problem Freud faces is as follows. The opposition between drives of self-preservation and sexual drives had until now been the cornerstone of Freudian psychoanalysis. Even in the first chapters of *Beyond the Pleasure Principle*, Freud works according to this plan. His reflections on the compulsion to repeat, however, forced him to at the same time introduce a new definition of drive and the instinctual. Drive as such is in essence conservative and regressive. Freud must now explain how this definition applies to self-preservation or ego-drives as well as to sexual drives. This provision is already rather odd in terms of the drives of self-preservation, of which it is indeed at first glance difficult to assume that they aim to return to the inorganic. And the latter actually applies even more to sexual drives, which aim at the continuation of life through reproduction. And when the drives of self-preservation as well as sexual drives are determined by an inertia principle and are conservative in character, does it then not mean that both drives are, in the terminology of the sixth chapter, 'death drives'? In other words, is the original dualism not in this way inevitably replaced by a drive monism? Did Freud not unexpectedly find himself in Jungian territory? A discussion of this problem also makes it possible to give more specific content than has been possible so far to the idea that drives are conservative in nature and to the inertia principle.

How can we be speaking about drives of self-preservation at all when the aim of all life is the inanimate or the inert?[67] When the drives only want to return us to the inorganic, why do we then not all jump out the window together? We already know Freud's answer. Every living being – think of the example of specific fish species given earlier – does not only long to return to the inorganic but also wishes to achieve this return in his or her own fashion. It wants to die a 'natural' death after the cycle of life is complete. Every other way will be unacceptable for this organism. This insight can, as we know, only be understood from Haeckel's biogenetic law. Not only does the embryo go through the various stages of the evolutionary line in a transient and abbreviated fashion, but also the episodes that determine our subsequent life are repetitions of the 'traumatic' events in the life of the species.[68] Indeed, this can help explain why we cling to life yet are driven by urges that want to discharge all tension and thus aim for a return to the inorganic. We only want to die once our life is completed 'naturally'. More concretely, this means, humans and all organic life are directed only toward the inorganic through the repetition of the history of the species. In other words, every organism wants to die from *internal* causes and therefore tries to avoid every external event that would make this impossible by artificially shortening life. Accidents, illnesses at an early age and suicide, to name but some examples, are contrary to the 'natural' lifecycle, and so they are resisted with all instinctual (*triebhafter*) force. Freud therefore concludes:

> Seen in this light, the theoretical importance of the instincts of self-preservation, of self-assertion and of mastery greatly diminishes. They are component instincts whose function it is to assure that the organism shall follow its own path to death, and to ward off any possible ways of returning to inorganic existence other than those which are immanent in the organism itself.[69].

The drives of self-preservation were also originally 'myrmidons of death'.[70]

Although at first glance, the sexual drives are opposed to the drives of self-preservation, we already pointed out that Freud also attributes a conservative character to them in the first version of the text. According to Freud, the sexual drives are aimed at preserving, protecting and fusing elementary organisms – germ-cells – which are the actual carriers of life. These germ-cells are the carriers of inherited and newly acquired drive dispositions. The sexual drives in this sense guard the emergence of more and more *new individuals* who nevertheless still *repeat the same kind of organic life*. According to Freud, they are conservative "in the same sense as the other drives in that they bring back earlier states of living substance" but they are in a way even more conservative "in that they are peculiarly resistant to external influences" and also because "they preserve life itself for a comparative long period".[71] The efficacy of the ego and sexual drives is formally analogue. Both drives are profoundly conservative and regressive. They answer *to the same inertia principle and principle of repetition.*

Freud is now able to rewrite the relationship between drives of self-preservation and sexual drives in a way that takes account of his new general definition of drive:

> It is as though the life of the organism moved with a vacillating rhythm. One group of instincts rushes forward to reach the final aim of life as swiftly as possible; but when a particular stage in the advance has been reached, the other group jerks back to a certain point to make a fresh start and so prolong the journey.[72]

The sexual drives repeatedly create individuals who want to reach the end of life, or of every tension, as quickly as possible – according to the historical determination that characterizes the life of the drive. They repeatedly establish the passage to death that determines life. The drives of self-preservation and the sexual drives thus become two sides of *the same instinctual process* that is essentially conservative and regressive.

In the first version of the text, Freud develops a tragic vision of humankind and of the whole of organic life. *Beyond the Pleasure Principle* is a sustained critique of every (teleological) progress optimism in which, as we know from the previous chapter, for instance Haeckel – but actually the large part of the culture of the time – still firmly believed.[73] According to Freud, development comes about through adapting to coincidental external circumstances, not through an inner sense of purpose. The drive does not aim for change but is controlled through an inertial principle: whatever the meaning we bestow upon our existence, drive is a constant force that leads us to death via a path imposed upon us from the history of the species.[74] What we call progress is, incidentally, fully dependent on the perspective we take towards a given series of modifications.[75] Progress for one person may be something completely different for another. Consequently, there is no such thing as a 'drive to perfection' (*Trieb zur Vervollkommnung*).

For our problematic, the next aspect of Freud's new definition of drive as conservative is of particular importance. This theory transcends the conflict between 'trauma' on the one hand and 'constitution' and 'drive' on the other. As has already become clear from the discussion of the study of the Wolf Man and the chapter on the psycho-Lamarckist influences on Freud's work is what Freud calls 'constitution' – the order of the drives – itself not to be understood in isolation from traumas. Freud increasingly interprets drive as the precipitation and effect of a still entirely unimaginable interplay of forces from which it arose and of the traumatic events to which the human species fell victim in the course of its history. 'Drive', 'trauma' and 'constitution' are thus neither opposed nor mutually exclusive. On the contrary, they are different aspects of the same reality.[76]

Freud's speculations and his attempt to examine all consequences of his audacious basis hypothesis have now brought him to a point far removed from some of the crucial insights of his own theory. Indeed, these speculations lead to a relativization of the drive dualism and the corresponding conflict model to which he had been strongly attached since the early years of psychoanalysis. This conflict model and the drive dualism were the core of Freud's theory of neurosis. Yet can we still speak of an essential conflict between the ego-drives and sexual drives when both are governed by *the same principle*? For Freud, these conclusions were difficult to accept. This undoubtedly explains why he abandoned the text unfinished for almost a year before adding a new chapter between May and July 1920 that had to break the impasse he had reached.[77]

8. A new drive theory: Eros and death drives

In the sixth chapter of his text, which was not written until 1920, Freud completely changes his reasoning.[78] From the beginning of this chapter, he states that the sexual drives are profoundly non-conservative. Moreover, in the second version of the text, Freud added an interjection towards the end of the fifth chapter to prepare us for this change of perspective. Where in the first version the question was raised whether "there are no instincts that do not seek to restore an earlier state of things", Freud now adds "apart from the sexual instincts".[79] Moreover, in the second published version from 1921, Freud italicized this short addition, further emphasizing its importance. This interjection from 1920 contradicts the 1919 paragraph that precedes it in which Freud calls sexual drive conservative 'to a higher degree' in comparison to the drives of self-preservation.[80]

However, in the sixth chapter Freud states that sexual drive cannot be understood from or as repetition:

> But we still feel our line of thought appreciably hampered by the fact that we cannot ascribe to the sexual instinct the characteristic of a compulsion to repeat which first put us on the track of the death instincts. (…) *But the essence of the processes to which sexual life is directed is the coalescence of two cell-bodies. That alone is what guarantees the immortality of the living substance in the higher organisms.*[81]

The sexual drives do not aim for a return to the inorganic but to the 'immortality of the living substance' and by a tendency of binding cells together into enduring units to prolong life. This is a different perspective from that which has dominated the text so far. We see, at the same time, that the sexual drives are placed in the service of self-preservation here. It is directed to the 'immortality of the living substance' and prolonging life. Freud will therefore further in the sixth chapter see both the sexual and self-preservation drives as expressions of the life drives or Eros. These life drives (sexual and ego-drives) are opposed to the death drives or Thanatos. In other words, Freud saves the drive dualism by placing the principle that governed both drives of the self-preservation and sexual drives in the 1919 version as separate drives – Thanatos – opposite the life drives of which the drives of self-preservation and sexual drives are now the manifestations.

Freud connects these insights with a new perspective on the origin of life: the force that produced life to emerge in the inanimate matter caused the substance just brought to life to be "torn apart into small particles".[82] In response to this fragmentation, the life drives arise that aim to unite the particles into a living cell. These life drives, seen in this way, arise spontaneously in response to the fragmentation but at the same time also continue a persistence of "the chemical affinity of inanimate matter", that is, of the ability of atoms and various chemical elements to enter compounds (chemical reactions) with other atoms and elements.[83] This perspective also implies that the dynamics of the animate are no longer understood exclusively from or as inertia (or repetition). The life drives underpin the later development into multicellular organisms and of the possibility of prolonging life.[84] From this perspective, the development of organisms into increasingly complex forms is not so much the result of 'imposed and acquired modifications' or of protection against externally induced stimuli, but of drives aimed at binding particles together into a cell, from cells to a 'cell-state' (multicellular organism) and from individuals to groups (culture). Life drives seek to integrate into larger units what is 'torn apart' and fragmented.[85] Since then, binding into larger units are all about protection against the constant threat of fragmentation and destruction of the unit by external forces (e.g., natural disasters) and from within. Freud assigns the internal force opposing the tendency to unite to the death drives. He also views the death drives, in their urge to restore the inanimate, as the urge to again undo union and coherence. The death drives tend to fragment into separate particles without mutual 'affinity' and thus without mutual tension. It is from this perspective that we can comprehend why Freud will be able to associate the death drives with aggression (primarily masochism, sadism) and violence. The death drives tend towards a violent fragmentation of that which has become a unit.[86]

How does this reaffirmation of dualism concretely come about in the sixth chapter of *Beyond the Pleasure Principle*? Freud attempts to ground this dualism primarily from insights of biological science. For this purpose, he takes the work of August Weismann as a starting point, notably his distinction between a mortal and immortal part of the living substance. The mortal part (the soma) is the body in the narrow sense. The germ-plasm (the sexual and genetic substances), on the other hand, are potentially immortal. They have a purely instrumental relationship to the soma. Their fusion creates a new carrier (soma) every time that before dying off is at the origin of yet another fusion (reproductive function).[87] Sexual drives are dynamic forces that bring about this fusion. Freud takes up this distinction again at the beginning of the sixth chapter. He now argues that the opposition between the ego-drives that seek death and sexual drives that want to retain life are at first glance a dynamic equivalent to Weismann's morphological theory of organic life.[88]

But can we sustain this equivalence, Freud wonders. After all, it assumes that the opposition between germ-plasm and soma is as original as that between death and sexual drives. The latter does not seem to be the case since, according to Weismann, this opposition only applies to multicellular organisms. In single-celled organisms the individual and the reproductive cell, on the other hand, are still one and the same.[89] When they multiply by division, not only do they remain the same as themselves, but in principle they also lose nothing to vitality. The study of protists further teaches us that fusion, the copulation of two individuals without a resulting division, has a rejuvenating effect on both.[90] Single-cell organisms, or protists as Freud calls them, would in this sense be immortal. The latter would also necessarily imply that only reproduction (multiplication) is an original characteristic of living matter, whereas death would rather be a matter of adaptation to the external conditions of life. Death "cannot be regarded as an absolute necessity with its basis in the very nature of life".[91] The idea that there is in the living substance originally a force directed at the return to the inorganic thus loses its ground.

Does this train of thought have plausibility, and can find enough scientific support? Woodruff showed, Freud writes, that single-celled organisms, upon division alone, do not lose any vitality or show signs of ageing when – and only when – every new generation is immersed in fresh nutrient medium. Organisms when harmed by metabolic products which they extruded into the surrounding fluid, and Woodruff could show that only products of their own metabolism have this effect of leading to the death of the generation.[92] This confirms the suspicion that the thesis that death is a later acquisition, applies only to its manifest expressions, and that single-cell substances also do die for internal reasons. Thus, according to Freud, biology provides no compelling reasons to abandon the idea of an original opposition between the ego- and the sexual drives. Freud concludes: "The striking similarity between Weismann's distinction of soma and germ-plasma and our separation of the death instincts from the life instincts persists and retains its significance".[93]

Freud will now go a step further. When biology does not provide compelling or ultimate arguments against the hypothesis of the drive dualism, he writes, then we can perhaps conversely transpose the psychoanalytic drive theory to all the living substances. Psychoanalytic drive theory will, in other words, be employed here to develop a comprehensive philosophy of life. Freud first recalls the history of his libido theory.[94] The initial contradiction between drives of self-preservation and sexual drives was put into perspective to a large extent through the introduction of narcissism. The study of homosexuality and psychoses had led Freud to the insight that not only could the ego be the object of libidinal energy, but that it must itself be thought of as a libidinal construct. The ego arises through the pooling of libidinal energy that for the first time objectifies the body as a whole: "There must be something added to auto-erotism – a new psychical action – in order to bring about narcissism".[95] This ego is the original reservoir of the libido.[96] It is the starting point of the libidinal object relations, of which the energy can also be drawn back into the Ego. In this way, the original opposition between ego- or self-preservative drives and sexual drives is replaced by an opposition between ego- or narcissistic libido and object libido. Freud understands the relation between these two poles as communicating vessels. The more energy is invested into the object, the less in the ego and vice versa.[97] From here, these drives can be interpreted as two sides of more general life drives that Freud now identifies with the "Eros of the poets and philosophers".[98] This Eros is a fundamental force that works in everything that is alive. The germ-cells, for example, on the one hand behave completely narcissistically. They are fully focused on their own survival. But simultaneously and profoundly for the same reason they also, on the other hand, take other germ-cells as their objects, to guarantee this survival. It comes as no surprise to see that Freud sometimes identifies Eros with sexual drives, which is understandable since it unites object- and ego-libido.[99]

Freud himself, in a 1923 passage added to the fifth chapter, indicates this this Eros is a surrogate for the drive towards perfection, the existence of which he previously denied.[100] It is therefore difficult not to think of Jung's libido when it comes to Freud's description of Eros. The Jungian 'libido' is a driving force that pervades all organic life in general and of which genital sexuality is a specification. Similarly, the Freudian Eros is a force that pervades the whole of organic life and of which human sexuality is a distant offshoot. Freud must have recognized this himself. Indeed, he himself immediately points out that here again the danger of a monism and a pansexualism arises.[101] We know his response to this threat: in opposition to the life drives are the death drives.

How should we understand these death drives. Freud writes in the sixth chapter that

> The dominating tendency of mental life, and perhaps of nervous life in general, is the effort to reduce, to keep constant or to remove internal tension due to stimuli (the 'Nirvana principle', to borrow a term from Barbara Low) – a tendency which finds expression in the pleasure principle; and our recognition of that fact is one of the strongest reasons for believing in the existence of death instincts.[102]

One notices the shift that takes place here in the sixth chapter compared to the first version of the text. In the first five chapters, the primary process or the drives themselves were situated 'beyond' the pleasure principle. The drive as a constant force that wants to lead organisms back to the inorganic 'along a path that is one's own' and is thus essentially conservative. In doing so, drive does not, at its deepest level, consider the demands of the secondary process and the associated pleasure principle. In the sixth chapter, Freud identifies the pleasure principle with the Nirvana principle. The pleasure principle is thus decoupled from the secondary process and the reality test with which it is bound. The pleasure principle is from here primarily characterized by a tendency to reduce all tension and is thus an extension of the death drives. It is now apparently by implication the life drives – that is, pre-eminently the sexual drives (narcissistic and object libido) – that lead us 'beyond the pleasure principle'. Freud concludes:

> This tallies well with the hypothesis that the life process of the individual leads for internal reasons to an abolition of chemical tensions, that is to say, to death, whereas union with the living substance of a different individual increases these tensions, introducing what may be described as 'vital differences' which must then be lived off.[103]

The tendency towards tension reduction that previously characterized all drives, is elevated here to a separate drive and identified with the death drives. It is striking that in the sixth chapter Freud no longer explicitly links this inertia principle to repetition and Haeckel's biogenetic principle. He even questions whether he overestimated the meaning of the 'facts of the compulsion to repeat'.[104] The death drives are not – like the inertia principle in the 1919 version – defined in terms of principles that characterize all drives as such. It is a force of its own aimed at the violent fragmentation of what Eros has brought about through unification. This violent fragmentation does lead to the reduction of the tension that accompanies Eros, but since it is *directed against* the units Eros creates, the recapitulation principle (repetition) loses much of its relevance for a proper understanding of the death drives. The model Freud develops in the sixth chapter is difficult to reconcile with the model the earlier version of the text presented.

To which manifest phenomena, Freud now asks, can the death drives be linked to make the necessity of their affirmation plausible? For this, Freud now does not refer to the problematic of repetition in traumatic neurosis or transference like in the first version of the text but to a polarity with which psychoanalysis is more familiar: the opposition between love and hate.[105] In this way, he hopes to give the opposition between life- and death drives more specific content that is simultaneously its expression. In *Three Essays* Freud had already assumed a sadistic component in the libido.[106] This sadistic component can individuate itself in the sexual perversion of the same name and usurp the entire sexual life. According to Freud in the text we are discussing here, it cannot be derived from Eros.[107] After all, unlike Eros, it is not oriented to the formation and maintenance of ever larger connections. Freud concludes:

> Is it not plausible to suppose that this sadism is in fact a death instinct which, under the influence of the narcissistic libido, has been forced away from the ego and has consequently only emerged in relation to the object? It now enters the service of the sexual function.[108]

Here Freud introduces the perspective of two opposing drives that are usually fused but that can also separate themselves so that they can show themselves in a 'pure' form. How this fusing and defusing can be thought of and described Freud pretty much disregards in *Beyond the Pleasure Principle*. This problematic will continue to occupy him at length in the following years.

Of particular interest to us here is that the death drives are explicitly connected to aggression in the sixth chapter. Not only was there no mention of the term 'death drives' in the first version of our text but Freud also drew no connection between inertia of the drive and aggression. This connection is also not so obvious. This changes when the dynamic of organic life is bound to the reunion of an original fragmentation. The death drives can then be thought of in opposition to this dynamic. They are, as we indicated earlier, aimed at the unbinding of what is bound. They envisage to undo the 'chemical tensions' and 'vital differences' that accompany Eros as drives to union. This is a specification of the inertia principle that in the first version belonged to all drives and that from there was thematized from the repetition and recapitulation principle. This specification allows connecting the inertia principle (tendency to reduce all tension) with aggression (towards the self and external objects). This aggressiveness is original and has its own purpose: destroy and fragment in order to reduce tension. It therefore owes its emergence not to life, even though it can be placed in service of life.

From this perspective, we are from the outset the bearer of an aggression that only seeks destruction and needs no external frustrations to be unleashed. At first, at the beginning of our existence, we are too weak to direct this aggression that rages within us outward. This aggression then attacks the still undeveloped organism from the within. In his text 'The Economic Problem of Masochism', Freud later calls this process 'primary masochism'.[109] We can only defend ourselves against this by blending this aggression with the life drives to direct them outward. However, this does not prevent an aggression from raging within us that can never completely be nullified or overcome.

9. Trauma, anxiety and repetition in Inhibitions, Symptoms and Anxiety

We would err to postulate an absolute opposition between the different versions of *Beyond the Pleasure Principle*. Yet it concerns more than a mere shift in accents. Traumatic neurosis (shell shock) and repetition fade into the background from the sixth chapter for the reasons we mentioned. At the same time, the death drives are coupled with hate and aggression. Should Freud have revisited the war neurosis in the sixth chapter, he would perhaps have described it as an expression of pure self-destruction and not as an expression of an attempt to bind and an expression of a repetition compulsion. In theoretical texts such as *The Ego and the Id* and *Civilization and Its Discontents*, written after 1920, the perspective in which the death drive (here in singular) is understood primarily as an aggression drive is paramount. At the same time, the problematic of fusing and defusing two kinds of drives is at the center. In these later writings Freud makes little or no reference to traumatic neurosis. Trauma and repetition play a secondary role in these texts. In other, more clinical texts from Freud's later works, on the other hand, he returns to the problematic of the traumatic neurosis and again emphasizes the problematic of repetition.[110] The latter is true of both *Inhibitions, Symptoms and Anxiety*[111] and *Moses and Monotheism* that Freud publishes shortly before his death. Before we discuss this text in our next, last chapter, we would first like to take a closer look at *Inhibitions, Symptoms and Anxiety*. Freud will indeed return in some depth to the problematic of the traumatic neurosis and the status of the trauma. In this way, this text offers an interesting transition to his text on *Moses and Monotheism*, in which he re-evaluates the old trauma model one last time.

In *Inhibitions, Symptoms and Anxiety* Freud again examines the etiology of traumatic neurosis.[112] According to him, it does not suffice to exclusively seek out this etiology in the life or death anxiety associated with trauma. He writes: "it would seem highly improbable that a neurosis could come into being merely because of the objective presence of danger without any participation of the deeper levels of the mental apparatus".[113] Freud consistently maintains his position: trauma comes from within ('the deeper layers of the mental apparatus'). In other words, not the external event, but the reaction to this event is traumatizing. The fear of death is one such possible reaction, but according to Freud this fear can play no part in the etiology of neurosis because we have no conception of death.[114]

What then are the 'deeper layers' of the unconscious, to which external trauma must be able to connect in order to produce a neurosis? For Freud, the domain of the unconscious is also the domain of the infantile. He now argues that a life-threatening situation can only lead to traumatic neurosis because such a situation puts us in a state of total helplessness. Unlike death, which none of us has experienced, we have all endured this helplessness at some point. According to Freud, birth creates a situation of helplessness that is the model of all traumatic situations.[115]

Freud makes the link here to a book that Otto Rank published in 1924: *Das Trauma der Geburt.*[116] Rank argued that everyone is affected to a greater or lesser degree by the trauma of birth, i.e., the mortal danger that would be caused by separation from the mother. According to Rank, the intensity of this trauma and the severity of the anxiety response that results from it will determine whether the individual will ever be able to control the fear and whether it will become neurotic or normal.[117] In the course of his text Freud raises several critical questions about this hypothesis. For example, it is not clear wherein the traumatic character of birth exists and in what way it may affect later pathologies. After all, the newborn does not possess perceptions of a visual nature the renewal of which can trigger the memory of the birth trauma and thus the anxiety reaction.[118]

Freud's main objection, however, concerns a problematic we already know well: "To lay so much stress, too, on the variability in the strength of the birth trauma is to leave no room for the legitimate claims of hereditary constitution as an aetiological factor (...) Rank's theory *completely ignores constitutional factors as well as phylogenetic ones*".[119] In other words, Freud blames Rank that he does not distinguish between accidental and hereditary factors (phylogeny) that underlie neurosis.[120] In our discussion of the case of the Wolf Man, we already pointed out in detail how, from his debate with Jung onwards, Freud seeks the ultimate account of sexual etiology of the neuroses in phylogeny. This is particularly the case for the castration complex, which as we know is rooted, according to Freud, in the historical destiny of humankind. Rank, on the other hand, regards castration anxiety as a mere reiteration of birth anxiety. The infantile primitive fear naturally focuses on the (female) genitalia because of their imagined or remembered biological relationship to birth. Castration anxiety (fear of the absence of male genitalia) is in this sense a reiteration of the fear of separating from the mother.[121] Rank then bases the universality of this complex not like Freud in phylogeny but in the unquestionable universality of birth.

These considerations compel Freud to further explore, reformulate and specify Rank's hypothesis. Freud first questions how birth can be a model for trauma, as Rank claims. Unlike states such as mourning and pain, motoric innervations – discharge processes along certain pathways (sensations of the respiratory system and heart) – are an intrinsic part of anxiety.[122] When we are anxious, our breath quickens, we begin to sweat, and our heart rate goes up. In other words, underlying anxiety is an increase in excitation that must be discharged. This, according to Freud, characterizes all forms of anxiety, and it can be traced back to a common model:

> We are tempted to assume the presence of a historical factor which binds the sensations of anxiety and its innervations firmly together. We assume, in other words, that an anxiety-state is the reproduction of such an increase of excitation and a discharge along particular paths, and that from this circumstance the unpleasure of anxiety receives its specific character.[123]

According to Freud, the historical factor that is repeated in every state of anxiety is birth. Birth is after all the first state of danger.[124] Here the small child is confronted by a massive increase in excitations that it experiences as unpleasant and threatening and of which it must consequently dispose.[125] The discharge reactions that lead here are firstly absolutely expedient. For example, the quickening of the pulse counteracts blood poisoning and quicker breaths and crying prepare for adequate lung function. This expediency can be maintained in later perilous situations only when the discharge reactions involved take on the significance of a signal of approaching danger: "Anxiety is the original reaction to helplessness in the trauma and is reproduced later in the danger-situation as a signal for help".[126]

The danger of birth has no psychical content yet. Unlike Rank, Freud does not believe that that it can be explicitly (visually) represented or remembered. It is nothing but a rising tension of need against which the child is utterly helpless and that renders it distraught: "the foetus (…) can only be aware of some vast disturbance in the economy of its narcissistic libido".[127] This helplessness is the original danger that repeats itself in every later situation of danger:

> We can still find out more about this if, not content with tracing anxiety back to danger, we go on to enquire what the essence and meaning of a danger-situation is. Clearly, it consists in the subject's estimation of

> his on strength compared to the magnitude of the danger and in his admission of helplessness in the face of it – physical helplessness if the danger is real and psychical helplessness if it is instinctual.[128]

The child soon learns that it can conquer this helplessness only with the help of the mother. For this reason, the memory image of the mother is hallucinatorily charged, whenever the child is left alone, and the original danger threatens to repeat itself. The child now anticipates the state of unpleasure and despair that would result from the absence of the mother. Anxiety is now no longer a response to the situation of helplessness. It is a result of the expectation that this situation will recur. The original discharge responses – respiratory muscles and vocal cords – are now used to call the mother closer. Consequently, according to Freud, anxiety is neither primarily nor only a signal of affect that there is the threat of danger, but it is the reaction to a loss or separation. [129]

Freud argues that different periods of life are characterized by different danger situations and anxiety determinants that are legitimate and normal for the phase in question. According to him, they all imply in a certain sense a separation from the mother.[130] We have already mentioned in this regard the anxiety of the infant. Here the mother's absence functions as an anxiety determinant. In a later stage of psychical development this anxiety determinant is replaced by a new one: castration. Freud writes:

> In this case the danger is of being separated from one's genitals (...) The high narcissistic value which the penis possesses can appeal to the fact that that organ is a guarantee to its owner that he can be once more united to his mother – i.e. to a substitute for her – in the act of copulation.[131]

Castration anxiety relates to an external danger. It is the expression of the anxiety that the male genitals can be taken away (particularly by the father). Later, this anxiety is transformed into fear of the superego, which incarnates the father that has become depersonalized and historical figures of authority more generally. Here, the fear of an external punishment for violating a law or norm is transformed into fear for an internal instance that induces guilt. Freud concludes:

> But if we ask ourselves what it is that the ego fears from the super-ego, we cannot but think that the punishment threatened by the latter must be an extension of the punishment of castration. Just as the father has become depersonalized in the shape of the super-ego, so has the fear of

> castration at his hands become transformed into an undefined social or moral anxiety. But this anxiety is concealed. The ego escapes it by obediently carrying out the commands, precautions and penances that have been enjoined on it.[132]

According to Rank, all infantile anxieties are merely reissues of the birth trauma. The latter, according to him, exhausts the meaning of these anxieties. Castration anxiety is actually a repetition of birth anxiety and of the original separation of the mother. According to Rank, castration and the confrontation with the female genitals reminds the (male?) child of this original anxiety- and danger situation. In contrast, according to Freud, the original trauma – the helplessness the newborn experiences when it is overwhelmed by the excitation associated with birth – is modified and reinterpreted in the successive stages of life. According to him, successive traumas and infantile anxieties are mutually irreducible. For example, castration is a modification of anxiety for the separation from the mother.[133] It no longer concerns the image of the mother, but the separation of the male genitals.[134] The attitude the child adopts towards this danger and this trauma differs from previous situations. In the face of birth trauma and the separation from the mother, the child was completely passive and helpless, while it can acknowledge or deny castration. By exchanging passivity for activity, the child can better handle its life impressions.[135] Therefore, rather than a reenactment of a primitive trauma, it is better to speak here of a *nachträgliche* reinterpretation thereof.

On the face of it there is nothing sexual about the birth trauma. This also seems to follow from Rank's idea that infantile sexuality must be understood from the question 'Where do babies come from?'.[136] This would imply, however, that the original trauma is not sexual. But not only the birth trauma thus risks falling outside of sexuality, the same could also be true in this perspective for the traumatic neurosis.[137] In the latter case, according to Freud, a situation analogous to the birth trauma arises in the unconscious that automatically leads to an anxiety reaction. One might infer that the traumatic neurosis is a result of the exposure of the drives of self-preservation, that is, to danger without any involvement of sexuality.[138] The exclusive primacy of sexuality thus comes under renewed pressure. We are familiar with this issue from previous chapters. But as in earlier texts, Freud also sexualizes traumatic neurosis here. He does so by identifying the drives of self-preservation with the narcissistic libido: "the foetus (…) can only be aware of some vast disturbance in the economy of its narcissistic libido".[139] Elsewhere Freud writes that birth trauma is connected to a drive that wants to re-establish the happy state that existed before birth. According to him, this 'drive for happiness' has an erotic meaning.[140] In this way, the birth trauma is nevertheless drawn back to sexuality.

We know that different phases of life are characterized by different danger- and anxiety situations that are both normal and effective for the period in question. Neurotic patients – to some extent, that is all of us – behave as if a defeated danger situation still exists:

> Although all the agencies for mastering stimuli have long ago been developed within wide limits in his mental apparatus, and although he is sufficiently grown-up to satisfy most of his needs for himself and has long ago learned that castration is no longer practiced as a punishment, he nevertheless behaves as if the old danger-situations still existed, they keeps hold of all the earlier determinants of anxiety.[141]

A simple and somewhat stereotypical example can clarify what Freud means here. Some adult men still experience every sexual relationship in the oedipal terms of early childhood. However, there is in principle no longer any *a priori* reason for these adults to still reject sexual drive representations for this reason and to fear castration as the punishment hanging over their heads. Yet they cannot prevent a new drive (the attraction by a new sexual object) from still unwinding as if the old danger situation still exists. The new representation becomes as it were contaminated by the old and is repressed for the same reason:

> The fixing factor in repression, then, is the unconscious id's *compulsion to repeat* – a compulsion which in normal circumstances is only done away with by the freely movable function of the ego. (…): the regressive attraction exerted by the repressed impulse and the strength of the repression are so great that the new impulse has no choice but to obey the compulsion to repeat.[142]

As in the first version of *Beyond the Pleasure Principle*, Freud again connects and founds the compulsion to repeat with phylogenetic motifs. In *Inhibitions, Symptoms and Anxiety*, he emphatically refers to puberty in this context. Puberty is the historical sediment of an important event from the history of humankind that caused sexual development to be interrupted in the fifth year of life (latency period) after a first bloom period. Tapping into the infantile sexuality from this first period it starts afresh at the onset of puberty. This bi-phased onset of sexuality is 'the most direct aetiology of the neuroses' because the sexual impulses of adolescence still run the danger of being drawn into repression by the attraction of infantile examples.[143] The 'unconscious id's compulsion to repeat' consequently finds its phylogenetic ground in historical trauma. In his letters to Abraham, Freud adds to this that the 'examples from infancy' have a phylogenetic ground. For example, castration anxiety and the incest barrier associated with it have their origins in the primal history of humankind.[144] Again, as in the first version of *Beyond the Pleasure Principle*, the trauma- and drive model are consequently two sides of the same coin founded in psycho-Lamarckism.

10. Conclusion

We started this chapter with the hypothesis that the contradictions, tensions and shifts *Beyond the Pleasure Principle* attests to can best be elucidated from the genesis of the text. Specifically, we argued that the sixth chapter should be read as a response to the difficulties to which the development in the first five chapters led. In the first part of the text, Freud initially relied on clinical phenomena, particularly on the compulsion to repeat in the dreams of war neurotics and in transference. Inspired by psycho-Lamarckism and Haeckel's recapitulation theory, he interprets this compulsion to repeat as a manifestation of the regressive and conservative character of all drives as such. However, this tragic view is in danger of culminating in a drive monism that Freud rejects. He replaces the clinical premise of his text in the sixth chapter with a speculative question: does death belong intrinsically to life? August Weismann's distinction between germ-plasm and soma should help answer this question. This distinction removes us from the psycho-Lamarckism that was the central point of reference in the first part. Germ-cells are the sole bearers of heredity. They cannot change under the influence of what the soma acquires or what happens to it during its existence. Thus, the germ-plasm Weismann assumes is not traumatizable. Weismann explicitly rejects psycho-Lamarckism.[145]

Freud calls the opposition between the ego-drives and the sexual drives the dynamic correlate of Weismann's morphological distinction. This means that Freud from now on does not, in line with psycho-Lamarckism and the recapitulation theory, understand particularly the sexual drives from the repetition of the primal history of humankind. He broadens these drives to the life drives (Eros), which also include ego-drives. This has important implications regarding the status and meaning of sexuality. The reference to biology as study of all living substances situates the problematic of sexuality in the context of reproduction. Human sexuality is immediately and structurally thought of as sexual reproduction, which is in itself a special case of reproduction. This perspective is at odds with the insights Freud addresses in his *Three Essays on the Theory of Sexuality*. Here, Freud discusses human sexuality in connection and sometimes in confrontation with animal sexuality. Sexuality is thus approached here primarily from an anthropological perspective and not from the perspective of a philosophy of organic life or even a cosmology. In *Three Essays*, sexuality is understood from the problematic of infantile sexuality. This is, according to Freud, essentially autoerotic and focused only on the acquisition of pleasure. The idea that sexuality should be described from or as procreation was therefore dismissed as a 'poetic fable'.[146]

In the sixth chapter, Freud first introduces the concept of death drives, which he thematizes as a tendency to fragmentation in opposition to Eros. The reference to this tendency specifies the notion to reduce tension through which drives are generally characterized in the first five chapters. This specification makes it possible to contrast the death drives with the life drives. Drive dualism, which was under pressure in the first part of the text, is thus restored. At the same time, the issue of repetition and trauma – including the problematic of the war neuroses – fade into the background at the expense of the problematic of aggression. After all, the relationship between the death drives and fragmentation makes it easier to place aggression as an essential dimension of the drives in opposition to sexuality. Freud thus solves a problem that has haunted his work since the first edition of *Three Essays* and the study of the Rat Man: sexuality and aggression are opposed to each other.[147]

The two versions of the text are not mutually exclusive in an absolute sense, but it is also clear that they present different theoretical approaches and argumentations. The respective positions defended therein do not occur in an unproblematic one-on-one relationship. Freud's work is characterized by tensions and shifts on which one needs to keep a close eye to properly understand both the meaning of this work and the wealth of the theoretical trains of thought as well as its evolution. Those who treat *Beyond the Pleasure Principle* as a homogenous text that can be read unequivocally cannot properly understand why it is that in text parts from 1920 drive dualism prevails and in clinical texts the reference to trauma and repetition is paramount. For the problematic of our book, the latter clinical texts are especially important. We showed how, in *Inhibitions, Symptoms and Anxiety*, Freud rather connects to the trauma- and drive model from the first version from the first version of *Beyond the Pleasure Principle*. Moreover, we showed how Freud again came up against the question about the sexual status of trauma. In *Moses and Monotheism*, the last text published in his lifetime, Freud uses this model again to understand the history and character of the Jewish people. Both the relationship between trauma, memory and repetition as well as the question regarding the status of trauma and the relationship between sexuality and aggression are here treated one last time as if in a grand finale.

Chapter 7

Trauma and character: The man Moses

1. Introduction

We have seen in the chapters on the case of the Wolf Man and *Beyond the Pleasure Principle*, that it is very important for a thorough reading to take the genesis of these texts as a point of departure. When we turn our attention in this chapter to *Moses and Monotheism* as a text in which Freud deals extensively with the meaning of trauma for the cultural history and formation of the character of a people and its religion, we will first need to pause and reflect on the history and remarkable construction of this text.

The text comprises three essays of which the first ('Moses an Egyptian') must have been written in 1936. This essay was published in the journal *Imago* in 1937. The second essay ('If Moses was an Egyptian…') was completed in August 1937 and appeared at the end of that year, also in *Imago*. The third and most comprehensive essay ('Moses, his People and Monotheist Religion') was probably written in part from 1936 but certainly not completed until the summer of 1938.[1] This essay comprises two parts. The first, presented by Freud as 'Summary and repetition', largely consists of an added part of the first version of the Moses text that Freud had written but not published in 1934.[2] From that first version we also know the outline and content: an 'historical novel' in three parts.[3]

In *Moses and Monotheism*, the second version of the text is thus supplemented with a substantial part of the first version Freud already penned in 1934. Finally, the following belongs to the remarkable construction of the text: preceding the third essay – thus literally in the middle of the text of the monograph – two forewords ('Prefatory Note I and II') are included. The first was written in Vienna before March 1938; the second in London in June 1938. Schematically, the construction of *Moses and Monotheism* appears as follows:[4]

<table>
<tr><td>First version (before October 1934)</td><td>Published version (1939)</td></tr>
<tr><td>Part 1</td><td rowspan="4">I Moses an Egyptian (end of 1936)</td></tr>
<tr><td>[Introduction]</td></tr>
<tr><td>a) Did Moses live?</td></tr>
<tr><td>b) The Origin of Moses</td></tr>
<tr><td>c) The New religion</td><td rowspan="5">II If Moses was an Egyptian.... (before August 1937)</td></tr>
<tr><td>d) The Exodus from Egypt</td></tr>
<tr><td>e) The Chosen People</td></tr>
<tr><td>f) The Sign of the Covenant and the Name of God</td></tr>
<tr><td>Critical Appendix (after September 1934)</td></tr>
<tr><td></td><td>III Moses, his people and the Monotheist Religion</td></tr>
<tr><td></td><td>Prefatory Note I (March 1938)
Prefatory Note II (March 1938)</td></tr>
<tr><td></td><td>Part 1 (June-July 1938)</td></tr>
<tr><td></td><td>A The Historical Premiss</td></tr>
<tr><td></td><td>B The Latency Period and Tradition</td></tr>
<tr><td></td><td>C The Analogy</td></tr>
<tr><td></td><td>D Application</td></tr>
<tr><td></td><td>E Difficulties</td></tr>
<tr><td>Part 2</td><td>Part 2</td></tr>
<tr><td></td><td>Summary and Recapitulation</td></tr>
<tr><td colspan="2">a/A The People of Israel
b/B The Great Man
c/C The Advance in Intellectuality
d/D Renunciation of Instinct (first part)</td></tr>
<tr><td></td><td>D Renunciation of Instinct (second part)</td></tr>
<tr><td>Part 3</td><td></td></tr>
<tr><td colspan="2">a/E Historical Truth</td></tr>
<tr><td>b) The Tradition in Group Psychology</td><td></td></tr>
<tr><td colspan="2">c/F The Return of the Repressed
d/G Historical Truth
e/H The Historical Development</td></tr>
</table>

In the secondary literature, the history and end-result of the text – a monograph compiled in London – has been interpreted throughout as Freud's very personal reflection on his Jewish heritage and identity,[5] and on the Jewish character and religion against the backdrop of rapidly growing antisemitism. The latter threatened not only Jewish communities and thus also Freud's own family but also seemed to be decisive for the destiny of psychoanalysis in Central Europe.[6] In a letter from September 1934, Freud writes to Arnold Zweig that the new wave of persecution of Jews raises the question how the Jews had become what they were and why they then were able to become the object of hate.[7] The question then, Freud writes to Lou Andreas Salomé in January 1935, is "what really created the particular character of the Jew".[8] To answer this question, one needs to return to the origin of the people as Jewish people. And that means a return to Moses. After all, "Moses created the Jews", that is, he is the one who gave them the character that would always be their hallmark.[9] To be able to answer the question about the emergence of the character of the Jews, we must first consider who Moses was and what he accomplished.[10]

That Freud did not immediately publish his first draft of the manuscript, written in 1934, was due in part to dissatisfaction with the content and the need he felt to rework and revise (from 1936). At least as important is also Freud's anxiety that his ideas about the Jewish religion would vex important and influential people in the church and politics, and that this indignation might translate into a ban on psychoanalysis.[11] Specifically, Freud has his 'greatest enemy' Father Wilhelm Schmidt in mind here, whom he suspects of using his contacts in the Vatican to thwart psychoanalysis in Italy.[12]

2. *The Moses project as character analysis*

From the outset, the Moses project was meant as a study of the emergence of the particular character of the Jews.[13] We are thus concerned with a character study or a 'character analysis'. Freud uses this latter concept in 'Analysis Terminable and Interminable' from 1937. A character analysis is a kind of therapeutic analysis. In both forms of analysis, the same 'themes' and 'laws' are expressed.[14] Both forms of analysis work with the same theoretical assumptions and deliver similar results. We can understand this as an effect of the psychoanalytical perspective as Freud had developed it in *Three Essays*, among other texts. The various psychoneuroses show in a magnified and caricatured way aspects of the psychic life of all human beings. Therefore, one can ideally gain insight into the common human psychological structures and dynamics through studying the various psychoneuroses. By extension, Freud could also group and describe 'character types' from the analysis.[15]

In addition, we have already seen that the analysis of character changes occupied an important place in Freud's case studies. The traumatic experience in the Rat Man's early years – the nervous reaction to his own anger attack against his father – was the cause of a change in his character.[16] In our discussion of the case study of the Wolf Man we considered at length the experiences and impressions that led to a change in character. This change of character was determined by moments of fixation and repression that then solidified into fixed 'reaction patterns'. Childhood neurosis then arose based on these fixations, repressions and reaction patterns.[17]

Another link for Freud's character analysis of an entire people was the turn to phylogeny (from *Totem and Taboo*), discussed in a previous chapter, and the cultural-historical development of human constitution. Notably, in 'Overview of the Transference Neuroses', Freud had elaborated this speculative theory about a series of traumatic experiences in the (prehistoric) Ice Age as determining the general structure of sexual and ego-development of all humans. In *Moses and Monotheism,* Freud connects with these intuitions. The character of Jews and their religion can be understood as the result of their own historical development strengthened by phylogenetic (constitutional) patterns.[18]

If *Moses and Monotheism* is indeed a character analysis of a people, the Moses project can be read as a case study. For Freud, this nation does not comprise a collection of individuals with own characters. The nation and its character are also not an average or cross-section of a whole of characters. Freud describes the Jewish people as the whole of consecutive generations with the same character. The nation is one set of consecutive generations in which the same character is repeated. That repetition is, as we shall see, possible through inheriting the shared and unconsciously persistent memory-traces of a traumatic experience and the associated calibrated response patterns. *Moses and Monotheism* is not the first text in which Freud takes a step from 'individual psychology' to 'group psychology'. What is indeed new is that in this study it concerns the question about the emergence and 'inheritance' of the one character from generation to generation within a specific people.[19] Central to this 'case study' is then the question of aetiology of that character, which clearly shows neurotic traits, according to Freud. We will see that also in this case study, Freud is particularly interested in the interaction between constitutional and accidental factors.

3. *The great man Moses (1934)*

Before a closer examination of the way in which Freud brings his trauma theory into *Moses and Monotheism* and rethinks it, we should first reflect on the first Moses version from 1934, that is, the sections A to H in part 2 ('Summary and Recapitulation') of the third essay.[20] Freud sets himself the goal of analyzing the particular character of the Jewish people and the cohesion between this character and their fate (namely persecutions). For this, he departs from several noticeable characteristics, namely a 'particularly high opinion of themselves' and 'a peculiar confidence in life' – even in times of the greatest adversity imaginable. He traces these characteristics back to the notion of a people chosen by God. It was Moses who religiously anchored the feeling of self-esteem and superiority in monotheism (adopted from pharaoh Akhenaten) and the idea of being chosen. However, in reality Moses was the one who had chosen a group of Semitic serfs to be liberated from Egypt. In this way, he imprinted them "with their definitive character".[21]

According to Freud, several important factors enabled Moses to stamp them in this way is. A first factor is the need, strongly present in every group of people, for authority and the desire for a father figure whom one can admire. The character of the 'great man' Moses fully meets this. His character is marked by strength of will, decisiveness, tempestuousness, a strongly developed independence, and a 'divine unconcern' bordering on the ruthless and unrelenting.[22] That such person could make an impression on the humble Semitic serfs in Egypt can, however, not be completely explained from his character. Crucially, he proclaimed an impressive depiction of one, omnipotent god very similar in character to the Moses admired by the people. To have had a long-lasting effect on the character of the Jewish people, it was not enough that Moses had once chosen and led a people away from Egypt. The idea that one 'greater god' had chosen and liberated the people was decisive here.[23]

The idea of a 'greater god' is expressed particularly in the prohibition against image-making. The greatness of Moses's god does not consist of a physical strength that makes him more powerful than other gods. His greatness is his exaltation above the material and thereby also above the violent. According to Freud, we can see it as 'a triumph of the spirit over the senses'. This triumph implies drive renunciation and an ideal of ethical perfection that is best expressed in a containment of the roughness and tendency to violence that characterized the surrounding peoples.[24] That the nation was prepared for such a renunciation of drives cannot be explained by reference to a willing acceptance of the lack of satisfaction. After all, that would lead to a 'lasting tension owing to unpleasure' that would rapidly become unbearable for the ego (here: the people). So how is this drive renunciation still possible? Freud refers to the idea explored in *Beyond the Pleasure Principle* that the presence of unpleasure is not always contrary to the pleasure principle. When we assume that unpleasure for one system is pleasure for the other system, the renunciation of drive impulses suddenly becomes plausible, according to Freud. We then only need to assume that another system can derive a 'yield of pleasure' from this renunciation. The ego can certainly achieve this yield when, through drive renunciation, it is no longer vulnerable to the impelling, accusatory and sabotaging influence of the superego.[25] Freud notes about this: "The ego feels elevated; it is proud of the instinctual renunciation, as though it were a valuable achievement".[26]

According to Freud, the monotheistic idea could have been lost in the first generation after the rebellion of people against their leader with his 'wrathful temper and his relentlessness' and the rejection of his demanding religion. That this did not happen, Freud argues (in 1934), is thanks to the action of men who "revived the fading tradition, who renewed the admonitions and demands made by Moses, and who did not rest till what was lost had been established once again".[27] Put differently, there was a strong tendency to keep the memory of the great man Moses and his monotheistic idea alive through the oral tradition and written record. The memory of Moses was thus kept alive and in this way his will, after the initial rejection of his ideas, nevertheless persevered.

According to Freud, the most glaring sign of this submission to Moses's will is circumcision. Circumcision shows that the drive renunciation cannot only be explained from an economic principle in which unpleasure in one system can result in 'yield of pleasure' for the other system. Circumcision specifically shows the meaning of a phylogenetic factor that is repeated in the "abbreviated development of the human individual" and again in every generation.[28] Here it is about the influence of a powerful father threatening with punishment and demanding drive renunciation from the child. In primordial times this father showed his power by castrating his sons, with circumcision being a later 'symbolic substitute'. It is this powerful will of the father to which the whole people is prepared to submit even though the price (unpleasure through drive renunciation) is so high and the demand so unreasonable.[29]

Noticeable in this first version from 1934 is the fact that the murder of Moses, that is so very central to the final version of the text (1938), is only mentioned once and practically in passing.[30] In this first version, the meaning of Moses is not determined by the murderous deed and its traumatic effects, but – more in line with *Group Psychology and the Analysis of the Ego* – through identification with and admiration of Moses's ruling and leadership qualities, i.e., the intellectual acts, self-assurance and independence that characterize the personalities of all great rulers and leaders since the primal fathers in primal times. In the first version, Freud focuses fully on the decisive influence of Moses as 'extraordinary genius' in the 'aetiology' of the Jewish character and the Jewish religion.[31]

The question Freud raises here (in 1934) is why Moses's god could not be and remain a mighty god among other gods (henotheism), and why strict monotheism could persist in Judaism. Connecting to the answer to this question, he refers to the doctrines of the conviction enshrined in monotheistic religion and compulsively repeated that the one true god is also an eternal god, that is, connected in a special way to humanity from the beginning of humanity. For the follower of religion, this conviction is true in a 'material' sense. Thereby Freud means to say that it is a religious statement ('I believe in an eternal god') that – through a process of rationalization – could attain the status of a dogma ('god exists and is eternal'). According to Freud, dogmas have the pretense to articulate 'material' or factual truths. They are assumed "assertions about facts and conditions of external (or internal) reality", Freud writes in *The Future of an Illusion*.[32] In the 1934 Moses text, Freud is however not interested in a further analysis of the illusory wish nature of the material truth of doctrines. His attention goes out to the conviction that the one and only god was connected to humanity in an exceptional way since the beginning of humanity. In this aspect of the conviction, a 'historical truth' is expressed, namely the relationship with the primal history of humanity. The truth that manifests in religious convictions exists in taking up in a 'distorted' and 'concealing' way the memories of the primal time, thereby giving statements of faith a well-nigh compulsive force.[33] This 'truth' distinguishes itself from a real or material truth because it is repressed and acts unconsciously without ever becoming conscious memory or knowledge. About this, Freud writes: "When Moses brought the people the idea of a single god, it was not a novelty but signified the revival of an experience in the primaeval ages of the human family which had long vanished from men's conscious memory".[34]

In these primaeval times, there was a single person, the primal father, "who was bound to appear huge at that time and who afterwards returned in men's memory elevated to divinity".[35] Left behind in the human constitution, the memory-traces of the impressions of a great man from the primaeval ages were awakened by Moses and his god. The actions of Moses and the monotheistic idea he proclaimed activated a constitutional factor.[36] The 'truth' of Jewish monotheism exists in 'repeating' an original prehistorical exaltation of the father to god.[37] Put differently, in the ontogeny of the character of the people of the Jewish faith, a phylogenetic scheme is repeated. The emphasis is placed on the reactivation of a historical truth, identifying with and admiration of the character of the father.

However, in the final Moses text from 1938, the identification with the father – and so with Moses – as 'great man' is no longer at the center. In the last draft of the text, the character of the Jewish people and strict monotheism will be fully understood from the devastating impact of a traumatic event. What makes the Jewish character, unites the people and separates from others is trauma.

4. Historiography, memory and text distortion

We now turn our attention to the Moses text as Freud publishes it in 1937-38, first in parts and then as a monograph. The first two essays, in analogy to his big case studies, read like 'case history'. They consist of reconstructions of the historical chronology and decisive moments and impressions in the establishment of the Jewish religion through its own coverage thereof in official historiography. The assumption that Moses must have been a high-ranking Egyptian in a pharaoh's court[38] is in the first essay the point of departure for a "purely historical study" in which Freud, with the help of the religious-historical and exegetic insights of his time, wants to reconstruct the earliest history of the Jewish people and particularly the origin of his religion.[39] Freud argues that if Moses was an Egyptian, he would have made his Egyptian religion – a monotheism – the religion of the Jewish people. That is possible if we assume that Moses lived during the time of Pharaoh Akhenaten, so around 1350 before Christ. Of this Akhenaten is known that he made a revolutionary turn towards monotheism when he pushed forward the Aten cult as the only permissible one. After his presumably violent death, this reformation is turned back under the Amun priests. This brings Freud to suggest that Moses possibly had to flee Egypt, but he did not do so without taking along a people chosen by him with the sole purpose of bringing them to Akhenaten's monotheism.[40]

That Jewish monotheism comes from Egypt is, however, debatable, as Freud knows. For example, the historian Eduard Meyer argued that monotheism must have originated in the Sinai Desert near Meribath-Kadesh. Jewish tribes there would have adopted the worship of a local volcano god, Yahweh. According to Meyer, Moses was the founder of this Yahweh monotheism. But this Moses was no Egyptian nobleman. He was a Midianite of low origin.[41] To solve the problem of the two primal murders, Freud calls on an exegetic study by Ernst Sellin from 1922, *Mose und seine Bedeutung für die israelitisch-jüdische Religionsgeschichte.* In this study, Sellin argues that Moses must have been the leader of the exodus from Egypt and that this Moses would have been killed by his own people. This murder would not have been committed because the people rejected the high spiritual (moral, intellectual) demands of Moses (as Freud argues) [42], but because the people no longer tolerated the harsh punishment they were dealt by Moses on account of their idolatry.[43] After this murder, the semitic tribes that left Egypt would then have united with other tribes in the mount Sinai area into what would quickly become the Jewish people. Freud essentially follows this thesis of the murder of the Egyptian Moses and the amalgamation of various Semitic tribes.

The merging of two tribes or 'peoples' did not take place immediately after the exodus but is, according to Freud, rather a process of multiple generations that provisionally ends in Kadesh, about one hundred years after the exodus from Egypt and the murder of Moses.[44] In Kadesh, this merging under the leadership of a Midianite priest (who in lore would have been given the name 'Moses') takes the form of a 'compromise'. From Egypt comes the custom of circumcision (as a sign of election), the monotheistic idea (Yahweh as the only god who can be addressed by the name Adonai) and the class of priests (Levites) who watch over the higher level of intellectuality brought from Egypt (notably legislation in writing).[45] But at the same time this compromise also means the strictly monotheistic idea does not persist. For now, Yahweh retains the brutal character of the Vulcan god that time and again reprises the battle against other gods of other peoples. The monotheistic idea was 'diluted' and had in fact made space for henotheism with polytheistic elements.[46]

So far, Freud tries to reconstruct a historical development with as much anchoring as possible in historical data known from literature and extensive research sources (of sources such as texts, clay tablets and stelae, archaeological finds).[47] But this reconstruction is more than an attempt at bringing different historical details and biblical-scientific theory forming together into one perspective. Freud wants to show that the compromise of Kadesh and the Jewish character should be understood from 'dualities': the merging of two peoples and of two gods (Aten and Yahweh); the existence of two founders with the name Moses and of two foundations of the religion; the collapse of the people into two kingdoms (Israel and Judah).[48] According to Freud, these dualities "are the necessary consequences of the first one: the fact that one portion of the people had an experience which must be regarded as traumatic and which the other portion escaped".[49] This 'first duality' lies at the root of all later opposing tendencies through Jewish history and is decisive for Jewish character.[50] Jewish character – or Jewish identity – is thus not founded in one stable and unequivocal base by Freud but is instead traced back to tense relationships between different locations and moments of origin outside of Israel, namely in Egypt and Kadesh (Arabia). Put differently, this character has no foundation in an idealized religious or national past of an always already assumed unity of a people and a place, but rather in a negation and erasure of original dualities.[51]

Freud is aware of the inevitable shortcomings of his reconstruction work. The problem is not so much a shortage of sources but the fact that most of the sources on Moses and the history of the Jewish people are written (or finally edited) in the first period after the Babylonian exile, so from about 515 before Christ.[52] Jewish historiography as it is captured in Bible texts reaches its definitive form in a period of, on the one hand, reflection on the developments that led to the fall of Jerusalem, the destruction of the temple of Solomon and the beginning of exile (from 587 before Christ) and on the other the actual (post-exilic) assignment of a religious, political and social reorganization of Israel. The stories around Moses are recorded and adapted to serve the 'actual task' of rebuilding (second building of the temple, religious laws, political institutions).

Analogous to earlier case studies the question intruding here is if the history of Moses is not the result of 'retrospective phantasizing'. The stories around Moses – of the wonderful rescue in the rush basket through the exodus up until his vanishing without a trace shortly before the entry into Canaan – could be read as an attempt of a people to paint its own history as grand and proud. In this way, the insignificance and failure of the past would be covered with phantasized material.[53] At the same time the actual rebuilding project following the Babylonic exile would find support in a blueprint for a good ending under the command of a powerful leader. According to Freud, Moses is however not a phantasized hero created by the people after the fact but in the first place a historical figure whose life story deviates substantially from that of a typical hero.[54]

An important argument for this is contained in the process and characteristics of transcription. According to Freud the process of transcribing the own history already started in Kadesh, the process finding a first highlight in the work of the Jahwist and the Elohist[55] around the year 1000 before Christ. The first version of the Hexateuch[56] comes about in this period. The first historiography is entirely dedicated to the 'compromise' of Kadesh and the still 'vivid memory' of Moses. They are 'mausoleums' lauding Moses as the imposing leader of the exodus. But they are also texts with a strong tendency to "repress... the memory of the fate with which their leader and lawgiver had met".[57] "The violent end of the great man" was thus – successfully "withdrawn from the knowledge of later generations".[58] That earliest historiography, moreover, makes every effort to cover up Moses's Egyptian heritage and his religion.[59] So Freud also concludes that the Bible indeed contains "precious and, indeed, invaluable historical data, which, however, have been distorted by the influence of powerful tendentious purposes and embellished by die products of poetic invention".[60] Here we recognize a problematic from other case studies: memories of traumatic events (during childhood) are forgotten throughout, and come to be expressed as 'mutilated' and 'revised' in later phantasies. Analogous to this, it is also applicable to Biblical sources being 'falsified, mutilated and amplified', as a function of the 'repression' and 'disavowal' of the painful and violent event of the murder of Moses in the past.

From Kadesh, there is thus a tendency in historiography to suppress the memory of the murder of Moses. From the onset, this suppression is an essential part of the process of textual preservation. Beside that was also an oral tradition in which what was 'left out' or 'altered' in the textual preservation could, in principle, have been kept 'untouched'. This oral tradition was withdrawn from the process of 'textual distortion' but was at the same time just as exposed to 'revisions and mutilations' inherent in the fragile process of oral tradition.[61] Also in this oral tradition, the murder of Moses could be suppressed in this way.

Later post-exilic historiography, which also partially consisted of revision (final edit) of all the existing textual parts of the Hexateuch, has another character. The historiography from this period actually even

> seeks to establish continuity between its contemporary period and the remote Mosaic past; it seeks to disavow precisely what we have described as the most striking fact about Jewish religious history, namely that there is a yawning gap between the law-giving of Moses and the later Jewish

> religion—a gap which was first filled by the worship of Yahweh, and was only slowly patched up afterwards.[62]

This continuity was created by asserting that the idea of a single god was brought to the people by Moses. Here sets in motion another force in the process of capturing the texts, namely a 'piety' that sought to preserve everything as it was transmitted. In the texts, this tendency becomes visible in gaps, contradictions, repetitions – in short, "indications which reveal things to us which it was not intended to communicate".[63] One example of such a memory-trace is the Hosea text in which the murder of Moses would have been confessed after all in secrecy. Thereby late Jewish historiography offers links to a 'construction' of the repressed and the obscured. Sellin was fortunate to have been able to 'guess' the murder of Moses.[64] The exegete produces valuable construction work here, dares to formulate a hypothesis and waits for testing, confirmation or rejection.

Through this tendency of retaining traces and guarding continuity, the effect of Moses's performance can fully unfurl during the post-exilic time: the monotheistic idea, the demand of higher spiritualization and the accompanying renunciation of drives. The Egyptian roots of the Jewish religion, Moses's Egyptian heritage and especially also his murder were and remained suppressed. What 'returned from repression' through activating the past was the message of Moses, the monotheistic idea that from now on would be adhered to in an almost compulsive manner. The god of Moses finally triumphed over the ferocious and sensual god, Yahweh.[65]

In the first version of *Moses* from 1934, Freud already noted the long timespans – about 800 years – between the introduction of the monotheistic idea by the great man Moses and the long period of 'incubation' needed for the idea to unfurl, and indeed such that they "gained more and more power over men's minds, and which finally succeeded in transforming the god Yahweh into the god of Moses and in calling back to life the religion of Moses which had been established and then abandoned long centuries earlier".[66] According to Freud this was possible because notably members of the priestly caste kept alive, through the verbal transmission and with the assistance of old records, the memory of a 'glorious past'. In the sections from 1937-38, Freud comments extensively on the problematic of these long timespans. The problem with the sources on Moses is indeed that there is a period of about 800 years between Moses's deeds and the eventual fixation (*Fixierung*) of the Bible texts.[67] What needs to be explained is why the Moses tradition did not gradually disappeared in this period but rather gained strength. That the people 'compulsively' adhered to the monotheistic idea can, according to Freud, not be interpreted with reference to the 'actual task' of late Jewish historiography. This compulsive conviction and resolve can also not be the result of pure notifications about the greatness of Moses and exhortations to submit to his will. In reflecting on this problem, the attention now completely shifts to the "experience which must be regarded as traumatic", of the murder of Moses, the reactions of the people and the meaning thereof for the long process of capturing the own history and for the revival of the monotheistic idea.[68] *Moses and Monotheism* is an attempt – through historical reconstructions – to analytically 'construct' a traumatic primal scene that is decisive for the later establishment of the character of a people.

5. *Construction and fixation*

In the article 'Constructions in Analysis', Freud briefly describes the aim of psychoanalytical treatment. Freud repeats what he wrote in *Beyond the Pleasure Principle* among other texts: the analyst's construction ('guessing' the repressed) is ideally confirmed by the patient.[69] Patients 'suffer from reminiscences' that constantly impose themselves on consciousness but encounter resistance. In such cases of resistances, these reminiscences can only be reproduced in repetitions of the repressed as contemporary experiences ('acting out'). The goal of therapy is not only to recall the repressed but also to make it into a memory, that is, to an event that belongs in the past.[70] About this, Freud writes: "That work would consist in liberating the fragment of historical truth from its distortions and its attachments to the actual present day and in leading it back to the point in the past to which it belongs" (Freud 1937d: 268). With the concept of 'historical truth' in this article Freud implies nothing other than 'the forgotten' or 'the repressed', which means, the repressed memory, continuing to work in the unconscious, of a specific event that took place in the past.[71] The task of an analyst is to 'guess' what has been forgotten "from the traces which it has left behind or, more correctly, to *construct* it".[72] We are reaching a theme we already discussed in the chapter on the Wolf Man: the construction of a traumatic primal scene in its meaning for character change and the aetiology of neurosis.

In this regard, Freud notes that Jewish historiography is 'construction work'. In its pursuit of continuity throughout its history, it is adamant that the monotheistic idea in all its rigor was received by Moses. It thus connects Moses and the monotheistic idea, thereby attempting to 'repair' the relationship between the actual (intellectual, religious) state of the people and decisive historical events. However, Freud believes that this construction fails and spots within it an analogy with delusion formation in psychosis. After all, delusions are an attempt at repairing the link to reality, an attempt at reversing the libidinal withdrawal from reality.[73] But it is a failed attempt, because what is repressed ultimately remains repressed. The attempt to restore the relationship with reality in both cases – historiography and delusion – runs ashore in distortions that are repeatedly carried out with 'resoluteness' and 'persuasiveness' and claim to be true. On the historiographical idea about the historical events around Moses, Freud writes:

> We have long understood that a portion of forgotten truth lies hidden in delusional ideas, that when this returns it has to put up with distortions and misunderstandings, and that the compulsive conviction which attaches to the delusion arises from this core of truth and spreads out on to the errors that wrap it round.[74]

According to Freud, the formation of delusions in psychosis exposes an important aspect of Jewish historiography, namely the "upward drive (*Auftrieb*) of the unconscious and the return of the repressed" as expressed in the "compulsive belief attaching to delusions" and that draws its strength from a childhood source.[75] The contribution historical truth makes to the formation of delusion consists in delivering the conviction with which belief is attached to the delusion (and with which a piece of reality is also disavowed).[76] The influence of the historical truth makes itself felt as a power that has its source in a further repression, a terrible event 'disavowed in the remote past' that must have happened at that time. What applied to the primal scene in the study of the Wolf Man, also applies here to the 'primal scene' of the Jewish people: it is not made into a conscious memory but forms the core of a forgotten past that leaves traces in the unconscious, and as such puts pressure on psychic life shaping character with its neurotic traits from the inside.

It is then certainly no coincidence that Freud speaks about a process of fixation in Jewish historiography. Thereby he aims in the first place on the process of fixation of the past by writing down traditions. But that is not all. Jewish historiography strives for continuity and (re)constructing the past. Here a tendency becomes visible, to remember a forgotten experience and relive a repetition of it. Historiography is also an effect of fixation (*Fixierung*) on a part of the past from which a people has not been able to disentangle itself. The historiography of the post-exile period is the effect of a persisting trauma and a pre-eminent indication that fixation and repetition compulsion are taken up as a permanent tendency in the Jewish character "precisely because, their true basis and historical origin are forgotten" and remain forgotten.[77] The 'positive' fixation and repetition compulsion can, after all, only continue existing through a 'negative' effect of a trauma: the defense reactions, the tendency specifically not to remember what was once forgotten. These reactions (resistances) can also be called fixations. These are fixations with an opposite tendency that ensure that the attempt to remember a forgotten experience is repeatedly sabotaged and postponed in Jewish historiography

This maps out the most important moments in the 'aetiology' of the Jewish character and the Jewish religion as these can be reconstructed through analyzing Jewish historiography (in analogy with a clinical case history): the traumatic murder of Moses and the return at a later stage of the repressed in an amalgam of obsessional neurotic symptoms (monotheism). The central issue in the remaining parts of the Moses text concerns the question of the interaction between accidental and constitutional factors in the 'aetiology' of the Jewish character.

6. *Historical truth and archaic heritage*

Just like for example in the case of the Wolf Man, it is the 'firm conviction' with which a certain idea is repeatedly hauled out in Jewish historiography that is the contact point for the construction of 'a real event' and 'something terrible' in the past. However, in *Moses and Monotheism*, Freud does not speak about a primal scene but about a 'historical truth'. In the first version of Moses, this concept referred to the constitutional (phylogenetic) factor, i.e. to the earliest experiences of humanity (the great and god-exalted primal father) and its effect later when it is awakened by an accidental factor (the great man Moses and the character of his god). In the final Moses text, the repressed historical facts around Moses – the fact that he was an Egyptian and was murdered by his people– were included in the notion 'historical truth' as an "important link between the forgotten event of primaeval times and its later emergence in the form of monotheist religions".[78] Unlike in the first version, this forgotten incident does not in the first place relate to the greatness of the primal father and his exaltation to god but to the murder of the primal father and its repetition in the murder of Moses.[79] That is the 'historical truth' as it would be communicated in a veiled manner in the late Jewish historiography (concretely: in Hosea) and as it would be expressed in the rock-solid conviction that Moses gave the monotheistic idea to his people.

We can take a further step in our analysis of the 'historical truth' and the continued effect of memory-traces. According to Freud, two factors are determinative in the psychical life and character of individuals and nations. The first factor is a constitutional factor. It concerns "elements with a phylogenetic origin—an *archaic heritage*".[80] Under archaic heritage, Freud in the first instance understands 'constitutional dispositions'. With these, he means "the capacity and tendency (…) to enter particular lines of development and to react in a particular manner to certain excitations, impressions and stimuli".[81] To be clear, the idea of disposition is not used in this context to indicate a 'development disorder' in a certain people (analogous to the development of an individual). As in earlier case studies (such as the Dora case), Freud understands the constitutional disposition to be the ability and inclination *of all people* to take certain developmental directions or respond to stimuli in a specific way.[82] In a previous chapter we already saw that Freud in his lectures from 1916-17 regards the human 'constitution' or 'constitutional disposition' as the result of an earlier interaction between constitutional and accidental factors. In *Moses and Monotheism* this idea is applied once more. Through a series of traumatic experiences in primaeval times, the sexual development and ego formation of all people is 'disturbed'. The traumatic past left a lasting trail in the libidinal life (phylogeny). Primal traumatic experiences led to somatic and psychical modifications that are inherited as acquired characteristics from one generation to the next. The general human constitutional disposition, created in primaeval times by constitutional and accidental factors, is transferred from generation to generation to be acquired and repeated in the lives of individuals (ontogeny). When we discuss Freud's explanations of 'latency' at length below, we shall see that especially delayed sexual development (the development of sexual organs and sexual functions during puberty) are to be understood as 'organic'[83] acquired characteristics in the form of a 'disturbance' in the libidinal life of all.

Beside these 'organic' constitutional dispositions, this archaic inheritance contains "things that were innately present at birth".[84] Under these contents he understands firstly thought-connections established "during the historical development of speech and which have to be repeated now".[85] His concrete reference here is to the appearance of 'typical' symbols in the dreams of children.[86] Another part of the contents comprises the "memory-traces of the experience of earlier generations" that are determinative for a 'typical' reaction to a particular experience.[87] Here Freud refers concretely to the Oedipus- and castration complex and the way in which phylogenetic schemes – like in the case of the Wolf Man – could reorganize individual experiences and impressions and furnish them with new meanings. Thus, not only do these complexes describe the relationship between individual children and their parents but they also contain typical contents and reactions that can, according to Freud, be traced back to traumatic events in the primaeval age, in the primal family, when the primal father was beaten to death. Beside the constitutional factor, there is a second that consists of self-experienced, accidental events and impressions that continue in later life. As concrete example Freud names the murder of Moses (and the 'judicial murder' of Christ – see below) as repetition of a prehistoric murder of the primal father.[88] In the murder of Moses, the primal murder is repeated as 'action', but without the people knowing or realizing that it is repeating the murder. The primal murder is after all never remembered as such. According to Freud, we can argue that the murder of Moses repeats a primal murder, when we assume that memory-traces from the primal murder were inherited and preserved. These memory-traces are awakened by the act of the murder of Moses and are determinative for the reactions to the murder and the later effect on the Jewish character. The meaning of the murder of Moses for the shaping of the Jewish character is thus largely determined by this constitutional factor. This allowed a current event to be modelled and amplified according to a 'phylogenetic scheme'.

In *Moses and Monotheism*, Freud includes the constitutional and accidental factors in their complementarity[89] and continuing effect (reaction formations, memory-traces) in the notion of tradition. We have seen that with the concept of tradition, Freud refers in earlier parts of the text to the process of oral history transmitted over generations. Not only does this oral tradition have many 'distortions' but it also, as 'information from outside', lacks the power to give religion a compulsive character.[90] According to Freud, the force for the compulsion must be seen as an inner 'upward drive' of the repressed that wants to return to the consciousness. The formation of a people's character can thus also not result from stories told by prophets or historians but indeed from an "inherited tradition (…) not one transmitted by communication".[91] Tradition is here described here in psycho-Lamarckian terms as the whole of psychical characteristics and contents acquired through inheritance.[92] The Jewish character of each subsequent generation is not shaped by socialization in a whole of practices and (religious) presentations but is a repetition of the character of previous generations through inheritance of an 'archaic heritage'. This heritage determines the character of each new generation *from the inside*.[93] In this way, the tradition itself is nothing other than the whole of successive generations with the same Jewish character, the same inherited memory-traces and reaction patterns that can be traced back to traumatic experiences and impressions from a distant past.[94] Freud thus calls on psycho-Lamarckism to defend the thesis that the tradition determines the character of the Jewish people from within. Thereby Freud implicitly repeats an idea from earlier studies: trauma works from inside. And because that character is marked by obsessive-compulsive aspects, we could say that the *tradition* corresponds with a *disposition* to a neurosis.

Whereas in the first version of *Moses and Monotheism* Freud still emphasizes the characteristics of conceit and self-confidence, the obsessive aspects of the character are central in the final version of the text. The focus is on a 'reaction formation' of a sense of guilt that emerged spontaneously after the murder of Moses and would increasingly become a fixed part of the religious system.[95] The most important inherited character trait is this sense of guilt. The historic origin of this sense of guilt was – as we have seen – covered up. As motivation for the sense of guilt, the various prophets would refer to current situations of sinning against God, the just punishments resulting from these sins in times of adversity and the need for even greater obedience and renunciation of passion. The high degree of 'spiritualization' and the strong ethical consciousness can be traced back to this sense of guilt.

According to Freud, there seemed to be a moment in Jewish history when the 'historical truth' almost breaks through into the consciousness, that is, becomes a conscious memory. Freud sees this moment in Paul, a religiously disposed man in whom "the dark traces of the past lurked in his mind, ready to break through into its more conscious regions".[96] Paul had recognized that Judaism is motivated by a strong unconscious sense of guilt. He knows to link this sense of guilt to a 'crime against God' that must have taken place somewhere in prehistoric times. But the murder of Moses also does not return to him in conscious memory. The intuition of a once committed crime against God is to wit not involved in the crime against Moses but links to the memory-traces of the primal crime against 'primal father deified' after his death. Paul could hardly contain this 'truth' and accommodated it in a new delusional distortion, namely the good news of deliverance from guilt and (original) sin. That this salvation was only possible through a sacrificial death covertly indicates that the primal crime must have been murder, Freud believes. This 'truth' is expressed only in this distorted and thereby covered way in Paul's message. What emerges is a new 'phantasy' about original sin and salvation – a wish phantasy in which feelings of guilt are abolished through the idea of the death and resurrection of Christ.[97]

Most of the Jews did not go along with Paul's new religious creation. They "halted at the recognition of the great father" and were not able to associate their feelings of guilt with a past crime. Instead, they 'acted', that means, repeated the disavowing their deed "and blocked their access to the point from which Paul was later to start his continuation of the primal history".[98] With the latter, Freud is not aiming so much at the murder of the primal father but on his subsequent exaltation to any god (monotheistic idea). This 'historical truth' is expressed in a veiled and distorted way in the Christian phantasy of forgiveness, salvation and resurrection. But with the emphasis on the death and resurrection of Christ, the guilt because of the murder (of the primal father, of Moses) could be largely reduced: Christ is the resurrected Moses. And the death of the messiah is not as much a repetition of a traumatic event as an instrumental necessity in a salvation history (wish phantasy). Seen that way, this wish phantasy is an attempt at healing.

7. Latency and trauma

We have seen that Freud wrote a first version of *Moses and Monotheism* in 1934. We also saw that he subsequently, through a process of revision and expansion, published the first two 'historical ' essays in 1937 and 1938. When the monograph finally appears, the third essay turns out to consist of one-third of the 1934 'historical novel'. The new material mostly consists of digressions on Paul, Christianity and the motives for antisemitism, and of the theoretical reflection on the role of constitutional (phylogenetic) and accidental factors in the emergence of the Jewish character and the Jewish faith. Freud would structure this reflection from the analogy with the aetiology of the neuroses (trauma theory). This reflection takes as point of departure the question why over 800 years of history, the Moses tradition (and specifically the idea of monotheism) did not fade but was eventually able to dominate. How can one understand an 'abandoned function' of an event from a distant past? Which psychotherapeutic insights and notions could provide clarification here?

But there is more. What also needs interpretation is the *compulsion to repeat* that manifests in different ways in Jewish history. Late Jewish historiography shows how the 'upward drive' of the repressed constantly insists but does, however, not lead to the recollection of the murder. In all the texts (written and edited by a plethora of authors) that emerged over time, we see the same tendency towards a compulsive insistence and repetition of the same conviction (the monotheistic idea) containing – distorted and disguised – traces of a traumatic event (historical truth). The Jewish historiography repeatedly 'acted out' and reproduced an unpleasurable and repressed event without remembering it. Striving for historical continuity, it cultivated a situation in which the forgotten experience could ardently continue to insist ('upward drive'). In this way, the compulsion to repeat became a 'permanent trend' in the Jewish character.[99]

Not only the compulsion to repeat in Jewish historiography and in the Jewish character deserves an analytical interpretation. Because the murder of Moses can be seen as a repetition of the primal murder and thereby of an unpleasurable traumatic experience, it can obtain the meaning and impact it has. Even if we had assumed the primal murder never really took place, it still – or rather preeminently – must be made understandable why this people could repeat and relive this 'primal phantasy' with all its unpleasurable effects. And then there is finally still the stubborn denial of the murder of Moses as reaction to Paul's fabricated 'good news' of redemption of guilt and sin. This denial thus equals the stubborn 'repetition' of a consciousness of guilt that would hereafter – up to Freud's own time – further be strengthened by the reproach repeatedly made by the Christians that the Jews murdered Christ.

According to Freud, the process of character formation as it takes shape in Jewish religious history can be clarified by psychoanalysis from the model of the aetiology of neuroses.[100] Here Freud does not search for analogies between concrete psychoneuroses – such as obsessional neurosis – and religion but rather wants to interpret religion from the general structure of pathogenesis. The emphasis lies, as we have seen, on the interaction of constitutional and accidental factors and on the temporality of trauma in its meaning for character formation and religious choice. The scheme of development of the neuroses is simple to reproduce, Freud believes: "early trauma—defence—latency—outbreak of neurotic illness—partial return of the repressed".[101] That does not mean the aetiology of the neuroses "in general may be regarded as traumatic". This does not mean that neuroses are necessarily only acquired. Certainly, traumas are "impressions experienced early and later forgotten", but such a traumatic impression cannot always be found in the earliest history of a neurotic subject.[102] After all, neuroses can – according to the model of the complemental series – also develop exclusively from constitutional factors. What are the most important characteristics of these traumas? Firstly, they occur in early childhood (until about the age of five). Secondly, these are forgotten experiences or impressions. Thirdly, they relate to "impressions of a sexual and aggressive nature". The sexual factor thus emphatically plays a role.[103]

What makes a certain experience or impression traumatic is not per se determined by the gravity or a special quality of the experience or impression. We have already seen in the various case studies that traumatic experiences do not per se have to be experiences of serious abuse but could also have a banal character – think of the 'primal scenes' in the Rat Man and the Wolf Man. In line with earlier case studies, Freud then also argues that the 'unusual, abnormal reaction' to an experience makes it a traumatic one. Here, it concerns defense reactions that sort a traumatic effect from inside. These are repressions, avoidances, inhibitions and anxieties aiming at pushing away the memory of an experience. In contrast, Freud places fixation and the compulsion to repeat as "attempts to bring the trauma into operation once again—that is, to remember the forgotten experience or, better still, to make it real, to experience a repetition of it anew".[104] Both reactions – defense (repression) and repetition – ensure the trauma has a durable compulsive effect and as such determines the character of a person (or people).

One may expect that Freud may, because of the problem of the large time spans of 800 years between the historical figure of Moses and late Jewish historiography, apply the model of the trauma and the later 'return of the repressed' to this period. And indeed, in the introductory maneuvers on the effect of the analogy between the aetiology of neuroses and the origin of the Jewish character, Freud suggests that, despite fundamental differences, the murder of Moses can be compared to a first trauma with a 'frightful accident', such as a railway accident. As we know from the analyses of traumatic neuroses, he writes, the person only develops a series of grave psychical and motoric symptoms over the course of a few weeks. The period between accident and the formation of symptoms can best be called an 'incubation period', or, as Freud now suggests, a period of latency (*Latenz*).[105] According to Freud we can find such an incubation or latency period also in Judaism, namely as the period between the murder of Moses and the return of the monotheistic idea in the time post-exile. The return of the monotheistic idea needs – according to the model of traumatic neurosis – no concrete cause to be activated. It comes as the delayed impact of the first shock. Seen in this way, the latency period is the period of apparent 'normality' in which the 'shock' however causes excitation and unpleasure to build and push up, so much so that symptom formation eventually takes place. Trauma functions, as we have seen in the previous chapter, from inside – as increasing 'upward pressure'. The Paul episode can also be understood from this model of 'incubation' and 'upward drive'. We could say that the period between the return from exile until Paul is the period of delayed symptom formation – the period of the return of the repressed in the main 'symptom' of the murder, monotheism.

The reference to traumatic neurosis is notable. Although only seems to want to focus the attention on the element of the incubation time of an accident, the reference seems to imply more. With the train accident as well as with the murder of Moses, it concerns a non-sexual trauma that, moreover, unlike with the duality of sexual trauma, does not change meaning or obtains a new meaning at a later stage. The murder was and remains a murder, like in the traumatic neurosis the accident always remains the accident.

Freud, however, does not continue this trail of the analogy between the genesis of a character of a people and a traumatic neurosis. Thereafter he seems more interested in that the Jewish people in the murder of Moses repeated the repressed primal murder and made it a reality. The attention thus shifts from the meaning of the 'self-experienced' (accidental) factor of the murder of Moses and its incubation time in Jewish history to an analysis of the phylogenetic, constitutional factor: the meaning of the primal murder for the murder of Moses and the reactions to this. In this way, Freud not only applies the scheme of the aetiology of the neuroses to the developments in Judaism from the murder of Moses to the post-exile historiography (or to Paul's appearance). Freud specifically uses it to bring constitutional factors into play: the phylogenetic/cultural-historical developments between the prehistoric primal murder and the murder of Moses.

With this step from ontogeny to phylogeny, Freud instantly finds himself on more familiar territory. After all, he emphasized that trauma is related to "impressions of a sexual and aggressive nature" and "early injuries to the ego (narcissistic mortifications)"[106] during childhood. During infancy, young children, unlike adults later, can "make no sharp distinction between sexual and aggressive acts".[107] This ties in with earlier insights into the meaning of the sadistic component of the libido (Rat Man) and of the anal component of the sexual constitution and the anal-sadistic organization (Wolf Man). The fact that the little Wolf Man can draw no distinction between an act of love and one of violence is defining for the traumatic effect of the primal scene.[108] What here applies to the individual also now applies mutatis mutandis to the 'infancy' of humanity. The murder of Moses is indeed an act of aggression (anger, violent outburst), and this is different from the primal murder, which has a sexual-aggressive character. Freud explicitly refers here to the father as castrator of the sons, to the rivalry for the women and daughters of the own horde, and to the sadistic and cannibalistic aspects of the primal murder: the consumption of the raw pieces of flesh of the father as expression of the most primitive form of identification.[109] The murder of Moses repeats this primal murder, but differently from before, namely as a deed of a people who have undergone cultural development and who, unlike the primaeval hominids, can draw a distinction between sexual and aggressive acts.

With this construction Freud seems to formulate an answer to a problem that already came up in *Beyond the Pleasure Principle*, namely the question if all traumas are sexual traumas. We could say that the answer is introduced with the suggestion that the murder of Moses could be compared to a 'frightful accident' like a train crash.[110] The murder of Moses is no sexual trauma, but the traumatic effect of this violent act is only possible because it repeats an earlier trauma, namely the sexually aggressive deed of the primal murder. The murder of Moses would then illustrate that only in a later development (in phylogeny as well as ontogeny), a distinction is drawn between aggression and sexuality. Thereby Freud wants to indicate that a non-sexual trauma could be taken up in his thinking about the aetiology of the neurosis and the place of sexual trauma in it.

The introduction of the concept of 'latency' in *Moses and Monotheism* is perhaps the most important indication that Freud wants to link the traumatic event of the murder of Moses with a theory of sexual trauma and a theory of sexuality. To understand why and how Freud introduces the concept of 'latency' in the text, we first need to connect with earlier views. We saw in the previous chapters how, aided by views from evolutionary biology, Freud could broaden his trauma theory to one in which all life and change originates in external disturbing and diverting (*ablenkende*) influences.[111] Every organism is – in its physique and development, its somatic processes, its instincts and memory-traces – the result of a series of acquired characteristics such as those caused or driven by external influences. That also applies to the organism 'human' that is, in its sexual development and ego formation, the result of a cultural-historic evolution that is the extension of the evolution of all life forms. We already saw in the previous chapters that Freud relays the development history of humanity and the origin of certain development directions and reaction patterns to a series of primal catastrophes or primal traumas.

In *Moses and Monotheism* Freud refers to *Three Essays*, where he described the latency period as one during which the initial sexual development (infantile sexuality) was brought about and the reaction formations (disgust, shame, guilt) were constructed, strengthened by cultural demands. Sexual development thus comes to a standstill during this period; sexual activities are reduced. This lasts until puberty when the sexual drive, serving procreation, 'breaks through in unmistakable fashion'.[112] Briefly, the latency period is an interruption in the sexual life and, as such, a physiological given. It is the period between the first expressions of sexual drive and the late development of reproductive organs and functions with associated intensified sexual desires and activities. But why is there this 'postponement' of the reproductive function? Why does the power of sexual drive diminish, and why is there a deferred 'eruption' of the sexual drive? To the question whether this delay of the reproductive function is useful, Freud can answer negatively, with reference to other animal species (where no latency period exists). The answer should be sought somewhere else, Freud believes.

In 'Overview of the Transference Neuroses', Freud not only explores the cultural-historic origin of the various neuroses in a series of catastrophes during the Ice Age. The latency period as 'delay phase' is also anchored in these traumatic experiences of primal humanity.[113] Freud claims that the latency period is an effect of the castration threat of the primal father. "We may imagine the effect of castration in that primeval time as an extinguishing of the libido and a standstill in individual development".[114] For Freud, the latency period as typically human phenomenon is linked to traumatic experiences during the primeval time. In *Inhibitions, Symptoms and Anxiety* Freud even views the latency period as the most important phylogenetic factor in the aetiology of the neuroses. Indeed, the reaction formations against the sexual drive are constructed during the latency period, and "the majority of the instinctual demands of this infantile sexuality are treated (…) as dangers and fended off as such".[115] The result of primal events is that the early activity of the sexual drive during a period in which the reproductive organs and function are not yet developed leads to the instinctual demands being experienced as dangerous and as threatening the psychic apparatus from within.

Here we come across a theme we already discussed extensively in the previous chapter: the traumatizing effect of instinctual urges. The reaction formations constructed during the latency period are not only responses to (perverse) aspects of sexuality. They are also reactions to the traumatizing way drives work. We could say that Freud, in his analysis of the latency period between two traumatic events – the primal murder and the murder of Moses – formulates an answer to the question of how it is possible that instinctual forces can threaten our psychic apparatus and traumatize us from within. The temporality of trauma parallels the interruption of sexual development, i.e. the period of latency between two regimes of sexuality. The sexual latency period and temporality of trauma has no equivalent in other organisms and animal species. They are a cultural-historical given and decisive for the fact that humans – and humans alone – can repress, remember or repeat traumas.

The latency period is one of repression of the memory of an original traumatic experience (the murder of the primal father-castrator). This period ends when, through a combination of 'upward drive' and reactivation, that which is repressed can return. A latency period in the cultural history is a long phase in which one cannot 'trace' a memory or the continued action of a traumatic experience.[116] This is particularly valid for the period between the primal murder and the murder of Moses. With his phylogenetic (cultural-historical) construction of a constitutionally given latency period, which repeats in the life of each individual member and in the nation, Freud (once again) manages to create an intimate connection between trauma theory and a theory of sexual development (drive theory) in *Moses and Monotheism*. Freud writes about this:

> Human beings appear to be the only animal organisms with a latency period and sexual retardation of this kind (…) It cannot be a matter of indifference psychologically that the period of infantile amnesia coincides with this early period of sexuality. It may be that this state of things provides the true determinant for the possibility of neurosis, which is in a sense a human prerogative and from this point of view appears as a vestige – a 'survival' – of primaeval times.[117]

The reference to 'infantile amnesia' is important in this passage. With that, Freud establishes a substantive and temporal connection between repressing sexual drive components and repressing ('forgetting') the memory of a traumatic experience. About this Freud writes that the period of 'apparently undisturbed development' between an infantile neurosis and the later neurosis of the adult, "is supported or made possible by the intervention of the physiological period of latency". From here on out, Freud can now use the concept of latency to indicate the period between two traumas (one in childhood, the other generally during puberty or early adulthood). He writes about this: "The phenomenon of a latency of the neurosis between the first reactions to the trauma and the later outbreak of the illness must be regarded as typical".[118] The temporality of trauma is anchored here by Freud in a physiological temporality of sexual development. Hereby – compared to the case of the Wolf Man – puberty again becomes relevant in the aetiology of the neuroses, and Freud reaches back for insights from his earliest trauma theory (seduction theory).

According to Freud, that the murder of Moses as a repetition of the murder of the primal father could become a crucial 'link' in the formation of the Jewish character is possible through a number of aspects of 'the great man' that he already thematized in the first Moses draft: with his paternal leadership qualities and the announcement of the monotheist idea, Moses awakens a repressed memory-trace of the authority of the primal father and the father who was already in primaeval times 'elevated' to deity. Of crucial meaning for the genesis of the strict Jewish monotheism was "the awakening of the forgotten memory-trace by a recent real repetition of the event. The murder of Moses was a repetition of this kind".[119]

But there is more. In the Moses version from 1934, Freud already draws attention to the circumcision that Moses imposed on his chosen people. Here, Freud defines circumcision as "the symbolic substitute for the castration which the primal father once inflicted upon his sons in the plenitude of his absolute power".[120] The emphasis in this first version is on the acceptance of this symbol and submitting to Moses as the one who chooses a people and frees them from slavery.[121] The reference to circumcision and castration is important and is included in the final version of the text in an analysis of the meaning of the murder of Moses. Indeed, the murder of Moses could also justly become a repetition of the first trauma (the primal murder) and elicit a violent reaction, because the murder of the man who introduced circumcision could activate the memory of the primal castrator. That Moses introduced castration to the people chosen by him recalled "the dreaded castration" and stirred "a portion of the primaeval past which is gladly forgotten".[122] In other words, the murder of Moses derives its meaning largely from the fact that it recalled the memory of a sexually aggressive trauma, the actual castration in the primaeval age, and the associated aggressive reactions. The murder of Moses has a traumatic effect, because it reminds of 'the severest trauma', the trauma of castration.[123]

8. *A final case*

The theme of sexuality also enters *Moses and Monotheism* in another way. In the conclusion of the chapter on the analogy between the latency period and tradition, Freud introduces a short case study that is, by his own admission, 'far removed' from the events of Jewish history , but still displays the structure of the pathogenesis.[124] The structure is as follows: early trauma – repression (and character change) – latency – outbreak of the neurosis – partial return of the repressed. It concerns the case of a little boy who, after witnessing sexual intercourse (primal scene) between his parents at a very tender age, in his aggressive-sexual activities (sexually attack of the mother) strongly identifies with his father. When his mother utters the threat of castration and tells him his father will punish him, it has a strong traumatic effect on this boy. His character changes; he becomes fearful of his father and seeks protection from his mother. What follows is the latency period in which the boy is free of disorders and develops well. But in puberty he suddenly becomes sexually impotent, creates all kinds of sado-masochistic phantasies and does not dare make sexual advances towards women. At the same time, he develops a strong hatred of his father – a hatred that self-destructively carries through into all kinds of conflicts with others. After his father dies and he finally finds a woman, he develops an 'egoistic, despotic and brutal personality' with a strong desire to punish and offend. He became, so Freud writes, "a faithful copy of his father as he had formed a picture of him in his memory". The repressed – the father's aggressive character – returns in the form of a copy through identification that "he had taken on as a little boy from sexual motives".[125]

Even if the case is substantively far removed from Jewish history, Freud has his reasons to include this case in the transition from the analysis of the tradition after the murder of Moses to the continuing effects of the primal murder. After all, several elements occur in this case that are decisive for the way in which the murder of Moses obtains meaning from this primal murder. First, there is the theme of the threat of castration by the father during early childhood and its effect on the boy's change of character. Secondly, after a time of relative rest in the latency period, a strong hatred of the father comes to the fore during puberty and, after the father's death, there is identification with the older man's aggressive-cruel character.

Substantively, the first part of the case of the little boy fits with the case of the Wolf Man. There is a primal scene; there are active sadistic aspirations and seduction traces; there is a threat of castration that has as traumatic effect a character change; there is the 'typical' oedipal complex in which the father is the castrator (and not the mother as the one expressing the threat). But where in the case of the Wolf Man the meaning of puberty falls away in the aetiology of the neurosis, in the case of the boy puberty is decisive for the formation of a manifest neurosis. In that manifest neurosis, a sexual problematic clearly becomes visible in the impotence and onanism with sadomasochistic phantasies. But with the eventual finding of a woman, the sexual problematic shifts to the background. Most striking and determinative for the manifest neurosis is the furious hatred of the father, the many conflicts with others, and, after the father's passing, the identification with his despotic-cruel character traits. And precisely in this revival of the identification Freud sees the return of repression. This second identification is a repetition of the earlier identification with the father, which means, with the person he observed at a tender age as a sexually aggressive person. The sexual motive, however, falls away in the second identification, and what 'returns' is only the aggressive and destructive character of the father.

Formulated differently, what comes to the fore in puberty is an aggression and inclination towards destruction that can be led back to a strongly developed original sadistic organization during childhood. Thanks to the cases of the Rat Man and the Wolf Man, we are familiar with this problematic of aggression (anger, hate) that Freud still relays to a sadistic component of the libido. It changes in and from *Beyond the Pleasure Principle*. Sadism becomes an outwardly focused destructive drive that was originally of a masochistic nature, thus aimed at the ego and the own body. From *Beyond the Pleasure Principle*, Freud would then also see consistent sadistic tendencies as "an instinctual fusion of purely libidinal purely destructive urges".[126] In sadism, a fusion (*Mischung*) of libidinal drives (Eros/life drives) and a destructive drive (death drive) become visible. This mixture is possible through the inclination to fusing and uniting in the life drives. Under pressure from the life drive, the death drive (aggression/destruction) enters the service of the life drives and can be diverted from the ego and weakened in this way. However, where drive mixture emerges, separation can also take place. The destructive drive then frees itself from the grip of the life drives, becomes stronger and steps into the foreground. The death drive can then immediately manifest itself in the 'blindest fury of destructiveness'.[127]

The case of the boy illustrates this vision of the sadistic organization in early childhood and the later separation into two drive streams where the destructive drive powerfully comes to the fore. However, that raises the question why Freud does not refer to the theory of death drive and the life drives anywhere in *Moses and Monotheism.*[128] To formulate an answer, we need to understand what would have been the effect of such a reference. The introduction of the death drive in the text would have meant the murder of Moses and its later effects on Judaism could be seen as a 'pure' manifestation of an original aggressive/destructive drive. We would then be able to trace the murder of Moses back to the fact that humans – like all other living beings – bear a destructive drive that can turn outwards against objects.[129] In principle, for such aggression against objects, only the slightest or even no provocation at all suffices for an act of violence. Arising immediately from a destructive drive, this aggression against objects does not find a motive or point of contact in the identification with, ambivalent feelings towards or frustration because of the father necessary. In other words, if Freud had introduced the death drive in his text, it would have been possible to view the murder of Moses as a direct, externally aimed release of a destructive drive. The entire traumatic effect of this murder would then have to be understood from the reactions (such as anxiety and sense of guilt) to this release of aggression against an object. That would have meant that Freud would have had to make space in his trauma theory for the possibility of a trauma from pure aggressive inclinations. Freud, however, wants to give the trauma of the murder of Moses a place in a theory of sexual trauma, that means, of a sexual trauma that continues along the path of phylogeny (archaic inheritance) in the ontogeny of a people.

It is difficult to separate this positioning in *Moses and Monotheism* from debates in which Freud was involved from the '20s with his students from the 'London School' – namely Ernest Jones, Melanie Klein, Susan Isaacs en Joan Riviere – about the origin of the Oedipus complex, the conscience (superego) and sense of guilt.[130] These students, who for the greatest part based their views on analyses of very young children in their own clinical practice, strongly emphasized the role of aggression (destructive drive) in a pre-oedipal development phase and more concretely in relation to the mother. In *Civilization and Its Discontents*, Freud already answered to these insights by arguing that this first pre-oedipal aggression follows "a phylogenetic model" and that a sense of guilt "springs from the Oedipus complex and was acquired at the killing of the father by the brothers banded together".[131] The aggression and sense of guilt in the pre-oedipal phase thus could be seen as a repetition of the original aggression against the father and the reactions to it. In other words, according to Freud, the earliest aggression against objects (mother) and the reactions to it (conscience formation, sense of guilt) are unfathomable without a theory of the Oedipus complex and with that of the identification with the father including both (a mixture of) aggressive (hatred) as well as erotic (love) tendencies. Freud can, however, only make the meaning of this complex and identification plausible with reference to phylogeny, that is to the primal murder, the inheritance of acquired dispositions and the repetition of the phylogeny in the ontogeny.

In *Moses and Monotheism*, Freud wants to show – with the case of the young boy among others – that the traumatic effect of Moses's murder can only be understood when the violence against Moses can be traced back to an original drive mixture in primaeval times. Whereas during the 'infancy' of humanity, sexuality still had an aggressive character and aggression still served sexual aspirations, the murder of Moses is a deed that can be understood from later separation of drives. With the case of the little boy, Freud draws the attention to the possibility of such a separation of sexual and aggressive drives whereby in one direction a sexual problematic reaches a certain settlement (the young man finally finds a woman) and in the other direction the destructive force of aggression can fully manifest itself (the identification with the despotic-cruel character of the father; the many conflicts with others).

9. Conclusion

The literature on *Moses* regularly pointed out the problematic that Freud confessed to a psycho-Lamarckism that – through developments in biology, namely the rise of modern Mendelian genetics from the beginning of the twentieth century – would long have been outdated.[132] In the Moses text, Freud himself writes about this that the 'present biological science' certainly does not want to have anything to do with the inheritance of acquired traits. To this he adds that, "nevertheless I cannot do without this factor in biological evolution".[133] The question is: why did Freud reckon we could not do without this theory of inheritance of psychological dispositions and contents?

We have already seen that in the case of the Wolf Man the meaning of the Oedipus complex in the aetiology of infantile neuroses in this patient is completely determined by the idea that this complex was 'acquired' in the primaeval age and inherited and continues as a 'scheme'. Here Freud called on a theory of inheriting psychical contents and dispositions and thereby gave the Oedipus complex a decisive role in the aetiology of the neurosis of the Wolf Man. We see the same in *Moses and Monotheism*. However, what is at stake in this text is not only the importance of an acquired Oedipus-

or castration complex as such but rather the fundamental question how the aggressive deed of the murder of Moses can be integrated into a psychoanalytic theory of sexual trauma as a traumatic event. Thereby this text is in line with *Beyond the Pleasure Principle* in which, as we have seen, Freud feels himself confronted with the limits of his trauma theory and of psychoanalysis itself. At first glance, the murder of Moses seems to be a purely aggressive deed, yet according to Freud it can indeed be traced back to a sexual problematic if one could approach it as repeating the primal murder of the primal castrator. This primal murder was after all a direct expression of a fusion of aggressive and sexual motives and elements: the (threat of) castration and the reaction of the sons to this; the rivalry for the possession of women; the sadistic and oral pleasure taken from dismembering a body and eating it. But, Freud realizes, this idea of repetition of the primal murder and the influence of sexual motives from the primaeval age is only plausible when we assume that memory-traces, reaction formations and psychical dispositions were preserved in the thousands of years that passed between the two murders. A reference to oral traditions does not offer much solace here. The 'archaic heritage' or 'tradition' cannot be defined in terms of written or oral fixations. From the primaeval age, there is nothing, neither in language nor in signs, which is passed on from generation to generation; the little we know about the brutality of existence in primaeval times, we know from rare archaeological finds. And while in the Christian communion Freud sees a repetition of the "sense and content of the old totem meal" of the primaeval people, nowhere in *Moses and Monotheism* do we find the suggestion that in Judaism, content might have been passed down through rituals.[134] So the question is how it is possible that memory-traces of our primal traumas could have been preserved for many thousands of years, so much so that castration – sexual primal trauma – could be an unconscious motive force. The answer Freud finds in a theory of inheritance of psychical disposition and contents. In short, he needs psycho-Lamarckism to defend his theory of sexual trauma.

Chapter 8

Freud's metaphysics of trauma

A metaphysics of the drive

Various authors have pointed out the fact that Freud, in his reflections on the origin, substance and working of the drives, gives psychoanalysis a dimension one could call a 'metaphysics of the drive'.[1] Freud would probably have frowned upon such a view. In the few references to metaphysics in his texts, it invariably concerns a 'philosophy of nature' or 'system of thought' that is controlled by what he calls the 'omnipotence of thoughts'. By this he refers to the 'primitive' tendency to imagine the coherence between phenomena in reality solely with the help of one's own thinking and on that basis to feel 'lord and master of the world'.[2] Such attempts to introduce a transparent order into reality through thought abstraction can be compared to the thought efforts of psychotics. They attempt to repair a relationship with reality through delusion, yet without the ability to experience either the world as matter subject to natural laws or people as living beings made of flesh and blood[3] Freud counters this by stating that psychoanalysis is a science in the tradition of Darwin that positioning humans in the animal kingdom brings a definite end to our every possible narcissist-illusory self-exaltation.[4] As with all living beings, our physical and psychical traits are determined by the evolutionary force field and the subjugation to the laws of nature.[5] For Freud, our instinctive constitution is therefore a variant within a larger whole of animalistic instinctive constitutions.[6] If we question from this self-positioning what Freud classifies as *meta*-psychology, meaning which discipline comes 'after psychology', then the answer is 'biology' and not 'metaphysics'.[7] Freud is part of a tradition that had little time for a metaphysics that develops propositions and concepts a priori using reason outside and apart from the domain of explanatory sciences.[8]

At the same time, Freud is however only aware in his later work of the fact that, with his notion of drive, he 'steered into the harbor' of a metaphysical tradition.[9] We can start by asking which route he sailed before arriving in this harbor. For Freud, the point of departure is his clinical practice. The phenomena that set off his analysis and theorization were clinical ones, that is, the various psychopathologies. From the beginning, the question of aetiology was central to his studies of the psychoneuroses. We saw that Freud rejected the then (end of the nineteenth century) dominant paradigm of a neuropathic disposition, countering firstly with a psychological theory of *sexual* trauma in two stages (seduction theory) and subsequently modifying this theory and extending it with constitutional elements. This step from a trauma theory, in which exceptional impressions and events are determining in the aetiology, to a theory in which constitutional factors play an important role is a crucial step for all subsequent psychoanalytical theory formation. By placing the general human constitution in the aetiology of the neuroses, the "pathological approach (…) has been displaced by the anthropological".[10] Psychoanalysis becomes a domain where the analysis of pathologies can provide insights into constitutionally determined psychical dynamics and structures. Elsewhere we extensively described Freud's patho-analytical perspective on being human: the idea that being human is adequate and could perhaps be best described from the perspective of pathological 'anomalies'.[11] With this step, psychoanalysis became a 'clinical anthropology'.[12]

In *Three Essays on the Theory of Sexuality* we see the first results of the exploration of these constitutional factors. Both sexual 'abnormalities' and 'normal' sex lives can be understood and described from a general human 'polymorphously perverse' and 'instinctual' sexual constitution. This means firstly that sexuality comprises different components, partial drives, erogenous zones and interacting organic processes. And secondly, sexual constitution is no functional and expedient unit. It is not, from the outset, in the service of preserving the species, but forms the basis of the possibilities for experiencing pleasure and unpleasure in one's own body. It is a composition of erogenous zones and partial sexual drives that is in no way aimed at synthesis. In fact, it is a constitution in which – through organic processes such as 'excitations' and 'organic repression' – conflicts and tensions ('reaction formations'), fixations, inhibitions and sublimations emerge.[13]

It is in this context of a theory of sexuality that Freud introduces the notion of 'drive' in his work. In 1905, he describes sexuality as an effect of a drive on a stimulus-receiving organ, the so-called erotogenic zone.[14] The organic consists mainly of stimulus-receiving zones where autoerotic pleasure can be experienced. Freud largely derives these first insights from his studies of hysteria and perversions. A "predominant development of the sexual instinct" becomes visible particularly in hysteria, and the sexual repression appears to be "in excess of the normal quantity".[15] In this regard we have seen how Freud in the analysis of Dora traces her hysteria back to a sexual constitution and disposition, to her 'too much' of sexual drive impulses and her 'effusive' reactions of anxiety and disgust. The psychical conflicts characteristic of her hysteria are inscribed in constitutional organic processes, which they partly determine.

In various case studies and other texts Freud holds onto a theory of *sexual* constitution and, precisely because of this, repeatedly encounters the limits of his analyses. After all, for Freud this meant that the anger of the Rat Man had to be traced back to a sexual-sadistic component of the drives and that the murder of Moses had to be seen as a repetition of a primal murder with sexual motives. We have seen how, in *Beyond the Pleasure Principle*, Freud tries to make it plausible that the experience of unpleasure in traumatic neurosis must have its sources in a released amount of sexual excitation. The anchoring of accidental traumatic moments in a sexually driven constitution is clearly less evident in this variety of cases than Freud suggests. Jean Laplanche will later draw the conclusion from this in his theory of primal seduction that psychoanalysis should limit itself to a psychological theory of sexual trauma that can do without a reference to biology. According to him, sexuality is not a constitutional given but only arises in early infancy when drives become sexual in autoeroticism and at the same time becomes phantasmatic with regard to the sexual object.[16]

Jacques Lacan draws a different conclusion from this problematic of the instinctual organic processes. Being human should not be understood from 'too much' organic activity influencing the psychic apparatus but from 'too little being' of the subject in relation to a limiting law. The subject is essentially characterized by a desire (*désir*) for the removal of this lack of being.[17] Without being able to go into this in more detail, we can state that Lacan's psychoanalytic theory formation has left its mark on the philosophical critiques of, among others, Deleuze and Guattari in *L'Anti-Oedipe* and Foucault in *Histoire de la Sexualité*, on Freudian psychoanalysis as a theory of the oedipal law and of desire as (an effect of) lack. We may wonder whether, as a result, Freud's 'metaphysics of the drive' and his theory of infantile sexuality as experience of pleasure in one's own body have not by and large become hidden from view. Or perhaps we find in them a possible other *retour à Freud*?

Foucault's 'counterattack' on the primacy of law and desire from an experience of 'body and pleasures' seems able to find support in Freud's non-oedipal theory of infantile sexuality.[18] And when Deleuze and Guattari speak of us as 'desire machines', that is, as organic and psychical apparatuses that – in their forms, functions and relations – express a productive force influencing them from within, then at first sight they seem to fit seamlessly into Freud's vision of the 'excess' of drive energy that sets in motion and shapes both the body and the psychical apparatus from within.[19]

Sexual constitution has an instinctive 'ground'. According to Freud, we should understand sexuality, sexual constitution and thus being human as such from the drives, that means, from the sexual drives and what he would call the 'ego-drives'. Despite tendencies towards a monistic conception of drives – we return to this shortly – Freud will always fall back on a drive dualism that is in fact borrowed from Darwin's distinction between natural selection (fight for survival) and sexual selection (fight for reproduction).[20] His clinical practice convinced him that the psychological lives of neurotics are determined by conflicts and tensions that cannot be traced back to a conflict between the person and the outside world, between inner urge and a limiting cultural morality.[21] The psychoneuroses are characterized by inner conflicts that have their basis in instinctual life. Drives exert pressure from organic sources of stimulation and are thus both the engine for psychical 'progress' and 'change' and for an opposite tendency: to eliminate all attempts of the apparatus to eliminate the constant unpleasure causing pressure.[22]

For Freud, drive is a 'concept on the frontier', a concept indicating a force that can only be recognized through the way in which it manifests in psychical life. Sexual constitution has an instinctual character, but that character essentially remains enigmatic. A drive makes itself known through sensory organs that receive stimuli and through psychical representations, but the study of its essence lies beyond the domain of the phenomena that psychoanalysis can study. The drive thus attains the status of a fundamental principle, more concretely a principle of cause of movement and change, action and reaction, possible pleasure and unpleasure sensations. It is a notion with which Freud can bring coherence to the phenomena studied in his clinical practice. In doing so, he moves from his clinical practice and anthropology into the domain of metaphysics. That means, if we understand metaphysics here as a theoretical reflection on the fundamental principles of being and the phenomena in their mutual coherence and correspondences.[23]

Freud's Darwinist background ensures that the reflections on drive cannot remain limited to the instinctual nature of the human constitution. The drives testify that the different animal species also have their own instinctual constitution, which is more efficient and organized in terms of adaptation to circumstances.[24] It is in this way that Freud's metaphysics of the drive can culminate in *Beyond the Pleasure Principle*. All organic life is understood here from the idea of a first force that brings inorganic matter to life. The organic is essentially 'stimulus reaction' and should as such be seen as an effect of forces continuously acting on matter (causing movement and change, disturbing, agitating).[25] The organic is that which can absorb and defend against stimuli (the ability to resist) depending on whether these stimuli arouse pleasure or unpleasure. The different concrete – simple or extremely complex – life forms are the result of the diverse reactions to the continuous stimuli and constant forces executed on these forms, forcing them to modify. And viewed from Haeckel's biogenetic law, this also means that the beginning and composition of each concrete organic unit is the result of (chemical, biological) forces in their mutual relations.

With the notion of the drive as causative 'force' of movement and change preceding concrete lifeforms, Freud can justifiably be included in a long-standing metaphysical tradition. At the beginning of this tradition stands Aristotle with his theory of causality.[26] The emphasis in this part of his metaphysics is on the thinking through of the active causes that bring about movement and change, and on life as an energetic process of realization and eventually bringing to perfection forces or potentials (*dunamis*). Life is an active being-event in which every change and movement has its raison d'être in this being itself and strives for the most perfect possible realization of inherent possibilities. For Aristotle, this thinking-through of cause and movement is then also inseparable from a teleological question about the aim and meaning of a movement. The question then is to what end a movement is initiated and continues. In modern philosophy – we follow Bernet here – this line of thought is taken up and reconsidered in particular by Leibniz and Schopenhauer. In Leibniz we find the idea of self-contained monads as a collection of active and passive forces that constantly strive to develop their potentialities with the aim of perfecting themselves.[27] In this theory of monads, we find a turn to the individual subject, to every animal species with its specific instincts and to the human as essentially instinctual. Schopenhauer further continues down this path already taken, in particular in *Die Welt als Wille und Vorstellung* from 1819/1844. In his work, active forces are condensed into a monistic view of a blind and irrational 'will to live' providing all phenomena in the cosmos with the force and ability to persist in existence and to act. According to Schopenhauer, Newtonian physics and the first evolution theories can only lead to the conclusion that everything that exists is a manifestation of this will to live. But the most direct way for each human being to know that this will manifests itself in all that exists is the experience of one's own body as an instinctive-physiological whole with sexual impulses that strive for satisfaction and pleasure, and of the object-oriented love life in which partners complement each other and reproduce.[28] Nietzsche will continue this line when he distances himself from Schopenhauer's metaphysics of the will to live and focuses on our instinctive nature, on the form-creating forces from within that seek release, and the conflicts and tensions that this creates within us. Both the urgent drive ('will to power') and the reactions to it can have a 'sickening', life-destroying effect.[29] In Nietzsche's view, the drive as a force or will to persevere in existence, [30] can become a force that destroys life from within.[31]

What disappears in Schopenhauer's monism is the teleological aspect of an inherent tendency to perfection. Seen in this light, he points ahead to Darwin and Freud, who reject a 'drive towards perfection'. Instead of such drive to perfection, Freud emphasizes the importance of accidental factors and thus the coincidental, the contingency of external circumstances. The way in which, in phylogeny as well as ontogeny, the drive is diverted from calibrated paths is determined by the possible and different reactions to coincidental impulses. Freud's case studies bear witness to this: accidental factors (consecutive scenes) evoke reactions that are decisive in further indefinite development.

The idea of a drive towards perfection nevertheless occupied an important place in the Darwinian reception of Freud's teachers in biology – think of Haeckel's drive monism. In this context it is perhaps not so surprising that Jung with his theory of primal libido refers to Schopenhauer's 'will' and once again assigns it a teleological dimension. Jung describes 'will' as if it were Aristotle's ability to realize potentialities. Primal libido is no blind force but an energetic principle that moves the individual to develop their own possibilities of existence through a complex process of differentiation and harmonization of psychical functions.[32] Freud's turn to metaphysics cannot be separated from the necessity to relate to the positions of his teachers and his students. Jung poses the greatest challenge and is repeatedly presented by Freud as the counter-position when it comes to the fundamental principles of psychoanalysis – a metaphysical debate particularly about working causes and final causes.[33]

Trauma and drive

What is Freud's contribution to and own position in this metaphysical tradition of reflection on causes, movements, changes and aims? In what way does Freud's thinking challenge philosophy and force it to reconsider its own conceptuality? From our own reconstruction of Freud's thoughts about trauma, we could note the following: Freud's 'metaphysics of the drive' is inextricably bound with a 'metaphysics of trauma'. It is from a reflection on his clinical practice and on the constitutional (phylogenetic) factors in the genesis of trauma that he becomes a critical and innovative thinker in this tradition. That Freud cannot but critically relate to an Aristotelean principle of a self-unfolding life striving for integration and perfection – we can understand this from the developments that we sketched in this book. From his knowledge of the traumatic neuroses, Freud will always start, in his theory of seduction and its later modifications, from the idea that psychic *reaction* to an impression or experience is the decisive traumatic moment in the aetiology of psychoneuroses. The analyses of neurotic patients repeatedly confirm the insight that the human is an impulse-reaction being. And the more powerful the impulse, the more extreme the reaction. The exaggerated reactions of his patients to an 'surplus' of sexual energy show that the trauma comes about from within. Drive is a blind and linear force that exerts pressure and in doing so pays no attention to one's psychic well-being. The psychical apparatus as regulated by the pleasure principle reacts to this with – not always adequate – attempts at binding, channeling and discharge.

Drive produces trauma. But according to Freud, the reverse is also true. The characteristics of human sexual drives and constitution must be understood as a historical acquisition.[34] The instinctive sexual constitution as such, the phylogenetic possession with its typical oedipal contents, the phased sexual development and the typical reaction patterns are the result of a series of traumatic experiences in the primeval age of the hominids. In turn, these traumatic experiences are part of an almost endless series of coincidental 'traumatic' moments in the evolutionary chain that have repeatedly led to physical and psychical modifications and thus formed the various living species. And all this has its origin in that one moment in which a force acts on matter in such a way that a first organic reaction occurs, namely a first attempt to relieve an internally arising tension.[35]

In this last point, we should note that in *Beyond the Pleasure Principle* Freud also formulates a second view of the traumatic beginning of life. Perhaps life can indeed be thought of from a self-unfolding 'erotic' principle of affinity and union into unity. But he immediately adds that there was also a traumatizing counterforce present from the beginning: the fragmentation in a first 'animation of life'.[36] He thus once again underlines that it is impossible to think of life solely in terms of an active-progressive self-unfolding drive.

Freud's metaphysics of drive and trauma is, as we have seen, the result of the extension of a purely psychological theory of trauma with a theory of constitutional factors in the aetiology. In the original seduction theory, the emphasis was mainly on moments of seduction by other people or on the experience of certain sexual scenes and their later pathogenic effect. By including constitutional factors in the analyses, the emphasis is placed more on seduction as a continuous force that derails sexual development and sexual life at an early age and leads them away from a supposedly normal development. In this context, Freud – as we saw in the case of the Wolf Man – includes seduction and the observation of sexual intercourse between the parents in what he calls 'phylogenetically inherited schemata'. With this reference to phylogeny, Freud in a sense provides an answer to the question that was already raised in the original theory of seduction. Are all those stories of patients about seductions in childhood really 'true'? Freud's original answer was 'often yes' when they really happened and 'often no' when they later turned out to be phantasized. The reference to phylogeny and primal phantasies allows for a different answer. After all, what Freud calls 'primal phantasies' are in fact 'primal memories' of real experiences in a prehistoric time.[37] Seductions are either real in the childhood of a person or real in the life of previous generations. In both cases, memory traces can be activated afterwards, and 'phylogenetic schemata' can also persist. We could say: the trauma is always 'true' in the sense of 'really happened', and that is also what Freud expresses in *Moses and Monotheism* when he refers to the primal scenes in the origins of the Jewish people as 'historical truth'.

In *Beyond the Pleasure Principle* Freud draws the ultimate consequence of his reconsideration of seduction as 'derailing' normal sexual development. For all multicellular organisms, life is a 'digression'. It is a '*détour*' forced by chance circumstances that is taken to ultimately achieve the elimination of tension in the inner self and to return to an inorganic state of lack of stimulation.[38] From this perspective, drive as 'constant force' is not only that which drives an organism forward and as such makes that organism 'alive'. It is also a force that puts pressure on the body and psychic apparatus, creates tension and conflicts and as such as a constant source of unpleasure for the organism. In fact, Freud argues here that organic life strives to abolish this force and tension – and with it itself. The organic does not want to coincide with its own and at the same time alien-hostile instinctive core, but with an original inorganic absence of stimulation. The organic strives to rid itself of that which essentially characterizes it – a force that causes unpleasure.

Trauma and repetition

We have said that, despite persisting with drive dualism, Freud's work tends towards drive monism. This tendency was clear in the first version of *Beyond the Pleasure Principle* when he calls all drives 'conservative' as they insist on restoring a former inorganic state. This restoration would mainly emerge via the 'detour' of a 'progress' that is manifested in ever more complex organisms. In fact, this tendency towards drive monism is already visible with the 1905 introduction of the concept of the drives in *Three Essays*. Here, Freud refers to a 'drive' (*ein "Trieb"*) that is originally of a non-sexual nature and only acquires a sexual character in connection with erotogenic zones.[39] In "Instincts and Their Vicissitudes" from 1915, this first definition was taken to the next level when Freud wrote that 'a drive' is a 'constant force', a 'workload' that encourages from within an appropriate ('adequate') alteration of the internal source of stimulation and a motive force behind advances. In this definition, no distinction is drawn in principle between various 'forces'. Only the quantity of the force and the workload varies.[40]

We can ask ourselves – with Deleuze – whether Freud did not in fact stumble upon the possibility of conceptualizing the drive in terms of an uncontrolled productive and repetitive drive. After all, even without reference to a 'drive towards perfection', Freud seems to be able to follow in the footsteps of Schopenhauer and Haeckel in *Beyond the Pleasure Principle*. All 'art forms of nature'[41] could then be though of as – endlessly repeated – productions of a (purposelessly) creative 'will' or 'natural drive'. Such a drive would not only produce the expanding multitude of life forms but would also be the driving force in the 'eternal return of the same' or the 'organic compulsion to repeat' that allows phylogeny to recapitulate endlessly in ontogeny.[42] A force preceding the individual would then force each individual to repeat an entire evolutionary development through the various embryonic stages to finally be able to repeat and complete the life cycle of their own species. Haeckel's biogenetic law would thus give rise to understanding life from drive repetition. Evolution could be though entirely from the principle of repetition. And each evolutionary line would consist of repeated forms caused by a creative force that propels organisms from within, making them mobile and changeable.

From this perspective, the drive to repeat would be a productive principle that precedes (empirically observable) conflicts and tensions in the physical and psychological apparatuses of individuals.[43] We are back to the drive as *dunamis*, but without this causative force serving needs or intentions, and without moral quality or purpose. The drive would only be a force that maintains itself and thereby propels life in endless repetitions. Or, what amounts to the same thing, there would be only repetition as a force manifesting itself again and again in the instinctive character of everything organic.

In *Beyond the Pleasure Principle*, it becomes clear why such a view of the repetition-drive as a creative force is unacceptable to Freud: drive and therefore also repetition are inconceivable without trauma. His starting point is a clinical insight. The shell shock victims of World War I show what happens when the reaction and defensive functions are swept away by an 'excess' of unbound drive energy. Here the defenses against stimuli collapse, the preparedness for anxiety is absent, and the unbound energy floods the psychic apparatus without it being able to receive and process this energy. The result is a repetitive spinning of the most intense experiences of unpleasure, namely that of the fright reaction to the situation of a serious accident.[44] A drive that is uncontrollably 'productive' and at the same time has no intention is a drive that destroys all the effective capacities of the psychic apparatus and the bodily functions. The instinctual, when it does not encounter resistance and boundaries, has a traumatic effect that is most clearly shown in a continuous and paralyzing repetition of the trauma. Unpleasure for one system cannot possibly be pleasure for the other system, because the second system has been swept away.

From here Freud takes the next step: from a phylogenetic perspective, the first system in which unpleasure arises precedes the second. All repetition in phylo- and ontogeny is the effect of a first trauma from which organic life could arise. The organic is matter in which unpleasure has been aroused through a first acting force. This forces organisms to react and to produce stimulus-resistant and drive-processing systems. In this regard Freud refers to those protists that began to envelop themselves with an inorganic shell against destructive stimuli from outside. These impulses forced these most primitive organisms to make a reactive effort, to produce an inorganic protective surface. According to Freud, we can understand our physiological and psychic architecture from this first effort made in response to impulses. We largely consist of devices and systems whose task is to process both impulses from outside and the constant force from within in a controlled manner. The pressure exerted by the drive (workload) forces both the body and psychical apparatuses to work.[45] All 'psychical work' is for Freud work imposed by the drive. And because the drive a constant force, every individual is forced to continuous psychical work.

You could say that for Freud, life is work – a work that can be done because and for as long as it is fed by drive energy. Psychic work therefore has a paradoxical character. It is an effort fueled by drive force to process the drives in such a way that pleasure can be experienced. But as an effort, this psychic work is itself also a source of unpleasure. The psychical systems that want to work towards pleasure are themselves also generators of unpleasure. In the final version of *Beyond the Pleasure Principle*, this is given shape in a new drive dualism. In this theory, the death drives underpin the pleasure principle because they insist on inertia (and therefore pleasure). These drives must be distinguished from the life drives, the action of which in the living substance actually "increases those tensions, introducing what may be described as fresh 'vital differences' which must then be lived off".[46] The life drives that underlie the development of more complex organisms that are capable of a longer and unpleasant 'detour' to death. Instead of a short, effective route to inertia, the life drives are 'breakers of the peace' and 'constantly producing tensions'.[47] They are 'troublemakers', and they can be this way because they can connect cells and organs, but also systems and functions, without a harmonious and efficient coordination arising. Moreover, in principle there always remains an 'excess' of force (drive) and a 'too little' of effective reactions to be able to relieve tension.[48] There are always (at least) two coupled psychical systems that represent opposing tendencies. Again, the organic exists by the grace of unpleasurable tension. The life drives are the guardians of the internal tension-filled architecture of all organic life. The repetition of phylogeny in ontogeny again and again results in the construction of tension-filled systems. And these tensions are not resolved by a harmonization of forces to finally arrive at rest and 'relaxation' in the highest state of perfection, but on the contrary by a discharge of tension that is equivalent to a return to the basic inorganic.

It is not only the shell shock patients who confront Freud with the problems of drive, trauma and repetition. Repetition was an important aspect of his trauma theory from the outset. After all, a certain repetition is already inherent in the idea of a 'trauma in two times'. The 'activation' of a first scene in a second experience can to a certain extent be understood as a repetition of that scene in a second moment. We have subsequently seen that in particular in the study of the Rat Man – and more generally of obsessive-compulsive disorder – the compulsion to repeat comes to occupy an important place. In the Rat

Man there is no trauma in two times but a continuous repetition without a change of meaning of the same anxious anticipation of an outburst of anger. Obsessive-compulsive disorder is characterized by the (threat of the) repeated return of the trauma. Many later scenes repeatedly show an anticipation of a similar outburst of anger out of fear of its explosive force. The Rat Man reproduces the insistent anger and especially his reactions to it, that is to say, the whole of his pathological character traits as well.[49]

In *Moses and Monotheism* as the study of the compulsive traits of the Jewish character, this theme emerged again. Freud's analyses of the processes of historiography culminate in the thesis that this character is largely the result of a tendency to repeat and relive trauma. The Jewish character is determined by the repetition of the reactions to the trauma in each subsequent generation. The people are thus propelled to 'advancement in intellectuality' but in the meantime suffer from 'too much' tradition and 'too little' adequate attempts to free themselves from a sense of guilt. This failure is determined by the fact that the traumatic murder cannot be remembered but has left memory traces that urge a 'return of the repressed'. In this way, each new generation repeats the manner of repeating ('acting out') inner conflicts of the previous generation. Just as repetition knows no end, so too tradition knows no end. The Jewish character can thus be seen as a final illustration of Nietzsche's 'perpetual recurrence of the same thing',[50] a chain of generations in which new experiences and impressions are given meaning by inherited traces of memory, and in which the same inner conflicts and tragic experiences keep repeating themselves. Tradition is therefore more than the whole of 'mausoleums' written down for a 'lack' of memories or for an absent founder, Moses the Egyptian.[51] For Freud, tradition is rather the opposite: the growing pressure of a threatening return of the repressed, of a traumatic event that cannot be remembered. After all, precisely because the trauma cannot be made into a memory, it cannot be given a place in the past and remains a possibility for the present and the future. The process of writing down is a symptom of this. Jewish historiography bears witness to an urge to repeat the repressed trauma and to a defense against it in a while of distortions that obscure the historical truth. Seen in this light, this historiography fails in its primary task of placing events in a chronology. Instead, it is driven to continue forgetting precisely that which threatens to repeat itself.[52] Behind a self-confidence that rests on 'advancement in intellectuality', another non-illusory process is hidden: the continuing effect of trauma.

If we ask ourselves how, according to Freud, an individual (or a people) can relate to this repetition of ancient phylogenetic experiences, he does not seek the answer in rejection (aversion, resistance) or in fact in will-less submission to a force of habit, but in an active 'acquisition' of the 'inherited'. He refers to the possibility of making these experiences one's own, that is, to include them in the whole of your experiences and thus in the way in which you travel your own life path and derive meaning from it.[53] Freud therefore does not seek the answer in a resentful aversion or *Verneinung* of life but precisely in an affirmation of its tragic character. This affirmation becomes possible through insight into the fact that every individual is formed from within by the experiences and reaction patterns of previous generations. This concerns experiences and patterns that determine the course of life, the way in which a 'detour' through life takes shape and is experienced; experiences and patters that never become transparent and escape your self-perception.

Freud's tragic anthropology

By not defining drive in terms of a progressive force in – usually idealized – processes of productivity in nature, progress and realization of possibilities of existence, but associating it with conflict, trauma and repetition, Freud develops a tragic vision of being human and of organic life as such. We are certainly not the first to point to such a tragic dimension, but we do so with different arguments than are usually provided. After all, in a good part of the existing reflections on the tragic in Freud's thinking, the references to an oedipal tragedy are central. The tragic dimension of being human is then determined by the first 'fatal' object relations, the desires and aggressive impulses manifested in them, and the cultural reaction to this in the form of the introduction of the (incest) taboo as the law that sets a limit to desire. Lacan follows this track when he points out that the tragic is eminently contained in the fatal structure of desire as essentially transgressive – as immoderate and limitless, and therefore (self-) destructive.[54] Another but related perspective can be found in René Girard: the tragic is the inevitable guilt resulting from an act of brutal violence that has its origins in a mimetic desire to possess the object that another also desires. Yet another variant is that in which the development of Western culture is described in terms of the growing repressing of the aggressive and sexual drives of the individual and of the need to free the libidinal forces from this hostile repression for the sake of a different and better organized society.[55]

What emerges from these various variants is the emphasis on the desire of the subject and its limitation in a context of intersubjectivity and culture (cf. Foucault 1976). Freud's vision of being human can neither be reduced to mutual hostility between the individual and culture, nor to the ambivalences and conflicts in oedipal object relations. In his view of drive, trauma and repetition, a tragic dimension becomes visible that can be described in terms of an inner dynamic. The fates of the individual can be seen as the totality of reactions to a traumatic 'too much' of drive that puts pressure on an individual from within and creates tension. It is precisely in this that Freud sees a repetition of the fate of the species and the evolutionary line. The 'perpetual recurrence of the same' has, under the influence of the traumatic experiences of previous generations, the 'disturbed' form of a 'detour' through life that repeats itself in every individual.

Freud's tragic view of humankind and life is therefore above all the consequence of a trauma theory in which the considerations on constitutional and phylogenetic aspects gradually came to occupy a more prominent place. In essence, these are considerations that are additions to a theory of seduction that – as we have tried to demonstrate in this book – was never abandoned by Freud as such. On the contrary, that theory of seduction retained its key role in his work and was expanded and modified over time with new theoretical components. Without this insight, Freud's clinical reflections and metapsychology cannot be understood.

Notes

Introduction

1 S. Freud (1985c), *The Complete Letters of Sigmund Freud to Wilhelm Fliess 1887-1904*, p. 264.

2 S. Freud (1896c), 'The Aetiology of Hysteria', *SE* 3; T. Geyskens (2001), 'Freud's Letters to Fliess. From Seduction to Sexual Biology, from Psychopathology to a Clinical Anthropology'; G. Izenberg (2006), 'Seduced and Abandoned: The Rise and Fall of Freud's Seduction Theory'.

3 M. Micale (1995), *Approaching Hysteria: Disease and Its Interpretation.*

4 For example, H. Israëls & M. Schatzman (1993), 'The Seduction Theory'; M. Borch-Jakobsen (2000), 'How to Predict the Past. From Trauma to Repression'.

5 J.-G. Schimek (2011), 'Fact and Fantasy in the Seduction Theory'.

6 A. Phillips (2014), *Becoming Freud. The Making of a Psychoanalyst*, p. 113.

7 For example, E. Kris (1952), 'Einleitung zur Erstausgabe'; D. Anzieu (1988), *L'auto-analyse de Freud et la découverte de la psychoanalyse*; Izenberg (2006), 'Seduced and Abandoned'; J. Whitebook (2017), *Freud: An Intellectual Biography.*

8 S. Freud (1918b), 'From the History of an Infantile Neurosis', *SE* 17; S. Freud (1939a), *Moses and Monotheism*, *SE* 23.

9 A. Esterson (2001), 'The Mythologizing of Psychoanalytic History: Deception and Self-deception in Freud's Accounts of the Seduction Theory Episode'.

10 S. Freud (1910a), 'Five Lectures on Psycho-Analysis', *SE* 11, p. 47.

11 S. Freud (1912-13a), *Totem and Taboo*, *SE* 13, p. 129.

12 Freud (1985c), *The Complete Letters*, p. 265.

13 S. Freud (1905d), *Three Essays on the Theory of Sexuality*, *SE* 7.

14 S. Freud (1906a), 'My Views on the Part Played by Sexuality in the Aetiology of the Neuroses', *SE* 7. Here, we are thinking in particular of 'Fragment of an Analysis of a Case of Hysteria ['Dora']' and the case study of the Rat Man, which are discussed in the second and third chapters of this book respectively.

15 S. Freud (1905e), 'Fragment of an Analysis of a Case of Hysteria', *SE* 7, p. 27 – in note)

16 S. Freud (1909d), 'Notes upon a Case of Obsessional Neurosis', *SE* 10, p. 155.

17 Freud (1906a), 'My Views', p. 274.

18 S. Freud (1985a), *A Phylogenetic Fantasy: Overview of the Transference Neuroses.*

19 I. Grubrich-Simitis (1985), 'Metapsychology and Metabiology'; I Grubrich-Simitis (2007), 'Trauma oder Trieb – Trieb oder Trauma: Wiederbetrachtet'.

20 H. Westerink (2009), *A Dark Trace: Sigmund Freud on the Sense of Guilt.*

21 Ph. Van Haute & H. Westerink (2021), *From Pleasure to the Object: Reading Freud's* Three Essays on the Theory of Sexuality.

22 S. Freud (1920g), *Beyond the Pleasure Principle, SE* 18, p. 38.

23 R. Bernet (2020), *Force, Drive, Desire: A Philosophy of Psychoanalysis.*

24 For a thematization of the various editions of *The Interpretation of Dreams*, see L. Marinelli & A. Mayer (2002), *Träume nach Freud. Die 'Traumdeutung' und die Geschichte der psychoanalytische Bewegung.* For different versions of *Beyond the Pleasure Principle*, see U. May (2015a), *Freud bei der Arbeit. Zur Entstehungsgeschichte der psychoanalytischen Theorie und Praxis, mit einer Auswertung von Freuds Patientenkalender* and U. May (2015b), 'The Third Step in Drive Theory: On the Genesis of Beyond the Pleasure Principle'.

25 Van Haute & Westerink (2021), *From Pleasure to the Object.*

26 One can think here of Derrida and Said, for instance. In their reflections on trauma, Freud's text on *Moses and Monotheism* from 1939, in addition to *Beyond the Pleasure Principle*, is central. J. Derrida (1980), *La carte postale: De Socrate à Freud et au-delà*; J. Derrida (1995), *Mal d'Archive: une impression freudienne*; E. Said (2003), *Freud and the Non-European.* It is also useful to compare, for example, Levinas's trauma theory with that of Freud. R. Visker (2005), 'De prijs van de onteigening: Levinas, Freud en het trauma'.

27 Here we are thinking particularly of Laplanche, who wants to put the sexual trauma back at the center of psychoanalytical reflection and who, with this aim, develops a general theory of seduction. J. Laplanche (1987), *Nouveaux fondements pour la psychoanalyse*; J. Laplanche (1992), *La revolution copernicienne inachevée*; J. Laplanche (2007), *Sexual. La sexualité élargie au sens freudien.* Trauma (and the real) is also central to Lacanian metapsychology. It refers to a dimension that cannot be included in the order of the imaginary and the symbolic (the order of law and language). J. Lacan (1973), *Le séminaire livre XI. Les quartre concepts fondamentaux de la psychoanalyse.* Cathérine Malabou works from a completely different (neuro-psychoanalytic) perspective. She attempts to develop a general theory of trauma that, on the one hand, ties in with Freudian psychoanalysis (in particular *Beyond the Pleasure Principle*), but that, on the other hand, subjects the assumptions of Freud's trauma theory to a thorough critique based on recent developments in neurology. C. Malabou (2017), *Les nouveaux blessés. De Freud à la neurologie, penser les traumatismes contemporains.*

28 Freud (1920g), *Beyond the Pleasure Principle*, p. 24.

29 As we shall see further on, 'The Economic Problem of Masochism' is an exception to this.

30 S. Freud (1926d), *Inhibitions, Symptoms, and Anxiety, SE* 20.

31 *Moses and Monotheism* is usually read as a very personal reflection of Freud on his own Jewish origins and identity and/or a confirmation of the religious theory from *Totem and Taboo*, in which the Oedipus complex and its embedded sense of guilt occupy such a central place. I. Grubrich-Simitis (1991), *Freuds Moses-Studie als Tagtraum*; Y.H. Yerushalmi (1991), *Freud's Moses. Judaism Terminable and Interminable*; J. Assmann (1998), *Moses the Egyptian: Memory of Egypt in Western Monotheism*; Westerink (2009), *A Dark Trace.*

Chapter 1: The psychologization of trauma and the origination of seduction theory

1 E. Fischer-Homberger (2004), *Die traumatische Neurose. Vom somatischen zum sozialen Leiden*; M. Micale & P. Lerner (2010), *Traumatic Pasts, History, Psychiatry and Trauma in the Modern Age, 1870-1930.*

2 It would nevertheless be remiss to mention only Freud in this context. Many authors have played a role in this evolution, well-known ones such as Pierre Janet as well as an entire group of psychiatric authors who have been forgotten over the years. We do not want to write a detailed history of the psychologization of trauma here but discuss some important positions in this debate in order better to place Freud's own insights. For an overview, see Fischer-Homberger (2004), *Die traumatische Neurose.*

3 J. Erichsen (1866), *On railway and other injuries of the nervous system.*

4 Fischer-Homberger (2004), *Die traumatische Neurose*, p. 37.

5 This term is often incorrectly attributed to Erichsen. Ibid., p. 17.

6 Ibid., p. 37.

7 R. Harrington (2010), 'The Railway Accident: Trains, Trauma and Technological Crises in nineteenth-century Britain', p. 46.

8 J. Erichsen (1875), *On concussion of the spine, nervous shock, and other injuries of the nervous system in their clinical and medico-legal aspects*; H. Hermans & S. Schmidt (1996), 'De traumatische neurose, een social-historische verkenning'; Fischer-Homberger (2004), *Die traumatische Neurose*, pp. 16, 37; Harrington (2010), 'The Railway Accident', p. 47.

9 Erichsen (1875), *On concussion of the spine*, p. 195.

10 Ibid., pp. 194 ff.

11 By 'functional disturbance', 19th century neurology understood disorders of function for which no demonstrable organic cause could be indicated. This of course does not prevent authors such as Oppenheim from simultaneously assuming that such an organic cause is indeed present.

12 H. Oppenheim (1889), *Die traumatische Neurosen*, p. 127.

13 Ibid., p. 123.

14 We return to this in detail in our sixth chapter on *Beyond the Pleasure Principle.*

15 H. Oppenheim (1915), *Der Krieg und die traumatischen Neurosen*, pp. 4-5 – our translation).

16 In her book on *Les nouveaux blessés*, Cahérine Malabou refers in this context to the recent notion of the 'emotional brain'. This notion emphasizes the inextricable unity between neuronal metabolism and the dynamics of emotions. The problems with the connection between psychical (emotional) and organic factors that had to remain enigmatic for Oppenheim can be resolved more easily from this perspective. Malabou, (2017), *Les nouveaux blessés*, p. 19 et *passim.*

17 Oppenheim (1889), *Die traumatische Neurosen*, pp. 128 ff.

18 J.W. Marshal (2016), *Performing Neurology. The Dramaturgy of Dr. Jean-Martin Charcot*, p. 122.

[19] Astasia-abasia refers to insufficient coordination when walking that ranges from complete unstableness (abasia) to trouble remaining upright (astasia). When it is possible to remain upright and walk, it is with legs spread and continuously striving to maintain balance.
[20] J.-M. Charcot (1889), *Clinical Lectures on Diseases of the Nervous System*, p. 221.
[21] According to Charcot, hysterical pathology could in principle be triggered by a multitude of factors: conditions related to exhaustion, infections, abundant masturbation, emotionally far-reaching events et cetera. J.-M. Charcot & P. Marie (1892), 'HYSTERIA mainly HYSTERO-EPILEPSY', p. 628.
[22] Ibid., p. 628.
[23] We also sometimes still find traces of this degeneration theory in Freud. For example, in the Dora case study, he does not rule out connection between the father's syphilis and the hysteria of his patient. Freud (1905e), 'Fragment of an Analysis of a Case of Hysteria', p. 19 – in note).
[24] R. Huertas & C.M. Winston (1992), 'Madness and degeneration, I: From "fallen angel" to mentally ill'.
[25] For more details on Lamarck's theory of acquired characteristics, we refer to our fifth chapter.
[26] This contrasts with Liébeault en Bernheim, who viewed hypnosis as a common human ability based on suggestion.
[27] The repetition of the traumatic event in dreams is a typical symptom of patients suffering from traumatic neurosis. We will return to the importance of this in detail in our sixth chapter, in which we discuss Freud's *Beyond the Pleasure Principle*.
[28] Charcot (1889), *Clinical Lectures*, pp. 375, 387.
[29] We limit our discussion to this conversion symptom. For a full discussion of the condition, we refer to ibid., pp. 374-386).
[30] Ibid., pp. 297, 380ff.; Charcot & Marie (1892), 'HYSTERIA mainly HYSTERO-EPILEPSY', p. 634.
[31] Insensitivity to touch in one half of the body.
[32] Charcot (1889), *Clinical Lectures*, p. 382.
[33] Ibid., p. 383.
[34] Ibid., p. 305.
[35] Ibid., p. 386.
[36] Ibid., p. 387.
[37] S. Freud (1893c), 'Some Points for a Comparative Study of Organic and Hysterical Motor Paralyses', *SE* 1, p. 168.
[38] Ibid., p. 169. Mark Solms and neuro-psychoanalysis have claimed Freud saw psychoanalysis as a preliminary construction that could sooner or later be confirmed by a reformed neurology. The idea that Freud's psychological theory is a radicalization of Charcot's insights seems to problematize this statement. This discussion will, however, take us too far here. M. Solms & O. Turnbull (2002), *The Brain and the Inner World. An Introduction to the Neuroscience of Subjective Experiences.*
[39] Charcot (1889), *Clinical Lectures*, p. 297.
[40] Freud (1893c), 'Some Points for a Comparative Study', p. 162.

[41] Ibid., p. 165 – italics Freud.
[42] Ibid., p. 169 – italics Freud.
[43] Ibid., p. 170.
[44] Ibid., pp. 169-170, 172; S. Freud (1893a/1895d), 'On the Psychical Mechanism of Hysterical Phenomena: Preliminary Communication', *SE* 2, p. 17. For the relationship between Freud and Janet, see O. van der Hart (1995), 'Pierre Janet en Sigmund Freud over hysterie, trauma en dissociatie'.
[45] Freud (1893c), 'Some Points for a Comparative Study', p. 170 – italics Freud.
[46] Freud was well aware of this: "Charcot was the first to teach us that to explain the hysterical neurosis we must apply to psychology". Ibid., p. 171.
[47] Ibid., p. 172.
[48] Freud (1893a/1895d), 'On the Psychical Mechanism of Hysterical Phenomena', p. 6.
[49] Ibid., p. 7 – italics Freud.
[50] Here it concerns 'Heredity and Aetiology of the Neuroses' (1896a), 'Further Remarks on the Neuro-Psychoses of Defence' (1896b) and 'The Aetiology of Hysteria' (1896c).
[51] Freud (1893a/1895d), 'On the Psychical Mechanism of Hysterical Phenomena', p. 6.
[52] Ibid., p. 13.
[53] In manuscript B from the letters to Fliess, Freud writes along the same lines: "Traumatic neurosis was well known; what we asserted beyond this was that *every* hysteria that is not hereditary is traumatic". Freud (1985c), *The Complete Letters*, p. 250 – italics Freud).
[54] Freud (1893a/1895d), 'On the Psychical Mechanism of Hysterical Phenomena', p. 17 – italics Freud.
[55] Ibid., p. 6. The latter also inevitably relativizes the aetiologic meaning of the 'affect of fright' we discussed earlier. The aetiological role of shock is related to a dissociative theory of hysteria: the fright affect that occurs in response to an external event complicates or prevents the synthesis of the representations. Fright is thus a reaction to an external event, while memory as trauma attacks us from within. Fright as the cause of a hysterical symptom is therefore tied with dissociation, not conflict and repression.
[56] Freud (1896c), 'The Aetiology of Hysteria', p. 206.
[57] J. Breuer & S. Freud (1895d), *Studies on Hysteria*, *SE* 2, pp. 106-124. For this problematic and a more detailed analysis of the case Lucy R., see J. Fletcher (2013), *Freud and the Scene of Trauma*. pp. 36ff.
[58] Breuer & Freud (1895d), *Studies on Hysteria*, pp. 118-119.
[59] Or to put it in another way, in the reconstruction of the causes, Freud does not encounter dissociation and the fragmentation of the self but rather the ability to associate and connect. These associations testify to the conflicts with the ego that lie at the origin of the symptoms of pathology.
[60] Ibid., p. 115.
[61] Ibid., p. 116.

[62] Freud (1893a/1895d), 'On the Psychical Mechanism of Hysterical Phenomena', p. 5; Breuer & Freud (1895d), *Studies on Hysteria*, pp. 112, 123; H. Westerink (2009), *A Dark Trace*, pp. 14-19. Repression here refers to a strong ego warding off associated representations. Consequently, according to Freud, the neurosis is characterized by a strong ego rather than by an ego that is no longer able to synthesize representations (Charcot, Janet).

[63] Freud (1905e), 'Fragment of an Analysis of a Case of Hysteria', p. 40; I. Alfandary (2017), 'Body Language'.

[64] Breuer & Freud (1895d), *Studies on Hysteria*, p. 11.

[65] Ibid., p. 118.

[66] Ibid., p. 120.

[67] Ibid., p. 123.

[68] Ibid., p. 124.

[69] Freud (1896c), 'The Aetiology of Hysteria', p. 193 – italics Freud)

[70] Ibid., p. 199.

[71] Ibid., p. 202. Freud compares the insight that hysteria is caused by premature sexual experience with the discovery of the source of the Nile (*caput Nili*) in the neuropathological realm. Ibid., p. 203.

[72] Freud remains somewhat ambiguous here. After all, after the first incident with the drugstore assistant, Emma returns to the store once more and now reproaches herself: 'Did I not provoke it myself?'. S. Freud (1950c), 'Project for a Scientific Psychology', *SE* 1, pp. 353-354.

[73] We will find an analogous problem in our discussion of the case of the Rat Man. In the case of the latter, the issue is not fear of the own sexual desire but fear of the own anger. We will return to this in detail in our third chapter.

[74] Freud (1950c), 'Project for a Scientific Psychology', pp. 353-354.

[75] Breuer & Freud (1895d), *Studies on Hysteria*, pp. 122-123.

[76] Also see Fletcher (2013), *Freud and the Scene of Trauma*.

[77] Freud (1896c), 'The Aetiology of Hysteria', p. 212. Freud compares this initial trauma with a 'disposition'. This is interesting because it shows that when Freud would in later texts interpret the notion of 'disposition' more organically, he continues to operate formally within the same frame of thought: trauma activates a pre-existing disposition. In the original seduction, this disposition is identified with an external event stored in the memory. In the modified seduction theory from Freud's later texts, it is associated with constitutional elements. We will return to this in detail.

[78] Ibid., p. 218.

[79] Freud (1985c), *The Complete Letters*, p. 223. We return to this problematic in detail in the third chapter on the Rat Man.

[80] I. Hacking (1995), *Rewriting the Soul: Multiple Personality and the Science of Memory*, pp. 191ff.

[81] Ph. Van Haute & T. Geyskens (2004), *Confusion of Tongues: The Primacy of Sexuality in Freud, Ferenczi and Laplanche*, pp. 12-13.

[82] S. Freud (1896b), 'Further Remarks on the Neuro-Psychoses of Defence', *SE* 3, p. 165 – italics Freud.

[83] Freud (1985c), *The Complete Letters*, p. 221.

[84] Ch. Darwin (1859), *On the Origin of Species*, pp. 63-70.

[85] F.J. Sulloway (1979), *Freud: Biologist of the Mind*; Van Haute & Geyskens (2004), *Confusion of Tongues*; Ph. Van Haute & H. Westerink (2016), 'Hysteria, Sexuality, and the Deconstruction of Normativity: Rereading Freud's 1905 Edition of *Three Essays on the Theory of Sexuality*'; Van Haute, & H. Westerink (2021), *From Pleasure to the Object*.

[86] T. Geyskens (2005), *Our Original Scenes. Freud's Theory of Sexulity*, pp. 23-26.

[87] Freud (1985c), *The Complete Letters*, p. 259.

[88] Ibid., pp. 259-260. Interestingly, in his text on 'The Aetiology of Hysteria', Freud goes into all these elements to refute them one by one. This text returns to a lecture of 21 April 1896 (he reports on it to Wilhelm Fliess in a letter of 26 April 1896) and is published in May and June of that same year in the *Wiener klinische Rundschau*. It remains unclear why, in his letter to Fliess of 21 September, he found these arguments convincing enough to abandon his *neurotica*.

[89] Kris (1952), 'Einleitung zur Erstausgabe', p. 545. In the course of our book, and especially in the chapters on the Wolf Man, on *Beyond the Pleasure Principle* and about *Moses and Monotheism*, it will become clear that this contradiction finds no support in Freud's texts.

[90] Freud (1985c), *The Complete Letters*, p. 260.

[91] For a more detailed discussion of what follows, see Van Haute & Geyskens (2004), *Confusion of Tongues*, pp. 10-32.

[92] For a detailed illustration, see the chapter on the Rat Man.

[93] In what follows, we discuss the internal reasons that brought Freud to the confirm the existence of infantile sexuality. However, Freud was by no means the only one debating the existence, content and importance of infantile sexuality around the end of the 19th century. On this historical context, see C.K. Carter (1983), 'Infantile Hysteria and Infantile Sexuality in Late Nineteenth-century German-language Medical Literature'; L. Sauerteig (2012), 'Loss of Innocence: Albert Moll, Sigmund Freud and the Invention of Childhood Sexuality around 1900'

[94] Freud (1985c), *The Complete Letters*, pp. 229-230.

[95] Ibid., pp. 223-224. Regarding paranoia, Freud simply does not answer the question: "The primary experience seems to be of a similar nature to that in obsessional neurosis; repression occurs after the memory of it has released unpleasure". Ibid., p. 226.

[96] Ibid., p. 221; Van Haute & Geyskens (2004), *Confusion of Tongues*, pp. 18-19.

[97] The discussion of the status of perversion is linked to the fact that Freud also gradually modified his understanding of the *content* of seduction. Initially, Freud ascribed a genital character to seduction (Freud 1896a: 152). Following the study of perversions, he came to a different conclusion on this matter during 1896: "they [sexual scenes from childhood – HW/PvH] include all the abuses known to debauched and impotent persons, among whom the buccal cavity and the rectum are misused

for sexual purposes". Freud (1896c), 'The Aetiology of Hysteria', p. 214. From here, it becomes inevitable to separate sexuality and genitality, as Freud will actually do from now on.

[98] Freud (1985c), *The Complete Letters*, pp. 268ff.

[99] Ibid., p. 222.

[100] Thus, as early as 6 December 1896, Freud writes the following: "So much for the superstructure. Now for an attempt to set it on its organic foundations. What must be explained is why sexual experiences, which, when they were current, generated pleasure, should, when remembered from a different phase (*als mit Phasendifferenz erinnert*), generate unpleasure in some people and persist as compulsion in others". Ibid., p. 238.

[101] Ibid., pp. 253-254 – letter 22 June 1897. Freud writes in this letter of 26 June 1897: "You [Fliess], the biological, I, the psychological".

[102] Van Haute & Westerink (2021), *From Pleasure to the Object.* The psychological theory describes the psychological mechanisms underlying the neurotic symptoms. Freud finds this theory first and foremost in the study of dreams, which are the central theme of his research in the years between 1897 and the publication of *Interpretation of Dreams* in November 1899.

[103] Freud (1985c), *The Complete Letters*, p. 326.

[104] Ibid., p. 434.

[105] Ibid., p. 268.

[106] Ibid., p. 269.

[107] Ibid., p. 269 – italics Freud.

[108] Ibid., pp. 269-270) Freud here concurs with contemporaries such as Krafft-Ebing. R. von Krafft-Ebing (1893), *Psychopathia Sexualis mit besonderer Berücksichtigung der conträren Sexualempfindung. Eine klinisch-forensische Studie*, pp. 1-18.

[109] Freud (1905d), *Three Essays*, p. 177.

[110] For detailed commentary on the problematic raised in this and the following paragraph, please refer to our fifth chapter on Freud's evolutionary insights.

[111] Freud (1985c), *The Complete Letters*, p. 280.

[112] Freud (1905d), *Three Essays*, p. 232; Van Haute & Westerink (2021), *From Pleasure to the Object.*

[113] Here we encounter a fundamental ambiguity in Freud's theory of sexuality that is beyond the scope of this study. As early as in the first edition of *Three Essays*, in which he publishes this theory, Freud writes that in principle the man takes a female object and vice versa, and this is because man and woman are complementary in reproduction (Freud 1905d: 207ff.). However, this assertion runs counter to the insights about the nature of sexuality that he formulates in the rest of the book: sexuality must be considered from the perspective of the search for desire. For a detailed discussion of this problematic, we refer to A. Davidson (2001), *The Emergence of Sexuality: Historical Epistemology and the Formation of Concepts*; Van Haute & Westerink (2021), *From Pleasure to the Object.*

[114] Ibid.

[115] As we will see in more detail in the following chapters on Dora, the Rat Man and the Wolf Man, Freud at no point rules out the possibility that the stories of traumas and abuse may indeed be real memories.

[116] Freud (1985c), *The Complete Letters*, p. 276.

[117] Ibid., p. 342.

[118] Ibid., p. 320.

[119] The following example from Freud's 1910 text *Leonardo da Vinci and a Memory of his Childhood* aptly illustrates this dynamic. It deals with a fundamental fantasy that plays a major role in the life of Leonardo in which a bird put its beak between his lips when he was still in the cradle: "The organic impression of this experience—the first source of pleasure in our life—doubtless remains indelibly printed on us; and when at a *later* date the child becomes familiar with the cow's udder whose function is that of a nipple, but whose shape and position under the belly make it resemble a penis, the preliminary stage has been reached which will later enable him to form the repellent sexual phantasy". S. Freud (1910c), *Leonardo da Vinci and a Memory of his Childhood, SE* 11, p. 86 – our italics; Van Haute & Geyskens (2004), Confusion of Tongues, pp. 28-30). Here too it is clear that for Freud the development of sexual fantasy occurs not in the infantile period but later in psychosexual development.

[120] S. Freud (1900a), *The Interpretation of Dreams, SE* 4–5, pp. 598ff.; S. Freud (1911b), 'Formulations on the Two Principles of Mental Functioning', *SE* 12, p. 219.

[121] In his later texts – for example in *Beyond the Pleasure Principle*, to which we will return in detail – Freud nuances this position and would also propose, for example, to consider a time factor: "The factor that determines the feeling is probably the amount of increase or diminution in the quantity of excitation *in a given period of time*". S. Freud (1920g), *Beyond the Pleasure Principle, SE* 18, p. 8 – italics Freud. In 'The Economic Problem of Masochism', Freud explicitly questions his general principle: "But such a view cannot be correct (…) it cannot be doubted that there are pleasurable tensions and unpleasurable relaxations of tension (…) The state of sexual excitation is the most striking example of a pleasurable increase of stimulus of this sort, but it is certainly not the only one (…) It appears that (pleasure and unpleasure) depend, not on this quantitative factor, but on some characteristic of it which we can only describe as a qualitative one (…) Perhaps it is the rhythm, the temporal sequence of changes, rises and falls in the quantity of stimulus". S. Freud, (1924c), 'The Economic Problem of Masochism', *SE* 19, p. 159.

[122] Freud (1950c), 'Project for a Scientific Psychology', p. 296.

[123] Ibid., pp. 325ff.

[124] Freud (1920g), *Beyond the Pleasure Principle*, p. 20.

[125] Freud (1905d), *Three Essays*, pp. 190-191.

[126] Ibid., pp. 235-236. For a detailed illustration, we refer to the next chapter on Dora.

[127] Ibid., p. 239.

[128] In our fourth chapter on the Wolf Man, we return in more detail on this notion of 'complemental series'.

[129] Breuer & Freud (1895d), *Studies on Hysteria*, p. 116.

[130] Freud (1906a), 'My Views', pp. 274, 277. In later chapters, and specifically in the discussion of the case of the Wolf Man (chapter 4) it will also be evident that our fantasy life harks back to phylogenetic schemes that result from the historical traumas to which humankind falls victim.

[131] Ibid., p. 272.

[132] In the 1923 'Two Encyclopedia Articles', Freud formulates this point of view as follows: "Thus a sexual trauma stepped into the place of ordinary trauma and the latter was seen to owe its aetiological significance to an associative or symbolic connection with the former, which had preceded it". S. Freud (1923a), 'Two Encyclpedia Articles: Psycho-Analysis and The Libido Theory', *SE* 18, p. 243.

[133] A. Scull (2009), *Hysteria: The Disturbing History*, pp. 152ff.

[134] Freud (1906a), 'My Views', p. 274.

Chapter 2: Seduction and hysterical disposition: Dora

[1] This chapter resumes several insights we have already explained in previous publications, particularly, Van Haute & Geyskens (2012), *A Non-Oedipal Psychoanalysis?*; Ph. Van Haute (2018), 'Trauma and Disgust: Dora between Freud and Laplanche'; Van Haute & Westerink (2021), *From Pleasure to the Object*.

[2] For the historical, political and cultural context backdrop to this analysis, see H.S. Decker (1991), *Freud, Dora and Vienna 1900*. Furthermore, also see D. Finzi & H. Westerink (2020), 'Die Dora Fall-Studie in Kontext'.

[3] Freud (1905e), 'Fragment of an Analysis of a Case of Hysteria', p. 23.

[4] Ibid., p. 13 – in footnote.

[5] Ibid., p. 7.

[6] Ibid., p. 24.

[7] Ibid., p. 27 – in footnote.

[8] Freud (1906a), 'My Views', p. 274.

[9] Ibid., p. 274). For a discussion of these passages, see A.I. Davidson (1984), 'The Assault on Freud'.

[10] Freud (1906a), 'My Views', p. 274 – italics Freud.

[11] Ibid.

[12] Ibid., p. 275.

[13] Freud (1985c), *The Complete Letters*, p. 433.

[14] The central meaning Freud assigns to the problematic of masturbation in this context is notable. The literature often suggests that there is a clear and unambiguous break between Freud and the psychiatric tradition in which this reference to the pathogenic role of masturbation plays a big role. Freud's discussion of Dora also illustrates that the relation between Freud and the psychiatric tradition is more complex than is sometimes thought and that it can certainly not be described in terms of pure opposition. However, this problematic falls beyond the reach of this book. Regarding the role of masturbation in the history of psychiatry, see J. Stengers & A. Van Neck (1998), *Histoire d'une grande peure. La masturbation.*

[15] P. Mahoney (1996), *Freud's Dora, A Psychoanalytic, Historical and Textual Study.*
[16] Freud (1905e), 'Fragment of an Analysis of a Case of Hysteria', p. 117.
[17] Ibid., p. 116.
[18] Ibid., p. 119 – italics Freud.
[19] Ibid, pp. 61, 122. Freud's countertransference relationship with Dora is a good illustration of Lacan's view that the countertransference should be identified with the sum of the analyst's biases. J. Lacan (1966), Écrits, p. 225.
[20] Freud (1905e), 'Fragment of an Analysis of a Case of Hysteria', p. 112.
[21] Ibid., p. 15. Two 'normal' phenomena allow the study of the psychical mechanisms that determine the formation of symptoms: the dream and the slip of the tongue. In 1901 Freud published an article about the latter subject that was later reworked into a comprehensive book: S. Freud (1901b), *The Psychopathology of Everyday Life*, *SE* 6.
[22] Freud (1905e), 'Fragment of an Analysis of a Case of Hysteria', p. 114.
[23] Freud (1985c), *The Complete Letters*, p. 433.
[24] Freud (1905e), 'Fragment of an Analysis of a Case of Hysteria', p. 113.
[25] Ibid., p 114). Also see Freud (1985c), *The Complete Letters*, pp. 433-434.
[26] On these patients, see i.a. A. Hustvedt (2011), *Medical Muses: Hysteria in nineteenth-century Paris.*
[27] E. Bleuler (1911), *Dementia Praecox oder die Gruppe der Schizophrenien.*
[28] In this regard, see i.a. A. Vergote (1982), 'Pulsion de mort et destins mortifères de la pulsion'; A. Vergote (1989), 'De splitsing taal-lichaam in de schizofrenie'.
[29] In this context it is perhaps meaningful to note that the fact that a large group of hysterical patients were henceforth diagnosed as 'schizophrenics' played an important part in the 'disappearance' of the Charcotian hysteria in the first decennium of the 20th century (Micale 1993). What Freud considered the basic symptom of hysteria – disgust with the sexual – could thus anticipate the impossibility of experiencing the body as a source of pleasure. Bleuler and many other authors who came after him regarded this impossibility as a basic symptom of schizophrenia.
[30] Freud (1905e), 'Fragment of an Analysis of a Case of Hysteria', p. 28.
[31] Ibid., p. 31 – italics Freud.
[32] Ibid., p. 32 – in footnote.
[33] Ibid., pp. 31-32 – italics Freud.
[34] Ibid., pp. 25, 27.
[35] Ibid., p. 28.
[36] Ibid., p. 29. Moreover, this scene also had other consequences: for example, Dora from then on refused to walk past a man when he was engaged in a passionate or tender conversation with a woman. From this point, she wanted to avoid observing such scenes at all costs. According to Freud this reluctance also refers to Dora's rejection of sexual arousal and pleasure feelings.
[37] We will further see in the chapters on Rat Man and the Wolf Man that in obsessional neurosis, the anal and not the oral drive component is reinforced. Different syndromes are associated with different dispositions.
[38] Ibid., p. 31

[39] Ibid.
[40] Ibid., p. 48 – italics Freud.
[41] Ibid., p. 51.
[42] Freud (1906a), 'My Views', pp. 275-276.
[43] Freud (1905e), 'Fragment of an Analysis of a Case of Hysteria', pp. 50-51. We know from our previous chapter that for Freud, the 'disturbance of the development of normal sexuality' is the definition of seduction.
[44] Ibid., p. 64 – italics Freud.
[45] Ibid., p. 72.
[46] It is not without merit to also comment here that Freud in this context is also referring to the old theory of degeneration. Freud's break with the old psychiatric theories is sometimes less radical than the secondary literature would have one suspect: "I was careful not to tell her that, as I have already mentioned (…), I too was of opinion that the offspring of luetics were very specially predisposed to severe neuropsychoses". Ibid., p. 75; also see Freud (1905d), *Three Essays*, pp. 235-236.
[47] Freud (1905e), 'Fragment of an Analysis of a Case of Hysteria', p. 75.
[48] Ibid., pp. 75, 76.
[49] Ibid.
[50] Ibid.
[51] Ibid., p. 79.
[52] Ibid., p. 27 – our italics.
[53] Israëls and Schatzman write: "In the Dora case Freud said he wishes to substantiate his 1896 theory, although the essence of that theory was absent in the Dora case history". Israëls & Schatzman (1993), 'The Seduction Theory', p. 23. Our previous discussion as well as what follows sufficiently shows that this interpretation is not in accordance with the text.
[54] Freud (1905e), 'Fragment of an Analysis of a Case of Hysteria', p. 80.
[55] Ibid.
[56] In a text from 1897, Freud summarizes this position as follows: "*Neurotic anxiety is transformed sexual libido*". S. Freud (1897b), 'Abstracts of the Scientific Writings', p. 250 – italics Freud.
[57] In this regard, Freud speaks of '*somatic compliance*' (Freud 1905e: 40 – italics Freud). The unconscious interpretation expresses itself in a real somatic symptom ("the symptom cannot occur without the presence of a certain degree of somatic compliance offered by some normal or pathological process in or connected with one of the bodily organs"). Dora's cough, for example, is not caused by a conversion from an unconscious interpretation in the body, but an interpretation uses the cough to make itself known. It is, as it were, welded to it. As a result, the cough does not disappear after some time as it normally would. The predominance of the oral zone in Dora's pathology that we discussed earlier can also be understood as a form of 'somatic compliance'. Freud (1905e), 'Fragment of an Analysis of a Case of Hysteria', p. 41.
[58] Ibid., p. 80.
[59] Ibid., p. 83.

60 Ibid., p. 84.

61 Ibid.

62 In the third edition of *Three Essays on the Theory of Sexuality* Freud adds the following passage to the original text: "The single aetiological series then falls into two, which may be called the dispositional and the definitive. In the first the constitution and the accidental experiences of childhood interact in the same manner as do the disposition and later traumatic experiences in the second". Freud (1905d), *Three Essays*, p. 239. This passage presumably refers to the study of the Wolf Man who was in analysis with Freud in the period between 1910 and 1914. In the following year – and thus coinciding with the preparation of the third edition of *Three Essays* – Freud started writing this case. Herein Freud would analyze the infantile neurosis of his patient, of which he further notes that it lies at the basis of the adult neurotic problematic. One can also apply the passage that was just cited to the study of Dora: like the infantile neurosis of the Wolf Man primed his adult neurosis, the constitutional elements (for example, the amplified oral drive) together with the experiences from Dora's infantile period (for instance her parents making love) primed the pathology that was expressed in puberty.

63 The problematic of hysteria in children was in itself no Freudian innovation. It was, on the contrary, a widely discussed theme in psychiatry at the end of the 19th century. About this, see Carter (1983), 'Infantile Hysteria and Infantile Sexuality'.

64 Freud (1905e), 'Fragment of an Analysis of a Case of Hysteria', pp. 224ff.)

65 See for example Bernheimer & Kahane (1990), *In Dora's Case.*

66 Freud (1905e), 'Fragment of an Analysis of a Case of Hysteria', p. 34.

67 Ibid., p. 35.

68 Ibid., p. 64.

69 Ibid., pp. 68-70.

70 Ibid., p. 56.

71 In the chapter on the Wolf Man, we return once more on the status of these typical dreams.

72 Freud (1900a), *The Interpretation of Dreams*, pp. 261ff.

73 Ibid., p. 262.

74 For a more extensive discussion of the passages on the Oedipus myth in *The Interpretation of Dreams*, see Ph. Van Haute (2016), '...die de diepste raadslen kende en de hoogste stond in macht. Het Oedipus-complex in de vroegste teksten van Freud'.

75 On the understanding that the young child in this period according to Freud exclusively interprets the gender difference in terms of the presence or absence of the male organ. S. Freud (1923e), 'The Infantile Genital Organization of the Libido', *SE* 19, pp. 144-145.

76 Freud (1905e), 'Fragment of an Analysis of a Case of Hysteria', p. 56.

77 We return to this in detail in our next chapter in connection with Freud's texts on the Rat Man and the 'Family Romances' of the neurotic that dates from the same period.

78 Freud (1905d), *Three Essays*, p. 224.

79 Van Haute & Westerink (2016), 'Hysteria, Sexuality, and the Deconstruction of Normativity'; Van Haute & Westerink (2021), *From Pleasure to the Object.* In the background there is a more general problem. Since Freud knows or accepts only two fundamental drives – a sexual drive and a self-preservation drive – he can exclusively think of attachment as inhibited sexuality. Freud's hesitation to call infantile infatuation with the parents of the opposite sex 'sexual' must perhaps also be understood in terms of this problematic. For a discussion of this, see also Van Haute & Geyskens (2005), *From Death Instinct to Attachment Theory.*

80 Freud (1905e), 'Fragment of an Analysis of a Case of Hysteria', p. 70.

81 Ibid., p. 86.

82 R. Blass (1992), 'Did Dora Have an Oedipus Complex? A Re-examination of the Theoretical Context of Freud's "Fragment of an Analysis"'; R. Blass (2018), 'The Analytic Denial of Freud's Struggle with the Understanding of Dora: Simplifying the Oedipus complex and the Process of its Adoption'; Van Haute & Geyskens (2012), *A Non-Oedipal Psychoanalysis?*

83 Freud (1905e), 'Fragment of an Analysis of a Case of Hysteria', p. 61.

84 Ibid., p. 26.

85 Freud (1905d), *Three Essays.*

86 John Fletcher, for instance, who wrote a seminal book on Freud's work, never or hardly ever mentions Dora. Fletcher (2013), *Freud and the Scene of Trauma.*

87 Freud (1896c), 'The Aetiology of Hysteria'. For more detail about this, we refer to our previous chapter.

88 We should also underline the importance of the case study of 'Little Hans' from 1909 here, which Freud publishes between these two case studies. This case forced Freud to accept the existence of a childhood neurosis.

89 Freud (1985c), *The Complete Letters*, p. 240.

90 Van Haute & Westerink (2021), *From Pleasure to the Object*, pp. 36ff.

Chapter 3: Trauma, aggression and father complex: the Rat Man

1 This chapter relies on and is complemented by earlier publications: Ph. Van Haute & T. Geyskens (2013), 'Woede, wellust en weifelzucht: Een freudiaanse symptomatologie van de dwangneurose'; H. Westerink (2013), 'De Rattenman, zijn schuldgevoel en zijn twee gevoelsconflicten'; H. Westerink (2015), 'De problematische plaats van de woede in het denken van Freud over agressiviteit'; H. Westerink & Ph. Van Haute (2020), '"Family Romances" and the Oedipalization of Freudian Psychoanalysis'.

2 In our exposition we do not rely exclusively on the text of the published case study itself but also on Freud's original record of the analysis, which was partially published posthumously in the *Standard Edition* (Freud 1955a). The complete records were published in 1987 in the *Nachtragsband* of the *Gesammelte Werke*. Freud also discussed this case during meetings of the Vienna psychoanalytic association on 30 October and 6 November 1907. H. Nunberg & E. Federn (1976), *Protokolle der Wiener Psychoanalytischen Vereinigung Bd. 1, 1906-1908*, pp. 212-224.

3 Freud (1909d), 'Notes upon a Case of Obsessional Neurosis', p. 155 – our italics.
4 Ibid., p. 221.
5 Ibid., pp. 200 ff.
6 P. Mahoney (1986), *Freud and the Rat Man.*
7 In this context, Freud's language is not always clear. He talks about *Konstitution, Disposition* and *Anlage* without clearly distinguishing these concepts. For example, it sometimes seems as if he uses constitution and disposition as synonyms. Gradually a clear difference emerges between 'constitution' and 'predisposition' on the one hand and 'disposition' on the other. Thus, Freud for instance writes about 'dispositions' in 'The Disposition to Obsessional Neurosis' that it concerns a developmental inhibition that comes about from an exchange of hereditary factors (disposition: for example, a constitutionally intensified anal-sadistic urge) and environmental factors (experiences, impressions). S. Freud (1913i), 'The Disposition to Obsessional Neurosis', *SE* 12. We will return to these distinctions in our chapter on the Wolf Man.
8 We will come back to this in detail in our sixth chapter, which deals with *Beyond the Pleasure Principle.*
9 Freud (1909d), 'Notes upon a Case of Obsessional Neurosis', p. 167.
10 Ibid., p. 168 – italics Freud
11 Ibid. – italics Freud.
12 Ibid., p. 158.
13 Ibid., p. 191.
14 Ibid., p. 187.
15 Ibid., p. 191.
16 Ibid., p. 192.
17 Ibid., p. 162.
18 Ibid., p. 160.
19 Ibid., p. 165.
20 Ibid., p. 163.
21 Ibid., p. 162. Freud already formulated this insight in a short text on 'Obsessive Actions and Religious Practices': "We may say that the sufferer from compulsions and prohibitions behaves as if he were dominated by a sense of guilt, of which, however, he knows nothing, so that we must call it an unconscious sense of guilt, in spite of the apparent contradiction in terms. This sense of guilt has its source in certain early mental events, but it is constantly being revived by renewed temptations which arise whenever there is a contemporary provocation. Moreover, it occasions a lurking sense of expectant anxiety, an expectation of misfortune, which is linked, through the idea of punishment, with the internal perception of the temptation". S. Freud (1907b), 'Obsessive Actions and Religious Practices', *SE* 9, p. 123.
22 Freud (1909d), 'Notes upon a Case of Obsessional Neurosis', p. 178.
23 Ibid., p. 182.
24 Ibid.
25 Ibid., p. 182.
26 Ibid., p. 163 – our italics.

[27] Ibid., pp. 205-206.
[28] Also, in the case of the Rat Man, the trauma thus comes from within. We will return to this problematic.
[29] S. Freud (1955a), 'Originalnotizen zu einem Fall von Zwangsneurose', p. 517.
[30] Freud (1909d), 'Notes upon a Case of Obsessional Neurosis', pp. 239-240.
[31] Ibid., p. 198.
[32] Ibid.
[33] Ibid., p. 210.
[34] Ibid., pp. 210-217.
[35] Ibid., p. 217.
[36] Ibid., p. 168.
[37] Freud (1896c), 'The Aetiology of Hysteria', p. 193 – italics Freud.
[38] Freud (1909d), 'Notes upon a Case of Obsessional Neurosis', p. 240.
[39] Ibid., p. 240 – our italics.
[40] Ibid., p. 248.
[41] Ibid., pp. 240-241.
[42] Van Haute & Geyskens (2013), 'Woede, wellust en weifelzucht'. This means that the Rat Man's anger is, according to Freud, an expression of his hatred towards the father, that is, founded on the sadistic component of the libido. We return to this later.
[43] Freud (1909d), 'Notes upon a Case of Obsessional Neurosis', p. 206.
[44] Freud (1955a), 'Originalnotizen zu einem Fall von Zwangsneurose', p. 547.
[45] Freud (1909d), 'Notes upon a Case of Obsessional Neurosis', p. 208 – in footnote.
[46] Freud (1908c), 'On the Sexual Theories of Children', *SE* 9, p. 211.
[47] S. Freud (1909c), 'Family Romances', *SE* 9, pp. 238-239; see also Westerink & Van Haute (2020), '"Family Romances" and the Oedipalization of Freudian Psychoanalysis'.
[48] In the first edition of the *Three Essays on the Theory of Sexuality*, Freud notes that infantile sexuality is not oriented at objects (autoerotic). Yet already in the original version of this text, he had to concede that some aspects of infantile sexuality appear thoroughly object-oriented or cannot be understood without such an orientation. The case on 'Analysis of a Phobia in a Give-Year-Old Boy ['Little Hans']', published in 1909, played a central role in the discovery of an object-oriented infantile sexuality. During the same period that Freud abandons the autoerotic character of infantile sexuality, there is a progressive 'oedipalization' of infantile relations. Freud's short texts on family romances and infantile sexual theories, which we analyze in the remainder of this section, play a central role in this oedipalization. Freud (1908c), 'On the Sexual Theories of Children'; S. Freud (1909b), 'Analysis of a Phobia in a Five-Year-Old Boy', *SE* 10; Freud (1909c), 'Family Romances'. For commentary on the meaning of this 'oedipalization', see Westerink & Van Haute (2020).
[49] This means a drive aimed at solving the mysteries that a confrontation with reality presents the small child. Freud only introduces this drive in the third edition of *Three Essays on the Theory of Sexuality.* Freud (1905d), *Three Essays*, p. 194.

[50] Freud (1908c), 'On the Sexual Theories of Children', p. 212.
[51] Freud (1909c), 'Family Romances', p. 224.
[52] Freud (1905d), *Three Essays*, p. 196; Freud (1908c), 'On the Sexual Theories of Children', p. 220.
[53] Freud (1905d), *Three Essays*, p. 196.
[54] Freud (1909d), 'Notes upon a Case of Obsessional Neurosis', pp. 106ff.
[55] Freud (1909c), 'Family Romances', p. 237.
[56] We use genital difference and not sexual difference here to respect Freud's terminology.
[57] Freud (1909c), 'Family Romances', p. 239 – our italics.
[58] Van Haute & Westerink (2021), *From Pleasure to the Object.*
[59] Freud closely follows Jung's insights into this problem. According to Jung, psychological development must be understood in terms of growing autonomy with regards to the parents. This development is also not motivated by sexual motives, according to Jung. C.G. Jung (1909), 'Die Bedeutung des Vaters für das Schicksal des Einzelnen', pp. 155 ff.; P. Vandermeersch (1991), *Unresolved Questions in the Freud-Jung Debate on Psychosis, Sexual Identity and Religion.* For a more extensive discussion of this theme, cf. Westerink & Ph. Van Haute (2020), '"Family Romances" and the Oedipalization of Freudian Psychoanalysis'.
[60] Freud (1908c), 'On the Sexual Theories of Children', p. 212.
[61] Freud (1909d), 'Notes upon a Case of Obsessional Neurosis', p. 206 – in footnote.
[62] Ibid.
[63] Freud (1893a/1895d), 'On the Psychical Mechanism of Hysterical Phenomena', p. 6.
[64] Westerink (2015), 'De problematische plaats van de woede', p. 729.
[65] Freud (1985c), *The Complete Letters*, pp. 164-165. For more details in this regard, see our first chapter.
[66] Freud (1909d), 'Notes upon a Case of Obsessional Neurosis', p. 157.
[67] Breuer & Freud (1895d), *Studies on Hysteria*, p. 202.
[68] M. Heidegger (1961), *Nietzsche 1*, pp. 56-59.
[69] Freud (1909d), 'Notes upon a Case of Obsessional Neurosis', p. 182.
[70] Ibid., p. 189; Freud (1955a), 'Originalnotizen zu einem Fall von Zwangsneurose', p. 569.
[71] Freud (1909d), 'Notes upon a Case of Obsessional Neurosis', p. 240.
[72] Freud (1905d), *Three Essays*, p. 193.
[73] Continuing these insights, Alfred Adler in 1908 developed his insights on an aggression drive. Adler takes up Freud's idea that in sadism we are dealing with an 'entanglement' of sexual drives and the non-sexual drive for mastery. He postulates that there is an original 'enmity' of the child towards the outside world. We find, an all relations to this outside world, a 'hostile combative attitude' that is needed to enable satisfaction and the experience of pleasure. A. Adler (1908), 'Der Aggressionstrieb im Leben und in der Neurose'.
[74] We return in detail to the relationship between sexuality and aggression in the chapter on *Beyond the Pleasure Principle.*

[75] Freud (1909d), 'Notes upon a Case of Obsessional Neurosis', p. 240. Only in *Totem and Taboo* does Freud provide an answer to the question about the origin of hate and love. These passions are determined by a past that really happened: a murder of a primal father. Since this primal murder, hate, love and blame are constitutionally anchored in human nature. Westerink (2009), *A Dark Trace*, pp. 87-138). We return extensively to this in our chapter on *Moses and Monotheism*.

[76] See in this regard our sixth chapter.

[77] These shifts should be understood from the discussion with Carl Gustav Jung about the existence and nature of infantile sexuality. To block all ambiguity, Freud redefines this sexuality in 'puberal' terms. In this way there is no doubt that infantile sexuality indeed concerns 'real' sexuality. The reference to the *reality* of a sexual trauma in the case of the Wolf Man is another strategy Freud uses to escape the Jungian rejection of infantile sexuality.

[78] Freud (1905d), *Three Essays*, p. 199.

[79] M. Schröter (2012), *Sigmund Freud - Eugen Bleuler: Ich bin zuversichtlich, wir erobern bald die Psychiatrie. Briefwechsel 1904 – 1937*, p. 100. Freud shares this interest with Jung, and it is especially in the discussion with the latter about the fundamentals of psychoanalytic metapsychology that 'applied psychoanalysis' comes about. This discussion with Jung falls beyond the scope of this study, however. For this, we refer to the scientific literature. Vandermeersch (1991), *Unresolved Questions in the Freud-Jung Debate*.

[80] This increasing importance first becomes clear in *Totem and Taboo*. S. Freud (1912-13a), *Totem and Taboo, SE* 13.

Chapter 4: Seduction, primal scene and constitution: The Wolf Man

[1] S. Freud (1918b), 'From the History of an Infantile Neurosis', *SE* 17, p. 95.

[2] S. Freud (1914d), 'On the History of the Psycho-Analytic Movement', *SE* 14.

[3] Freud (1918b), 'From the History of an Infantile Neurosis', p. 7 – in footnote.

[4] Ibid., p. 8.

[5] In principle, the libido in Jung has a non-sexual character. It is an energetic principle of 'interest' that moves the individual to develop the own possibilities of existence (Jung 1912; 1913).

[6] C.G. Jung (1913), 'Versuch einer Darstellung der psychoanalytischen Theorie', §365; see also Vandermeersch (1991), *Unresolved Questions in the Freud-Jung Debate*, pp. 241ff.

[7] Jung (1913), 'Versuch einer Darstellung', §411.

[8] Freud (1918b), 'From the History of an Infantile Neurosis', p. 54.

[9] Ibid., p. 10.

[10] Ibid., p. 11.

[11] Ibid., p. 4, Editor's Note – italics Freud.

[12] S. Freud (1913d), 'Dreams in Folklore', *SE* 12. Freud will include that part of the text in its entirety in chapter 4 of his case study.

[13] When the text was republished in 1924, Freud added a long footnote at the end of the text in which he reconstructed the chronology of the disease history, followed by a short statement about the period of the second analysis of the Wolf Man – from September 1919 until April 1920.

[14] Freud (1913d), 'Dreams in Folklore', p. 283. Some of the details Freud does not note can be found in the memoires the Wolf Man wrote at an advanced age. M. Gardiner (1971), *The Wolf-man.*

[15] Freud (1918b), 'From the History of an Infantile Neurosis', p. 77.

[16] Ibid., p. 14.

[17] Ibid., p. 15.

[18] The Wolf Man also recalls several anger attacks during this time. There is one scene where he becomes angry for not having received double the number of gifts to which he thought he was entitled: this is on account of his birthday coinciding with Christmas (6 January – according to the Russian calendar).

[19] Ibid., p. 17.

[20] Ibid., p. 12.

[21] Ibid., pp. 21, 33.

[22] Ibid., p. 49.

[23] Freud already raised this question in the letter to Fliess in which he denounces the belief in his neuroticism. Freud (1985c), *The Complete Letters*, p. 264.

[24] Freud (1918b), 'From the History of an Infantile Neurosis', p. 19.

[25] Ibid., p. 20.

[26] Ibid., p. 51.

[27] Ibid. In the case of the dreams about the governess and the sister, the analysis failed to arrive at a fixed dream content. The same material (the aggression against the two of them) was produced in a different way each time without firm conviction of the reality of past scenes. Ibid. p. 19.

[28] Ibid., pp. 33, 36.

[29] Ibid., p. 20.

[30] Ibid.

[31] Ibid., p. 24.

[32] Ibid., p. 17.

[33] Freud returns here to insights from his study of Little Hans from 1909. Freud (1909b) 'Analysis of a Phobia in a Five-Year-Old Boy', pp. 7-8, 31, 120. Also see Van Haute & Westerink (2021), *From Pleasure to the Object*, pp. 54-58.

[34] Freud (1918b), 'From the History of an Infantile Neurosis', p. 25.

[35] In the case study of Little Hans, Freud showed that Hans's 'worldview' is a 'sexual theory' informed infantile auto-eroticism and the components of the sexual constitution. Freud (1908c), 'On the Sexual Theories of Children'; Freud (1909b)., 'Analysis of a Phobia in a Five-Year-Old Boy', pp. 105ff.

[36] Freud (1918b), 'From the History of an Infantile Neurosis', p. 25.

[37] Ibid. – italics Freud.

[38] Ibid., pp. 26, 47.

[39] Ibid., p. 68.

[40] A screen memory is powerful, and its content is apparently meaningless, yet on closer inspection, it provides a screen for another, sexually traumatic memory. Such a screen memory has a compromising character: on the one hand it shows a tendency to remember a repressed experience, on the other hand a resistance to a return of this memory to consciousness. S. Freud (1899a), 'Screen Memories', *SE* 3.

[41] Freud (1918b), 'From the History of an Infantile Neurosis', p. 96.

[42] Ibid., p. 93.

[43] Ibid., p. 112.

[44] Ibid., p. 108.

[45] Ibid., p. 27.

[46] Ibid., p. 109.

[47] The introduction of a developmental psychological perspective in the theory of sexuality (i.a. Freud (1913i), 'The Disposition to Obsessional Neurosis'; Freud (1905d), *Three Essays,* pp. 197-200), makes it possible for Freud to refer to an assumed normal sexual development (i.a. Freud (1918b), 'From the History of an Infantile Neurosis', pp. 43, 47) and deviations therefrom in perverse fixations, inhibitions or regressions. Since this sexual development normally results in a heterosexual object choice and sexual activities that serve reproduction, according to Freud, the introduction of a developmental perspective is accompanied by an increased heteronormative tendency. Van Haute & Westerink (2021), *From Pleasure to the Object*, pp. 64-67.

[48] Freud (1918b), 'From the History of an Infantile Neurosis', p. 108; see also J. Laplanche (1980). *La sublimation*, p. 87.

[49] Freud (1918b), 'From the History of an Infantile Neurosis', p. 27.

[50] Ibid., p. 108.

[51] Freud (1905d), *Three Essays*, p. 242.

[52] Freud concludes in *Three Essays*: "The causation [of lasting perverse and neurotic disorders] is shared between a compliant constitution, precocity, the characteristic of increased pertinacity of early impressions and the chance stimulation of the sexual instinct by extraneous influences". Ibid., p. 243.

[53] Breuer & Freud (1895d), *Studies on Hysteria*, p. 127 – in footnote.

[54] Tailor is *Schneider* in German, someone who 'cuts' or 'cuts off'.

[55] In the case of Little Hans, Freud shows that the fear of and fascination with horses can be seen as resulting from the 'shift' of the ambivalent feelings for the father to an animal. Freud (1909b), 'Analysis of a Phobia in a Five-Year-Old Boy', p. 125; Freud (1912-13a), *Totem and Taboo*, p. 128. See also H. Westerink (2014), 'Projection, Substitution and Exaltation: Freud's Case Study of Little Hans and the Creation of God in *Totem and Taboo*'.

[56] Freud (1918b), 'From the History of an Infantile Neurosis', p. 32.

[57] Ibid., p. 34.

[58] Ibid., pp. 35-36.

[59] Ibid., pp. 36, 37.

[60] In the Dora case, the little girl hears her parents' 'shortness of breath' during sexual intercourse. Freud notes that children 'divine' that the 'uncanny sound' has a sexual

meaning. Freud suggests here that children understand 'intuitively' ('innate pieces of mechanism') when something has a sexual meaning. Freud (1905e), 'Fragment of an Analysis of a Case of Hysteria', p. 80.

61 Freud (1918b), 'From the History of an Infantile Neurosis', p. 45.

62 Ibid., p. 36.

63 Ibid., p. 46.

64 Ibid., p. 44 – in footnote.

65 Ibid., p. 47.

66 In *Three Essays* from 1905 Freud had argued that knowledge of genital difference only comes about during puberty. Freud (1905d), *Three Essays*, pp. 219-221). In the case of the Wolf Man, it becomes clear that the wolf dream also marks the moment the boy comes to understand the genital difference and its implications for himself. It implies reinforcing a heteronormative perspective on sexuality.

67 Freud (1918b), 'From the History of an Infantile Neurosis', p. 28.

68 Ibid., p. 47.

69 Ibid.

70 Ibid., p. 109.

71 Ibid., p. 95.

72 Westerink (2014), 'Projection, Substitution and Exaltation'.

73 Freud (1918b), 'From the History of an Infantile Neurosis', p. 120 – in footnote.

74 Ibid., p. 45 – in footnote – italics Freud).

75 For an extensive discussion on *Nachträglichkeit* in the work of Freud, see J. Laplanche (2006), *Problématiques VI: L'après coup*.

76 Cf. Fletcher (2013), *Freud and the Scene of Trauma*, p. 252.

77 Freud (1918b), 'From the History of an Infantile Neurosis', p. 55.

78 Cf. Fletcher (2013), *Freud and the Scene of Trauma*, pp. 248ff.

79 Freud (1906a), 'My Views on the Part Played by Sexuality in the Aetiology of the Neuroses', p. 275.

80 Freud (1905d), *Three Essays*, pp. 170-171.

81 Freud (1905e), 'Fragment of an Analysis of a Case of Hysteria', p. 50.

82 Freud (1909d), 'Notes upon a Case of Obsessional Neurosis', p. 240

83 It is important in this context that there are also people with shocking experiences during childhood who did not develop a neurosis.

84 Van Haute & Geyskens (2012), *A Non-Oedipal Psychoanalysis?*, pp. 36ff.

85 S. Freud (1913j), 'The Claims of Psychoanalysis to Scientific Interest', *SE* 13, p. 183.

86 Freud (1918b), 'From the History of an Infantile Neurosis', p. 81.

87 Ibid., p. 41.

88 S. Freud (1912i), 'Einleitingspassagen zu: "Über einige Übereinstimungen im Seelenleben der Wilden und der Neurotiker"', p. 745.

89 Freud (1912-13a), *Totem and Taboo*, p. 158. That an individual's life experiences are necessary to activate constitutional factors can be seen as a response to Jung. After all, Jung had argued that phylogenetic material acts autonomously and as a self-determining force on psychic life.

[90] Freud (1918b), 'From the History of an Infantile Neurosis', p. 119; also L. Silveira (2013), 'Phylogenetic schema and transcendental field: The problem of the universal character of fantasy in Freud and Lacan'; E. Marder (2015), 'L'Homme aux loups. L'animal sexuel et la scène primitive'.

[91] Freud (1918b), 'From the History of an Infantile Neurosis', p. 119.

[92] Ibid., p. 96. The father as castrator in this phylogenetic schema is described by Freud in *Totem and Taboo* and 'Overview of the Transference Neuroses' from 1915. In these texts, he notes that in the Oedipus complex and the castration complex, the father has the same role, that is "the part of a dreaded enemy to the sexual interests of childhood" and as actual castrator of the sons in his horde as must have been in the case in the remote primordial history (Ice Age, Stone Age) of the hominids. Freud (1912-13a), *Totem and Taboo*, p. 130; Freud (1985a), *A Phylogenetic Fantasy*, pp. 16ff.

[93] Freud (1918b), 'From the History of an Infantile Neurosis', p. 120. Also compare earlier remarks on Dora's reaction to overhearing the sexual intercourse between her parents (p. xxxx).

[94] Ibid.

[95] Ibid.

[96] Freud (1905e), 'Fragment of an Analysis of a Case of Hysteria, p. 50 – italics Freud.

[97] In the text 'Overview of the Transference Neuroses', which was written in 1915 (but not published until 1985), Freud speaks of a disposition as "a fixation point, in either ego or libido development", and he views this point of fixation as a decisive moment in the choice of neuroses. Freud (1985a), *A Phylogenetic Fantasy*, p. 9).

[98] S. Freud (1913a), 'A Dream which bore Testimony', *SE* 12, p. 317.

[99] Van Haute & Westerink (2021), *From Pleasure to the Object.*

[100] Freud writes about this: "To begin with, I had only distinguished, first the phase of auto-erotism, during which the subject's component instincts, each on its own account, seek for the satisfaction of their desires in his own body, and then the combination of all the component instincts for the choice of an object, under the primacy of the genitals acting on behalf of reproduction". Freud (1913a), 'A Dream which bore Testimony', pp. 320-321.

[101] In his views on the stages of development, Freud is strongly influenced by the work of his pupil Karl Abraham. See about this May (2015a), *Freud bei der Arbeit.*

[102] Freud (1905d), *Three Essays*, pp. 197-200.

[103] Ibid., p. 235; Freud (1905e), 'Fragment of an Analysis of a Case of Hysteria', p. 50.

[104] Freud (1913a), 'A Dream which bore Testimony', p. 324.

[105] Freud (1918b), 'From the History of an Infantile Neurosis', p. 27.

[106] Ibid., p. 47.

[107] Ibid., p. 80.

[108] Ibid., p. 79 – our italics.

[109] Ibid., p. 78. In this regard, we would like to point out that in different texts such as *Three Essays*, the Leonardo text, the Schreber case study, and 'On Narcissism' Freud developed widely divergent perspectives on homosexuality. For a brief overview, see Van Haute & Westerink (2021), *From Pleasure to the Object*, pp. 67-70.

[110] Freud (1918b), 'From the History of an Infantile Neurosis', p. 113.
[111] Ibid., p. 61.
[112] Freud (1916-17a), *Introductory Lectures*, p. 346.
[113] Ibid., p. 362.
[114] Ibid., p. 361. In the preface to the third edition of *Three Essays* from 1915, Freud writes that a disposition is nothing but the precipitation of earlier experiences of previous generations, supplemented by the individual's recent experiences. A disposition is from this perspective "the sum of the accidental factors". Freud (1905d), *Three Essays*, p. 131.
[115] S. Freud (1895f), 'A Reply to Criticisms of My Paper on Anxiety Neurosis', *SE* 3, p. 138.
[116] Freud (1906a), 'My Views', p. 279. Compare: "Disposition and experience are here linked up in an indissoluble aetiological unity. For *disposition* exaggerates impressions which would otherwise have been completely commonplace and have had no effect, so that they become traumas giving rise to stimulations and fixations; while *experiences* awaken factors in the disposition which, without them, might have long remained dormant and perhaps never have developed. Freud (1914d), 'On the History of the Psycho-Analytic Movement', p. 18 – italics Freud).
[117] Freud (1905d), *Three Essays*, pp. 239-240.
[118] Freud (1900a), *The Interpretation of Dreams*, pp. 37-38, 241. In this context, Freud discusses the Oedipus myth (Sophocles) as exemplary for the occurrence of amorous and hostile wishes directed at the parents. Ibid., p. 261.
[119] Ibid., pp. 360-367; cf. lecture X in Freud (1916-17a), *Introductory Lectures*.
[120] S. Freud (1915f), 'A Case of Paranoia running counter to the Psychoanalytic Theory of the Disease', *SE* 14, p. 269; see also J. Laplanche & J.-B. Pontalis (1985), *Fantasme originaire, Fantasmes des origines, Origines des fantasmes*.
[121] Freud (1916-17a), *Introductory Lectures*, p. 371.
[122] The reference to phylogeny implies a reinforcement of a tendency to universalization of 'typical' psychical contents and thus also of the Oedipus complex.
[123] Freud (1918b), 'From the History of an Infantile Neurosis', p. 97. Laplanche and Pontalis proposed ridding the 'primal phantasies' of the reference to inheritance of psychical contents (sexual experiences/impressions of previous generations) and defining the concept from confrontation of the child with the enigmatic messages from adults and the a priori structuring character of the Oedipus complex. Laplanche & Pontalis (1985), *Fantasme originaire, Fantasmes des origines, Origines des fantasmes*.
[124] Cf. Freud (1985c; *The Complete Letters*, pp. 264-265.
[125] Freud (1918b), 'From the History of an Infantile Neurosis', p. 97.
[126] In lecture 23, Freud describes the relationship between the individual experience and the experiences of ancestors as 'complemental relationship' (*Ergänzungsverhältnis*). Freud (1916-17a), *Introductory Lectures*, p. 370.
[127] Freud (1918b), 'From the History of an Infantile Neurosis', p. 34.

[128] In lecture 23, Freud writes about this that the observation of animals copulating combined with viewing pleasure and sexual curiosity can be supplemented by phylogenetic material so that a phantasy emerges of the copulating parents. It is 'typical' for these phantasies that the sexual intercourse is *more ferarum* (*a tergo*). Freud (1916-17a), *Introductory Lectures*, p. 369.

[129] Fletcher (2013), *Freud and the Scene of Trauma*, p. 227.

[130] Freud (1918b), 'From the History of an Infantile Neurosis', p. 97.

[131] Ibid., p. 96.

[132] Freud (1910a), 'Five Lectures on Psycho-Analysis', p. 47; Freud (1912-13a), *Totem and Taboo*, p. 157.

[133] Ibid.

Chapter 5: Constitution, phylogeny and evolutionary biology

1 In *Totem and Taboo*, it becomes explicitly clear that the introduction of the Oedipus complex as "nuclear complex of perhaps every psychoneurosis" and as description of the child's original object-choice is inseparable from a systematic exploration of the phylogenetic aspects of "the peculiarities which characterize his [the child's and primitive man's] modes of thought and his emotional life". Freud (1912a), 'Postscript to Psychoanalytic Remarks', p. 82; Freud (1912-13a), *Totem and Taboo*, p. 132.

2 Freud (1985c), *The Complete Letters*, p. 279.

3 Cf. Sulloway (1979), *Freud: Biologist of the Mind*, p. 199.

4 Freud (1985c), *The Complete Letters*, pp. 223, 230, 279-280.

5 Freud (1916-17a), *Introductory Lectures*, p. 354.

6 Freud (1905d), *Three Essays*, p. 198 – inserted 1915; P. Adriaens (2008), *Het nut van waanzin. Essays over darwinisme en psychiatrie*.

7 Freud (1913j), 'The Claims of Psychoanalysis to Scientific Interest', p. 184; Freud (1905d), *Three Essays*, p. 131 – inserted in 1915. Frank Sulloway shows in *Freud: Biologist of the Mind* that Fliess as well as Freud presume Haeckel in their research into smell and the origin of disgust in early childhood. Sulloway (1979), *Freud: Biologist of the Mind*, pp. 198-202.

8 *Die Ontogenesis ist die kurze und schnelle Recapitulation der Phylogenesis, bedingt durch die physiologische Functionen der Vererbung (Fortpflanzung) und Anpassung (Ernährung)*. E. Haeckel (1866), *Generelle Morphologie der Organismen: Allgemeine Grundzüge der organischen Formen-Wissenschaft, mechanisch begründet durch die von Charles Darwin reformirte Descendenz-Theorie, Bd.*, p. 300.

9 S.J. Gould (1977), *Ontogeny and Phylogeny*; Sulloway (1979), *Freud*, pp. 198-202, 258-264; A. De Block (2006), *Waanzin en natuur. Darwin en de psychiatrie*, pp. 42-45.

10 Freud (1920g), *Beyond the Pleasure Principle*, p. 37.

11 L.B. Ritvo (1990), *Darwin's Influence on Freud. A Tale of Two Sciences*, pp. 125-131.

12 In this regard, Claus does not refer to (his rival) Haeckel but cites Fritz Müller (from *Für Darwin*, 1864): *die Entwicklungsgeschichte des Individuums [erscheint] als eine kurze und vereinfachte Wiederholung, gewissermassen als eine Recapitulation des*

Entwicklungsganges der Arten. C. Claus (1872), *Grundzüge der Zoologie*, p. 96.

13 Ritvo (1990), *Darwin's Influence on Freud*, pp. 151-169.

14 Ch. Darwin (1859), *On the Orgin of Species*, pp. 330-331.

15 G. Fechner (1873), *Einige Ideen zur Schöpfungs- und Entwicklungsgeschichte der Organismen*, pp. 40-41; A. Weismann (1892), Über Leben und Tod, Eine biologische Untersuchung, pp. 58-60.

16 In 'Versuch einer Entwicklungsgeschichte der Libido' from 1924 Karl Abraham would argue that the progress from an oral-sadistic to an anal-sadistic organization can be understood from embryology and evolutionary biology: the anus develops from a very primitive 'primal mouth'. K. Abraham (1924), 'Versuch einer Entwicklungsgeschichte der Libido', pp. 181-183; cf. Freud (1933a), *New Introductory Lectures*, p. 100.

17 In this regard, also see Sulloway (1979), *Freud: Biologist of the Mind*, pp. 398-399.

18 Freud (1926d), *Inhibitions, Symptoms, and Anxiety*, p. 174. This citation shows that the meaning of the Oedipus complex is anchored in a theory of phylogeny and heredity. We will come back to this in more detail later.

19 For Haeckel, these are primarily the Darwin-derived 'functions' of reproduction (species maintenance) and food intake (self-preservation). Freud follows this 'Darwinian' line in his drive dualism as it takes shape from *Three Theories* onwards. Freud (1915c), 'Instincts and their Vicissitudes', pp. 123-124.

20 S. Freud (1939a), *Moses and Monotheism*, *SE* 23, p. 92.

21 Geyskens (2005), *Our Original Scenes*, pp. 23-26.

22 S. Freud (1926e), *The Question of Lay Analysis*, *SE* 20, p. 212.

23 Freud (1916-17a), *Introductory Lectures*, p. 199. Also cf: "In a few short years the little primitive [every human individual] must grow up into a civilized human being; he must pass through an immensely long stretch of human cultural development in an almost uncannily abbreviated form". Freud (1940a), *An Outline of Psycho-Analysis*, p. 185.

24 Freud (1985c), *The Complete Letters*, p. 227; Freud (1900a), *The Interpretation of Dreams*, p. 256.

25 Freud (1912-13a), *Totem and Taboo*, p. xiii – our italics.

26 Cf. Freud (1916-17a), *Introductory Letters*, p. 199.

27 Cf. Freud (1912a), 'Postscript to Psychoanalytic Remarks'; Freud (1912-13a), *Totem and Taboo*.

28 Freud (1985a), *A Phylogenetic Fantasy*, p. 10.

29 Here Freud connects with a 1913 text by Sandor Ferenczi, 'Entwicklungsstufen des Wirklichkeitssinnes'. In this text, Ferenczi sees the sexual development and ego-formation of the individual and the disposition to the neuroses determined by the phase of development as the repetition (Haeckel's biogenetic law) of phylogenetic factors that originate in a series of catastrophes in prehistoric times (Ice Age). The events of prehistoric times forced the development (including the repression) of the 'character of the human race' in a certain direction and have been passed on from generation to generation as memory traces of the history of the human race. S. Ferenczi (1913), 'Entwicklungsstufen des Wirklichkeitssinnes'.

[30] Cf. Grubrich-Simitis (1985), 'Metapsychology and Metabiology'; Grubrich-Simitis (2007), 'Trauma oder Trieb – Trieb oder Trauma: Wiederbetrachtet'; De Block (2006), *Waanzin en natuur*, pp. 44-45; Adriaens (2008), *Het nut van waanzin.*

[31] S. Freud (1915b), 'Thoughts for the Times on War and Death', *SE* 14, p. 292.

[32] Where Freud emphasizes the continuity between nature and culture, Lacan, especially under the influence of Lévy-Strauss's view on the origins of culture, would emphasize the break between nature and culture that arises with the introduction of the law (incest taboo). In Lacan, the symbolic order of culture and language and the universality of the law of the father it enshrines replaces the reference to phylogeny; Freud grounds the universality of human instinctive life in phylogeny, i.e. in the evolution of organic life and (by extension) cultural history.

[33] Freud (1915c), 'Instincts and Their Vicissitudes', p. 126; Freud (1939a), *Moses and Monotheism*, p. 75.

[34] Freud (1905d), *Three Essays*, p. 234.

[35] Freud (1985a), *A Phylogenetic Fantasy*, pp. 16-17.

[36] G. Moore (2002), *Nietzsche, Biology and Metaphor*, pp. 2-3; J. Willner (2020), 'Neurotische Evolution. Bioanalyse als Kulturkritik in "Jenseits des Lustprinzips"'.

[37] E. Haeckel (1863), 'Die Jungfernrede: Über die Entwicklungstheorie Darwin's'.

[38] Freud (1920g), *Beyond the Pleasure Principle*, p. 42.

[39] In line with this, cultural development can also primarily be understood as continuous and effective protection against the life-threatening 'violence of the forces of nature' through the production of tools and techniques with which the human can compensate for their physical and organic shortcomings. S. Freud (1930a), *Civilizations and Its Discontents*, *SE* 21, p. 90.

[40] Freud (1912-13a), *Totem and Taboo*, p. 158.

[41] Ibid., p. 31.

[42] Freud (1905d), *Three Essays*, p. 225 – footnote from 1915.

[43] Cf. Freud (1918b), 'From the History of an Infantile Neurosis', p. 119. See also Westerink (2009), *A Dark Trace*.

[44] Gould (1977), *Ontogeny and Phylogeny*, p. 80. Frank Sulloway rightly points out that Freud's Lamarckism is partly derived from Darwin, who had incorporated some of Lamarck's insights into heredity and evolution into his own theories. Sulloway (1979), *Freud: Biologist of the Mind*, p. 274 – in footnote.

[45] A. Wagner (1909), *Geschichte des Lamarckismus*, pp. vi-viii; R.J. Butzer & R. Burkholz (1991), 'Urvater der Eiszeit: Biologisch-evolutionäres und psycholamarckistisches Denken bei Freud', p. 39.

[46] S. Freud & S. Ferenczi (1996), *The Correspondence Vol. 2 1914-1919*, F634.

[47] Ibid., F740. In a letter dated January 1, 1917, Freud announced that he would read Lamarck's main work in a German edition from 1910, *Zoologische Philosophie*. Ibid., F636. On the correspondence between Freud and Ferenczi on Lamarckism, see also Grubrich-Simitis (1985), 'Metapsychology and Metabiology'.

[48] J.-B. Lamarck (1910) *Zoologische Philosophie*, p. 73.

[49] Darwin rejects Lamarck's theory of organic modifications through purposeful use. However, he does not object to Lamarck's idea that experiences with a strong af-

fective charge generate certain response patterns that can be transferred to subsequent generations (inheritance of acquired traits). For example: the fear and flight responses of baboons for snakes. Ch. Darwin (1871), *The Descent of Man, and Selection in Relation to Race*, pp. 41ff., 50. Freud refers to this mechanism in. Freud (1915c), 'Instincts and Their Vicissitudes', p. 120.

50 This forms the core of Schopenhauer's criticism of Lamarck (in *Über den Willen in der Natur*, 1836). In contrast to Lamarck's emphasis on perception and insights gained from it, Schopenhauer proposes to explain the physical modifications of organisms based on a will to live that precedes the particular organism (*Wille zum Leben*). A. Schopenhauer (1854), Über den Willen in der Natur, pp. 42-43.

51 Freud & S. Ferenczi (1996), *Correspondence,* F646;

52 Pauly (1905), *Darwinismus und Lamarckismus*, pp. 8-14, 20; Sulloway (1979), *Freud: Biologist of the Mind*, pp. 274-275. Here we can add that, according to Pauly, not only humans or higher animal species have 'needs', but also the simplest organisms. For example, a single-celled organism will modify (harden, strengthen) its cell wall out of the need to defend itself against stimuli from outside. In fact, this means that all organisms are assigned psychological functions – needs, immune responses, judgment, and etc. Butzer & Burkholz (1991), 'Urvater der Eiszeit', pp. 40-44.

53 S. Freud & K. Abraham (1965), *Briefe 1907-1926*, p. 247.

54 Cf. Freud (1912-13a), *Totem and Taboo*, pp. 86-87.

55 Silveira (2013), 'Phylogenetic schema and transcendental field'.

56 Freud knew Hering's work from his student days. Hering had even once offered him an appointment as his assistant in Prague. His 1870 lecture was included as a chapter in Samuel Butler's *Unconscious Memory* (1880). In a 1926 translation of Israel Levine's *The Unconscious* by Anna Freud, the paragraph about Butler was translated by Freud. In a footnote to that paragraph, Freud writes that instead of Butler, Hering should have been foregrounded in Levine's book, and this because of Hering's contribution to the knowledge of 'unconscious soul activities'. S. Freud (1926g), 'Freud and Ewald Hering (Appendix A to 'The Unconscious')', *SE* 14.

57 Wagner (1909), *Geschichte des Lamarckismus*, p. 221.

58 E. Hering (1870), 'On Memory'; Gould (1977), *Ontogeny and Phylogeny*, pp. 96-97.

59 Freud (1900a9, *The Interpretation of Dreams*, p. 539; cf. also Freud (1920g, *Beyond the Pleasure Principle*, p. 25.

60 In the study of the demonological neurosis of Christoph Haitzmann from 1923 Freud writes that the image Haitzmann had of his father shows that early childhood impressions are 'merged' with "the inherited memory-trace of the primal father". S. Freud (1923d9, 'A Neurosis of Demoniacal Possession in the Seventeenth Century', *SE* 19, p. 85.

61 S. Freud (1923b), *The Ego and the Id, SE* 19, p. 38.

62 Freud (1940a), *An Outline of Psycho-Analysis*, p. 201.

63 Gould (1977), *Ontogeny and Phylogeny*, pp. 96-97.

64 Freud (1915c), 'Instincts and Their Vicissitudes', pp. 121-122.

[65] Ibid., p. 122.

[66] Ibid., p. 120.

[67] Freud & Ferenczi (1996), *Correspondence*, F551.

[68] Freud (1985a), *A Phylogenetic Fantasy*, p. 14. On a single occasion, Freud uses *verführen* ('seduce') and *verleiten* ('led into') in the same meaning: "It is an instructive fact that under the influence of seduction (*Verführung*) children can become polymorphously perverse, and can be led into (*verleiten*) all possible kinds of sexual irregularities". Freud (1905d), *Three Essays*, p. 191.

[69] The first and most important hardship in the Ice Age is food scarcity. This leads to reproduction no longer simply being permitted and that genital function is disabled. In these circumstances, the disposition to conversion hysteria arises. Freud (1985a), *A Phylogenetic Fantasy*, p. 14.

[70] Freud (1915b), 'Thoughts for the Times on War and Death', p. 282.

[71] Freud (1905d9, *Three Essays*, p. 242.

[72] Freud describes the pre-traumatic situation as beneficial outside world, which provided all satisfaction (Freud 1985a: 13).

[73] Freud (1916-17a), *Introductory Lectures*, p. 354-355.

[74] Cf. Grubrich-Simitis (2007), 'Trauma oder Trieb – Trieb oder Trauma: Wiederbetrachtet'; J. Press (2010), 'Trauma et pulsion'. The most important difference between animals and humans is not only the polymorphous perverse character of the sexual drives but also the repression of drive components and the delayed development of 'normal' sexuality and reproductive functions until puberty. Cf. Geyskens (2005), *Our Original Scenes*, pp. 7-8.

[75] Cf. S. Ferenczi (1924), 'Versuch einer Genitaltheorie', p. 362; Freud (1939a), *Moses and Monotheism*, p. 100.

Chapter 6: Traumatic neurosis, compulsion to repeat and drive theory: Beyond the Pleasure Principle

[1] S. Freud (1923a), 'Two Encyclopedia Articles: Psycho-Analysis and The Libido Theory', *SE* 18, p. 243.

[2] Only in the war years of 1914-18 Freud regularly returns to this problematic. See for instance, Freud (1916-17a), *Introductory Lectures*, pp. 381-382.

[3] Micale (2010), 'Jean-Martin Charcot et *les névroses traumatiques*', pp. 131-132.

[4] Fischer-Homberger (2004), *Die traumatische Neurose;* Scull (2009), *Hysteria.*

[5] Ibid., p. 171; Freud (1926d) *Inhibitions, Symptoms, and Anxiety*, p. 129.

[6] Grubrich-Simitis (1996), *Back to Freud's Texts*, pp. 182ff.

[7] Ulrike May and Michael Schröter edited an edition of *Jenseits des Lustprinzips* in which one can trace when passages were written or added. May's extensive commentary on the various editions is essential to a good understanding of the composition and meaning of the text. U. May (2015b), 'The Third Step in Drive Theory'.

[8] This is the case for example in the following more recent philosophical interpretations: P. Moyaert (2014), *Opboksen tegen het inerte. De doodsdrift bij Freud*; M. David-Ménard (2016), 'Comment lire "Au-delà du principe du plaisir"?'; Mala-

bou (2017), *Les nouveaux blessés*; Bernet (2020), *Force, Drive, Desire*, and J. Butler (2020), *The Force of Nonviolence. An Ethico-Political Bind.*

9 This principle means that from itself, the psychical system only aims to pursue pleasure. Freud identifies 'unpleasure' in a general sense with an increase in the tension in the system and 'pleasure' with releasing tension. Freud (1920g), *Beyond the Pleasure Principle*, pp. 7-8. The psychic system thus tries as far as possible to avoid every possible increase in tension. He however adds the following: "What we are implying by this is not a simple relation between the strength of the feelings of pleasure and unpleasure and the corresponding modifications in the quantity of excitation; least of all—in view of all we have been taught by psycho-physiology—are we suggesting any directly proportional ratio: the factor that determines the feeling is probably the amount of increase or diminution in the quantity of excitation *in a given period of time*". Ibid., p. 8.

10 Ibid., p. 11.

11 Ibid., p. 20

12 And vice versa: each attempt to renounce drive can only be successful when a pleasure profit can be foreshadowed for the ego.

13 Ibid., p. 11.

14 Ibid., p. 13.

15 Freud (1900a), *The Interpretation of Dreams*, p. 476 – in footnote)

16 Laplanche and Pontalis define transference as "a process of actualization of unconscious wishes. Transference uses specific objects and operates in the framework of a specific relationship established with these objects. Its context *par excellence* is the analytic situation. In the transference, infantile prototypes re-emerge and are experienced with a strong sensation of immediacy". Laplanche & Pontalis (1973), *The Language of Psychoanalysis*, p. 455.

17 Freud (1920g), *Beyond the Pleasure Principle*, p. 18.

18 Ibid., p. 19. We also came across the problematic of repetition in the context of our discussion of the case of the Rat Man.

19 Ibid., p. 20.

20 Ibid., pp. 15-16.

21 Ibid., p. 23.

22 Ibid., p. 23 – our italics.

23 Ibid., p. 35.

24 Ibid., p. 22. In *The Gay Science* Nietzsche also links the 'perpetual recurrence of the same thing' and the daemon or the daemonic. F. Nietzsche (1882), *Die fröhliche Wissenschaft*, pp. 273-274 [§341]). For the relationship between Nietzsche's 'perpetual recurrence' (*amor fati*) and the Freudian repetition compulsion, see D. Chapelle (1993), *Nietzsche and Psychoanalysis.*

25 Freud (1920g), *Beyond the Pleasure Principle*, p. 22.

26 Ibid., p. 31.

27 Ibid., p. 12.

28 Ibid., p. 31.

[29] Ibid. These insights about anxiety as a signal of impending danger Freud would refine only in *Inhibitions, Symptoms and Anxiety*. We return to this in the last section of this chapter.

[30] Ibid., p. 32.

[31] Ibid.

[32] In an earlier publication we defend the view that the foundation of repetition in drive is an unnecessary addition. Van Haute & Geyskens (2005), *From Death Instinct to Attachment Theory*. We argued that the reference to the necessity to bind the trauma sufficed to comprehend the repetition. We can no longer defend this view because, as will become clear, the drive itself is, according to Freud, an effect of trauma. Trauma and drive are not mutually exclusive.

[33] Freud (1920g), *Beyond the Pleasure Principle*, p. 26; Breuer & Freud (1895d), *Studies on Hysteria*, p. 194 – in footnote; Freud (1900a), *The Interpretation of Dreams*, pp. 601-603.

[34] Ibid., pp. 367-368.

[35] In this instance Freud refers to Immanuel Kant's a priori forming of sensoriness. Freud links these forms with the structuring and binding of unconscious presentations in the (pre-)conscious system (Freud 1920g: 28). It is understandable since it structures the sensory relationship to the world according to Kant. This relationship is as it were suspended in the unconscious.

[36] Freud (1920g), *Beyond the Pleasure Principle*, p. 35.

[37] A systematic discussion of this distinction can be found in Freud (1911b), 'Formulations on the Two Principles of Mental Functioning'.

[38] Freud (1920g), *Beyond the Pleasure Principle*, p. 10.

[39] Ibid.

[40] Freud identifies the tendency to keep the tension as low as possible with Fechner's principle of constancy.
It is remarkable. After all, the constancy principle implies that 'too much' as well as 'too little' tension can be unpleasurable. For Fechner, this principle implies that the organism wants to keep the tension within certain below- and above boundaries. On this point, see Sulloway (1979), *Freud: Biologist of the Mind*.

[41] Freud (1920g), *Beyond the Pleasure Principle*, p. 33.

[42] Freud (1905d), *Three Essays*, p. 202.

[43] This hypothesis is connected to the complete reformulation of the paragraph about the chemical theory in the fourth edition of *Three Essays on the Theory of Sexuality*, which Freud was working on at the same time and that appeared in 1920. Freud seemed to think that through the shock, "… special chemical substances are produce in the interstitial portion of the sex-glands; these are then taken up in the blood stream and cause particular parts of the central nervous system to be charged with sexual tension. (We are already familiar with the fact that other toxic substances, introduced into the body from the outside, can bring about a similar transformation of a toxic condition into a stimulus acting on a particular organ.) Ibid., p. 215.

[44] Freud (1920g), *Beyond the Pleasure Principle*, p. 35.

45 Ibid., p. 36.
46 Freud (1915c), 'Instincts and their Vicissitudes', p. 120.
47 That is also why Freud, as we noted earlier, is in this regard concerned with the 'perpetual recurrence of the same thing'. Freud (1920g), *Beyond the Pleasure Principle*, p. 22.
48 Ibid., p. 36.
49 Ibid., p. 38.
50 Ibid.
51 Ibid., p. 36.
52 Such as the radiolaria described by Haeckel in the appendix to Lamarck's *Zoological philosophy* or the rhizopods. Lamarck (1910), *Zoologische Philosophie*, pp. 97-98; Haeckel (1866), *Generelle Morphologie der Organismen Bd. 1*, pp. 186 ff.
53 Freud (1920g), *Beyond the Pleasure Principle*, pp. 26-27.
54 Ibid., p. 48.
55 Ibid., pp. 28-29.
56 Ibid., p. 31.
57 Ibid., pp. 38-39.
58 Ibid., p. 37.
59 Ibid., pp. 38-39.
60 Ibid., p. 39.
61 Ibid., p. 37.
62 Ibid., p. 40. In chapter 5 (from 1919) of *Beyond the Pleasure Principle* we find no explicit references to specific biological theories to which Freud thinks he can appeal. It seems that Freud's reference to germ-cells surrounding themselves with a protective body connects to the work of August Weismann. In chapter 6 (from 1920) Freud would discuss at length some of his writings (see below).
63 Ibid., p. 37.
64 Here we also find a fine example of the way in which later versions of the book obscure the former from view. Freud writes that the hypothesis that there are also drives that strive for 'the production of new forms' should certainly not be discounted. In 1921, he adds: "and it [this hypothesis – HW/PvH] will be taken into account at a later stage". Ibid. The reader then inevitably thinks that the sixth chapter evidently referred to here was already included in the reasoning from the beginning. However, when the remainder of the passage under discussion was written in 1919, there was no mention of the sixth chapter.
65 Ibid., pp. 42-43.
66 Ibid., p. 40.
67 Ibid., p. 39.
68 Ibid., p. 37. For example, in *Inhibitions, Symptoms and Anxiety*, Freud writes the latency period and thus the fact that the institution of sexuality in humankind runs in two times, must be the historical sediment of disturbing events in the vicissitudes of the human species. Freud (1926d) *Inhibitions, Symptoms, and Anxiety*, p. 253.
69 Freud (1920g), *Beyond the Pleasure Principle*, p. 39.

70 Ibid. We already find the first beginnings of such speculations in Ferenczi's text about the 'Entwicklungsstufen des Wirklichkeitssinnes' from 1913. The insights we discuss here Freud worked out considerably in dialogue with Ferenczi. The examination of this dialogue is beyond the scope of our study, however. In this regard, see for example May (1915b), 'The Third Step in Drive Theory' and Willner (2020), 'Neurotische Evolution'.

71 Freud (1920g), *Beyond the Pleasure Principle*, p. 40.

72 Ibid., pp. 40-41.

73 Willner (2020), 'Neurotische Evolution', pp. 14-15.

74 It is at least noteworthy that none of the recent philosophical interpretations of *Beyond the Pleasure Principle* that we mentioned at the beginning of this chapter refer to Freud's psycho-Lamarckism. If our interpretation is correct, these interpretations thereby deny themselves the possibility of understanding exactly what Freud understands by drive as characterized by an 'inertia principle'. Freud's revival of the drive theory in 1919 is directly connected to his turn to psycho-Lamarckism.

75 Freud (1920g), *Beyond the Pleasure Principle*, p. 41.

76 Grubrich-Simitis (2007), 'Trauma oder Trieb – Trieb oder Trauma: Wiederbetrachtet'.

77 May (2015b), 'The Third Step in Drive Theory'.

78 Paul Ricoeur is one of the few authors who in his philosophical reading of *Beyond the Pleasure Principle* (and without being aware of the existence of two versions of Freud's text) systemically does justice to the fact that Freud effects a change of perspective through which, as we shall see further on, emphasis is no longer on repetition but on aggression. P. Ricoeur (1965), *De l'interprétation. Essai sur Freud*, p. 290.

79 Freud (1920g), *Beyond the Pleasure Principle*, p. 41.

80 Ibid., p. 40. At the beginning of the sixth chapter, Freud confirms that the preceding fifth chapter of his text culminated in an opposition between the ego-drives and sexual drives. Ibid, pp. 44, 52-53. Thus, he presents his position as if drive dualism were never in danger and then as if it were only a matter of replacing one dualism with another. We believe, however, that the sixth chapter is about 'saving' drive dualism.

81 Ibid., p. 56 – our italics.

82 Ibid., p. 58.

83 Ibid.

84 Ibid., pp. 51-52.

85 Ibid., p. 43.

86 For an exhaustive study of aggression in the work of Freud, see J. De Vleminck (2013), *De schaduw van Kaïn: Freuds klinische antropologie van de agressiviteit.*

87 The death of this body is, according to Weismann 'expedient' because after a certain duration it is 'worn out' (*Abnutzung*) and thus can no longer fulfill any function for the germ-cell and the survival of the species. A. Weismann (1892), Über Leben und Tod, Eine biologische Untersuchung, pp. 20, 36; Freud (1920g), *Beyond the Pleasure Principle*, pp. 201vv; Churchill (2015), *August Weismann.*

[88] Weismann (1882), *Das Keimplasma.* Here again we see how sexuality is placed in the service of self-preservation. Freud's statement that germ-cells are narcissistic fits into this view. We will return to this below.
[89] Weismann (1892) Über Leben und Tod, Eine biologische Untersuchung 16 ff., 36; Freud (1920g), *Beyond the Pleasure Principle*, p. 46.
[90] Ibid., p. 55.
[91] Ibid., p. 46.
[92] Ibid., p. 48.
[93] Ibid., p. 49.
[94] Ibid., pp. 50-53.
[95] Freud (1914c), 'On Narcissism', p. 77.
[96] Freud (1920g), *Beyond the Pleasure Principle*, p. 52.
[97] Freud (1914c), 'On Narcissism', p. 76.
[98] Freud (1920g), *Beyond the Pleasure Principle*, p. 50.
[99] Ibid., p. 58.
[100] Ibid., p. 40.
[101] Ibid., p. 52. Incidentally, this also shows that Freud constantly kept the problem of monism (and avoiding it) in the back of his mind while working on *Beyond the Pleasure Principle*
[102] Ibid., pp. 55-56. As we also noted earlier, keeping the quantity of excitation 'constant' is not unreservedly on a par with reducing or removing it. 'Keeping constant' goes against both a reduction and an increase in the quantity of excitation, assuming certain limits are exceeded.
[103] Ibid., p. 55.
[104] Ibid., p. 59.
[105] Ibid., pp. 53-54. In *The Ego and the Id* Freud writes: "For the opposition between the two classes of instincts we may put the polarity love and hate". Freud (1923b), *The Ego and the Id*, p. 42.
[106] Freud (1905d), *Three Essays*, pp. 157-158.
[107] In *The Ego and the Id* it reads: "Over and over again we find, when we are able to trace instinctual impulses back, that they reveal themselves as derivatives of Eros. If it were not for the considerations put forward in *Beyond the Pleasure Principle*, and ultimately for the sadistic constituents which have attached themselves to Eros, we should have difficulty in holding to our fundamental dualistic point of view". Freud (1923b), *The Ego and the Id*, p. 46.
[108] Freud (1920g), *Beyond the Pleasure Principle*, p. 54.
[109] S. Freud (1924c), 'The Economic Problem of Masochism', *SE* 19, pp. 160-161.
[110] An exception to this is 'The Economic Problem of Masochism', which can nevertheless be considered as a clinical text. This perhaps also indicates that Freud himself did not see absolute opposites here. For example, even in 'Instincts and Their Vicissitudes', immediately after defining drive as a force aimed at change, he writes the following "There is naturally nothing to prevent our supposing that the instincts themselves are, at least in part, precipitates of the effects of external stimulation, which in the course of phylogeny have brought about modifications

in the living substance". Freud (1915c), 'Instincts and Their Vicissitudes', p. 120. Freud thus apparently saw no absolute opposition between his 'old' conception of drive and the psycho-Lamarckism that underpins its new determination.

[111] One should not infer from this that every reference to Eros and the death drive is absent from the text, but they play a secondary part and even more so where trauma and repetition are concerned. See for instance Freud (1926d), *Inhibitions, Symptoms, and Anxiety*, pp. 124-125.

[112] See also for what follows Van Haute & Geyskens (2005), *From Death Instinct to Attachment Theory*, pp. 18 ff.

[113] Freud (1926d), *Inhibitions, Symptoms, and Anxiety*, p. 129.

[114] In 'Thoughts for the Times on War and Death', Freud writes: "It is indeed impossible to imagine our own death; and whenever we attempt to do so we can perceive that we are in fact still present as spectators. Hence the psycho-analytic school could venture on the assertion that at bottom no one believes in his own death, or, to put the same thing in another way, that in the unconscious every one of us is convinced of his own immortality". Freud (1915b), 'Thoughts for the Times on War and Death', p. 289.

[115] Freud (1926d), *Inhibitions, Symptoms, and Anxiety*, p. 142.

[116] O. Rank (1924), *Das Trauma der Geburt und seine Bedeutung für die Psychoanalyse.*

[117] Freud (1926d), *Inhibitions, Symptoms, and Anxiety*, pp. 151-152.

[118] Ibid., pp. 135-136.

[119] Ibid., p. 151 – our italics.

[120] Freud & Abraham (1965), *Briefe*, p. 323.

[121] Rank (1924), *Das Trauma der* Geburt, p. 22

[122] Freud (1926d), *Inhibitions, Symptoms, and Anxiety*, pp. 132-133.

[123] Ibid., p. 133.

[124] Ibid., p. 150.

[125] Ibid., p. 133.

[126] Ibid., pp. 166-167.

[127] Ibid., p. 135.

[128] Ibid., p. 166.

[129] Ibid., pp. 130, 137.

[130] Ibid., pp. 150, 166.

[131] Ibid., p. 139). Also see: "Following Ferenczi's line of thought, we might say that the man in question, having tried to bring about his return into his mother's womb by using his genital organ, is now [in this fantasy] replacing that organ regressively by his whole person". Ibid.

[132] Ibid., p. 128.

[133] One could understand this to mean that castration anxiety sexualizes the birth trauma in a *nachträgliche* way. Cf. Van Haute & Geyskens (2005), *From Death Instinct to Attachment Theory*, pp. 18ff. Thus, an original vital trauma would take on a sexual meaning only in a second moment. The exclusively sexual origin of the neurosis would thus again be compromised. As we shall see further, also in *Inhibitions, symptoms and anxiety* Freud tries with all his might to avoid this conclusion.

[134] Freud (1926d), *Inhibitions, Symptoms, and Anxiety*, p. 138.
[135] Ibid., p. 165.
[136] Rank (1924), *Das Trauma der Geburt*, p. 30.
[137] Freud (1926d), *Inhibitions, Symptoms, and Anxiety*, pp. 130, 141, 161-162.
[138] Ibid., pp. 129, 138.
[139] Ibid., p. 135.
[140] Freud & Abraham (1965), *Briefe*, p. 322.
[141] Freud (1926d), *Inhibitions, Symptoms, and Anxiety*, p. 147.
[142] Ibid., pp. 153-154 – our italics.
[143] Ibid., p. 155.
[144] Freud & Abraham (1965), *Briefe*, p. 323.
[145] Weismann (1892), Über Leben und Tod, pp. 45-46. It for instance already became apparent in a letter to Jones from 1912 – thus long before the publication of *Beyond* – that Freud's Lamarckism is irreconcilable with the theories of Weismann. S. Freud & E. Jones (1993), *The Complete Correspondence 1908-1939*, p. 150.
[146] Freud (1905d), *Three Essays*, p. 135.
[147] In 'The Economic Problem of Masochism' Freud contrasts a death- or destruction drive that primarily seeks to 'disintegrate' (fragment) the own organism with the libido that is tasked with defusing this death drive by directing it largely outwards. "A portion of the instinct," he argues, "is placed directly in the service of the sexual function, where it has important art to play. This is sadism proper". Freud (1924c), 'The Economic Problem of Masochism', p. 163. Sexual sadism is thus a hybrid product of sexuality and the externally oriented death drive.

Chapter 7: Trauma and character: The man Moses

1 The three essays were published together as a monograph in 1939 by Allert de Lange in Amsterdam.
2 With regards to the 1934 version, Freud considered the title 'The Man Moses, a Historical Novel'. The term "novel" was chosen since there are very few 'factual' historical details available about Moses, and that different components are combined 'in accordance with psychological probability' and must be brought in relation to each other. Freud (1939a), *Moses and Monotheism*, p. 105; S. Freud (2021), *L'homme Moïse. Un roman historique*, pp. 12, 14; Y.H. Yerushalmi (1989), 'Freud and the "Historical Novel": From the Manuscript Draft (1934) of *Moses and Monotheism*'.
3 Freud (2021), *L'homme Moïse.*
4 Cf. Grubrich-Simitis (1991), *Freuds Moses-Studie als Tagtraum*, pp. 80-103; H. Westerink (2023), 'Reconstructing Freud's Moses-texts (1934-1938): From Character Study to Contribution to Trauma Theory'. The time stamps refer to the moment of completion; the italics indicate that a fragment was planned but not written in an original draft or preserved.
5 It has been suggested that the generous focus on the place and meaning of trauma for the emergence of the Jewish character religion was inseparable from Freud's

own traumatic experiences in the thirties and his enduring interest in the figure of Moses. Grubrich-Simitis (1991), *Freuds Moses-Studie als Tagtraum*; Yerushalmi (1991), *Freud's Moses*. In this regard, there are references throughout to Freud's fascination with the Moses sculpture of Michelangelo in the San Pietro in Vincoli in Rome. S. Freud (1914b), 'The Moses of Michelangelo', *SE* 13.

6 Books written by Jewish authors, among them psychoanalytic literature, were burned as early as 1933 in Germany. In the same year, the exodus of Jewish German psychoanalysts started to the United States and Great Britain.

7 S. Freud & S. Zweig (1968), *Briefwechsel*, p. 102.

8 S. Freud & L. Andreas-Salomé (1972), *Letters*, p. 204.

9 Freud & Zweig (1968), *Briefwechsel*, p. 102.

10 Freud & Andreas-Salomé (1972), *Letters*, p. 204.

11 Freud (1939a), *Moses and Monotheism*, pp. 55, 103-104.

12 Freud & Zweig (1968), *Briefwechsel*, pp. 103, 141. That Freud sees Father Wilhelm Schmidt, who was professor of ethnology at the University of Vienna from 1921 to 1938, as an 'enemy' can be traced primarily to Schmidt's sharp criticism of *Totem and Taboo*. That criticism stemmed from Schmidt's own theories about the origins of religion. According to Schmidt, we must assume that the first form of religion was a 'primal monotheism' that originated in the experience of a revelation of God. M.-F. Chevron (2012), 'Urkultur, Ur-Monotheismus und Zivilisationskritik bei W. Schmidt (1868-1954)'.

13 Freud (1939a), *Moses and Monotheism*, pp. 103, 123; Freud (2021), *L'homme Moïse*, p. 14.

14 S. Freud (1937c), 'Analysis Terminable and Interminable', *SE* 23, p. 250.

15 S. Freud (1908b) 'Character and Anal Erotism', *SE* 9; S. Freud (1916d), 'Some Character-Types met with in Psychoanalytic Work', *SE* 14; S. Freud (1931a), 'Libidinal Types', *SE* 21.

16 Freud (1909d), 'Notes upon a Case of Obsessional Neurosis', p. 206.

17 "No one individual, of course, makes use of all the possible mechanisms of defence. Each person uses no more than a selection of them. But these become fixated in his ego. They become regular modes of reaction of his character, which are repeated throughout his life whenever a situation occurs that is similar to the original one". Freud (1937c), 'Analysis Terminable and Interminable', p. 237.

18 Seen in this way, *Moses and Monotheism* is the development of an intuition that Freud already articulated in 1912 at a meeting of the *Wiener Psychoanalytische Vereinigung*, cited by Sandor Ferenczi in a 1913 article: "the character of a race [or nation] [is] the precipitation of the history of that race [or nation]". Ferenczi 1913: 'Entwicklungsstufen des Wirklichkeitssinnes', p. 162; H. Nunberg & E. Federn (1981), *Protokolle der Wiener Psychoanalytischen Vereinigung Bd. 4, 1912-1918*, p. 80.

19 Eliza Slavet has pointed out that Freud's theory of the Jewish character can be seen as a "racial theory of memory" in which unity, character and fate of a nation/people is founded on a shared (mythical) past and a biological inheritance. E. Slavet (2009), *Racial Fever. Freud and the Jewish Question*, p. 7. This raises the question,

however, whether this inadvertently put Freud on the trail of fascist and national socialist race theory. After all, in Freud's theory of Jewish character, one looks in vain for attempts to give this character – or this identity – a stable and unambiguous foundation. On the contrary, the origins and moments lie outside Judaism and outside Israel, in Egypt and Arabia. Said (2003), *Freud and the Non-European.*

[20] Freud (1939a), *Moses and Monotheism*, pp. 103-137.

[21] Ibid., p. 106.

[22] Ibid., pp. 109-110.

[23] Ibid., p. 123.

[24] Ibid., p. 122.

[25] This is also valid for the reverse: should drive renunciation be abandoned (resulting in pleasure), the superego would produce violent unpleasure in the form of remorse, reproach and guilt.

[26] Ibid., p. 117. In *The Ego and the Id* Freud argued that the superego constantly encouraged the ego to meet an ideal that came about through identification (with the father). Nowhere does Freud say about the superego that it would be able to 'appreciate' or 'love' the ego. At most, there is a decrease in exhortations, admonitions, sabotages and accusations. Freud (1923), *The Ego and the Id*, pp. 28-39.

[27] Freud (1939a), *Moses and Monotheism*, p. 111.

[28] Ibid., p. 119.

[29] Ibid., p. 122.

[30] Ibid., p. 110. In the original planning of the Moses project (1934), no chapter or section was planned on the analogy between trauma in the aetiology of neuroses and the effect of the murder on the primal father or resp. the murder of Moses. Freud (2021), *L'homme Moïse.*

[31] Freud (1921c), *Group Psychology and the Analysis of the Ego*, pp. 122-123; Freud & Andreas-Salomé (1972), *Letters*, p. 205.

[32] S. Freud (1927c), *The Future of an Illusion, SE* 21, p. 25.

[33] Already in *The Future of an Illusion* Freud noted that religious doctrines not only express humankind's most infantile (narcistic) wishes but are also supported by 'historical recollections' and a 'historic truth'. There is evidence of this when for example the commandments and prohibitions that must regulate the mutual relationships in the group are attributed to one god that already issued these commandments and prohibitions at the beginning of time. Ibid., p. 42.

[34] Freud (1939a), *Moses and Monotheism*, p. 129.

[35] Ibid. Noticeable in this passage is the absence of a reference to the murder of the father.

[36] Ibid. With this statement – which harks back to the theory, developed in *Totem and Taboo*, of the return of the father in the totem and subsequently the exaltation of this totem father to god – Freud approaches Father Wilhelm Schmidt's thesis of primal monotheism. The first form of religion in cultural history is also for Freud a form of monotheism – the exaltation of father to god. Polytheism would develop later with the merging of tribes to larger groupings and through the need for 'heroes' from a glorious past.

[37] Cf. Freud & Andreas-Salomé (1972), *Letters*, p. 206.
[38] The most important argument for this statement is that Moses is an Egyptian name.
[39] Freud (1939a), *Moses and Monotheism*, p. 52.
[40] This is justified by the similarity between Aten and the biblical Adonai ('lord' as the name of god).
[41] The Midianites were a people that lived east of the Sinai desert in the northwest of the Arabic peninsula.
[42] According to Freud, the 'savage Semites' refused the high grade of spiritualization that Moses demanded as it did not satisfy their sensual and basic needs. Ibid., p. 46.
[43] See J. Assmann (2020), *Moses Tragicus: Freud, Schönberg und der scheiternde Moses. Sigmund Freud Vorlesung 2019.* That Moses would have been murdered Sellin derives from the biblical book of Hosea (chapter 12, verse 15b).
[44] Freud (1939a), *Moses and Monotheism*, p. 51.
[45] Ibid., pp. 38-40.
[46] Freud mentions in this regard discoveries during archaeological excavations in a Jewish military colony on Elephantine Island that point to the worship of a goddess, Anat-Yahu. Ibid., p. 63.
[47] Yerushalmi (1991), *Freud's Moses*, pp. 19-35.
[48] Freud (1939a), *Moses and Monotheism*, p. 38. From roughly 930 before Christ the united kingdom of Israel under Saul, David en Solomon comprised a northern realm (Israel with Samaria as capital) and a southern realm (Juda with Jerusalem as capital).
[49] Ibid., p. 52.
[50] In *Moses* we hardly find references to a drive theory. Freud instead draws attention to historic 'dualities' as reference points for an analysis of internal tensions and compromise foundations in the Jewish character.
[51] M. De Certeau (1988), 'The Fiction of History. The Writing of Moses and Monotheism'; Said (2003), *Freud and the Non-European.*
[52] Freud (1939a), *Moses and Monotheism*, pp. 42-43.
[53] Cf. Freud (1918b), 'From the History of an Infantile Neurosis', p. 20.
[54] Here, Freud concretely turns away from Otto Rank's interpretation of the history of Moses as a typical heroic tale in *Der Mythus von der Geburt des Helden* (1909) and Theodor Reik's vision of the figure of Moses as a remnant of an older polytheistic Judaism in *Probleme der Religionspsychologie* (1919).
[55] The Jahwist and the Elohist are two of the most important written texts of the Pentateuch (traditionally and viewed by Freud as 'the five books of Moses': Genesis, Exodus, Leviticus, Numbers and Deuteronomy).
[56] The five books of Moses and the book of Joshua.
[57] Freud (1939a), *Moses and Monotheism*, p. 68.
[58] Ibid., p. 41.

59 Ibid., p. 62. The idea that Jewish historiography is a 'mausoleum' for an absent founder and/or traumatic event not stored in the memory forms the core of the De Certeau (1988) and Derrida's (1995) readings of Freud's text on Moses. De Certeau (1988), 'The Fiction of History'; J. Derrida (1995), *Mal d'Archive: une impression freudienne.*

60 Freud points out that the word 'distortion' (*Entstellung*) has two meanings that both reveal aspects of the process of transcription. Distortion means 'change the appearance of something' as well as to 'put something in another place, to displace'.

61 Freud (1939a), *Moses and Monotheism*, p. 43.

62 Ibid., pp. 65-66.

63 Ibid., p. 42.

64 Ibid., p. 47, 93.

65 Ibid., p. 113.

66 Ibid., p. 124.

67 Ibid., p. 47.

68 Ibid., p. 52.

69 (Freud (1920g), *Beyond the Pleasure Principle*, p. 18; S. Freud (1937d), 'Constructions in Analysis', *SE* 23, pp. 260-261.

70 Compare: "The patient (…) is obliged to *repeat* the repressed material as a contemporary experience instead of, as the physician would prefer to see, *remembering* it as something belonging to the past". Freud (1920g), *Beyond the Pleasure Principle*, p. 18 – italics Freud).

71 The concept of 'historical truth' already took on this meaning in the case of the Wolf Man (see p. xxx).

72 Freud (1937d), 'Constructions in Analysis', p. 259 – italics Freud.

73 Cf. Ibid., p. 268. In the case study of Schreber, Freud already put forward that psychotic delusion should be seen as "an attempt at recovery", that means an attempt to reconstruct the relation to reality. Freud (1911c), 'Psychoanalytic Remarks on an Autobiographically Described Case of Paranoia', p. 71.

74 (Freud 1939a: 85. In the first version from 1934, Freud already connected the religious idea (of one great god) and delusion; "in so far as it brings a return of the past, it must be called the *truth*". Freud (1939a), *Moses and Monotheism*, p. 130 – italics Freud.

75 Freud (1937d), 'Constructions in Analysis', p. 267.

76 The other factors for the development of delusion are the 'turning away from reality' and 'the influence of wish-fulfilment'. Freud extensively mapped out these two factors in his case study of Schreber. Freud (1911c), 'Psychoanalytic Remarks on an Autobiographically Described Case of Paranoia'.

77 Freud (1939a), *Moses and Monotheism*, p. 75.

78 Ibid., p. 89.

79 Ibid., pp. 81-90.

80 Ibid., p. 90 – italics Freud.

81 Ibid., p. 98.

[82] We limit ourselves to humans here. In the text Freud takes a broader perspective (as we already know from *Beyond the Pleasure Principle*): the qualities, abilities and tendencies of all living beings – more specifically, of the various kinds of organisms – can be explained with reference to an 'archaic heritage' that comprises certain dispositions and instinctive reaction formations. Ibid., p. 99.

[83] In the case study on the Wolf Man, Freud writes that the (constitutional) predisposition that emerged in prehistoric times under the influence of accidental factors and that was subsequently transferred through inheritance "emerge once more as a concrete event in the experience of the individual". Freud (1918b), 'From the History of an Infantile Neurosis', p. 97.

[84] Freud (1939a), *Moses and Monotheism*, p. 98.

[85] Ibid., p. 99.

[86] Perhaps due to strategic considerations, Freud does not refer to primal phantasies here. After all, he wants to emphasize the real-life fact of the murder of Moses as repetition of factual events in the primaeval age.

[87] Ibid., p. 99.

[88] Ibid., p. 101.

[89] In this regard, Freud speaks of a 'complemental series'. Ibid., p.73.

[90] Ibid., p. 101.

[91] Ibid., p. 100.

[92] Yerushalmi correctly writes that Freud does not want to anchor Jewish character and being Jewish in a chain of written and oral history but – in an appeal to psycho-Lamarckism – in a chain of inherited characteristics (Yerushalmi 1991: 31).

[93] Cf. Assmann (1998), *Moses the Egyptian*, p. 239.

[94] Slavet (2009), *Racial Fever*, pp. 94-95, 175-177.

[95] Freud (1939a), *Moses and Monotheism*, p. 134.

[96] Ibid., pp. 86-87. Beside his fascination with the figure of Moses, which is well documented in the secondary literature. Yerushalmi (1991), *Freud's Moses*; Grubrich-Simitis (1991), *Freuds Moses-Studie als Tagtraum*; Assmann (1998), *Moses the Egyptian*; R. Bernstein (1998), *Freud and the Legacy of Moses*. Freud had an enduring fascination with Paul's "genuinely Jewish character" and his unique position between Judaism and Christianity. Freud & Pfister (1963), *Psychoanalysis and Faith*, p. 76; see also S. Freud (1911f), 'Great is Diana of the Ephesians', *SE* 12; H. Westerink (2007), 'The Great Man from Tarsus. Freud on the Apostle Paul'.

[97] Freud (1939a), *Moses and Monotheism*, p. 90.

[98] Ibid., p. 89.

[99] Ibid., p. 75. With his remarks about repetition compulsion as an aspect of Jewish historiography (and especially manifest in Jewish historiography), Freud connects to the first version of *Beyond the Pleasure Principle* (see the preceding chapter). Freud, however, does not make any connection between repetition compulsion and the death drive in *Moses and Monotheism* – the latter concept does not occur in the text. Cf. Fletcher (2013), *Freud and the Scene of Trauma*, pp. 314-315.

[100] Freud (1939a), *Moses and Monotheism*, p. 72.

[101] Ibid., p. 80.

[102] Ibid., p. 72.

[103] Ibid., p. 74.
[104] Ibid., p. 75.
[105] Ibid., pp. 67-68.
[106] In *The Future of an Illusion*, the narcistic insult is connected to the realization of 'our weakness and helplessness' when the culture we created cannot protect us from the damage that can be wreaked by 'nature (...) majestic, cruel and inexorable'. Freud (1927c), *The Future of an Illusion*, pp. 15-16.
[107] Freud (1939a), *Moses and Monotheism*, p. 74.
[108] Freud (1908c), 'On the Sexual Theories of Children', pp. 220-221; Freud (1918b), 'From the History of an Infantile Neurosis', pp. 41-47.
[109] Freud (1939a), *Moses and Monotheism*, p. 81.
[110] Ibid., p. 66.
[111] Freud (1920g), *Beyond the Pleasure Principle*, pp. 38-39.
[112] Freud (1905d), *Three Essays*, p. 225; Freud (1939a), *Moses and Monotheism*, p. 75.
[113] In this regard, Sandor Ferenczi also led the way in his 1913 article "Entwicklungsstufen des Wirklichkeitssinnes". The strong 'thrust to repress' (*Verdrängungsschub*) that characterizes the latency period would find its historical origin in a catastrophe in the Ice Age and repeat in every one of us since then. Ferenczi (1913), 'Entwicklungsstufen des Wirklichkeitssinnes', p. 162.
[114] Freud (1985a), *A Phylogenetic Fantasy*, p. 17.
[115] Freud (1926d), *Inhibitions, Symptoms, and Anxiety*, p. 155.
[116] Freud (1939a), *Moses and Monotheism*, p. 68.
[117] Ibid., p. 75 – italics Freud.
[118] Ibid., p. 77.
[119] Ibid., p. 101.
[120] Ibid., p. 122.
[121] Cf. Freud & Andreas-Salomé (1972), *Letters*, pp. 204-205; Freud (2021), *L'homme Moïse.*
[122] Freud (1939a), *Moses and Monotheism*, p. 91.
[123] Freud (1940a), *An Outline of Psycho-Analysis*, p. 190.
[124] Freud (1939a), *Moses and Monotheism*, p. 78.
[125] Ibid., p. 80.
[126] Freud (1940a), *An Outline of Psycho-Analysis*, p. 154.
[127] Freud (1930a), *Civilization and Its Discontents*, p. 121; Moyaert (2014), *Opboksen tegen het inerte*, pp. 95-97.
[128] Fletcher (2013), *Freud and the Scene of Trauma*, pp. 314-316.
[129] This is an interpretation of the death drive that Melanie Klein would systemically unpack from the end of the '20s. From the beginning, the death drive is an aggressive and destructive drive that would, to escape the danger of self-destruction, would be aimed against an external world perceived as hostile and the objects present therein. See among others M. Klein (1933), 'The Early Development of Conscience in the Child', pp. 250ff.
[130] Westerink (2009), *A Dark* Trace, pp. 261-273.
[131] Freud (1930a), *Civilization and Its Discontents*, p. 131.

[132] Yerushalmi (1991), *Freud's Moses*; R. Bernstein (1998), *Freud and the Legacy of Moses*. Eliza Slavet points out that up until the 1930s, Lamarckism (in various guises) still played an important part in scientific debates about heredity. Only from the '40s does Lamarckism definitively lose ground. Slavet (2009), *Racial Fever*, pp. 68ff.

[133] Freud (1939a), *Moses and Monotheism*, p. 100.

[134] Ibid., p. 84. Although in his *Lectures on the Religion of the Semites* (1894) William Robertson-Smith introduced the notion of the 'totem meal' based on Old Testament sources, and Freud assigns it a crucial role in his construction of the primal murder, we find references to a Jewish equivalent of this ritual neither in *Totem and Taboo* nor in *Moses and Monotheism*.

Chapter 8: Freud's metaphysics of trauma

1 Bernet (2020), *Force, Drive, Desire*; Moyaert (2014), *Opboksen tegen het inerte*.

2 Freud (1912-13a), *Totem and Taboo*, p. 87.

3 Freud (1911c), 'Psychoanalytic Remarks on an Autobiographically Described Case of Paranoia', pp. 65-71. With this minimal positioning with regards to classic metaphysics, Freud in fact connects with the visions of Kant, Comte and in particular Dilthey of metaphysics as the expression of a 'totality of the human spirit' in the conception of a reasonable order in reality. G.-J. van der Heiden (2021), *Metafysica*, pp. 343-351.

4 For Freud, this historical positioning of psychoanalysis (in a series of scientific revolutions starting with Copernicus) implies that it can make philosophical thought (thought and knowledge processes) and its constructions the object of critical analysis and must attempt to understand them in their origin and development from a psychical dynamic. S. Freud (1913j), 'The Claims of Psychoanalysis to Scientific Interest', *SE* 1, p. 178; cf. Ferenczi (1912), 'Philosophie und Psychoanalyse'. For a detailed analysis of Freud's vision of philosophy as thought system, see P.-L. Assoun (1976), *Freud, la philosophie et les philosophes*.

5 S. Freud (1917a), 'A Difficulty in the Path of Psycho-Analysis', *SE* 17, pp. 139-141.

6 With the understanding that instincts are determined patterns of behavior, while drives have great plasticity and variability.

7 S.S. Draenos (1978), 'Psychoanalysis, Evolution and the End of Metaphysics'. Frank Sulloway correctly points this out when he calls Freud a 'biologist of the mind' and 'crypto-biologist'. Sulloway (1979), *Freud: Biologist of the Mind*.

8 It is known of Freud's teacher Carl Claus that he strongly rejected a metaphysics that assumed a 'will' (Schopenhauer) beyond a world organized by causal connections and laws. G. Gödde (1999), *Traditionslinien des "Unbewußten". Schopenhauer – Nietzsche – Freud*, p. 422.

9 Cf. Freud (1920g), *Beyond the Pleasure Principle*, p. 50. Here and elsewhere Freud concretely refers to the work of Schopenhauer and his notion of the 'will to live'. Cf. also Freud (1917a), 'A Difficulty in the Path of Psycho-Analysis', pp. 143-144). Paul-Laurent Assoun has pointed out that Schopenhauer has been positively re-

ceived by Freud's teachers as a 'materialistic' philosopher who also explicitly considered the natural sciences capable of providing insight into the basic principles (life will) of nature. Assoun (1976), *Freud, la philosophie et les philosophes*, pp. 206-213; cf. A. Schopenhauer (1854), Über den Willen in der Natur, pp. 1-3.

10 Freud (1905d), *Three Essays*, p. 139.

11 Inter alia Van Haute & Westerink (2021), *From Pleasure to the Object.*

12 Van Haute & Geyskens (2012), *A Non-Oedipal Psychoanalysis?.*

13 Van Haute & Westerink (2021), *From Pleasure to the Object.*

14 Freud (1905d), *Three Essays*, p. 183.

15 Ibid., pp. 164-165.

16 J. Laplanche (1987), *Nouveaux fondements pour la psychanalyse*; Van Haute & Geyskens (2004), *Confusion of Tongues.*

17 Ph. Van Haute (2001), *Against Adaptation: Lacan's Subversion of the Subject.*

18 M. Foucault (1976), *The Will to Knowledge*, p. 157; H. Westerink (2019), *De lichamen en hun lusten. In het spoor van Foucaults* Geschiedenis van de seksualiteit.

19 G. Deleuze & F. Guattari (1972), *L'Anti-Oedipe – Capitalisme et schizophrénie*; A. Kleinherenbrink (2016), *Machine Philosophy. Gilles Deleuze and the Externality of Entities.*

20 Darwin (1859), *On the Origin of Species*, pp. 63-70.

21 This view goes against a standard reading of Freudian psychoanalysis that we find in almost the entire post-Freudian tradition and in a very pronounced way in Herbert Marcuse. This reading would have us believe that the essential conflict characterizing human existence is one between drive and culture. H. Marcuse (1955), *Eros and Civilization. A Philosophical Inquiry into Freud.* Lacan occupies a somewhat special place in this context. According to him the subject of psychoanalysis only comes into being through its inscription in the symbolic order. This subject is essentially split and characterized by inner conflicts. This is no longer a contradiction between drive and culture as in the post-Freudians and Marcuse. However, in Lacan – and in contrast to Freud – this subject of psychoanalysis is thought of as a break with nature.

22 Freud (1915c9, 'Instincts and Their Vicissitudes', pp. 118, 122.

23 Cf. Assoun (1976), *Freud, la philosophie et les philosophes*, pp. 63-68; Moyaert (2014), *Opboksen tegen het inerte*, pp. 21-23.

24 Compared to Freud, Lacan and Laplanche draw a sharp distinction between drive and instinct. Both associate instinct with the domain of biology and, more concretely, hereditary determined needs and adaptive functions. In contrast they position drive as object-focused, changeable, and historically and culturally determined. J. Lacan (1966), Écrits, pp. 851-854; J. Laplanche (1999), *La sexualité humaine. Biologisme et biologie.*

25 Anson Rabinbach has convincingly showed that, with his view of drive as force or energy (drive energy) connects to a nineteenth century 'transcendental materialism' in which the concepts of force and energy are seen as the basis of reality and source of all productivity. A. Rabinbach (1990), *The Human Motor. Energy, Fatigue, and the Origins of Modernity.*

[26] Bernet (2020), *Force, Drive, Desire*. One can draw a distinction within Aristotle's metaphysics between the theory of substance and the theory of causality. Ibid., p. 9; Van der Heiden (2021), *Metafysica*, p. 46. Our focus is on the theory of causality.
[27] Leibniz argues that this self-development of each individual monad 'corresponds' with the changes and movements towards perfection in the universe as a whole. G.W. Leibniz (1996), 'Neues System der Natur', pp. 447-461.
[28] A. Schopenhauer (1977), *Die Welt als Wille und Vorstellung Bd. II-2*, pp. 621-664.
[29] Here we refer in particular to a number of collected short fragments about 'organic processes' that appeared in 1901's posthumous *The Will to Power*. F. Nietzsche (1968), *The Will to Power*, pp. 341-447.
[30] Schopenhauer is still following the tradition of Spinoza and his definition of *conatus* as 'an innate inclination of a thing to maintain and enhance itself'. Moore (2002), *Nietzsche, Biology and Metaphor*, p. 46. Nietzsche, on the other hand, explicitly rejects the idea that the 'will to power' could be defined as the 'drive for self-preservation', because this adheres to a 'teleological principle' that excludes the possibility of a force that turns against life cf. i.a. F. Nietzsche (18869, *Jenseits von Gut und Böse*, pp. 27-28.
[31] Gödde (1999), *Traditionslinien des "Unbewußten"*, pp. 501-540; Moore (2002), *Nietzsche, Biology and Metaphor*, pp. 21-55.
[32] C.G. Jung (1912), *Wandlungen und Symbole der Libido. Beiträge zur Entwicklungsgeschichte des Denkens*, p.138. In later texts, Jung's references to an Aristotelean tradition become more explicit by applying concepts such as form (*forma*) and matter, act and potential, and entelechy. About this, see M. Nagy (1991), *Philosophical Issues in the Psychology of C.G. Jung.*
[33] This debate does not stand in isolation but can be seen as an offshoot of post-Darwinian debates about drive and evolution. We could for instance recall in this regard Nietzsche's critique of Haeckel's biogenetic law of evolutionary progression in nature and culture.
[34] Freud (1985a), *A Phylogenetic Fantasy*; Freud (1920g), *Beyond the Pleasure Principle*, p. 37.
[35] Ibid., pp. 36, 38.
[36] Ibid., p. 58.
[37] Fletcher (2013), *Freud and the Scene of Trauma*, p. 267.
[38] Freud (1920g), *Beyond the Pleasure Principle*, pp. 36, 38.
[39] Freud (1905d), *Three Essays*, p. 168. Jung's drive monism can be seen as an elaboration of this formulation in which a *Trieb* only becomes sexual in a subsequent (differentiating) development. Jung (1912), *Wandlungen und Symbole der Libido*; Van Haute & Westerink (2021), *From Pleasure to the Object*, pp. 60-61.
[40] Freud (1915c), 'Insincts and Their Vicissitudes', pp. 118, 120. The dualistic classification of the instincts (ego drives and sexual drives) seems to be an 'auxiliary construction' that proves its utility in a clinical practice in which psychical complexity of neurotic patients has a very clear conflicting character. Ibid., p. 125.
[41] E. Haeckel (1899), *Kunstformen der Natur.*
[42] Cf. Freud (1920g), *Beyond the Pleasure Principle*, p. 37.

[43] Cf. Deleuze (1968), *Différence et répétition*; L. De Bolle (2010), 'Desire and Schizophrenia'.

[44] Freud (1920g), *Beyond the Pleasure Principle*, p. 12.

[45] In his thinking about the relationship between drive (force, energy) and work (conversion of energy for efficient use), Freud stands in the tradition of the late nineteenth-century materialism of Helmholtz, Fechner and Haeckel among others. About this, see Rabinbach (1990), *The Human Motor*.

[46] Freud (1920g), *Beyond the Pleasure Principle*, p. 54.

[47] Ibid., p. 62.

[48] Cf. Bernet (2020), *Force, Drive, Desire*, p. 147.

[49] In the study of the Wolf Man, we also come across these repetitions in the sexual activities of the boy and in his compulsive neurosis.

[50] Cf. Freud (1920g), *Beyond the Pleasure Principle*, p. 22.

[51] M. De Certeau (1988), 'The Fiction of History. The Writing of Moses and Monotheism'.

[52] This theme of (repeatedly) obliterating the memory of Jewish historiography (as 'archive') is central to the reflections of Derrida on Freud's Moses text. J. Derrida (1995), *Mal d'Archive: une impression freudienne*.

[53] Here we refer in particular to two sections in which Freud cites a text by Goethe: "What thou hast inherited from thy fathers, acquire it to make it thine". Freud (1912-13a), *Totem and Taboo*, p. 158; Freud (1940a), *An Outline of Psycho-Analysis*, p. 207.

[54] Here we concretely think of Lacan's analysis of Sophocles' tragedy *Antigone*. J. Lacan (1986), *Le séminaire livre VII. L'éthique de la psychoanalyse*, pp. 285-333). See about this Van Haute (2001), *Against Adaptation*, and M. De Kesel (2009), *Eros & Ethics: Reading Jacques Lacan's Seminar VII*, among others.

[55] R. Girard (1972), *La violence et le sacré*; Marcuse (1955), *Eros and Civilization*.

Bibliography

Abraham, Karl (1924), 'Versuch einer Entwicklungsgeschichte der Libido', in: *Psychoanalytische Studien zur Charakterbildung und andere Schriften*, ed. J. Cremerius. Frankfurt: Fischer Verlag, 1969, pp. 113-226.

Adler, Alfred (1908), 'Der Aggressionstrieb im Leben und in der Neurose', *Fortschritte der Medizin* 26, pp. 577-584.

Adriaens, Pieter (2008), *Het nut van waanzin. Essays over darwinisme en psychiatrie.* Leuven: Acco.

Alfandary, Isabelle (2017), 'Body Language', *DIVISION/Review*, N. 17, pp. 22-25.

Anzieu, Didier (1988), *L'auto-analyse de Freud et la découverte de la psychanalyse.* Paris: Presses universitaires de France.

Assmann, Jan (1998), *Moses the Egyptian: Memory of Egypt in Western Monotheism.* Cambridge (MA): Harvard UP.

Assmann, Jan (2020), *Moses Tragicus: Freud, Schönberg und der scheiternde Moses. Sigmund Freud Vorlesung 2019.* Vienna: Turia + Kant.

Assoun, Paul-Laurent (1976), *Freud, la philosophie et les philosophes.* Paris: Presses universitaires de France.

Bernet, Rudolf (2020), *Force, Drive, Desire: A Philosophy of Psychoanalysis.* Evanston: Northwestern UP.

Bernheimer, Charles & Kahane, Claire (eds.) (1990), *In Dora's Case: Freud – Hysteria – Feminism.* New York: Columbia UP.

Bernstein, Richard (1998), *Freud and the Legacy of Moses.* Cambridge: Cambridge UP.

Blass, Rachel (1992), 'Did Dora Have an Oedipus Complex? A Re-examination of the Theoretical Context of Freud's "Fragment of an Analysis"', *Psychoanalytic Study of the Child* 47, pp. 159-187.

Blass, Rachel (2018), 'The Analytic Denial of Freud's Struggle with the Understanding of Dora: Simplifying the Oedipus complex and the Process of its Adoption', in: eds. D. Finzi & H. Westerink, *Dora – Hysteria – Gender: Reconsidering Freud's Case Study.* Leuven: Leuven UP, pp. 33-44.

Bleuler, Eugen (1911), *Dementia Praecox oder die Gruppe der Schizophrenien.* Giessen: Psychosozial-Verlag (2014).

Breuer, Joseph & Freud, Sigmund (1895d), *Studies on Hysteria*, in: *Standard Edition (SE)* 2, ed. J. Strachey. London: Hogarth, 1953-1974.

Borch-Jacobsen, Mikkel (2000), 'How to Predict the Past. From Trauma to Repression', *History of Psychiatry* 11, pp. 15-35.

Butler, Judith (2020), *The Force of Nonviolence. An Ethico-Political Bind,* New York & London: Verso.

Butzer, Ralph J. & Burkholz, Roland (1991), 'Urvater der Eiszeit: Biologisch-evolutionäres und psycholamarckistisches Denken bei Freud', *Luzifer-Amor. Zeitschrift zur Geschichte der Psychoanalyse* 4(8), pp. 24-40.

Carter, Codell K. (1983), 'Infantile Hysteria and Infantile Sexuality in Late Nineteenth-century German-language Medical Literature', *Medical History* 27, pp. 186-196.

Castel, Pierre-Henri (1998), *Introduction à 'L'interprétation du rêve' de Freud*. Paris: Presses universitaires de France.

Chapelle, Daniel (1993), *Nietzsche and Psychoanalysis*. Albany: SUNY Press.

Charcot, Jean-Martin (1889), *Clinical Lectures on Diseases of the Nervous System*, Vol. III. London: The New Sydenham Society.

Charcot, Jean-Martin & Marie, Pierre (1892), 'HYSTERIA mainly HYSTERO-EPILEPSY', in: ed. D. Hack Tuke, *A Dictionary of Psychological Medicine*. London: J.A. Churchill, pp. 627-641.

Chevron, Marie-France (2012), 'Urkultur, Ur-Monotheismus und Zivilisationskritik bei W. Schmidt (1868-1954)', *Wiener Jahrbuch für Theologie* 9, pp. 161-174.

Churchill, Frederick B. (2015), *August Weismann: Development, Heredity, and Evolution*. Cambridge (MA) & London: Harvard UP.

Claus, Carl (1872), *Grundzüge der Zoologie*. Marburg: N. G. Elwert'sche Verlag.

Darwin, Charles (1859), *On the Origin of Species*, ed. G. Beer. Oxford: Oxford UP, 2008.

Darwin, Charles (1871), *The Descent of Man, and Selection in Relation to Race*, eds. J. Tyler Bonner & R.M. May. Princeton: Princeton UP, 1981.

David-Ménard, Monique (2016), 'Comment lire "Au-delà du principe du plaisir"?', *L'évolution psychiatrique* 81, pp. 865-879.

Davidson, Arnold I. (1984), 'The Assault on Freud', *London Review of Books* 6(12), pp. 9-11.

Davidson, Arnold (2001), *The Emergence of Sexuality: Historical Epistemology and the Formation of Concepts*. Cambridge (MA) & London: Harvard UP.

De Block, Andreas (2006), *Waanzin en natuur. Darwin en de psychiatrie*. Amsterdam: Boom.

De Bolle, Leen (2010), 'Desire and Schizophrenia', in: ed. L. De Bolle, *Deleuze and Psychoanalysis. Philosophical Essays in Deleuze's Debate with Psychoanalysis*. Leuven: Leuven UP, 7-32.

De Certeau, Michel (1988), 'The Fiction of History. The Writing of Moses and Monotheism', in: *The Writing of History*, transl. T. Conley. New York: Columbia UP.

De Kesel, Marc (2009), *Eros and Ethics: Reading Jacques Lacan's Seminar VII*. New York: SUNY Press.

De Vleminck, Jens (2013), *De schaduw van Kaïn: Freuds klinische antropologie van de agressiviteit*. Leuven: Leuven UP.

De Vleminck, Jens & Van Haute, Philippe (2013), 'Freud filosoof?', in: eds. Ph. Van Haute & J. De Vleminck, *Freud als filosoof. Over seksualiteit, psychopathologie en cultuur*. Kalmthout: Pelckmans, pp. 9-13.

Decker, Hannah S. (1991), *Freud, Dora and Vienna 1900*. New York: The Free Press.
Deleuze, Gilles (1968), *Différence et répétition*. Paris: Presses universitaires de France.
Deleuze, Gilles & Guattari, Felix (1972), *L'Anti-Oedipe – Capitalisme et schizophrénie*. Paris: Éditions de Minuit.
Derrida, Jacques (1980), *La carte postale: De Socrate à Freud et au-delà*. Paris: Flammarion.
Derrida, Jacques (1995), *Mal d'Archive: une impression freudienne*. Paris: Editions Galilée.
Draenos, Stan S. (1978), 'Psychoanalysis, Evolution and the End of Metaphysics', *Canadian Journal of Political and Social Theory* 2(2), pp. 31-54.
Eghigian, Greg A. (2010), 'The German welfare state as a discourse of trauma', in: eds. M. Micale & P. Lerner, *Traumatic Pasts, History, Psychiatry and the Trauma in the Modern Age, 1870-1930*. Cambridge & New York: Cambridge UP, pp. 92-114.
Erichsen, John (1866), *On railway and other injuries of the nervous system*. London: Walton and Maberly.
Erichsen, John (1875), *On concussion of the spine, nervous shock, and other injuries of the nervous system in their clinical and medico-legal aspects*. London: Longmans, Green and Co.
Esterson, Allen (2001), 'The Mythologizing of Psychoanalytic History: Deception and Self-deception in Freud's Accounts of the Seduction Theory Episode', *History of psychiatry* 11, pp. 329-352.
Fechner, Gustav (1873), *Einige Ideen zur Schöpfungs- und Entwicklungsgeschichte der Organismen*. Leipzig: Breitkopf und Härtel Verlag.
Ferenczi, Sandor (1912), 'Philosophie und Psychoanalyse', in: *Schriften zur Psychoanalyse Bd. 1*, ed. M. Balint. Frankfurt: Fischer Verlag, 1982, pp. 116-124.
Ferenczi, Sandor (1913), 'Entwicklungsstufen des Wirklichkeitssinnes', in: *Schriften zur Psychoanalyse Bd. 1*, ed. M. Balint. Frankfurt: Fischer Verlag, 1982, pp. 148-163.
Ferenczi, Sandor (1924), 'Versuch einer Genitaltheorie', in: *Schriften zur Psychoanalyse Bd. 2*, ed. M. Balint. Frankfurt: Fischer Verlag, 1982, pp. 317-400.
Finzi, Daniela & Westerink, Herman (2020), 'Die Dora Fall-Studie in Kontext', in: S. Freud, *Bruchstück einer Hysterie-Analyse*, eds. D. Finzi, Ph. Van Haute & H. Westerink. Vienna: Vienna UP, pp. 13-21.
Fischer-Homberger, Esther (2004), *Die traumatische Neurose. Vom somatischen zum sozialen Leiden*. Giessen: Psychosozial-Verlag.
Fletcher, John (2013), *Freud and the Scene of Trauma*. New York: Fordham University Press.
Foucault, Michel (1976), *The History of Sexuality 1: The Will to Knowledge*. London: Penguin.
Freud, Sigmund (1893a/1895d), 'On the Psychical Mechanism of Hysterical Phenomena: Preliminary Communication', in: *Standard Edition (SE)* 2, ed. J. Strachey. London: Hogarth, 1953-1974.

Freud, Sigmund (1893c), 'Some Points for a Comparative Study of Organic and Hysterical Motor Paralyses', *SE* 1.
Freud, Sigmund (1895f), 'A Reply to Criticisms of My Paper on Anxiety Neurosis', in: *SE* 3.
Freud, Sigmund (1896a), 'Heredity and the Aetiology of the Neuroses', in: *SE* 3.
Freud, Sigmund (1896b), 'Further Remarks on the Neuro-Psychoses of Defence', in: *SE* 3.
Freud, Sigmund (1896c), 'The Aetiology of Hysteria', in: *SE* 3.
Freud, Sigmund (1897b), 'Abstracts of the Scientific Writings of Dr. Sigm. Freud (1977-1897)', in: *SE* 3.
Freud, Sigmund (1899a), 'Screen Memories', in: *SE* 3.
Freud, Sigmund (1900a), *The Interpretation of Dreams*, in: *SE* 4–5.
Freud, Sigmund (1901b), *The Psychopathology of Everyday Life*, in: *SE* 6.
Freud, Sigmund (1905d), *Three Essays on the Theory of Sexuality*, in: *SE* 7.
Freud, Sigmund (1905e), 'Fragment of an Analysis of a Case of Hysteria', in: *SE* 7.
Freud, Sigmund (1906a), 'My Views on the Part Played by Sexuality in the Aetiology of the Neuroses', in: *SE* 7.
Freud, Sigmund (1907b), 'Obsessive Actions and Religious Practices', in: *SE* 9.
Freud, Sigmund (1908b), 'Character and Anal Erotism', in: *SE* 9.
Freud, Sigmund (1908c), 'On the Sexual Theories of Children', in: *SE* 9.
Freud, Sigmund (1909b), 'Analysis of a Phobia in a Five-Year-Old Boy', in: *SE* 10.
Freud, Sigmund (1909c), 'Family Romances', in: *SE* 9.
Freud, Sigmund (1909d), 'Notes upon a Case of Obsessional Neurosis', in: *SE* 10.
Freud, Sigmund (1910a), 'Five Lectures on Psycho-Analysis', in: *SE* 11.
Freud, Sigmund (1910c), *Leonardo da Vinci and a Memory of his Childhood*, in: *SE* 11.
Freud, Sigmund (1911b), 'Formulations on the Two Principles of Mental Functioning', in: *SE* 12.
Freud, Sigmund (1911c), 'Psychoanalytic Remarks on an Autobiographically Described Case of Paranoia (Dementia paranoids)', in: *SE* 12.
Freud, Sigmund (1911f), 'Great is Diana of the Ephesians', in: *SE* 12.
Freud, Sigmund (1912a), 'Postscript to Psychoanalytic Remarks on an Autobiographically Described Case of Paranoia', in: *SE* 12.
Freud, Sigmund (1912i), 'Einleitingspassagen zu: "Über einige Übereinstimmungen im Seelenleben der Wilden und der Neurotiker"', in: *Gesammelte Werke Nachtragsband*. Frankfurt: Fischer Verlag, 1987, pp. 743-745.
Freud, Sigmund (1912-13a), *Totem and Taboo*, in: *SE* 13.
Freud, Sigmund (1913a), 'A Dream which bore Testimony', in: *SE* 12.
Freud, Sigmund (1913d), 'Dreams in Folklore', in: *SE* 12.
Freud, Sigmund (1913i), 'The Disposition to Obsessional Neurosis', in: *SE* 12.
Freud, Sigmund (1913j), 'The Claims of Psychoanalysis to Scientific Interest', in: *SE* 13.
Freud, Sigmund (1914b), 'The Moses of Michelangelo', in: *SE* 13.
Freud, Sigmund (1914c), 'On Narcissism: An Introduction', in: *SE* 12.

Freud, Sigmund (1914d), 'On the History of the Psycho-Analytic Movement', in: *SE* 14.
Freud, Sigmund (1914g), 'Remembering, Repeating and Working-Through', in: *SE* 12.
Freud, Sigmund (1915b), 'Thoughts for the Times on War and Death', in: *SE* 14.
Freud, Sigmund (1915c), 'Instincts and their Vicissitudes', *SE* 14.
Freud, Sigmund (1915f), 'A Case of Paranoia running counter to the Psychoanalytic Theory of the Disease', in: *SE* 14.
Freud, Sigmund (1916d), 'Some Character-Types met with in Psychoanalytic Work', in: *SE* 14.
Freud, Sigmund (1916-17a), *Introductory Lectures on Psycho-Analysis*, in: *SE* 15-16.
Freud, Sigmund (1917a), 'A Difficulty in the Path of Psycho-Analysis', in *SE* 17.
Freud, Sigmund (1918b), 'From the History of an Infantile Neurosis', in: *SE* 17.
Freud, Sigmund (1919d), 'Introduction to *Psychoanalysis and the War Neuroses*', in: *SE* 17.
Freud, Sigmund (1919e), 'A Child is Being Beaten', in: *SE* 17.
Freud, Sigmund (1920g), *Beyond the Pleasure Principle*, in: *SE* 18.
Freud, Sigmund (1921c), *Group Psychology and the Analysis of the Ego*, in: *SE* 18.
Freud, Sigmund (1923a), 'Two Encyclopedia Articles: Psycho-Analysis and The Libido Theory', in: *SE* 18.
Freud, Sigmund (1923b), *The Ego and the Id*, *SE* 19.
Freud, Sigmund (1923e), 'The Infantile Genital Organization of the Libido', in: *SE* 19.
Freud, Sigmund (1923d), 'A Neurosis of Demoniacal Possession in the Seventeenth Century', in: *SE* 19.
Freud, Sigmund (1924c), 'The Economic Problem of Masochism', in: *SE* 19.
Freud, Sigmund (1926d), *Inhibitions, Symptoms, and Anxiety*, in: *SE 20.*
Freud, Sigmund (1926e), *The Question of Lay Analysis*, in: *SE* 20.
Freud, Sigmund (1926g), 'Freud and Ewald Hering (Appendix A to 'The Unconscious')', in: *SE* 14.
Freud, Sigmund (1927c), *The Future of an Illusion*, in: *SE* 21.
Freud, Sigmund (1930a), *Civilization and Its Discontents*, in: *SE* 21.
Freud, Sigmund (1931a), 'Libidinal Types', in: *SE* 21.
Freud, Sigmund (1933a), *New Introductory Lectures on Psycho-Analysis*, in: *SE* 22.
Freud, Sigmund (1937c), 'Analysis Terminable and Interminable', in: *SE* 23.
Freud, Sigmund (1937d), 'Constructions in Analysis, in: *SE* 23.
Freud, Sigmund (1939a), *Moses and Monotheism*, in: *SE* 23.
Freud, Sigmund (1940a), *An Outline of Psycho-Analysis*, in: *SE* 23.
Freud, Sigmund (1950c [1895]), 'Project for a Scientific Psychology', *SE* 1.
Freud, Sigmund (1955a), 'Originalnotizen zu einem Fall von Zwangsneurose', in *Gesammelte Werke Nachtragsband*, Frankfurt: Fischer Verlag, 1987, pp. 509-569.

Freud, Sigmund (1985a), *A Phylogenetic Fantasy: Overview of the Transference Neuroses*, ed. I. Grubrich-Simitis. Cambridge (MA) & London: The Belknap Press of Harvard UP.

Freud, Sigmund (1985c), *The Complete Letters of Sigmund Freud to Wilhelm Fliess 1887-1904*, ed. J. M. Masson. Cambridge (MA) & London: The Belknap Press of Harvard UP.

Freud, Sigmund (2021), *L'homme Moïse. Un roman historique*, eds. M. Fagard & Th. Gindele. Paris: Édition Imago.

Freud, Sigmund (2024), *Beyond the Pleasure Principle*, ed. U. May, M. Schröter, M. ffytche, J. Forrester & M. Molnar, in: eds. H. Westerink, J. Willner & Ph. Van Haute, *Towards the Limits of Freudian Psychoanalysis: Critical Edition and Readings of Beyond the Pleasure Principle*. Leuven: Leuven UP, pp. 29-80.

Freud, Sigmund & Abraham, Karl (1965), *Briefe 1907-1926*, eds. H.C. Abraham & E.L. Freud. Frankfurt: Fischer Verlag.

Freud, Sigmund & Andreas-Salomé, Lou (1972), *Letters*, ed. E. Pfeiffer. New York: Harcourt Brace Jovanovich.

Freud, Sigmund & Ferenczi, Sandor (1996), *The Correspondence Vol. 2 1914-1919*, eds. E. Falzeder, E. Brabant & P. Giampieri-Deutsch. Cambridge (MA) & London: The Belknap Press of Harvard UP.

Freud, Sigmund & Jones, Ernest (1993), *The Complete Correspondence 1908-1939*, ed. R.A. Paskauskas. Cambridge (MA) & London: The Belknap Press of Harvard UP.

Freud, Sigmund & Pfister, Oskar (1963), *Psychoanalysis and Faith: The Letters of Sigmund Freud and Oskar Pfister*, eds. E.L. Freud & H. Meng. New York: Basic Books.

Freud, Sigmund & Zweig, Arnold (1968), *Briefwechsel*, ed. E.L. Freud. Frankfurt: Fischer Verlag.

Gardiner, Muriel (1971), *The Wolf-man*. New York: Basic Books.

Geyskens, Tomas (2001), 'Freud's Letters to Fliess. From Seduction to Sexual Biology, from Psychopathology to a Clinical Anthropology', *International Journal for Psychoanalysis* 82, pp. 861-876.

Geyskens, Tomas (2005), *Our Original Scenes. Freud's Theory of Sexuality*. Leuven: Leuven UP.

Girard, René (1972), *La violence et le sacré*. Paris: Editions Grasset.

Gödde, Günter (1999), *Traditionslinien des "Unbewußten". Schopenhauer – Nietzsche – Freud*. Tübingen: edition diskord.

Gould, Stephen Jay (1977), *Ontogeny and Phylogeny*. Cambridge (MA) & London: The Belknap Press of Harvard UP.

Grubrich-Simitis, Ilse (1985), 'Metapsychology and Metabiology', in: S. Freud, *A Phylogenetic Fantasy: Overview of the Transference Neuroses*, ed. I. Grubrich-Simitis. Cambridge (MA) & London: The Belknap Press of Harvard UP, pp. 73-107.

Grubrich-Simitis, Ilse (1991), *Freuds Moses-Studie als Tagtraum*. Weinheim: Verlag Internationale Psychoanalyse.

Grubrich-Simitis, Ilse (1996), *Back to Freud's Texts: Making Silent Documents Spreak*. New Haven & London: Yale UP.

Grubrich-Simitis, Ilse (2007), 'Trauma oder Trieb – Trieb oder Trauma: Wiederbetrachtet', *Psyche. Zeitschrift für Psychoanalyse und ihre Anwendungen* 61(7), pp. 637-656.

Hacking, Ian (1995), *Rewriting the Soul: Multiple Personality and the Science of Memory*. Princeton: Princeton UP.

Haeckel, Ernst (1863), 'Die Jungfernrede: Über die Entwicklungstheorie Darwin's', in: ed. G. Heberer, *Der gerechtigtfertigte Haeckel. Einblicke in seine Schriften aus Anlaß seines Hauptwerks "Generelle Morphologie der Organismen" vor hundert Jahren*. Stuttgart: Gustav Fischer Verlag, 1968, pp. 45-59.

Haeckel, Ernst (1866), *Generelle Morphologie der Organismen: Allgemeine Grundzüge der organischen Formen-Wissenschaft, mechanisch begründet durch die von Charles Darwin reformirte Descendenz-Theorie. 2 Bände*. Berlin: Georg Reimer Verlag.

Haeckel, Ernst (1899), *Kunstformen der Natur*. Leipzig & Vienna: Verlag des Bibliographischen Instituts.

Harrington, Ralph (2010), 'The Railway Accident: Trains, Trauma and Technological Crises in nineteenth-century Britain', in: eds. M. Micale & P. Lerner, *Traumatic Pasts, History, Psychiatry and the Trauma in the Modern Age, 1870-1930*. Cambridge & New York: Cambridge UP, pp. 31-56.

Heidegger, Martin (1961), *Nietzsche 1*. Pfullingen: Neske.

Hering, Ewald (1870), 'On Memory', in: S. Butler, *Unconscious Memory*. London: A.C. Fifield, 1910, pp. 63-86.

Hermans, Hubertien & Schmidt, Sonja (1996), 'De traumatische neurose, een social-historische verkenning', *Amsterdams sociologisch tijdschrift* 23(3), pp. 525-550.

Huertas, Rafael & Winston, C.M. (1992), 'Madness and degeneration, I: From "fallen angel" to mentally ill', *History of psychiatry* 3, pp. 391-411.

Hustvedt, Asti (2011), *Medical Muses: Hysteria in nineteenth-century Paris*. New York: Norton.

Israëls, Han & Schatzman, Morton (1993), 'The Seduction Theory', *History of Psychiatry* 4, pp. 23-59.

Izenberg, Gerald (2006), 'Seduced and Abandoned: The Rise and Fall of Freud's Seduction Theory', in: ed. J. Neu, *Cambridge Companion to Freud*. Cambridge: Cambridge UP, pp. 25-43.

Jung, Carl Gustav (1909), 'Die Bedeutung des Vaters für das Schicksal des Einzelnen', *Jahrbuch für psychoanalytische und psychopathologische Forschungen* 1, pp. 155–73.

Jung, Carl Gustav (1912), *Wandlungen und Symbole der Libido. Beiträge zur Entwicklungsgeschichte des Denkens*. München: DTV, 1991 (English translation: *Psychology of the Unconscious*. Mineola: Dover Publications, 2002).

Jung, Carl Gustav (1913), 'Versuch einer Darstellung der psychoanalytischen Theorie', in: *Gesammelte Werke Bd. 4*. Solothurn/Düsseldorf: Walter-Verlag, 1995, pp. 107-255.

Klein, Melanie (1933), 'The Early Development of Conscience in the Child', in: *Love, Guilt and Reparation, and other Works 1921-1945*, ed. H. Segal. London: Virago Press, 1994, pp. 248-257.
Kleinherenbrink, Arjen (2016), *Machine Philosophy. Gilles Deleuze and the Externality of Entities*. Dissertation, Nijmegen.
Krafft-Ebing, R von (1893), *Psychopathia Sexualis mit besonderer Berücksichtigung der conträren Sexualempfindung. Eine klinisch-forensische Studie*. Stuttgart: Enke.
Kris, Ernst (1952), 'Einleitung zur Erstausgabe', in: *Sigmund Freud: Briefe an Wilhelm Fließ*. Frankfurt: Fischer, 1986, pp. 519-561.
Lacan, Jacques (1966), Écrits. Paris: Seuil.
Lacan, Jacques (1973), *Le séminaire livre XI. Les quartre concepts fondamentaux de la psychanalyse*. Paris: Seuil.
Lacan, Jacques (1986), *Le séminaire livre VII. L'éthique de la psychanalyse*. Paris: Seuil.
Lamarck, Jean-Baptiste (1910), *Zoologische Philosophie*. Leipzig: Alfred Kröner Verlag.
Laplanche, Jean (1980). *La sublimation*. Paris: Presses universitaires de France.
Laplanche, Jean (1987), *Nouveaux fondements pour la psychanalyse*. Paris: Presses universitaires de France.
Laplanche, Jean (1992), *La revolution copernicienne inachevée* (Travaux 1967-1992). Paris: Aubier.
Laplanche, Jean (1999), *La sexualité humaine. Biologisme et biologie*. Paris: Les Empêcheurs de penser en rond.
Laplanche, Jean (2006), *Problématiques VI: L'après coup*. Paris: Presses universitaires de France.
Laplanche, Jean (2007), *Sexual. La sexualité élargie au sens freudien*. Paris: Presses universitaires de France.
Laplanche, Jean & Pontalis, Jean-Bertrand (1973). *The Language of Psychoanalysis*, New York: Norton.
Laplanche, Jean & Pontalis, Jean-Bertrand (1985), *Fantasme originaire, Fantasmes des origines, Origines des fantasmes*. Paris: Hachette.
Leibniz, Gottfried Wilhelm (1996), 'Neues System der Natur und der Gemeinschaft der Substanzen', in: *Hauptschriften zur Grundlegung der Philosophie Teil II*, ed. E. Cassirer. Marburg: Meiner Verlag, pp. 447-458.
Leys, Ruth (2000), *Trauma. A Genealogy*. Chicago & London: Chicago UP.
Lerner, Paul (2010), 'From Traumatic Neurosis to Male Hysteria: The Rise and Fall of Herman Oppenheim, 1889-1919', in: eds. M. Micale & P. Lerner, *Traumatic Pasts, History, Psychiatry and the Trauma in the Modern Age, 1870-1930*. Cambridge & New York: Cambridge UP, pp. 140-170.
Mahoney, Patrick (1986), *Freud and the Rat Man*. New Haven: Yale UP.
Mahoney, Patrick (1996), *Freud's Dora, A Psychoanalytic, Historical and Textual Study*. New Haven & London: Yale UP.
Malabou, Catherine (2017), *Les nouveaux blessés. De Freud à la neurologie, penser les traumatismes contemporains*. Paris: Presses universitaires de France.

Marcuse, Herbert (1955), *Eros and Civilization. A Philosophical Inquiry into Freud.* Boston: Beacon Press.

Marder, Elissa (2015), 'L'Homme aux loups. L'animal sexuel et la scène primitive', in: ed. G. Ribault, *Freud au cas par cas. Lectures philosophiques des cas freudiens.* Leuven: Leuven UP, pp.127-148.

Marinelli, Lydia & Mayer, Andreas (2002), *Träume nach Freud. Die 'Traumdeutung' und die Geschichte der psychoanalytische Bewegung.* Vienna: Turia + Kant.

Marshal, Jonathan W. (2016), *Performing Neurology. The Dramaturgy of Dr. Jean-Martin Charcot.* New York: Palgrave/Macmillan.

May, Ulrike (2015a), *Freud bei der Arbeit. Zur Entstehungsgeschichte der psychoanalytischen Theorie und Praxis, mit einer Auswertung von Freuds Patientenkalender.* Giessen: Psychosozial-Verlag.

May, Ulrike (2015b), 'The Third Step in Drive Theory: On the Genesis of Beyond the Pleasure Principle', *Psychoanalysis and History* 17(2), pp. 205-272.

Micale, Mark S. (1993), 'On the "Disappearance" of Hysteria. A Study in the Clinical Deconstruction of a Diagnosis', *Isis* 84(3), pp. 496-526.

Micale, Mark S. (1995), *Approaching Hysteria: Disease and Its Interpretation.* Princeton: Princeton UP.

Micale, Mark S. (2008), *Hysterical Man, The Hidden History of Male Nervous Illness.* Cambridge (MA) & London: Harvard UP.

Micale, Mark S. (2010), 'Jean-Martin Charcot et *les névroses traumatiques*: From Medicine to Culture in French Trauma Theory of the Late Nineteenth Century', in: eds. M. Micale & P. Lerner, *Traumatic Pasts, History, Psychiatry and the Trauma in the Modern Age, 1870-1930.* Cambridge & New York: Cambridge UP, pp. 115-139.

Micale, Mark S. & Lerner, Paul (eds.) (2010), *Traumatic Pasts, History, Psychiatry and Trauma in the Modern Age, 1870-1930.* Cambridge & New York: Cambridge UP.

Moore, Gregory (2002), *Nietzsche, Biology and Metaphor.* Cambridge: Cambridge UP.

Moyaert, Paul (2014), *Opboksen tegen het inerte. De doodsdrift bij Freud.* Nijmegen: Vantilt.

Nagy, Marilyn (1991), *Philosophical Issues in the Psychology of C.G. Jung.* Albany: SUNY Press.

Nietzsche, Friedrich (1882), *Die fröhliche Wissenschaft*, in: *Werke. Kritische Gesamtausgabe Bd. 3*, eds. G. Colli & M. Montinari. Munich: DTV, 1999.

Nietzsche, Friedrich (1886), *Jenseits von Gut und Böse*, in: *Werke. Kritische Gesamtausgabe Bd. 5*, eds. G. Colli & M. Montinari. Munich: DTV, 1999.

Nietzsche, Friedrich (1968), *The Will to Power*, ed. W. Kaufmann. New York: Vintage Books

Nunberg, Herman & Federn, Ernst (eds.) (1976), *Protokolle der Wiener Psychoanalytischen Vereinigung Bd. 1, 1906-1908.* Frankfurt: Fischer Verlag.

Nunberg, Herman & Federn, Ernst (eds.) (1981), *Protokolle der Wiener Psychoanalytischen Vereinigung Bd. 4, 1912-1918.* Frankfurt: Fischer Verlag.

Oppenheim, Hermann (1889), *Die traumatische Neurosen*. Berlin: Verlag von August Hirschwald.

Oppenheim, Hermann (1915), *Der Krieg und die traumatischen Neurosen*. Berlin & Heidelberg: Springer Verlag.

Pauly, August (1905), *Darwinismus und Lamarckismus*. Munich: Ernst Reinhardt Verlagshandlung.

Phillips, Adam (2014), *Becoming Freud. The Making of a Psychoanalyst*. New Haven & London: Yale UP.

Press, Jacques (2010), 'Trauma et pulsion', *Libres Cahiers pour la psychanalyse* 21(1), pp. 35-51.

Rabinbach, Anson (1990), *The Human Motor. Energy, Fatigue, and the Origins of Modernity*. Berkeley & Los Angeles: University of California Press.

Rank, Otto (1924), *Das Trauma der Geburt und seine Bedeutung für die Psychoanalyse*. Leipzig, Vienna & Zurich: Internationaler Psychoanalytischer Verlag.

Ricoeur, Paul (1965), *De l'interprétation. Essai sur Freud*. Paris: Édition du Seuil.

Ritvo, Lucille B. (1990), *Darwin's Influence on Freud. A Tale of Two Sciences*. New Haven & London: Yale UP.

Roudebush, Marc (2010), 'A Battle of Nerves: Hysteria and Its Treatment in France during World War I', in: eds. M. Micale & P. Lerner, *Traumatic Pasts, History, Psychiatry and the Trauma in the Modern Age, 1870-1930*. Cambridge & New York: Cambridge UP, pp. 253-279.

Said, Edward (2003), *Freud and the Non-European*. London & New York: Verso.

Sauerteig, Lutz (2012), 'Loss of Innocence: Albert Moll, Sigmund Freud and the Invention of Childhood Sexuality around 1900', *Medical History* 56(2), pp. 156-183.

Schimek, Jean-Georges (2011), 'Fact and Fantasy in the Seduction Theory', in: ed. D. L. Browning, *Memory, Myth and Seduction. Unconscious Fantasy and the Interpretive Process*. New York & Hove: Routledge.

Schopenhauer, Arthur (1854), Über den Willen in der Natur. Frankfurt: Joh. Chr. Hermann'sche Buchhandlung.

Schopenhauer, Arthur (1977), *Die Welt als Wille und Vorstellung Bd. II-2*. Zurich: Diogenes Verlag.

Schröter, Michael (ed.) (2012), *Sigmund Freud - Eugen Bleuler: Ich bin zuversichtlich, wir erobern bald die Psychiatrie. Briefwechsel 1904 – 1937*. Basel: Schwabe.

Schröter, Michael (2018), 'Die Psychoanalyse und die "Kriegsneurosen" des ersten Weltkriegs', *Psyche* 72(2), 122-145.

Scull, Andrew (2009), *Hysteria: The Disturbing History*. Oxford: Oxford UP.

Silveira, Lea (2013), 'Phylogenetic schema and transcendental field: The problem of the universal character of fantasy in Freud and Lacan', Lecture presented at the conference of the *International Society of Psychoanalysis and Philosophy*, Nijmegen/Gent.

Slavet, Eliza (2009), *Racial Fever. Freud and the Jewish Question*. New York: Fordham UP.

Solms, Mark & Turnbull, Oliver (2002), *The Brain and the Inner World. An Introduction to the Neuroscience of Subjective Experiences*. New York: Other Press.

Stengers, Jean & Van Neck, Anne (1998), *Histoire d'une grande peure. La masturbation (Collection 'Les empêcheurs de penser en rond')*. Paris: Institut Synthélabo.

Sulloway, Frank J. (1979), *Freud: Biologist of the Mind*. New York: Basic Books.

Van der Hart, Onno (1995), 'Pierre Janet en Sigmund Freud over hysterie, trauma en dissociatie', *Nederlands Tijdschrift voor Geneeskunde* 139(43), pp. 2183-2186.

Van der Heiden, Gert-Jan (2021), *Metafysica. Van orde naar ontvankelijkheid*. Amsterdam: Boom.

Van Haute, Philippe (1997), 'Antigone, heldin van de psychoanalyse? – Lacans lectuur van Antigone', in: eds. E. Berns, P. Moyaert & P. van Tongeren, *De God van denkers en dichters. Opstellen voor Samuel IJsseling*. Amsterdam: Boom, pp. 172-191.

Van Haute, Philippe (2001), *Against Adaptation: Lacan's Subversion of the Subject*. New York: Other Press.

Van Haute, Philippe (2016), '...die de diepste raadslen kende en de hoogste stond in macht. Het Oedipus-complex in de vroegste teksten van Freud', in: eds. P. Verstraten & S. Houppermans, *Oedipus heerst*. Apeldoorn: Garant, pp. 59-80.

Van Haute, Philippe (2018), 'Trauma and Disgust: Dora between Freud and Laplanche', in: eds. D. Finzi & H. Westerink, *Dora – Hysteria – Gender: Reconsidering Freud's Case Study*. Leuven: Leuven UP, pp. 59-72.

Van Haute, Philippe & Geyskens, Tomas (2004), *Confusion of Tongues: The Primacy of Sexuality in Freud, Ferenczi and Laplanche*. New York: Other Press.

Van Haute, Philippe & Geyskens, Tomas (2007), *From Death Instinct to Attachment Theory: The Primacy of the Child in Freud, Klein and Hermann*. New York: Other Press.

Van Haute, Philippe & Geyskens, Tomas (2012), *A Non-Oedipal Psychoanalysis? A Clinical Anthropology of Hysteria in the Works of Freud and Lacan*. Leuven: Leuven UP.

Van Haute, Philippe & Geyskens, Tomas (2013), 'Woede, wellust en weifelzucht: Een freudiaanse symptomatologie van de dwangneurose', in: eds. Ph. Van Haute & J. De Vleminck, *Freud als filosoof. Over seksualiteit, psychopathologie en cultuur*. Kalmthout: Pelckmans, pp. 117-129.

Van Haute, Philippe & Westerink, Herman (2016), 'Hysteria, Sexuality, and the Deconstruction of Normativity: Rereading Freud's 1905 Edition of *Three Essays on the Theory of Sexuality*', in: S. Freud, *Three Essays on the Theory of Sexuality (1905)*, eds. Ph. Van Haute & H. Westerink, transl. U. Kistner. London: Verso, pp. xiii-lxxvi.

Van Haute, Philippe & Westerink, Herman (2021), *From Pleasure to the Object: Reading Freud's* Three Essays on the Theory of Sexuality. London & New York: Routledge.

Vandermeersch, Patrick (1991), *Unresolved Questions in the Freud-Jung Debate on Psychosis, Sexual Identity and Religion*. Leuven: Leuven UP.

Vergote, Antoon (1982), 'Pulsion de mort et destins mortifères de la pulsion', *Psychanalyse à l'université* 28(7), pp. 579-580.

Visker, Rudi (2005), 'De prijs van de onteigening: Levinas, Freud en het trauma', in: R. Visker, *Vreemd gaan en vreemd blijven. Filosofie van de multiculturaliteit*. Nijmegen: SUN.

Wagner, Adolf (1909), *Geschichte des Lamarckismus*. Stuttgart: Franckh'sche Verlagshandlung.

Weber, Matthias (2010), 'Hermann Oppenheims Konzept der traumatischen Neurose', *Psychotherapie* 15(2), pp. 205-213.

Weismann, August (1882), *Das Keimplasma. Eine Theorie der Vererbung*. Jena: Gustav Fischer Verlag.

Weismann, August (1892), Über Leben und Tod, Eine biologische Untersuchung. Jena: Gustav Fischer Verlag.

Westerink, Herman (2007), 'The Great Man from Tarsus. Freud on the Apostle Paul', *The Psychoanalytic Quarterly* 76(1), pp. 217-236.

Westerink, Herman (2009), *A Dark Trace: Sigmund Freud on the Sense of Guilt*. Leuven: Leuven UP.

Westerink, Herman (2013), 'De Rattenman, zijn schuldgevoel en zijn twee gevoelsconflicten', in: eds. Ph. Van Haute & J. De Vleminck, *Freud als filosoof. Over seksualiteit, psychopathologie en cultuur*. Kalmthout: Pelckmans, pp. 131-144.

Westerink, Herman (2014), 'Projection, Substitution and Exaltation: Freud's Case Study of Little Hans and the Creation of God in *Totem and Taboo*', *Psychoanalysis and History* 16(1), pp. 55-68.

Westerink, Herman (2015), 'De problematische plaats van de woede in het denken van Freud over agressiviteit', *Tijdschrift voor Filosofie* 77(4), pp. 719-746.

Westerink, Herman (2019), *De lichamen en hun lusten. In het spoor van Foucaults* Geschiedenis van de seksualiteit. Nijmegen: Vantilt.

Westerink, Herman (2023), 'Reconstructing Freud's Moses-texts (1934-1938): From Character Study to Contribution to Trauma Theory', *Psychoanalysis and History* 25(3), 297-322.

Westerink, Herman & Van Haute, Philippe (2020), '"Family Romances" and the Oedipalization of Freudian Psychoanalysis', *Psychoanalysis and History* 22(2), pp. 175-187.

Whitebook, Joel (2017), *Freud: An Intellectual Biography*. Cambridge: Cambridge UP.

Willner, Jenny (2020), 'Neurotische Evolution. Bioanalyse als Kulturkritik in "Jenseits des Lustprinzips"', *Psyche. Zeitschrift für Psychoanalyse und ihre Anwendungen* 74(11), pp. 895-921.

Yerushalmi, Yosef Hayim (1989), 'Freud and the "Historical Novel": From the Manuscript Draft (1934) of *Moses and Monotheism*', *International Journal of Psycho-Analysis* 70(3), pp. 375-395.

Yerushalmi, Yosef Hayim (1991), *Freud's Moses. Judaism Terminable and Interminable*. New Haven & London: Yale UP.

Index

www.ingramcontent.com/pod-product-compliance
Lightning Source LLC
Chambersburg PA
CBHW060503221125
35799CB00042B/2640
* 9 7 8 9 4 6 2 7 0 4 8 6 2 *